NEW TESTAMENT ESSAYS

T. W. MANSON

NEW TESTAMENT ESSAYS

STUDIES IN MEMORY OF

Thomas Walter Manson

1893–1958

sponsored by

PUPILS, COLLEAGUES

AND FRIENDS

edited by

A. J. B. HIGGINS

*Lecturer in New Testament Language
and Literature in the University
of Leeds*

MANCHESTER UNIVERSITY PRESS

© 1959
Published by the University of Manchester at
THE UNIVERSITY PRESS
316-324 Oxford Road, Manchester 13

Printed in Great Britain by Butler & Tanner Ltd., Frome and London

EDITOR'S FOREWORD

THE material for this volume was complete and about to be sent to the publisher when I received the news of Professor Manson's illness which ended in his death a few days later on May 1st. His passing at a comparatively early age is a heavy loss to Biblical scholarship not only in this country but far beyond its shores.

As one of Professor Manson's old Manchester students (the beginning of my theological studies coincided with his coming to the Rylands Chair) and as one proud to be numbered among his friends, I was looking forward to presenting the *Festschrift* to him and he, I know, was looking forward to receiving it. But it was not to be, and the papers which were written in his honour must now be dedicated to his memory. It would have been an honour to be the editor of his *Festschrift*; to me it is, if that were possible, an even higher privilege to be able to render tribute to his memory in this way.

Of Professor Manson's written contributions to learning it is unnecessary to say much here. Suffice it to say that every sentence he wrote expresses his meaning exactly; that he disliked theological jargon as much as he disliked cant; and that his books, of which *The Teaching of Jesus* was the first, and his numerous articles in the *Bulletin of the John Rylands Library* and elsewhere, are permanent contributions to learning, distinguished by a freshness of approach and independence of judgment as they are by clarity of expression.

As a teacher, as all who were privileged to sit at his feet will agree, he was *sui generis*. His lectures were frequently illuminated by flashes of his own characteristic wit and pungency of language. Many of his students will remember such pronouncements as: 'Christianity is either unique or it is superfluous.' He was an outstanding and thought-provoking preacher. He bore his great learning humbly, gracefully and lightly, and he had the gift of speaking simply and directly to the ordinary man both in his broadcast talks and sermons and in those of his writings which were intended for a wider public.

It is an agreeable duty to acknowledge the interest of my colleagues on the sponsoring committee, Professors M. Black, J. W. Bowman, C. H. Dodd, J. Jeremias, and W. C. van Unnik. It is, we feel, appropriate that in offering this volume to the world of scholarship, we should be allowed to express the hope that it may serve as a further indication to Mrs. Manson of our deep appreciation of her distinguished husband as scholar and churchman.

I am grateful to Professor Black and Dr. R. McL. Wilson, of St. Andrews University, for going through the proofs of this volume during my absence in Canada. Thanks are also due to the Press of the University which Professor Manson served so loyally for many years for undertaking the publication of this tribute.

A. J. B. HIGGINS

Whitsun 1958

NOTE

A memoir of Professor Manson will preface a volume of his collected papers (those principally on the Life of Jesus and the Epistles, contributed to the Bulletin of the John Rylands Library), which will be published probably in early 1960 under the editorship of Professor Matthew Black. This memoir will be both an appreciation of the man and a tribute to his work, particularly his tenure of the Chair of Biblical Criticism and Exegesis at Manchester University.

CONTENTS

Frontispiece THOMAS WALTER MANSON (Photo Lafayette).

THOMAS WALTER MANSON

1893–1958

Born 22 July, 1893, at North Shields, Northumberland. University of Glasgow, 1912; M.A. with first class honours in Mental and Moral Philosophy. Clark and Ferguson Scholarships 1919. D.Litt., 1931. Served in First World War, Lieut. R.F.A. (wounded 1916). Theological training, Westminster College, Cambridge, 1919–22. Research student, Christ's College, Cambridge. B.A. by dissertation (unpublished) on the Occasionalist Philosophy. Oriental Languages Tripos Pt. II (Hebrew and Aramaic), first class, 1923. Research scholar of Christ's College (work on the Targum on Lamentations). Burney Prize, 1923. Tyrwhitt Scholarship and Mason Hebrew Prize, 1924.

Tutor of Westminster College, Cambridge, 1922–5.

Ordained 1925. Minister of the Presbyterian Church of England at Bethnal Green, London, 1925–6, and at Falstone, Northumberland, 1926–32.

Yates Professor of New Testament Greek and Exegesis, Mansfield College, Oxford, 1932–6, and University Lecturer in New Testament Studies, 1935–6.

Rylands Professor of Biblical Criticism and Exegesis, University of Manchester, 1936–58. Dean of the Faculty of Theology, 1941–52. Pro-Vice-Chancellor, 1945–9. Presenter of Honorary Graduands, 1938–58.

Russell Lecturer, Auburn Theological Seminary and Shaffer Lecturer, Yale University, 1939.

In Second World War served as Operations Officer, N.W. Regional H.Q. (1939–41), and Capt. 61st (Manchester University) Bn., Lancashire Home Guard.

Grinfield Lecturer in the Septuagint, Oxford, 1943–5.

Fellow of the British Academy, 1945.

Ayer Lecturer, Colgate-Rochester Theological Seminary and Zenos Lecturer, McCormick Theological Seminary, Chicago, 1952.

Moderator of the General Assembly of the Presbyterian Church of England, 1953.

T.V. Moore Lecturer, San Francisco Theological Seminary, 1955.

Honorary Degrees, etc. Hon. D.D., Glasgow, Durham, Cambridge, Pine Hill, Halifax, N.S., Trinity College, Dublin; Docteur, hon. caus., Strasbourg; Hon. Member of the Society of Biblical Literature and Exegesis; Corresponding Member of the Göttingen Academy; Burkitt Medallist of the British Academy.

SELECT BIBLIOGRAPHY OF THE WORKS OF
T. W. MANSON

ABBREVIATIONS

BJRL *Bulletin of the John Rylands Library*
CQ *Congregational Quarterly*
ET *Expository Times*
JEA *Journal of Egyptian Archaeology*
JTS *Journal of Theological Studies*
ZNTW *Zeitschrift für die Neutestamentliche Wissenschaft*
C.U.P. Cambridge University Press
O.U.P. Oxford University Press

1929

Mark 8:14–21. JTS 30, 45–7.

1931

The Teaching of Jesus: Studies of its Form and Content. C.U.P.

1933

The Foundation of Christianity (Inaugural Lecture at Mansfield College, Oxford). CQ 11, 11–23.
The Message of the Epistles: 1 Corinthians. ET 44, 500–4.

1934

Jesus as Teacher. *Religion in Education* 1, 21–30.

1935

The Problem of Aramaic Sources in the Gospels. ET 47, 7–11.
Religion and Morality in the New Testament. *The Bible and Modern Religious Thought,* 6, 10–20.
The Christology of the New Testament. CQ 13, 153–64.

1936

'The Jewish Background' in *Christian Worship* (ed. N. Micklem), 35–49, O.U.P.
On a Passage in Peter of Laodicea's Commentary on Matthew. ZNTW 35, 307.
A Parallel to a New Testament use of σῶμα. JTS 37, 385.

1937

Review of *Fragments of an Unknown Gospel and other Early Christian Papyri,* ed. H. I. Bell and T. C. Skeat. JEA 23, 130–2.

A Note on Mark 4:28 f. JTS 38, 399 f.
Part II (The Sayings of Jesus) of *The Mission and Message of Jesus* (with H. D. A. Major and C. J. Wright). Nicholson and Watson.
Christ and Society. *Toc H. Journal* 15, 3–8.

1938

'Jesus, Paul, and the Law' in *Judaism and Christianity*, vol. iii—*Law and Religion* (ed. E. I. J. Rosenthal), 125–41. Sheldon Press.
Sadducee and Pharisee: the Origin and Significance of the Names. BJRL 22, no. 1.

1939

A Companion to the Bible (editor and contributor). T. & T. Clark.
St. Paul in Ephesus: (1) The Date of the Epistle to the Philippians. BJRL 23, no. 1.

1940

St. Paul in Ephesus: (2) The Problem of the Epistle to the Galatians. BJRL 24, no. 1.
God and the Nations. S.C.M. Press.

1941

Tübingen Revisited (Presidential Address to the Oxford Society of Historical Theology). *Abstract of Proceedings for the Academic Year 1941–1942*, 5–25.
St. Paul in Ephesus: (3) The Corinthian Correspondence. BJRL 26, no. 1.

1942

Review of *Novum Testamentum Graece: Ev. sec. Matt.* (ed. S. C. E. Legg). JTS 43, 83–92.
'Freedom of Thought and Expression' in *What we Defend* (ed. E. F. Jacob), 33–45. O.U.P.
Is it possible to write a Life of Christ? ET 53, 248–51.
St. Paul in Ephesus: (4) The Corinthian Correspondence. BJRL 26, no. 2.

1943

The Life of Jesus: a study of the available material. BJRL 27, no. 2.

1944

'The Failure of Liberalism to interpret the Bible as the Word of God' in *The Interpretation of the Bible* (ed. C. W. Dugmore), 92–107. S.P.C.K.
The Life of Jesus: (2) The Gospel of Mark. BJRL 28, no. 1.
The Life of Jesus: (3) The Work of St. Luke. BJRL 28, no. 2.

1945

Miscellanea Apocalyptica I–II (Pss. Sol. xviii. 6; Ass. Mos. x. 1–10). JTS 46, 41–5.
'ΙΛΑϹΤΗΡΙΟΝ.. JTS 46, 1–10.
The Argument from Prophecy. JTS 46, 129–36.

1946
The Life of Jesus: (4) The Gospel according to St. Matthew. BJRL 29, no. 2.

1947
Entry into Membership of the Early Church. JTS 48, 25–33.
Miscellanea Apocalyptica III (Test. XII Patr.: Levi viii). JTS 48, 59–61.
The Unity of the New Testament: The New Testament Ethics. ET 58, 284–7.
The Life of Jesus: (5) The Fourth Gospel. BJRL 30, no. 2.
Mark 2: 27 f. in *Coniectanea Neotestamentica* xi in honorem Antonii Fridrichsen, 138–46.

1948
St. Paul's Letter to the Romans—and Others. BJRL 31, no. 2.
The Church's Ministry. Hodder and Stoughton.

1949
Review of P. E. Kahle, *The Cairo Geniza. Dominican Studies* 2, 183–92.
Baptism in the Church. *Scottish Journal of Theology* 2, 391–403.
Presbyterian Contribution to *One Catholic and Apostolic Church*, 27–34. Epworth Press.
The Problem of the Epistle to the Hebrews. BJRL 32, no. 1,
The Sayings of Jesus (Pt. II of *The Mission and Message of Jesus*, reissued as a separate volume with some additional notes). S.C.M. Press.
Manchester University Loose Leaf Texts: Series A, Hellenistica (with G. Zuntz). Manchester University Press.

1950
The New Testament Basis of the Doctrine of the Church (Presidential Address to Studiorum Novi Testamenti Societas, 1949), *Journal of Ecclesiastical History*, 1, 1–11.
'Some Reflections on Apocalyptic' in *Aux Sources de la Tradition Chrétienne* (Mélanges Goguel), 139–45.
The Son of Man in Daniel, Enoch, and the Gospels. BJRL 32, no. 2.
The Beginning of the Gospel (*A Primer of Christianity, Pt. I*). O.U.P.
Articles 'Exegesis' and 'Jesus Christ' in *Chambers's Encyclopaedia*. Newnes.

1951
The Cleansing of the Temple. BJRL 33, no. 2.

1952
The Old Testament in the Teaching of Jesus. BJRL 34, no. 2.
The Gospel Miracles. *Religion in Education* 19, 45–51.

1953
Review of J. Jeremias, *Die Gleichnisse Jesu. Göttingische Gelehrte Anzeigen* 207, 141–7.
'2 Cor. 2:14–17: Suggestions towards an Exegesis' in *Studia Paulina in honorem Iohannis de Zwaan*, 155–62.

xiv *Thomas Walter Manson*

St. Paul in Greece: the Letters to the Thessalonians. BJRL 35, no. 2.
The Pericope de Adultera (Joh. 7:53–8:11). ZNTW 44, 255 f.
The Servant-Messiah. C.U.P.

1954

The Bible and Personal Immortality (Drew Lecture). CQ 32, 7–16.
'Preaching and Exegesis' in *Neutestamentliche Studien für R. Bultmann*, 10–14.
John the Baptist. BJRL 36, no. 2.
'Historical Background of the Gospel' and 'The Ministry of Jesus' in *Bible Supplement to the Times.*
Manchester University Faculty of Theology: the first fifty years, a sketch. BJRL 37, no. 1.

1955

The Lord's Prayer (I). BJRL 38, no. 1.
Some Reflections on Biblical Religion. *Manchester Memoirs*, 96 (1954–5), 1–10.
Jesus and the Non-Jews (Ethel M. Wood Lecture: University of London). Athlone Press.
'Realized Eschatology and the Messianic Secret' in *Studies in the Gospels: Essays in memory of R. H. Lightfoot* (ed. D. E. Nineham), 209–22. Blackwell.

1956

The Lord's Prayer (II). BJRL 38, no. 2.
'The Events in the Gospels' in *Jesus Christ: History, Interpretation, and Faith*, 25–43. N.S. and S.P.C.K.
'The Life of Jesus: some tendencies in present-day research' in *The Background of the New Testament and its Eschatology* (Essays in honour of C. H. Dodd), 211–21. C.U.P.

1957

Martyrs and Martyrdom (I). BJRL 39, no. 2.

1958

Ministry and Priesthood: Christ's and Ours. Epworth Press.

ABBREVIATIONS

BDB	Brown, Driver, Briggs, *Hebrew Lexicon*.
BGDW	Bauer, *Griechisch-deutsches Wörterbuch*.
BJRL	*Bulletin of the John Rylands Library*.
BZNW	*Beihefte zur Zeitschrift für die neutestamentliche Wissenschaft*.
C Ber	*Corpus Berolinense* (*Die griechischen christlichen Schriftsteller der ersten drei Jahrhunderte*).
Cent. B	*Century Bible*.
DCG	*Dictionary of Christ and the Gospels*.
ERE	*Encyclopaedia of Religion and Ethics*.
ET	*Expository Times*.
HDB	Hastings' *Dictionary of the Bible*.
HNT	Lietzmann, *Handbuch zum NT*.
HRCS	Hatch and Redpath, *Concordance to the Septuagint*.
ICC	*International Critical Commentary*.
JBL	*Journal of Biblical Literature*.
JEH	*Journal of Ecclesiastical History*.
JR	*Journal of Religion*.
JSS	*Journal of Semitic Studies*.
JTS	*Journal of Theological Studies*.
MGC	Moulton and Geden, *Concordance to the Greek Testament*.
Nov. Test.	*Novum Testamentum*.
NTS	*New Testament Studies*.
RB	*Revue Biblique*.
RGG	*Die Religion in Geschichte und Gegenwart*.
RHPR	*Revue d'Histoire et de Philosophie religieuses*.
SB	Strack-Billerbeck, *Kommentar zum NT aus Talmud und Midrasch*.
SJT	*Scottish Journal of Theology*.
TLZ	*Theologische Literaturzeitung*.
TS	*Texts and Studies*.
TU	*Texte und Untersuchungen zur Geschichte der altchristlichen Literatur*.
TZ	*Theologische Zeitschrift* (Basel).
TWNT	*Theologisches Wörterbuch zum Neuen Testament*, Kittel.
VC	*Vigiliae Christianae*.
VT	*Vetus Testamentum*.
ZNTW	*Zeitschrift für die neutestamentliche Wissenschaft*.

THE BACKGROUND OF MARK 10:45

by

C. K. BARRETT

The Son of man came not to be ministered unto, but to minister, aud to give his life a ransom for many.

THIS saying raises acutely two of the most difficult, and most disputed, questions of New Testament scholarship: (1) What is the meaning of the term Son of man as used in the gospels? (2) Did Jesus foresee his death, and, if so, how did he interpret it? These questions cannot be handled in this essay, in which it will not be possible to discuss even the authenticity, and the interpretation, of Mark 10:45 itself. One subject only is proposed for inquiry: What factors (other than the creative thought of Jesus, or of the primitive Church) contributed to the formation of this saying? Or (in other words), against what background does the saying become most readily intelligible? It will be necessary to impose a further limitation by making the assumption—in which probably all students of the subject would agree—that the background is to be found within the field of the Old Testament and Judaism.

To many, the question can be answered in a word: the background of Mark 10:45 is to be sought in Isa. 53 (more strictly, in Isa. 52:13–53:12). In this verse, Jesus represents himself (or, is represented) as the Suffering Servant of Deutero-Isaiah. This opinion is held so widely and by such distinguished writers[1] that it must appear temerarious to throw oneself into the scale against the weight of their learning. Yet there is a danger lest the cautious judgment of a scholar in one generation become the unexamined opinion of the many in the next, and it may render some service to scholarship if at least a few question-marks are set beside this *communis sensus doctorum*. For the influence of Isa. 53 upon Mark 10:45 is by no means so clear and unambiguous as is often

B

supposed. To say this is not to make the absurd suggestion that Jesus and Mark had never read Isa. 53 or heard of the Servant. The question is not whether there may not be in our verse some distant echo of that passage, but whether the statement about the serving and dying of the Son of man is directly based upon it. It is quite possible that there should be slight resemblances not implying that whoever was responsible for the verse had before his eyes the actual figure of the Servant who was despised and afflicted.[2]

The present essay falls into two parts. In the former, the *language* of Mark 10:45 is examined, with reference to the allusions which have been found in it to the language of Isa. 53; in the latter, an attempt is made to explore the background of *thought* in which the ideas of Mark 10:45 find their place.

I

1. The term 'Son of man', ὁ υἱὸς τοῦ ἀνθρώπου, certainly does not in itself suggest Isa. 53 and the Servant. It has however been argued that it is no more than one remove from Isa. 53, and therefore suggests it indirectly.

Thus 'Son of man' certainly recalls Dan. 7; and at least one passage in Daniel calls to mind the Suffering Servant. In Dan. 12:3 *hammaśkîlîm* and *maṣdîḵē hārabbîm* are singled out for special glory in the age to come. But in Isa. 52:13 it is said *yaśkîl ʿabhdî*, and in 53:11, *yaṣdîk ṣaddîk ʿabhdî lārabbîm*. So we might conclude: Mark rests on Daniel, and Daniel on the song of the Suffering Servant.[3] This is an unconvincing argument.

(*a*) Not even two swallows make a summer; two words, one from the beginning and one from the end of the Song, do not prove the use of the Song as a whole. The words (both of which deal with the glory rather than the suffering of the Servant), are not uncommon; *hiśkîl* occurs 58 times (excluding Psalm titles), and *hiṣdîk* 13 times in the Old Testament. It would be unwise to build a heavy structure on such a foundation.

(*b*) The words are used in different senses in the two books. In Isa. 52:13 *hiśkîl* means, according to K-B,[4] 'to act with insight, piously'; Dr. Mowinckel, perhaps more probably, renders 'will attain his aim';[5] Dr. Engnell[6] thinks of the cultic glorification of the king. When the context as a whole is taken into account it is hard to doubt that the word describes the success, perhaps the triumph, of the Servant.[7] But in Dan. 12:3 the word points back to 11:33 (*maśkîlē 'ām yābhînū lārabbîm*) and 11:35, and these passages strongly suggest that it means 'the teachers'. It is used in this sense in the Zadokite Document,[8] and in some of the Dead Sea MSS.[9]

The meaning of *yaṣdîḳ* in Isa. 53:11 is far from clear, and cannot be discussed here.[10] K-B[11] translate 'to help one to his right'; others[12] prefer an intransitive rendering. The meaning in Dan. 12:3 also is uncertain. Montgomery[13] renders 'set the many right', comparing P. Aboth 5:18 (*kol-hammᵉzakkeh 'eth-hārabbîm*). It may however be suggested that, as *hammaśkîlîm* are the teachers, so *maṣdîḳē hārabbîm* are 'the judges of the community'. For 'the many' as the community as a whole we may quote Dan. 9:27; 11:33, 39. The use became common in later Hebrew; cf. Zad. Frag. 13:7; 14:12; Man. of Disc. 6:1 *et passim*. Indeed, the Qumran documents go far to support the view, which is otherwise by no means improbable, that the *maśkîlîm* and the *maṣdîḳē hārabbîm* are the same persons, those leading members of the community who were both teachers and judges.[14]

In all probability, then, Dan. 12:3 pronounces a special blessing on teachers and judges—the leading members of the Jewish community—at the time of the resurrection. This has little to do with Isa. 53 and the Suffering Servant.

(*c*) The two significant words of Dan. 12:3 are five chapters removed from the chapter of the Son of man, and are in the plural. It is not hard for modern scholars, who adopt some sort of corporate interpretation of the Danielic Son of man, to make out a connection between the man-like figure of 7:13 and the leaders of the people mentioned in 12:3; but it is doubtful whether anyone put the passages together in antiquity.

It follows from these arguments that we cannot use Daniel as a connecting link between Isa. 53 and Mark 10:45, at least as far as the words *maśkîlîm, maṣdîḳîm*, are concerned. On the Son of man in Daniel see further below.[15]

If it be true that it is impossible to draw a straight line from Mark 10:45 to Isa. 53 through Daniel, the figure of the Son of man in 1 Enoch will scarcely call for consideration. There are indeed in 1 Enoch 37-71 reminiscences of Isaianic Servant passages,[16] but the crucial point is that, whatever verbal echoes may exist, the Son of man in 1 Enoch does not suffer.[17] This book provides no link between Mark and the *Suffering* Servant.

2. 'Came', ἦλθεν, need not detain us. It does not suggest Isa. 53, nor can it be seriously held to suggest any other background passage. It may be worth while to recall the language of Dan. 7:13: k^ebhar '$^enāš$ '$āthēh$ $h^awā$' (LXX: ὡς υἱὸς ἀνθρώπου ἤρχετο; Th.: ὡς υἱὸς ἀνθρώπου ἐρχόμενος). Daniel's vision is of a future coming, but the aorist ἦλθεν could represent the characteristically paradoxical New Testament view of the fulfilment of prophecy—the Son of man *has* come. Nothing however can be built on this word.

3. The next clause, 'not to be served but to serve', οὐ διακονηθῆναι ἀλλὰ διακονῆσαι, offers at first sight a much stronger argument to those who maintain that Mark 10:45 is based on the figure of the Servant;[18] but the linguistic connection with Isa. 53 is less close than is often thought.

In the Servant Songs the Servant is always described as God's '*ebhedh*. This word becomes in the Targum (except in 53:11, where there is a free paraphrase) '*abhdā*'; the same word is used in the Peshitto. In the LXX it is at 42:1; 49:6; 52:13 παῖς; at 49:3, 5 δοῦλος; at 53:11 it is paraphrased εὖ δουλεύοντα. In the Old Testament generally the root '-b-d is rendered by a quite bewildering variety of Greek words; but it is never rendered by διακονεῖν or any of its cognates.

These Greek words are in fact very uncommon in the LXX. The verb does not occur at all. διακονία is found as a variant at Esther 6:3, 5 (see below), and at 1 Macc. 11:58, where it appears to mean a dinner service. διάκονος is used disparagingly at 4 Macc. 9:17 of the servants of Antiochus IV; at Prov. 10:4, where there is no Hebrew equivalent; and (with οἱ ἐκ τῆς διακονίας as a variant at 6:3, 5) in Esther 1:10; 2:2; 6:3, 5 (and as an inferior reading at 6:1), where it renders either *na'ar*, or the Pi'el participle of *šārath*, or the two in apposition. *Linguistically*, διακονεῖν does not recall Isa. 53, or any of the Servant passages.

4. The Son of man came 'to give his life', δοῦναι τὴν ψυχὴν αὐτοῦ. This clause is said to reflect Isa. 53:12, παρεδόθη εἰς θάνατον ἡ ψυχὴ αὐτοῦ (*he'erāh lammāweth naphšō*). It would be absurd to deny a measure of linguistic parallelism between the Old and New Testament passages at this point; but even here it is well to avoid premature conclusions.

The expression in Isa. 53:12 is unique in the Old Testament. '-r-h is not a very common root; in the Hiph'il it occurs only here and at Lev. 20:18, 19, where its objects are *meͤkōrāh* and *šeͤ'ērō* respectively, and it means 'to uncover', 'to make naked'. The meaning 'to pour out' is found with the Pi'el at Gen. 24:20 (object, *kaddāh*) and 2 Chron. 24:11 (object, *hā'ārōn*); and more significantly at Ps. 141:8, where the object is *naphšî* (LXX: ⸢μὴ ἀντανέλῃς τὴν ψυχήν μου). Even this however is not a true parallel to Isa. 53:12, where *naphšō*, agreeing in person with the verb, is probably reflexive. The word *lammāweth* is generally excised by editors on metrical grounds; the fact that it was added shows that without it *he'eͤrāh naphšō* was not perfectly clear: 'he surrendered himself—to death'. The LXX use of παραδιδόναι (rather than διδόναι) may support this view.

The simpler phrase used in Mark, ψυχὴν διδόναι, seems to have been coming into use in the post-biblical period, perhaps under Greek influence (see also below on λύτρον ἀντὶ πολλῶν). Büchsel (TWNT ii. 168) writes, 'The expression is current among the Jews for the death of martyrs, among the Greeks for the death of soldiers'. It can also mean 'to devote one's life in service'. See for examples of the Greek phrase 1 Macc. 2:50 (cf. 6:44, where ἑαυτόν probably represents *naphšō*); Ecclus. 29:15. The expression *nāthan naphšō* is also fairly common in post-biblical Hebrew.[19]

It cannot be claimed that δοῦναι τὴν ψυχήν had a background of its own other than Isa. 53; but neither can it be said that it points unambiguously to that chapter.

5. According to Professor R. H. Fuller,[20] 'λύτρον is a perfectly adequate rendering of '*āšām*' (Isa. 53:10: '*im-tāśîm 'āšām naphšō*). This confident statement is open to question. In the Old Testament '*āšām* occurs 46 times; it is rendered in the LXX by ἄγνοια, ἀδικία, ἁμαρτία, βάσανος, καθαρισμός, πλημμελεῖν, πλημμέλημα, πλημμελία, but *never* by λύτρον or any cognate word.

Again, λύτρον renders the roots *g-'-l*, *k-p-r*, *p-d-h*, and the word *meͤhîr*; if we add the Greek cognates λύτρωσις, λυτρωτής, λυτρωτός, and λυτροῦν we may add in Hebrew the roots '*-r-p*, *p-l-ṭ*, *p-ṣ-h*, *p-r-ḳ*, *k-n-h*, *ś-g-b*, *š-g-b*. But *never* does λύτρον render '*āšām* or any cognate word.

The linguistic data are too striking to be regarded as merely fortuitous; they represent a real difference in meaning between '*āšām* and λύτρον.[21] The basic idea represented by the root '-*š-m* is *guilt*, and although it has been argued[22] that the notion of compensation is essential to the 'āšām it is important here to keep in mind a clear distinction which exists in the biblical, and especially in the post-biblical, texts. The fundamental law is set out in Lev. 5:14-26 (cf. Num. 5:5-10), and analysed more clearly in Zebahim 5:5: an 'āšām is offered in respect of false dealing, sacrilege, intercourse with a betrothed bondwoman, failure to keep a Nazirite vow, and the cleansing of a leper. In at least three cases the Mishnah (following the Pentateuch) expressly distinguishes between the act of restitution, and the offering of the 'āšām;[23] and in Zebahim 10:5 it is said that the 'āšām of the leper is offered 'to render him fit [to enter the Temple and to eat of Hallowed Things]'. It is not a compensation.

In λύτρον the idea of equivalence is central.[24] What the word meant to a Greek-speaking Jew is shown by an often quoted sentence in Josephus (*Ant.* xiv. 107), which describes the unsuccessful attempt made (in 54 B.C.) by the priest Eleazar to buy off Crassus: τὴν δοκὸν αὐτῷ τὴν χρυσῆν λύτρον ἀντὶ πάντων ἔδωκεν. Eleazar gave him the golden bar in the hope that he would take nothing else, that he would take it *instead of* all the other things he might have taken.

This sense of equivalence, or substitution, is proper to λύτρον, and also to the Semitic roots mainly connected with it—g-'-l, k-p-r, p-d-h. None of these, nor indeed any Hebrew word ever translated by λύτρον, occurs in Isa. 53; but in a number of passages they help to illuminate Mark 10:45. Among these may be noted:

Exod. 21:30   δώσει λύτρα τῆς ψυχῆς αὐτοῦ
              weᵉnāthan pidhyōn naphšō.
Exod. 30:12   δώσουσιν ἕκαστος λύτρα τῆς ψυχῆς αὐτοῦ
              weᵉnāthᵉnu 'iš kōpher naphšō.
Cf. Exod. 21:23 δώσει ψυχὴν ἀντὶ ψυχῆς
              weᵉnāthattāh napheš taḥath napheš.
and 4 Kdms 10:24 ἡ ψυχὴ αὐτοῦ ἀντὶ τῆς ψυχῆς αὐτοῦ
              naphšō taḥath naphšō.
ψ 48:8   ἀδελφὸς οὐ λυτροῦται · λυτρώσεται ἄνθρωπος;
              οὐ δώσει τῷ θεῷ ἐξίλασμα αὐτοῦ
Ps. 49:8   'āḥ lō'-phādhōh yiphdeh 'iš
              lō'-yittēn lē'lōhim kophrō.

Isa. 52:3   οὐ μετὰ ἀργυρίου λυτρωθήσεσθε
               lō' bhᵉkheseph tiggā'ēlū.

In virtue of something given (which may or may not be a ψυχή) a ψυχή is set free. Thus the linguistic connection between λύτρον in Mark 10:45 and Isa. 53 is non-existent; and the theme of ransoming is far too widespread in the Old Testament to allow us to suppose that it must have been drawn from one particular passage.

6. The last words of Mark 10:45, 'for many', ἀντὶ πολλῶν, have been touched on in the last quotations. ἀντί is bound up in sense with λύτρον; λύτρον demands an ἀντί to follow. ἀντί and its Hebrew equivalent *taḥath* occur in Isa. 52:13–53:12, but not significantly. We have 53:9 . . . ἀντὶ τῆς ταφῆς αὐτοῦ . . . ἀντὶ τοῦ θανάτου (. . . ḳibhrō . . . bᵉmōthāyw), which may require emendation; and in 53:12 the idiomatic ἀνθ' ὧν, rendering the equally idiomatic *taḥath 'ᵃšer*. There is nothing here to our purpose.

Great weight is sometimes laid upon Mark's πολλῶν. It is true that here we can cite Isa.

52:14   ἐκστήσονται ἐπὶ σὲ πολλοί (šamᵉmū 'āleykhā rabbîm)
52:15   θαυμάσονται ἔθνη πολλά (yazzeh gōyîm rabbîm)
53:11   δικαιῶσαι δίκαιον εὖ δουλεύοντα πολλοῖς (yaṣdîḳ ṣaddîḳ
         'abhdî lārabbîm)
53:12   κληρονομήσει πολλούς ('ᵃḥalleḳ-lō lārabbîm)
53:12   ἁμαρτίας πολλῶν ἀνήνεγκεν (ḥēṭ'-rabbîm nāśā')

It is however difficult to feel that there is anything conclusive in these quotations. It is perhaps trite to point out that in Greek πολλοί and in Hebrew *rabbîm* are common words. It is more significant that in Isa. 53 we have only one example, though an outstanding example, of a theme which runs through the whole of the Old Testament, namely, the relation of the One to the Many.[25]

Our examination of the *language* of Mark 10:45 is now at an end. It would be difficult indeed, on the basis of it, to claim that Mark's words point clearly to Isa. 53 rather than to any other part of the Old Testament and Jewish literature. Accordingly, we turn to the background of thought.

II

The real crux of the problem lies in the use of the title Son of man. Superficially at least this (like other sayings which declare that the Son of man is to suffer) is a paradoxical inversion of the meaning of the term. Outside the gospels, the Son of man is in general a figure of glory rather than of suffering: among many passages see Dan. 7:13 f.; 1 Enoch 46:3; 48:5; 69:29;[26] 4 Ezra 13:3 f. It would of course be quite wrong to expect to find a 'background' containing all the thought of Mark 10:45. Full allowance must be made for originality, but even originality almost always works within a given framework of ideas, selecting, rearranging, developing, modifying, contradicting, but never in a vacuum. The question before us therefore is whether the apocalyptic background of thought, which is certainly suggested by the term Son of man, provides a framework of ideas in which Mark 10:45 becomes intelligible without direct recourse to Isa. 53, which, as we have seen, is much less strongly suggested by the terminology of our verse than is often supposed.

There are two main problems, (*a*) that of the serving, and (*b*) that of the suffering and dying, of the Son of man.

1. *The Son of man came to serve.* In Mark 10:45 it is said that the Son of man οὐκ ἦλθεν διακονηθῆναι ἀλλὰ διακονῆσαι. The formulation of this sentence is determined by the words οὐ-ἀλλά; the truth is expressed first negatively, then positively. Why should this form of utterance be chosen? There is a partial answer to this question in the context,[27] but it is scarcely sufficient, and we are therefore obliged to consider it further.

The οὐ-ἀλλά is intended to bring out a *contrast*. This incidentally goes a long way towards removing the saying from the field of Isa. 53 and the Servant, for it would be more than a little precious to insist that the Servant did not come to be served. There can be little doubt what contrast is intended. The verse sets out to teach a different view of the Son of man from that which was at the time commonly accepted: '. . . not, *as you might think*, or *do think*, to be served, but to serve.' This view finds strong confirmation in what is said elsewhere about the Son of man; see, for example, Dan. 7:14: There was given him dominion, and glory, and a kingdom, that all the peoples, nations, and languages should *serve him* (*yiphl*ᵉ*ḥūn*); cf. v. 27, and 1 Enoch 46:3–6; 48:5; 62:8.[28]

According to Mark 10:45, this picture of the glorious Son of man, who comes that all may serve him, is wrong (or rather, incomplete); the Son of man has come not to be served but to serve.

It may be said that it was precisely the figure of the Servant which thus modified the conception of the Son of man. To this suggestion the following replies may be made. (*a*) The most powerful motive for the οὐ-ἀλλά correction was not literary at all, but arose out of the circumstances of the ministry of Jesus. He who was the Son of man, and was to come in glory, had come in humility to serve. (*b*) We have already seen that the evidence alleged to connect Mark 10:45 with Isa. 53 is unconvincing. There is moreover very little evidence anywhere else in the gospels to suggest Isa. 53.[29] (*c*) In the Old Testament the idea of service is to be found in many places other than Isa. 53. To mention no others, Abraham, Isaac, Jacob, Joshua, Caleb, David, Hezekiah, and Zerubbabel are all described as God's servants. In particular, Moses is very frequently said, in the Old Testament and elsewhere, to be God's servant, whose meekness, humility, and death (cf. also Exod. 32:32) atoned for Israel.[30] We *know* that the figure of Moses, and those of the humble men of the Psalms, affected the gospels, and due weight should be given to them in the attempt to discover what led to the change in the character and function of the Son of man.

2. *The Son of man came to give his life*. In this second part of the verse the οὐ-ἀλλά contrast is not explicitly continued; nevertheless (especially as οὐ precedes ἦλθεν) it is possible that its sense is carried on. Certainly it is true that in other sources the Son of man does not give his life but destroys his enemies; e.g. 1 Enoch 46:4 ff.; 69:27 (. . . he caused the sinners to pass away and be destroyed from off the face of the earth . . .). If a contrast with this destroying Son of man is implied, where does it arise?

The question can be answered simply by those who believe that it is possible to trace a more or less direct line of development from an *Urmensch*, or a Tammuz, ideology, through the cultic experiences of the sacred king, to the humiliation and exaltation of the Servant in Isa. 53, and thence in turn to Dan. 7. According to this view, suffering is inherent in the role of the Son of man, and has its roots in primitive mythological thought and in ancient Israelite cultus. It is as proper to the Son of man that he should suffer as that he should subsequently be glorified. This theory is attractive but unconvincing.

(*a*) Identification of the Servant with an *Urmensch*, or with Tammuz, is too speculative—as the disagreement on these issues between a number of very eminent scholars is sufficient to suggest. Discussion of the matter would be out of place here, but it may be said that there are at least two major issues on which so much doubt remains, and so little evidence exists, that it is unwise to proceed on the basis of preliminary judgments about them. These are (i) the provenance and date of the oriental *Urmensch* speculations, and (ii) the question how far it is legitimate to draw conclusions about an Israelite cultus, concerning which we have no first-hand information, from the rites of other nations who were for the most part the objects of Israelite suspicion and distrust.

(*b*) Even if the figure of the Servant in Isa. 53 could be accounted for on the basis of an Israelite crystallization in cultic form of non-Israelite mythology it would still be necessary to demonstrate a continuity of thought leading from Deutero-Isaiah through Daniel and 1 Enoch to Mark; and this is quite impossible. The cultus of the sacred king, if it ever existed, must have ceased at the Exile, and though living tradition may have lasted till the writing of Deutero-Isaiah it could hardly have survived till the second century B.C., still less to the first century A.D. There seems to be no evidence that the figure of the Servant exerted any direct influence upon Daniel,[31] or indeed upon the thought of the Maccabean period in general.[32] It has been maintained[33] that in the time of Christ there were Jews who found in Isa. 53 the promise of a suffering and dying Messiah; but the case does not seem to have been made out.[34]

It is better to begin with the documents. A primary observation is that Jewish eschatology contains an *Unheilseschatologie*. It looks to an ultimately happy future, but its brightness is set off by dark clouds. There are two main features in the unhappy future: (*a*) the torment and ultimate destruction of the wicked; (*b*) the temporary afflictions of the righteous, who must pass through a time of trial before reaching the bliss of the age to come. This time of trial is often, and naturally, compared to the travail pains which precede birth. The apocalyptists tend to think, somewhat naïvely, that mankind fall into two groups, the Righteous, or Elect; and the Wicked. The former suffer in the present age, and prosper in the age to come; the latter prosper in this age, and suffer in the future.[35]

Bliss is preceded and off-set by suffering. Along with this fact may be set another, to which reference has already been made.[36] Jewish thought readily works in terms of representation: an individual may represent his people in his own person. He may even bear their punishment or suffering, and they can bear his.[37] No one who is at home in the Old Testament will be surprised to read in the New Testament that one may act, or even suffer, ἀντὶ πολλῶν—provided of course that it is the right 'one'.

A third observation is that, within Judaism, the Son of man as a distinct figure first appears at the time of the Maccabees.

It is true that the words *ben 'ādhām* have appeared long before this. The title is very common as a vocative in Ezekiel. It is used in synonymous parallelism with *'îš* at Num. 23:19; Job 35:8; Ps. 80:18; Jer. 49:18, 33; 50:40; 51:43, and with *'enōš* at Job 25:6; Ps. 8:5; Isa. 56:2. Ps. 146:3, where the parallel is *nedhîbhîm*, is similar; we must understand 'men who are princes'. Only Dan. 8:17 is left over,[38] and it remains true that the Son of man as an apocalyptic figure arises first in Daniel, that is, at the time of the attempted suppression of Judaism under Antiochus IV.[39]

In this period two great religious issues, so closely related to each other that it is not easy to set them out separately, became prominent. These are the problem of suffering, and the development of individualism in religion. It is simplest to view them together as they crystallized in the experience of Jews under the Syrian kingdom.

The mere fact of suffering does not call for elaboration. Jews who refused to join the 'United Hellenistic Front' which Antiochus IV sought, not without political reason, to impose upon the Levant, were exposed to no common pains. It suffices to recall the story of the seven brothers and their mother in 2 Macc. 7. It is not however the barbarity of the tortures that were devised that calls for notice, but the fact that they were imposed upon, and freely accepted by, individuals. In earlier periods the people suffered as a whole; in the horrors of a siege, or a transportation, all had their part, willy-nilly. It was not so in this period. Those who were prepared to abandon the practice of Judaism could avoid punishment and secure advancement (e.g. 2 Macc. 7:24).

Some took advantage of such opportunities (e.g. 1 Macc. 1:52 f.). It was the voluntary acceptance of martyrdom that stimulated Jewish thought in the direction of individualism. If the whole nation (or at least a very substantial part of it) was transported to Babylon, the divine act of vindication and restoration naturally took the form of the return of the whole nation to its own land. It was the nation that suffered and died, and the nation that was vindicated and raised up. But this was a process that did not apply to the new situation, in which circumstances had forced upon individual Jews the choice between apostasy and martyrdom. Some had been faithful, others had not. It was only right that the future also should be differentiated; and the differentiation appears in classic form in Dan. 12:2: Many of them that sleep in the dust of the earth shall awake, some to everlasting life, and some to shame and everlasting contempt.

This individualistic evaluation of the destiny of the martyrs could not however do justice to the strong collective or corporate sense of traditional Jewish thought. The martyr's death was not after all a purely personal affair; it was believed to influence the destiny of the people as a whole. Thus 2 Macc. 7:37 f.:

I ... give up body and soul ($\sigma\tilde{\omega}\mu\alpha$ $\varkappa\alpha\grave{\iota}$ $\psi\upsilon\chi\grave{\eta}\nu$[40] $\pi\varrho\upsilon\delta\acute{\iota}\delta\omega\mu\iota$) for our fathers' laws, calling on God to show favour ($\tau\grave{\upsilon}\nu$ $\theta\epsilon\grave{\upsilon}\nu$ $\emph{i}\lambda\epsilon\omega\nu$ ... $\gamma\epsilon\nu\acute{\epsilon}\sigma\theta\alpha\iota$) to our nation soon, and to make them acknowledge, in torments and plagues, that he alone is God, and to let the Almighty's wrath, justly fallen on the whole of our nation, end in me and in my brothers.

The self-sacrifice of the martyrs, who acted as intercessors before God, would form a means of atonement for Israel. The same theme is developed elsewhere.

4 Macc. 6:27 ff.: Thou, O God, knowest that though I might save myself I am dying by fiery torments for thy Law. Be merciful ($\emph{i}\lambda\epsilon\omega\varsigma$ $\gamma\acute{\epsilon}\nu\upsilon$) unto thy people, and let our punishment be a satisfaction on their behalf. Make my blood their purification ($\varkappa\alpha\theta\acute{\alpha}\varrho\sigma\iota\upsilon\nu$), and take my soul ($\psi\upsilon\chi\acute{\eta}\nu$) to ransom their souls ($\grave{\alpha}\nu\tau\acute{\iota}\psi\upsilon\chi\upsilon\nu$ $\alpha\grave{\upsilon}\tau\tilde{\omega}\nu$).

17:22: Through the blood of these righteous men and the propitiation of their death ($\tau\upsilon\tilde{\upsilon}$ $\emph{i}\lambda\alpha\sigma\tau\eta\varrho\acute{\iota}\upsilon\upsilon$ $\theta\alpha\nu\acute{\alpha}\tau\upsilon\upsilon$ $\alpha\grave{\upsilon}\tau\tilde{\omega}\nu$), the divine Providence delivered Israel that before was evil entreated.

18:4: Through them the nation obtained peace.

It would not be an exaggeration to say that the martyrs are here described as—$\lambda\acute{\upsilon}\tau\varrho\upsilon\nu$ $\grave{\alpha}\nu\tau\grave{\iota}$ $\pi\upsilon\lambda\lambda\tilde{\omega}\nu$.

These documents are of course Greek books, but we can see the imprint of the ideas they contain in the Rabbinic use of *kappārāh*. It is here that the true linguistic background of λύτρον is to be found. In the old Testament, the root *k-p-r* frequently stands behind the LXX use of λύτρον and its cognates.[41] The later use of *kappārāh* is equally important. Such expressions as 'The children of Israel (may I make atonement for them!) . . .' are not uncommon.[42] Suffering in general is a means of atonement.[43] Death in particular acts as an atonement, both for the individual who dies, and for others, if the man who dies is righteous.[44] Even the execution of a criminal makes atonement for the man himself; the man being led out for stoning is bidden to say (Sanhedrin 6:2), 'May my death be an atonement for all my sins' (*kappārāh 'al-kol-'awōnōthay*). But 'as the Day of Atonement makes atonement (*mekhappēr*), so the death of the righteous (*saddîkîm*) makes atonement (*mekhappereth*)' (Lev. R. 20:7 (end)). The most important example from our point of view is that of death in martyrdom. The Rabbis undoubtedly preserved the Maccabean view that martyrdom effected atonement; see for example Siphre Deuteronomy 333:

'And his land shall atone for its people' (Deut. 32:43). How canst thou know that the martyrdom [lit. slaying] of Israel at the hands of the Gentiles is an atonement in the world to come? Because it says 'O God, the heathen have come into thine inheritance . . . they have given . . . the flesh of thy saints to the beasts of the earth' (Ps. 79:1 f.) (translation from C. G. Montefiore and H. Loewe, *A Rabbinic Anthology* (1938), 226).

R. Akiba and his companions, who were martyred in A.D. 135, form an outstanding example. It was in the Maccabean period that Judaism became 'eine Religion des Martyriums',[45] and this it remained throughout the period with which we are concerned.

We are now in a position to return to the theme of the Son of man. Daniel as a whole is a book of martyrdom. This is evident in the narrative sections, but it is true of the rest of the book too. In 11:33; 12:3 we have seen in the *maśkîlîm* the teachers of the people; but they suffered the same fate as their successors, R. Akiba and his companions.[46] Dan. 7 also speaks of the sufferings of the people. Before the appearance of the one described as *kebhar 'enāš*, who represents the people of the saints of the Most

High, there appear four beast-like figures, which correspond to four kings (7:17). It is simply a matter of history that the four kingdoms thus represented had in turn tyrannized over and oppressed the saints; that is, in the terms of the vision, the Son of man, before coming into glory, suffers, and his sufferings are, historically, the sufferings of the martyrs. The celestial work of the Son of man is a mythological, eschatological expression of the deeds of the martyrs; the assured triumph of the Son of man is an expression of the fact that God will surely accept the atoning sufferings of the martyrs, and because of them deliver his people.

If it be asked why a figure so described is chosen to represent the heavenly aspect of the suffering of Israel on behalf of the Law, an answer may be sought in what was said above on the question of individualism, which was so acutely raised by the events of the Maccabean period. Individual responsibility and individual reward were brought into the foreground, but at the same time the solidarity of the people was not lost sight of: what the One did affected the Many. Now more vividly even than King or Priest or Servant, the figure of the Man suggests the representation of the Many by the One. Quite apart from any mythological background which may underlie Dan. 7, one who is defined as Man, whether he be thought of as the *Urmensch* and progenitor, or as Archetypal Man, evidently stands in a special relation to mankind as a whole. If he suffers, he suffers in a representative capacity, and his sufferings, like those of the martyrs, are a *kappārāh*: he gives his life as λύτρον ἀντὶ πολλῶν.

It remains only to add a few details from 1 Enoch. (a) This book belongs to the same context of suffering as Daniel;[47] see for example 1:1; 46:8 (They persecute the houses of his congregations); 47:2 (. . . the blood of the righteous . . . that they may not have to suffer for ever).

(b) As has often been remarked, the Son of man in 1 Enoch stands in close relation to the people: he is the Righteous One, they are the righteous; he is the Elect One, they are the elect; and so on.[48]

(c) In 1 Enoch 71, Enoch is exalted to heaven, and (apparently) identified with the Son of man. We cannot here go into the problems raised by this very difficult chapter,[49] but it must have helped to prepare the way for the conception of one who lived an earthly life (even though, unlike Enoch's, it ended in death), was exalted to heaven, and there awaited the due moment to appear as Judge of the living and the dead.

To sum up: it appears (*a*) that the connection between Mark 10:45 and Isa. 53 is much less definite and more tenuous than is often supposed;[50] and (*b*) that the background sketched in the second part of this essay is such that a creative mind working upon it could produce a saying such as that recorded by Mark.

NOTES.

[1] In the interests of brevity I quote only T. W. Manson, 'The Son of Man in Daniel, Enoch and the Gospels', BJRL 32 (1950), 192: Jesus 'defined the "Son of man" in terms of the "Servant of the Lord" '. Cf. *The Servant-Messiah* (1953), 73: this definition 'appears clearly in the sayings about the Son of man, especially those which emphasise his task of service and sacrifice'. I regret that my study of the present question leads me to differ in some respects from one for whose work on the New Testament I have the greatest possible admiration.

[2] Cf. the fact (for which see below, pp.3 f. with notes 16 and 17) that though the Similitudes of Enoch contain verbal echoes of Deutero-Isaiah they reveal no conception of a *suffering* Servant.

[3] See C. R. North, *The Suffering Servant in Deutero-Isaiah* (1948), 6 f. Cf. also the article by I. Engnell cited in note 6, and A. Bentzen, *Messias, Moses redivivus, Menschensohn* (1948), 53.

[4] *Lexicon in Veteris Testamenti Libros* (1953), 922b.

[5] *He that Cometh* (1956), 196, cf. 204.

[6] I. Engnell, 'The 'Ebed Yahweh Songs and the Suffering Servant in "Deutero-Isaiah" ', BJRL 31 (1948), 54–93. On *yaśkîl*, 75 ff. 'Thus we have the right to assume that the contested *yaśkîl* in our text means *either* "to execute a *maśkîl*", i.e. an Annual Festival psalm, *or* "take the throne, the power in (re)possession" or the like, to wit, after the passion and resurrection. . . . The latter seems to be decidedly preferable' (77). See also H. H. Rowley, *The Servant of the Lord* (1952), 43–6.

[7] So BDB, and most commentators.

[8] 13:7, of the M*e*bhakkēr (*yaśkîl...'ēth hārabbîm*).

[9] *Manual of Discipline* 3:13; 9:18; *Hodayoth* (*Meg. Gen.*) 2:50, 3.

[10] On the root ṣ-d-ḳ in general see G. Quell in TWNT ii, 176–80, and the literature there cited.

[11] *Op. cit.*, 794b.

[12] E.g. Mowinckel *op. cit.*, 199, 204: 'will stand forth as righteous before the many'.

[13] J. A. Montgomery, *A Critical and Exegetical Commentary on the Book of Daniel* (ICC) (1927), 472 f.

[14] For Rabbis in this twofold capacity cf. e.g. Sanhedrin 6:4 (Simeon ben Shetah), Baba Kamma 8:6 (Akiba). See also passages such as Aboth 1:1; Baba Bathra 8b.

[15] See pp. 13 f., and note 39.

[16] See TWNT v, 686 f. (J. Jeremias); W. Manson, *Jesus the Messiah* (1943), 173 f.

[17] See below, pp. 8 ff. and cf. Mowinckel, *op. cit.*, 410–15.

[18] See below, pp. 8 f., where the theme of service is considered.

[19] See e.g. Tos. Berakoth 7:7 (Zuck. 15:15); Siphre Deuteronomy 306; Mekilta on Exod. 12:1 (1b), and on 15:20 (43b). Cf. also Isaac's self-offering as interpreted in early Judaism; see H. J. Schoeps, *Aus frühchristlicher Zeit* (1950), especially 234; also J. Jeremias, *Judaica* 3 (1947), 253.

[20] *The Mission and Achievement of Jesus* (1954), 57. On this question in general see J. Jeremias, 'Das Lösegeld für Viele (Mark 10:45)', *Judaica* 3 (1947), 249–64.

[21] It is significant that in his Hebrew New Testament Delitzsch translates λύτρον not by 'āšām but by kōpher. Similarly G. Dalman (*Jesus-Jeshua* (1929), 118) translates λύτρον into Aramaic as purḳān (cf. the Syriac rendering at Mark 10:45; Matt. 20:28), though 'ªšāmā was available if it had seemed appropriate. Cf. J. Jeremias, *Judaica* 3 (1947), 250: 'Im Hebräischen wird das an Gott gezahlte Lösegeld meist mit kōpher, vereinzelt mit pidhyōn und 'āšām bezeichnet.' But for 'āšām he quotes only Isa. 53:10.

[22] Recently by H. C. Thompson, in *Transactions of the Glasgow University Oriental Society* 14 (1953), 20–6. See also E. Lohse, *Märtyrer und Gottesknecht* (1955), 119.

[23] Baba Kamma 9:8: If he confessed it [misuse of a deposit] of himself, he must repay the value and the added fifth and offer a Guilt-offering. Shebuoth 8:3 [loss of a borrowed ox]; Kerithoth 5:2 [sacrilege].

[24] The primary meaning of course refers to the ransoming of a slave by the payment of an equivalent price.

[25] See below, pp. 11–15.

[26] For text and meaning see E. Sjöberg, *Der Menschensohn im äthiopischen Henochbuch* (1946), 9.

[27] Certain disciples (Mark 10:37) have shown themselves, unlike the Son of man, more anxious to be served than to serve. But in the answer to them (10:39) it is promised that they will suffer with Jesus—a promise scarcely consistent with 10:45. It may be that Luke's partial parallel (22:27) is more accurately placed.

[28] Cf. also Ps. 8:5 ff. When this Psalm was understood to refer to the Son of man as a supernatural figure it was seen to represent him as entitled to universal service. Cf. Ps. 110:1; and 1 Cor. 15:27; Eph. 1:22; Heb. 2:6–9.

[29] I may refer here to an important work by Miss Morna D. Hooker, to be published shortly by S.P.C.K. as *Jesus and the Servant*. Miss Hooker's arguments go far to support conclusions which I had arrived at independently.

[30] For evidence, see J. Jeremias in TWNT iv, 856–68.

[31] For a consideration of Dan. 12:3 see above, pp. 2 f.

[32] See below, note 50.

[33] See especially J. Jeremias, 'Zum Problem der Deutung von Jes. 53 im palästinischen Spätjudentum', in *Aux Sources de la Tradition Chrétienne* (Mélanges offerts à M. Goguel; 1950), 113–19; also TWNT v, 680–98.

[34] This opinion ought of course to be substantiated in detail. Space forbids

this here, and for the present reference to Mowinckel, *op. cit.*, 325–33, 410–15, must suffice.

[35] Cf. the Rabbinic view (e.g. Berakoth 7a; T. J. Kiddushin 1, § 7, f. 61b, line 62) that in this life the virtuous are punished for their minor sins and the wicked rewarded for their minor virtues, that both may have an unmixed requital in the future.

[36] See pp. 6 f.

[37] Out of the literature on this subject may be mentioned H. W. Robinson, 'The Hebrew Conception of Corporate Personality', in *Werden und Wesen des Alten Testaments* (BZAW 66; 1936), 49 ff.; A. R. Johnson, *The One and the Many in the Israelite Conception of God* (1942); and D. Daube's acute discussion of 'Communal Responsibility' in his *Studies in Biblical Law* (1947), 154–89.

[38] Ps. 80:18 (which can no longer be regarded as Maccabean in origin) might appear to be another exception; but the parallelism shows that here 'Son of man' is metaphor, and does not refer to a specific figure.

[39] Whether the Son of man may be described as an individual figure is disputed: see especially T. W. Manson, *The Teaching of Jesus* (1935), 211–34; and the article cited in note 1. That the Son of man in Daniel represents a community is certainly true (cf. Dan. 7:13, 27). But a community may be represented by an abstraction of itself with no independent existence (e.g. John Bull), or by a distinct person (e.g. an ambassador). That the Son of man in Daniel is the latter kind of representative is suggested by the following considerations. (*a*) Daniel certainly knows of heavenly representatives, especially Michael, who acts on behalf of the people of God (10:13, 21; 12:1). (*b*) It is possible to identify other visionary features of Dan. 7 with individual persons; e.g. the 'little horn' (7:8) is almost certainly Antiochus IV. (*c*) In 8:15 we read of one *k͏ᵉmar'ēh ghebher*; in 10:16 of one *kidh͏ᵉmûth b͏ᵉnēy 'ādhām*; and in 10:18 of one *k͏ᵉmar'ēh 'ādhām*. It is probable that these Hebrew phrases were intended to mean much the same as the Aramaic *k͏ᵉbhar 'ᵉnāš* (7:13), and do not stand for abstractions.

There is even less probability that the Son of man in 1 Enoch is a mere abstraction of the people.

[40] *V.l.* τύχην.

[41] See above, p. 6.

[42] E.g. Negaim 2:1 (*'ᵃnî khappārāh*).

[43] See A. Büchler, *Studies in Sin and Atonement* (1928), 175–89, especially 188 f.; also J. Bonsirven, *Le Judaïsme Palestinien* (1934/5), ii, 96 ff.; G. F. Moore, *Judaism* (1927), i, 546–52; S. Schechter, *Some Aspects of Rabbinic Theology* (1909), 307–11; E. Lohse, *op. cit.*, 29–32. There is a good example in Midr. Ps. on 118:18 (243b, § 16): Beloved are sufferings, for they appease like offerings; yea, they are more beloved than offerings, for guilt and sin offerings atone only for the particular sin for which they are brought in each case, but sufferings atone for *all* sins, as it says, 'The Lord has chastened me sore, but he has not given me over unto death.'

[44] Büchler, *op. cit.*, 189–207; Bonsirven, *ibid.*; Moore, *ibid.*; E. Lohse, *op. cit.*, 32–110.

[45] W. Bousset—H. Gressmann, *Die Religion des Judentums* (1926), 374. Some would at this point refer to the 'Dead Sea Scrolls'; but in fact these do not contain such clear references to the atoning power of martyrdom as has

c

been supposed. See T. H. Gaster, *The Scriptures of the Dead Sea Sect* (1957), 28 f.

[46] See especially 11:33: They shall fall by the sword and by flame, by captivity and by spoil, many days.

[47] Not necessarily to the same date.

[48] On this see especially T. W. Manson, BJRL 32 (1950), 188 ff.

[49] See especially E. Sjöberg, *op. cit.*, 147–89.

[50] The view (see e.g. R. H. Kennett, *The Servant of the Lord* (1911)) that Isa. 53 was itself written in the Maccabean period has little to commend it; and there seems no good reason to believe that Isa. 53 was responsible for the theology of martyrdom developed at that time (though this is stated, without proof, by e.g. N. Johansson, in *Parakletoi* (1940), 72).

THE ARREST AND TRIAL OF JESUS AND THE DATE OF THE LAST SUPPER

by

M. BLACK

IT has long been recognized that the author of the Gospel according to St. Mark (followed, in this respect, by the other two Synoptic Gospels) presents us with a compressed or 'telescoped' account of the Ministry of Jesus. The mention of one Passover only in the Marcan narrative (14:1) creates the strong impression that the Ministry did not extend beyond a single year. St. John, on the other hand, records three Passovers (2:13, 6:4, 11:55), implying a duration for the Ministry of the same number of years, and this is generally held to constitute a much more credible account of the actual length of Christ's Ministry.

In an important study entitled 'The Cleansing of the Temple',[1] Professor T. W. Manson has convincingly argued that St. Mark's 'telescoping' of the Ministry of Jesus extends to his account of its closing phases, in the period traditionally referred to as 'Holy Week.'

St. Mark ends his account of the Galilean ministry with chapter ix; and from that point onwards his narrative moves swiftly and relentlessly towards its inevitable climax of the Passion and Resurrection of the Lord. Because the story moves swiftly we are apt to imagine that events described followed closely upon one another. As a result we compress the events of Mark 10:46–16:8 into a single week. On one Sunday morning Jesus, leaving Jericho for Jerusalem, heals blind Bartimaeus; on the following Sunday morning the women find the empty tomb. I am going to suggest that Mark himself furnishes indications that the period covered by these events is not one week but something more like six months (p. 271).

Dr. Manson concludes that the Cleansing of the Temple (Mark 11:1–25), usually thought of as one of the opening incidents in

Christ's last Passover, took place, not during the Feast of the Passover, but at the previous Feast of Tabernacles. 'We are then left with a period of some six months (Oct.–April) between the cleansing of the Temple . . . and the opening of the Passion narrative proper (Mark 14:1).' Confirmation is sought from the record of the Fourth Evangelist; according to John 7:10–13, when Jesus leaves Galilee for the last time it is to visit Jerusalem for the Feast of Tabernacles.

While he is there we have incidents recorded in John which bear a certain resemblance to stories told by Mark in connexion with the cleansing of the Temple. For example, we have a challenge to the authority of Jesus (John 7:14–18) which recalls the challenge in Mark 11:27–33. Or again, we may compare John 7:37–44 with Mark 12:35–7, and the setting of John 8:12–20 with that of Mark 12:41–4 (p. 281 ff.).

If this is what happened with Mark's account of 'Holy Week', it seems natural to go on and ask if the same kind of thing may not also have happened with his subsequent narrative of the Last Supper, Arrest, Trial, and Crucifixion of Jesus.

It is with this problem (and related questions) I am concerned in this essay.

Legal procedure can never have been so precipitately expedited as in the Trial of Jesus as portrayed by St. Mark. It is not, therefore, surprising to find a Jewish scholar, J. L. Saalschütz,[2] among the first to question the accuracy of the Synoptic tradition of a nocturnal trial, according to which, within a few hours, Jesus was interrogated (before witnesses) by the Jewish Sanhedrin and handed over to the civil authorities. Saalschütz felt even as acutely the well-known legal difficulty of an execution taking place (even at Roman hands) on such a Day as 15th Nisan, the first (great) Day of the Feast of Passover. To meet these difficulties he put forward the theory that Jesus, while arrested, as the Synoptic Gospels testify, on the eve of Passover, was not actually brought to trial until the following week, and was in fact crucified on Friday, Nisan 21st, which was also a feast day; a whole week had intervened between Arrest and Crucifixion.

The theory raised as many difficulties as it professed to solve, and has found few, if any, advocates since. But one observation seems of value. Saalschütz wrote, 'That a series of days passed between the arrest and the crucifixion of Christ, a closer study of the Gospels might well rather confirm than refute.' [3]

Before we examine some evidence in the Gospels for such a contention, something must be said about a hypothesis which has attracted increasing attention in Synoptic criticism in recent years, viz. that St. Luke's Passion narrative is largely based on a non-Marcan tradition into which extracts from St. Mark's Gospel have been inserted.

As is well-known, this idea was first adumbrated by Sir John Hawkins in *Oxford Studies* and developed by B. H. Streeter in his Proto-Luke theory.[4] It formed the basis of a more detailed study by A. M. Perry who further elaborated Hawkins's three main points, that verbal correspondence with Mark dropped from 53 per cent in the rest of the Gospel to 27 per cent in the Passion story; that transpositions of Marcan material in Luke's account of the Passion took place four times more frequently than elsewhere in Luke; and that Luke not only omitted much Marcan matter but contained twice as much again of new interwoven material.[5] Dr. Vincent Taylor has given his continued support to the theory, adding: 'The whole problem calls for closer study', and, 'The view that the Lukan Passion Narrative is fundamentally non-Marcan has naturally invited attention, although not with the fullness of discussion which so important a question demands.' [6]

The discussion has been carried forward, however, so far as Luke 22 (the Last Supper) is concerned, in the recent work of Heinz Schürmann.[7] The following observations are designed to show the extent of Synoptic (mainly Marcan) 'telescoping' in this section of the Gospels, by carrying the hypothesis of an independent Lucan Passion tradition a step further into the narrative of the Arrest and Trial.

(a) The first passage is Mark 14:53-72[8] where the account of the Arrest (14:43-52) is followed immediately by an appearance of Jesus before the High Priest and the Sanhedrin (v. 53). The legal proceedings which follow (vv. 55-65) are placed within the story of Peter's Denial (v. 54, resumed in 66-72). Since the Denial follows immediately on the nocturnal arrest, we are led to infer that the trial before the Sanhedrin was also a nocturnal affair, though it is strange to find witnesses already on the spot (v. 56).

Further, it was (according to Mark) 'immediately, early (on the following morning)' that Jesus was bound and handed over to Pilate (15:1), tried summarily, and, on the demand of the mob, sent off to immediate execution (15:6–15). The entire process, both ecclesiastical and civil, appears to occupy no more than a few hours.

That this is a 'telescoped' account (with literary priority going to the story of the Denial, not the Trial) may be held to be borne out by a comparison with Luke's fuller version of the same train of events.

Luke 22:54 reports that Jesus, after his nocturnal arrest, was carried off to the house of the High Priest. Verses 55–62 are occupied with the Denial of Peter, 63–5 with the Mockery, but at verse 66 we are informed that, *on the next day* (καὶ ὡς ἐγένετο ἡμέρα) the Sanhedrin was convened, and Jesus led before it for interrogation. There then follows Luke's account, not of a nocturnal trial before the Sanhedrin, but of a daylight session, in which, as a result of Christ's own replies (to virtually the same questions put, according to Mark, at the nocturnal session), Jesus was handed over for judgment to Pilate (23:1). (If we accept this Lucan tradition as independent of Mark, then we may be prepared to find an echo of this daylight Trial at Mark 15:1.)

How are we to account for these fundamental differences in the records of the two Evangelists?

A recent discussion of the problem is to be found in the late Canon Wilfred L. Knox's posthumously published book, *The Sources of the Synoptic Gospels*, i (1953), 133 f. The Lucan καὶ ὡς ἐγένετο ἡμέρα is explained as Luke's editing of Mark 15:1; Luke then added Mark's story of the Trial; the whole account is a piece of 'Lucan fine writing'.

Can we, however, dismiss Luke's version as 'edited history' so easily? It contains at least one sign of independence of Mark and dependence on a non-Marcan source or tradition, in one of those curious minor agreements of Luke with Matthew against Mark. It is the significant addition at v. 69 of the words ἀπὸ τοῦ νῦν (Matt. 26:64, ἀπ' ἄρτι). (The two expressions look very like 'translation variants' of an original Aramaic *min kaddu(n), deinde, in posterum*.)

Such minor agreements of Matthew and Luke against Mark have been studied recently by Professor N. A. Dahl in an important article in NTS 2.[9] They cannot all, as Dr. Dahl points out, be set down to harmonistic scribal errors. What has more probably happened is that Matthew and Luke, in their reproduction of Mark, have introduced fresh non-Marcan material from '*eine neben Markus weiterbestehende oder auf Grund von Markus entstandene Überlieferung*'.[10] Dr. Dahl accounts for much of the additional material in Matthew's Passion narrative on this hypothesis of '*eine Bekanntschaft mit einer von Markus unabhängigen Überlieferung*'.[11]

No less must be claimed for the Lucan Passion story.

Moreover, even if Luke is simply editing Mark 15:1 in his *καὶ ὡς ἐγένετο ἡμέρα*, his placing of an account of the same Trial in the day-time, which Mark invites us to believe took place at night, looks like deliberate correction of the Marcan tradition. It seems unlikely that Luke would so correct Mark, if he did not have an alternative tradition to draw on.

Which record, we must go on to ask, is, historically the more credible, Mark's nocturnal trial by the Jewish authorities and sum- mary hearing before Pilate early on the following morning, or Luke's version that Jesus spent the first night after his arrest in the palace of the High Priest, and was brought up for trial the follow- ing day? If we set aside for the moment considerations about the date of the Last Supper, Luke's account seems inherently a more likely one.

(*b*) At Luke 23:5-12 Luke introduces a story which is not found in the Marcan-Matthaean tradition, namely, Jesus' examination by Herod. In the course of a first hearing of Jesus before Pilate, the 'chief priests and the crowd' (i.e. the Sanhedrin or a delega- tion of the Sandehrin with their entourage and followers) report, according to Luke only, that the influence of Jesus' teaching had been felt 'throughout all Judaea' and from Galilee to Jerusalem (23:5). (This 'universalism' introduces a characteristically Lucan motif, but though it is this verse which prompts Pilate's question whether Jesus is a Galilaean (v. 6), we need not thereby be led to dismiss the question as unhistorical.) Armed with the information that Jesus belonged to the jurisdiction of Herod, Pilate promptly sent Jesus to the Tetrarch, who happened (Luke adds) to be in Jerusalem at that time (v. 7). Pilate shows an obvious reluctance to deal with the case, no doubt at least for the reason he gives (v. 4, *οὐδὲν εὑρίσκω αἴτιον ἐν τῷ ἀνθρώπῳ τούτῳ*), but the whole passage suggests that he was unwilling to yield to Jewish pressure, and welcomed any reason for delay.

There is nothing corresponding to this Lucan episode in Matt.-Mark, and this has given rise to the suspicion that it has no foundation in history. The case against its authenticity has been argued by Creed,[12] who suggests that its origin is to be sought in Acts 4:25 ff., the only other passage in the New Testament where Pilate and Herod are mentioned together as being concerned in the death of Jesus. Ps. 2 is quoted there with reference to the Passion: 'The kings of the earth stand up, and the rulers take counsel together against the Lord and against His anointed'; the 'kings' and rulers are then identified with Herod and Pilate. Such an interpretation of the Psalm has (according to Creed) given rise to the Lucan story.

It seems doubtful, however, if the interpretation itself would have arisen at all had there not been some foundation for it in a historical connection between Herod (as well as Pilate) and the death of Jesus; Acts 4:25, i.e. takes for granted that Herod also was implicated in Christ's death, and, in fact, assumes an acquaintance with the story at Luke 23:5 ff.

One of the main reasons for the rejection of the Lucan story has been its omission by Mark. In view of the strong presumption that Luke had access to an alternative tradition of the Passion to that of Mark, this objection to its historicity now falls to the ground.

If it is a genuine incident, however, then we are bound to conclude that Mark's narrative is again an abridged or apocopated one; an episode, which could probably occupy an entire day, has fallen out of the Marcan narrative.

(c) There is one other passage where we meet with the same kind of evidence of 'telescoping' of the narrative, but in this case in the Gospel of St. Luke.

At Luke 23:13–16, Luke has just told us about Jesus' hearing before Herod, and goes on to add that, on Jesus' return from Herod, Pilate summoned the chief priests, rulers and people (i.e. the people with their Sanhedrin), and, after a brief report on Herod's examination, proposed that he should scourge Jesus and set him at liberty (v. 16). This proposal, according to Luke, provoked the immediate outcry, 'Crucify him . . . release Barabbas to us', which precipitated the Crucifixion (v. 17 in Luke, explaining the custom of releasing a prisoner at the feast, is not in our best manuscripts, and seems manifestly a later gloss intended to harmonize Luke with Mark).

Comparison with Mark 15:6–14 shows that, in attaching the Barabbas episode to Pilate's report on Herod's decision, Luke has 'telescoped' two separate incidents, by making them take place on the same occasion. Mark 15:8 clearly implies that, on the occasion of the Barabbas incident, it was the Jews who approached Pilate (ἀναβάς, as the best attested reading). This must, therefore, be a quite different occasion from that described at Luke 23:13, where it was Pilate who approached the Jews.

It seems a reasonable inference that, after Pilate's report from Herod and proposal to scourge and release Jesus, the Jews demurred, asked for time to consider his proposal, and went off dissatisfied, to consult again and try another plan. The next approach of the Jews succeeded. The mob had been incited to demand a prisoner. They did so, and Pilate seizing an apparent opportunity to release Jesus, fell into the Jewish trap. The sequel was the Crucifixion.

Some explanation of this compressed and 'telescoped' method of recording historical events is to be found in a principle of contemporary historiography, which paid less attention to an ordered and orderly account of events than to conveying or portraying an impressive dramatic sequence. The story was narrated in the interests of history as 'rhetoric', or as 'near to poetry' (cf. Quintilian, x, 1, 31), and not as a sequence of objectively observed data; the principle is that of the artist making the best use of his canvas and colours rather than that of the historian seeking to account for every stage and step in a process. The Gospel writers are to a large extent simply adopting such recognized principles of historical narrative of their time. Thus, Mark's 'telescoped' version of the nocturnal trial is very much in the interests of his dramatic story of the Denial of Peter, to which it takes an almost subordinate place.

There is an interesting parallel to the Gospel of Mark in Sallust's history of the Jugurthine War. As with Mark's single passover, there is one definite date only in Sallust's history, January, 110 B.C., when Albinus made his unfortunate winter expedition. For the rest, the historian is vague and careless in his use of

M. Black

temporal conjunctions, such as *interea, postremo, post paucos dies*.
Indeed, as in Mark Sallust's Jugurthine War appears to have lost
at least a whole year as a result of this 'rhetorical' method of
writing history: we are presented with a 'telescoped' account,
which we have to draw out for ourselves, by comparison with
other sources.

There seems little doubt that this method of writing history
explains much in the Synoptic record.

The recognition that the period between the Arrest of Jesus
and his Crucifixion must have been longer than a single night and
morning, and may have extended to one or even two full days
has important consequences for the dating of the two main events
of Passion week, the Last Supper and the Crucifixion itself. As we
have already seen, Saalschütz felt obliged to place the events of
the Trial of Jesus in the week following Friday, Nisan 15th (the
Synoptic date for the Crucifixion), and the Crucifixion on Friday,
Nisan 21st. Few scholars, however, have been prepared to depart
so radically from the tradition, both Scriptural and patristic, that
Jesus was crucified on the first Friday of the Feast of the Passover.
If room is to be found for a Trial lasting for one or even two full
days, then it must be found within Passion week itself.

Traces of a tradition of the Arrest (and Supper) as taking place
earlier in the week are to be found in St. John's Gospel.

That the Fourth Gospel has preserved elements of a reliable
historical tradition independent of the Synoptics (possibly even
setting out to correct them) is now widely accepted. There is no
doubt in that Gospel that the night of the Last Supper and Arrest
(the narrative of 13:1 ff.—with intervening discourse material—
resumed at 18:1) was not the eve of the Passover, i.e. 14–15th
Nisan as in the Synoptics, but took place *earlier in the week*, πρὸ
τῆς ἑορτῆς τοῦ πάσχα (13:1). (According to St. John, Jesus was
crucified on the Day of Preparation for the Passover (19:14).)
St. John thus again confirms the suspicion that the Marcan narrative 'telescopes' events.

John also supplies us with information about events in the High
Priest's house which supplement Synoptic tradition, for, according to the Fourth Gospel, there was first a private nocturnal
interrogation of Jesus before the High Priest Annas, the father-in-
law of Caiaphas. From our information about the relations of these

two influential Jewish leaders, the Johannine tradition looks authentic. Like Mark, John appears, however, to assume a nocturnal Trial before Caiaphas (18:24–28). But the night may in fact have been occupied solely with the private hearing before Annas (and the Denial of Peter), followed on the next day by a session of the Sanhedrin under Caiaphas.

One thing is certain. The Last Supper in the Fourth Gospel cannot have been a Passover, or at least the Passover publicly celebrated in Jerusalem in that year (see further below, p. 31 ff.). Yet the meal as described by St. John has several paschal features. No importance can be attached to the reclining of the disciples, though this posture was in fact obligatory at Passover; it was also, however, a Roman custom, and it would be natural for St. John to portray the occasion in this way. It is curious to find, however, that the meal took place at night: that was also a Passover custom, but in this case one that ran counter to ordinary custom in which the main meal in Palestine was partaken in the late afternoon. The dipping of the sop (bitter herbs dipped in the *haroseth* sauce) was definitely a Passover custom only: 'In the Passover Haggadah the Passover Supper is distinguished from all other meals in several ways including "on all other nights we do not dip . . . even once, but on this night twice".' (See C. K. Barrett, *The Gospel according to St John*, 373.)

The usual explanation of these Passover elements in the Johannine Supper is that they are reminiscences or echoes of the Synoptic tradition. They cannot alter the fact that the Supper in St. John was not a Passover, or, at any rate, a regular Passover meal. Perhaps the explanation of these elements is to be sought in the irregularity of this particular Passover celebration, with its transformation of the traditional meaning of the rite and its celebration some days before the official Passover. I shall return to this suggestion.

No further support is to be found in the Gospels themselves for an earlier date for the Arrest and Last Supper of Jesus, but there is a patristic tradition which places both on the Tuesday evening (in the Jewish reckoning the beginning of Wednesday). (For what follows I am largely indebted to the acute observations of Mlle. A. Jaubert, especially in her article 'La Date de la dernière Cène', in *Revue de l'histoire des religions*, cxlvi, 140 ff.)

It occurs in the *Didascalia Apostolorum*[13] and in the fourth century Church Father Epiphanius.[14] The former is usually dated about the beginning of the third century; it contains earlier sources, however, so that we are in touch with an older tradition. A similar dating of the events of Holy week, but apparently independent of the *Didascalia*, is found in the *Fabrica Mundi*, the work of Victorinus of Pettau, Bishop of Styria, who died about A.D. 304.[15] The following is R. H. Connolly's summary and critical estimate of the relevant chapter of the *Didascalia* (XXI).

Chapter XXI is on the Pascha, or more precisely on the paschal feast. The subject is introduced rather oddly by a discourse of a couple of pages in which Christians are warned against profane speech and swearing. The transition is made thus: 'Therefore it is not lawful for a believer to swear, . . . not to make mention with his mouth of the name of idols; nor to utter a curse out of his mouth . . . ; and especially in the days of the Pascha, wherein all the faithful throughout the world fast' (p. 180). The author's purpose is evidently to show reason why the fast before Easter should extend over the whole six days, from Monday to Saturday. To this end he adopts, and probably invents, a strange chronology of Holy Week for which there is no shadow of authority in the Gospels. The fast should coincide with our Lord's passion; but His passion extended, in a sense, over six days, thus: on Monday, the 10th of the moon, Judas arranges with the priests to betray Him; in the evening of Tuesday, the 11th, He ate the Passover with His disciples (the priests having maliciously published a false date for the Feast, anticipating the true one by two days), and in that night He was seized and taken to the house of Caiaphas. All Wednesday and the following night He was kept in ward in the high priest's house. On Thursday He was brought to Pilate; and He was kept in ward by Pilate till the beginning of Friday. On Friday morning he was judged and condemned (Herod, not Pilate, passing the sentence). Incidentally we are given also a curious explanation of the 'three days and three nights' that our Lord was 'in the heart of the earth': they are obtained by counting (apparently) the period of His trial as the first day, and also counting the three hours of darkness and the ensuing hours of light as a night and a day. Besides the paschal fast of six days there is prescribed a weekly fast on Wednesday and Friday. The week of the paschal fast is to be determined by observing when the Jews keep the Passover. There is much confusion of thought and treatment in this chapter, but an attentive study of it will show that the main end in view is to defend, or establish, the practice of a six-days fast before Easter.

In view of the manifest object of this chronology to establish

the six-day fast, it seems very doubtful if we can place any faith
in it as history; similarly, Epiphanius's chronology appears to
have served the interests of a two-day fast in Holy Week, Wednesday and Friday;[16] historical justification for holding Wednesday as well as Friday as a Christian fast is obtained by associating
Wednesday with Christ's Arrest. As these two fast days are
already established in the Didache, the tradition may go back to
the first half of the second century.[17]
   The evidence of Victorinus of Pettau and the case for its independence of the *Didascalia* have been stated by Mlle. Jaubert:[18]

Dans son petit traité *De fabrica mundi*, Victorin traite des jours de la
création, et insiste sur le quatrième jour (mercredi), jour de la création
des luminaires qui règlent le cours des saisons. Ce nombre 4 possède des
propriétés bien remarquables: les 4 éléments, les 4 saisons, les 4 animaux,
les 4 évangiles, les 4 fleuves du paradis . . . et, pour clore cette enumera-
tion: 'L'homme Jésus-Christ, auteur des choses que nous avons men-
tionnées plus haut, a été *arrêté* par les impies le *quatrième jour*. C'est pourquoi nous faisons du quatrième jour un jour de jeûne, à cause de son
emprisonnement, à cause de la majesté de ses oeuvres, et afin que le
cours des saisons amène la santé aux hommes, l'abondance aux mois-
sons, le calme aux intempéries.' Victorin connaît aussi les jeûnes du
vendredi et du samedi, mais il les cite sans aucune référence aux inter-
prétations de la *Didascalie*. L'emprisonnement de Jésus, le mercredi, jour
de la tétrade, lui est légué par une tradition absolument indépendante,
dans un contexte tout différent.
   Nous sommes donc obligés de remonter à une tradition commune
à Victorin et à la *Didascalie*, donc antérieure à l'un et a l'autre. Si
nous datons la *Didascalie* du debut du IIIe siècle, cette tradition
devai exister dans le cours du second siècle.

   Can we, however, be so certain that Victorinus is independent
of the *Didascalia*? The sentence 'C'est pourquoi nous faisons du
quatrième jour un jour du jeûne' is suspicious. The same dependence on the *Didascalia* probably also explains other traces of the
Wednesday tradition in the Fathers of the Church (Jaubert, *op.
cit.*, 148 ff.).
   Once again it might appear that an attractive and promising
line of research had turned out to be a cul-de-sac. Can we, however, be absolutely certain that the sole or whole explanation of
this patristic tradition was to provide historical justification for
two Christian fast days during Holy Week? It is arguable that it
was the actual history as transmitted in the tradition of the Early

Church which was the origin of the two Christian fast days on Wednesday and Friday; the Church fasted on Wednesday to commemorate the Arrest of Jesus and on Friday to commemorate His Crucifixion. Furthermore, it is difficult to see how a Wednesday tradition could arise after the Thursday to Friday tradition had become established. The reverse process is easy to imagine taking place, since the tradition of an Arrest on the eve of his Crucifixion is an obvious inference from the Gospels. The tradition of the Last Supper and Arrest on the Thursday evening is already reflected in the Pilgrimage of Etheria, but there is a visit to the Mount of Olives on the Wednesday, and this looks very like a survival of the Wednesday tradition (ed. Pétré, 228–30).

Support for this patristic tradition and for an earlier dating in Holy Week of the Lord's Supper has now been found in the festival calendar of the Dead Sea Scrolls. Mdlle. A. Jaubert has recently developed a suggestion of Père D. Barthélemy that the Qumran sectarians (or Essenes) followed the calendar of the Book of Jubilees, representing the priestly calendrical tradition of Israel.[19] Mlle Jaubert is now supported by Père J. T. Milik, who claims that this hypothesis is confirmed by the number of scrolls dealing with calendar questions from Cave 4; Milik adds that, in this respect, Qumran sectarians followed the same calendrical system as the Boethusian Sadducees.[20] According to this sectarian calendar, the dates of the great festivals are not movable (as in the Pharisaic calendar) but immovably fixed: the day of Pentecost, e.g. always falls on a Sunday and the 1st and the 15th Nisan always on a Wednesday. Thus, according to this calendar, 14–15th Nisan, in the year of the Crucifixion, must have fallen on Tuesday/Wednesday of Holy Week, which, according to the *Didascalia* and Epiphanius, was the night of the Arrest and the Last Supper of Jesus.[21]

A note of caution has been struck with regard to these identifications (not always at every point verifiable), in an article by the late Professor Julian Obermann, entitled 'Calendaric Elements in the Dead Sea Scrolls'.[22] Obermann was not convinced that the Calendar of Qumran could in fact be conclusively identified with that of Jubilees.

Nevertheless, on the general question of the existence and observance of such a type of sectarian calendar in the time of

Christ there can be no doubt; and it is certain too, that it was a calendar differing fundamentally from the official Pharisaic-Sadducaean system of calculations in current use. In Plate VI of the *Manual of Discipline* dealing with the admission of new members to the community, catechumens or converts are exhorted 'not to depart as regards their (calendar) periods from any of God's commandments', and this is explained as meaning that they are neither 'to advance their seasons, nor to retard any of their festivals'.[23]

The meaning of this injunction becomes evident in the light of Pharisaic calendar references and innovations vis-à-vis the older priestly tradition. Thus the Pharisees interpreted Lev. 23:11, 15, 'the morrow after the Sabbath' to mean Nisan 16, following the Passover Festival Day (or Sabbath) Nisan 15; Pentecost, 50 days later always fell on Sivan 6, without regard to the day of the week. The Sadducees appear to have contended that both the 16th Nisan and Pentecost should be observed on the day following a weekly sabbath, and, therefore, must always fall on a Sunday.[24]

Such a difference meant that the Pharisaic Pentecost (and the Waving of the Omer) generally always fell in advance of the time observed by the Sadducees.[25] Similarly the Pharisees might postpone certain festivals for reasons of expediency, one well-known device being that of intercalation.

The warnings of the *Manual of Discipline*, therefore, about advancing and retarding festival dates, are manifestly aimed at just such Pharisaic practices.

Was there, then, a dispute about the date of the Passover in the year of the Crucifixion, one party dating the first Day of the feast on the Friday, another earlier in the week? The theory is one that has been advanced more than once to account for the divergences between the Synoptic and Johannine chronologies,[26] but so far no convincing evidence has been found to support it.[27] Some kind of substantiation may now be held to be forthcoming from Qumran; for we can be certain that the Qumran sectarians or Essenes, an important and numerous minority in the Palestinian scene of the first century, did celebrate Passover in the year of the Crucifixion at a different time from the official time promulgated by the Jerusalem Temple authorities, which were dominated by Pharisaic influence and interests. Moreover, if the sectarian dating was the old priestly one, and, as Père Milik contends, Essenes and Sadducees were agreed in such calendrical matters, then the non-Pharisaic date may have been more widely observed, especially outside Jerusalem. Some liberty was allowed about the dates of celebration in the Diaspora,[28] and there appear to have been special regulations for Galilee,[29] though it is unlikely that any other law ran in Jerusalem than the Pharisaic—except perhaps in secret.

We do not require to assume that Jesus belonged to any sectarian group, even if he and his disciples actually did celebrate a Passover earlier in the week, since it may have been the Passover of the old orthodox priestly calendar which was, in any case, being celebrated outside Jerusalem. If this was to be the Last Passover of all, the consummation of Israel's Deliverance in a new Exodus, Jesus might naturally choose what may have been widely and popularly held to be the old 'Mosaic' season. Was it, in fact, an *illegal* Passover—so far as the date and place was concerned— which Jesus and His disciples celebrated in Holy Week? Mark 14:12 ff. emphasizes the secret nature of the preparations for it. The meal in John, falling before the official Passover, does, as we have seen, show certain paschal features. Was it the illegality of the transformed rite, a new kind of Passover, abrogating by transcending the old Mosaic ordinance, and set at an illegal season (the old Calendar) which gave Judas his final opportunity to betray Christ? In carrying off the sop, he took with him evidence to the priests and Pharisees that an illegal feast had been celebrated. In that case, Jesus was challenging Pharisaic Law in its stronghold, Jerusalem itself. Such an illegal Passover may have been celebrated, like the celebrations in the synagogue, especially in the Diaspora, without a paschal lamb.

These can be no more than interesting speculations prompted by this study. It seems unlikely that they will ever be more than speculations: a high degree of probability, on the other hand, may perhaps be accorded to the main contention of this essay, that the period occupied by the Arrest and Trial of Jesus was longer than our Gospels make it out to be. And this is bound to have consequences for our ideas about the time of the Arrest and the date and character of the Last Supper.

NOTES

[1] BJRL 33, No. 2 (March, 1951), 271–82.

[2] *Das Mosäische Recht* (Berlin, 1853) (*Der Process Jesu*, 623 ff.; especially, however, p. 413, n. 527).

[3] *Op. cit.*, p. 415 (foot).

[4] *The Four Gospels* (1924). The theory was defended by Dr. Vincent Taylor in *Behind the Third Gospel* (1926).

[5] *The Sources of Luke's Passion Narrative* (1920).

[6] ET 67 (1955), 15.

[7] *Neutestamentliche Abhandlungen*, XIX. Band, 5. Heft, XX. Band, 4. Heft, 5. Heft (Münster, 1953, 1955, 1957).

[8] These passages should be studied with a Gospel synopsis at hand.

[9] 17 ff.: 'Die Passionsgeschichte bei Matthäus.'

[10] P. 21.

[11] P. 24.

[12] *The Gospel according to St. Luke*, 279 ff.

[13] Ed. R. H. Connolly (Oxford, 1929).

[14] *Panarion*, 51, 26; 50, 1–2; *Frag.*, ed. Holl, p. 206.

[15] *Tractus de Fabrica Mundi*, 3, CSEL 49 (1916), p. 4 (ed. Hausleiter).

[16] Cf. K. Holl, 'Ein Bruchstück aus einem bisher unbekannten Brief des Epiphanius' in *Gesammelte Aufsätze zur Kirchengeschichte* ii (1927), 213.

[17] *Didache*, VIII:I 'But let not your fasts be together with the hypocrites for they fast on the 2nd and 5th days of the week, but ye shall fast the 4th day and the παραϰεύη (Friday).'

[18] *Op. cit.*, 148.

[19] 'Le Calendrier des Jubiles et les jours liturgiques de la semaine' in VT 7, 35 ff.

[20] *Dix Ans de Decouvertes dans le Desert de Juda* (Paris, 1957), 70 ff.

[21] 'La Date de la dernière Cène', 140 ff.

[22] Cf. Milik, *op. cit.*, 70. JBL 75, 285 ff.

[23] See Obermann, *op. cit.*, 292 ff.

[24] Different forms of this tradition depend on whether the sabbath in question is the sabbath within Passover Week or the first sabbath after it. See R. H. Charles, *Apocrypha and Pseudepigrapha of the Old Testament*, ii, 35 ff.

[25] Cf. Obermann *loc. cit.*

[26] Cf. J. Jeremias, *Die Abendmahlsworte Jesu* (Göttingen, 1949), 14 (Eng. trans. by A. Ehrhardt, *The Eucharistic Words of Jesus*, p. 9).

[27] *Ibid.*, 15.

[28] Jos. Ant. III, 10, 5, cf. II, 15, 1.

[29] Bab. Talmud, *Pes.* iv. 5 f. (cf. Jeremias, *op. cit.*, 15).

THE INDEBTEDNESS OF 2 PETER TO 1 PETER

by

G. H. BOOBYER

THE second epistle of Peter has a relationship with 1 Peter on the one hand and Jude on the other, and two views concerning its nature now have widespread acceptance. The first is that 2 Peter borrows from Jude. This seems the most likely explanation of the close correspondence between 2 Pet. 1:12 and Jude 5; 2 Pet. 2:1–18 and Jude 4–13, 16; 2 Pet. 3:1-3 and Jude 17 f., though it is uncertain whether the author of Peter 2 wrote with the text of Jude before him, or relied on his memory of it.[1] The second commonly held view is that 2 Pet. 3:1 f. alludes to our canonical 1 Peter, and claims it as the first epistle which the writer of 2 Peter addressed to his readers. This opinion also commends itself, inasmuch as 1 Peter had probably won extensive acceptance and authority as a genuine work of the apostle before 2 Peter was written. Further, in 2 Pet. 3:1 f., one seems to hear a strong echo of 1 Pet. 1:10–12.[2]

2 Peter was therefore written under the influence of Jude on the one side and with at least a reference to 1 Peter on the other. The debt to Jude is considerable. Most of it has been reproduced, though with some variations in wording. It supplies, in fact, the substance of about twenty-two verses, or, roughly, one third of 2 Peter. That 2 Peter was attacking antinomians similar to those assailed in Jude evidently occasioned the plagiarism. Indeed, in the church, or association of churches to which the author of 2 Peter belonged, Jude's tract may have been not infrequently used in speech and writing as a weapon against the antinomianism in question. If so, by incorporating most of Jude in his own epistle, the pseudo-Petrine writer was but following an established polemical line.

Jude, then, is laid under heavy contribution in 2 Peter. But what of 1 Peter? Was 1 Peter a second source from which 2 Peter borrowed? If so, to what extent? Modern commentators, whilst usually agreeing that 2 Pet. 3:1 f. alludes to our 1 Peter,[3] differ curiously in their assessments of the extent to which 2 Peter writes under the influence of the earlier letter. R. Knopf remarked: 'Dass der Verfasser I Pt kennt, folgt aus II Pt 3:1, aber nur daraus. Denn im übrigen haben die beiden Schreiben, die unter dem gleichen Namen gehen, nichts mit einander gemein'.[4] Windisch commented in similar terms: 'Freilich ist I Petr in II Petr kaum benützt, auch trifft die Charakterisierung auf I Petr gar nicht zu.'[5] But Mayor who, like Knopf and Windisch, did not attribute 2 Peter to the apostle Peter thought that 'the second Epistle shows signs of careful study of 1 P.'[6], and C. Bigg endorsed B. Weiss's view that as far as its general Christian teaching is concerned, 'no document in the New Testament is so like 1 Peter as 2 Peter'.[7]

Scholars who have called attention to the resemblances between 1 and 2 Peter have, of course, been well aware of the striking differences. Bigg, for instance, who believed both epistles to be genuine, readily conceded that 2 Peter diverged significantly from 1 Peter in matters such as vocabulary, use of the O.T., christology, 2 Peter's stress on ἐπίγνωσις and its picture of the End with the expected world conflagration.[8] Since Bigg wrote, these disparities, along with other considerations, have of course led Mayor and most scholars to deny the common authorship of the two epistles, and to adjudge 2 Peter a pseudonymous document of the sub-apostolic age.

But what resemblances have been noted between the two writings? Mayor compared them in detail.[9] The main parallels to which he drew attention were some coincidences in language in spite of prevailing differences (2 Pet. 1:2 and 1 Pet 1:2; 2 Pet. 3:14 and 1 Pet. 1:19 are examples from a longer list); the prominence of the second-advent theme in both; the mention of Noah and seven others saved from the flood (2 Pet. 2:5, cf. 3:5 ff.—and 1 Pet. 3:19 ff.); the μακροθυμία of God related in 2 Pet. 3:15 to the coming conflagration and in 1 Pet. 3:20 to the flood; and the accounts in 2 Pet. 1:16-21 and 1 Pet. 1:10-12 (cf. 2 Pet. 3:1 f.) of prophecy as a divinely inspired foretelling of Gospel events now announced by apostles.

Whatever can be said about any of these points taken separately, the summary suggests that judgment on the 2 Peter–1 Peter relationship ought not perhaps to be left without reconsideration where scholars like Knopf and Windisch left it. Moreover, the resemblances and differences between these writings seem to have been examined mainly, sometimes entirely, as an aspect of the problem of the authorship of 2 Peter. This may have led those concerned to establish a common authorship for the two to overstress the resemblances, whilst those convinced that the second epistle was not by the same hand as the first could have exaggerated the disconnectedness. Anyhow, the internal relationship between 1 and 2 Peter deserves study in itself, detached from authorship questions, especially in view of the direct reference to 1 Peter in 2 Pet. 3:1 f. and 2 Peter's borrowing propensities, so evident in his use of Jude.

This essay then asks once more, Do the contents of 2 Peter show indebtedness to 1 Peter?

It will be advisable to start with another look at 2 *Pet. 3:1-2.* 2 Peter was written to save the readers from libertines of a Gnostic type who were mockers of the parousia hope;[10] and 2 Pet. 3:1 f. indicates the author's method, though he has in fact already indicated it in 1:12-15. He grapples with the situation by putting the readers in remembrance, particularly of the message of the OT prophets, and 'the commandment'—or 'the truth' (1:12)—as revealed in Jesus Christ and then proclaimed by the apostles. He took, he says, a similar line in 1 Peter. As an approach to the dangers in question, this owes something to Jude 5, 17 f., but it is also a consquence of the religious standpoint of the author. To him, sound doctrine is the truth as formerly given by God in the OT scriptures, in 'our Lord Jesus Christ' and in the message of the apostles as accredited witnesses of Christ.[11] 'False teachers' (2:1) and those they may seduce must therefore be confronted with these authorities—the sources of the traditional deposit of faith which the Church has received and teaches. Such being his viewpoint, this sub-apostolic author inevitably sees his pastoral and instructional duty as one of recalling to the mind, or 'putting you in remembrance'.

But whilst granting that 'putting in remembrance' is a description to which 2 Peter answers, is not 2 Pet. 3:1 f. strange or inappropriate as an account of 1 Peter, thereby implying that the later writer was indifferent to the actual contents of the former epistle? Some, like Windisch, think so. The question necessitates careful attention to the nature of the reminding. What, then, is its content in 2 Peter?

From 2 Pet. 3:1-4, it becomes clear that the readers are enjoined to remember 'words which were spoken before' relating above all to the hope of Christ's second coming and the obligation to avoid every error of belief and lust. The passage draws on Jude 17 f., but the way in which 2 Peter alters Jude should be noted. In Jude, the warning concerning mockers, walking in ungodly lusts, is given as though it were a quotation from the words of apostles. In 2 Pet. 3:1-4, however, no more is implied than that the words of the prophets, the Lord (i.e. Christ) and the apostles will be found to contain exhortations with a bearing on mockers of the second advent and their reprobate ways and helpful to the readers in resisting them. The reminding in 2 Pet. 1:12-21 is of the same kind. Here, too, the prophets (19-21), the Lord Jesus Christ (14-18) and the apostles (12-16, 18 f.) are the authorities who appear. Further, through the transfiguration of Jesus the apostles are said to have been given a revelation of the certainty of the parousia.[12] This revelation confirms 'the word of prophecy' relating thereto (19); and ταῦτα, of which the 'apostle' himself reminds his readers in 1:12 and 15 seems a comprehensive term referring to the foregoing plea for godliness in 1:1-11 as well as to the second-advent theme of 16-21. In sum, 2 Pet. 1:12-21 again stirs up the readers to remember the inevitability of the parousia and the need of avoiding the corruption and lust of the world. Finally, in chapter two, the reminding relates predominantly to the condemnation of the false teachers and their evil lives.

Throughout 2 Peter, then, reminding, or 'putting in remembrance' is concerned mostly with the parousia (and associated subjects) and the necessity of avoiding error and lust, in lives devoted to godliness. On both these topics, the OT prophets, Jesus Christ and the apostles are held to say the authoritative words. This is, to be sure, fully in conformity with the overriding purpose of the epistle which, as already remarked, set out to save the readers from antinomians who scoffed at the parousia hope. We are thus brought to the conclusion that when in 2 Pet. 3:1 f. the writer couples 1 Peter with his present letter, as giving similar reminders, his meaning is that the former epistle likewise contains 'words which were spoken before by the holy prophets and the commandment of the Lord and Saviour through your apostles' relevant to the same two themes.

It is now possible to answer the question previously raised. Is it justifiable to say that 2 Pet. 3:1 f. is strange or inappropriate as a description of 1 Peter? Why strange, coming from the writer of 2 Peter, with *his* aim and *his* conception of the nature of orthodox teaching? Deeming the putting in remembrance of traditional authorities essential to his role as 'Peter' now, will he not have attributed the same function to Peter then? And why is the description inappropriate as an account of what 1 Peter contains? In 1 Peter, exhortation to turn from evil and live holy lives occupies most of the epistle; and in 1 Peter, as in 2 Peter, the second advent, the incorruptible inheritance in heaven thereafter, and God's coming judgment, unsparing of sinners, are all prominent subjects, not to mention lesser parallels. But are these reminders given in 1 Peter on the authority of 'words which were spoken before by the holy prophets, and the commandments of the Lord and Saviour through your apostles' (2 Pet. 3:2)? They are. The holy living there enjoined is prominently depicted as a necessary 'imitatio Christi', Christ being our ὑπογραμμός (2:21),[13] and the OT is quoted as an additional sanction for it (1:16; 3:12–12; 5:5). The OT is further cited in support of future salvation (2:6) and the judgment of the wicked (3:12; 4:18). Finally, there are the specially significant verses 1 Pet. 1:10–12. Here, in one and the selfsame passage, all three authorities to whom 2 Peter appeals find mention—the prophets who wrote the OT scriptures, Christ (this time as the Spirit of Christ prompting the prophets) and the apostles (implied in 'them that preached the gospel unto you').[14] And what precisely was the nature of the 'salvation' (10) to which these authorities testified? When the passage is read in its context the answer becomes plain: it was that Christian salvation which would be attained in its completeness at Christ's second advent and the subsequent entry into the inheritance 'reserved in heaven for you' (1:4). In 1:10 and 12 the thrice repeated ὑμεῖς is also worth noting. That is, 1 Peter emphasizes that it was especially for his readers and their generation of believers that the Spirit of Christ testified through the prophets to the future salvation, now announced by the apostles. The emphasis seems not to have been lost on 2 Peter, when he speaks as he does in 2 Pet. 3:1 f., at the same time identifying the recipients of 1 Peter with his own readers.

Is further evidence now needed to reach a conclusion about 2 Pet. 3:1 f. as a reference to 1 Peter? Is there not every reason for confidence that 2 Pet. 3:1 f. does refer to the former Petrine epistle, and, moreover, refers to it in what for the writer of the second are wholly intelligible and appropriate terms? Indeed, the argument seems to carry further, pointing to two more possibilities, namely: (i) 2 Pet. 3:1 f. (and probably 2 Pet. 1:19-21) was written with 1 Pet. 1:10-12 immediately in mind; and (ii) the 'Peter' of 2 Pet. 3:1 f., in his expressed desire to be the Peter of the former epistle, will be found to draw further on 1 Peter, just as in his desire to be the Peter of the Gospels, he uses and stresses his presence at the transfiguration of Jesus.

Can these last two suggestions be substantiated? An exhaustive study of the question cannot be attempted here, but let us examine two more passages with a bearing on it.

Shall we turn next to *the structure of the first chapter of 2 Peter*? If 2 Peter is further indebted to 1 Peter, the signs of it are likely to appear at the beginnings of both epistles, because in chapter two, 2 Peter draws mainly on Jude, and the third chapter of 2 Peter contains much that is peculiar to the second epistle. Let us then compare the structure of 2 Pet. 1:1-21 with the opening chapter of the first epistle.

This line of investigation yields a small, positive result at once. As expositors have noticed, 2 Pet. 1:2 exactly reproduces the greeting formula of 1 Pet. 1:2—χάρις ὑμῖν καὶ εἰρήνη πληθυνθείη —though adding words characteristic of the thought of 2 Peter, namely, ἐν ἐπιγνώσει τοῦ θεοῦ καὶ Ἰησοῦ τοῦ κυρίου ἡμῶν. Significance attaches to the duplication in that πληθύνειν as the verb of a NT formula of greeting occurs only in 1 and 2 Peter and Jude.[15] Further, although Jude, from whom 2 Peter borrows so heavily, uses a greeting somewhat similarly worded to that in 1 Peter, 2 Peter at this point follows 1 Peter rather than Jude. Even Knopf, who is elsewhere sceptical about any indebtedness of the second writer to the first, is here constrained to comment, 'vermutlich liegt eine bewusste Anlehnung vor'.[16] But is the dependence of 2 Peter on 1 Peter likely to have ceased abruptly, when 2 Peter had written his greeting? We have already found cause to think that at least 1 Pet. 1:10-12 had 2 Peter's attention, and prompted his thought. But perhaps his mind jumped from

1 Pet. 1:2 to 1:10, unaffected by the intervening verses? At least, a comparison of 1 Pet. 1:3–9 and 2 Pet. 1:3–11 should be made to see what impression emerges. Nor, as we make it, should we forget that it is characteristic of 2 Peter to express himself differently from 1 Peter, the later writer having his own distinctive vocabulary and more Hellenistic categories of thought. For such factors, reasonable allowance must be made. Set out in parallel columns, the two sequences of thought are as follows:

1 Pet. 1 : 3-9

Through the resurrection of Jesus Christ, we have hope of an incorruptible and undefiled inheritance, reserved for us in heaven.

This inheritance is for those guarded by faith until salvation 'in the last time', and is a cause of rejoicing in the grief of present trials or temptations.

But faith, tested, and proved, will issue in glory, honour and the salvation of your souls 'at the revelation of Jesus Christ' (i.e. the second advent).

2 Pet. 1 : 3-11

Christ's divine power and glory are sources of all things pertaining to life and godliness, as well as of precious promises, enabling us to become partakers of the divine nature and avoid terrestrial corruption.

To faith other virtues must be added. This will promote the necessary knowledge of Jesus Christ and be in keeping with cleansing from former sins.

In this manner, make your calling and election sure, as well as your entry into Christ's eternal kingdom (i.e. at the parousia).

The comparison reveals at once differences in expression and emphasis. The principal difference of emphasis is in 2 Pet. 1:5–9 where the later author stresses that to faith—mentioned twice in the passage from 1 Peter (in 1:5 and 7)—must be added other virtues, mostly moral ones. The teaching of this section is reminiscent of the treatment of faith and works in the Epistle of James,[17] although of the virtues specifically named after faith only ὑπομονή occurs in James. But James shows faith without works to be 'dead' (2:17, 26) or 'barren' (2:20); whilst 2 Peter leads up to the conclusion that it is blind (1:9. Cf. Jas. 1:23–25). Further, James may, as some hold, have been correcting a misunderstanding of Paul's doctrine of faith. That 2 Peter was doing so seems

certain: 3:15 f. evidently means that the libertines were twisting
Paul's teaching—in part, again, that on faith and works—to make
it support their own perversities. If, then, the double reference to
faith in 1 Pet. 1:5 and 7 did occasion 2 Peter's mention of it in
1:5, there is a fully intelligible reason for the supplementary teaching which immediately follows. 2 Peter was dealing with dangerous opponents whose misuse of Paul's doctrine of faith and
works made it essential to leave the readers of 2 Peter in no doubt
that faith unsupported by good works was of no avail. The digression from 1 Pet. 1:3–9—if such it is—occurring in 2 Pet. 1:5–9 is
therefore fully intelligible: it arose from the pressing requirements of the emergency which 2 Peter handles. This digression
apart, however, is there so great a disparity between the substance
of the two trains of thought in 1 Pet. 1:3–9 and 2 Pet. 1:3–11?
At least a measure of likeness is apparent in the opening lines and
both writers arrive at the same point in 1 Pet. 1:9 and 2 Pet. 1:11.
Perchance, however, broad correspondences occur because the
sequence of ideas expressed in both epistles would come naturally
enough to any early Christian writer at the outset of an epistle?
And yet the run of thought in the opening section of 2 Peter
seems less close to the introduction of any other NT letter than
it is to that of 1 Peter. Note, too, what is said in 2 Pet. 1:12 f.
Here, the writer mentions his permanent obligation 'to put you
in remembrance'. From our study of 2 Pet. 3:1 f., we now know
that these words must imply that at this point, anyhow, the mind
of 2 Peter was still (cf. 1:2) reverting to 1 Peter. But what more
does he say in 1:12 f.? He stirs up their memory concerning 'these
things'. The reference of περὶ τούτων is, as we have already
observed (p. 37), partly retrospective: it points back to the exhortation in 1:3–11. Does he then mean here that he was writing
1:3–11 as a review and amplification of 1 Pet. 1:3–9? Were it so,
it would at least supply one reason why he added the words
'though ye know them and are established in the truth which is
with you'. They knew 'them', partly because they had been
reminded of them in First Peter.

Will it, then, be overpressing the case to say that a combination
of points justifies the view that the thought parallelism between
1 Pet. 1:3–9 and 2 Pet. 1:3–11 is not fortuitous, but derives from
the fact that from 1 Pet. 1:2 onwards the second 'Peter' continued
to write under the influence of the former one? The probability

will be strengthened, if there is reason to believe that the indebtedness continued after 2 Pet. 1:3–11. It remains therefore to compare 2 Pet. 1:12–21, with the rest of chapter one of the previous epistle.

1 Peter, having spoken in 1:3–9 of the full salvation awaiting the readers at the return of Jesus Christ from heaven, proceeds in 1:10–12 to the supporting testimony of the OT prophets, inspired by 'the Spirit of Christ which was in them', and of 'them that preached the gospel unto you by the Holy Ghost'. These all witnessed to τὰ εἰς χριστὸν παθήματα καὶ τὰς μετὰ ταῦτα δόξας. Whilst the somewhat unusual phrase τὰ εἰς χριστὸν παθήματα may mean principally the sufferings of Christ himself, it could also connote the sufferings of Christians;[18] and 2 Peter is likely to have attached the double meaning to it. Originally, τὰς μετὰ ταῦτα δόξας probably signified all the triumphs of Christ after his death, which Christians would in some measure share with him, including the glory of his second advent; and once more, 2 Peter will readily have seen such meanings in the words. In short, Second Peter's reading of 1 Pet. 1:10–12 saw there a reminder of the authoritative witness of the prophets, Christ (through the prophets) and Christian apostles to the fact that Christ and his followers would suffer and pass through suffering to glory, including the glory of Christ's second coming.

But what happens now in 2 Peter at the stage corresponding to that reached by 1 Pet. 1:10–12? In 2 Pet. 1:12–15, the writer introduces his stress on the reminding aspect of his epistle, and for him this means putting his readers in remembrance of the words of the OT prophets and of Jesus Christ through the apostles (cf. 3:1 f.) about 'these things' (1:12 and 15)—the phrase undoubtedly looking forward to the parousia theme in 1:16–21 (as well as backward to 1:3–11), especially in its use in 1:15. He also makes prominent mention of his own approaching decease which will be ταχινή; and in 1:16–21 there is the vindication of the parousia hope which makes direct appeal to the authority of Christ transfigured (16–18), OT prophecy (19–21) and the witness of apostles (16, 18, 19). The parallel between the emphasis on prophecy as given by men 'moved by the Holy Ghost' (21) and the prophets of 1 Pet. 1:11 as moved by 'the Spirit of Christ' is also worthy of note. Much in this section, in fact, could be an outflow from 1 Pet. 1:10–12.

But, it may be asked, if this overlap of thought between 1 Pet. 1:10-12 and 2 Pet. 1:12-21 is to be traced to the influence of the former passage on Second Peter, what leads 2 Peter to introduce the transfiguration of Christ in order to substantiate the parousia belief? At this point at least his mind seems to be elsewhere—on the Apocalypse of Peter perhaps?[19] Admittedly, it has travelled further than 1 Pet. 1:10–12, but has it left 1 Peter? Not necessarily. Remembering that 2 Peter held the view that at the transfiguration Peter and his companions saw Jesus in his parousia glory, how must he have read 1 Pet. 5:1, especially the words ὁ καὶ τῆς μελλούσης ἀποκαλύπτεσθαι δόξης κοινωνός? Commentators have sometimes found the phrase awkward as a description of Peter in his lifetime; but E. G. Selwyn adopts a possible exegetical line. He suggests that even for 1 Peter the words carried an allusion to Peter's presence at the transfiguration. That is to say, 1 Peter considered that the transfiguration foreshadowed the second advent, and gave Peter a proleptic participation in the glory of Christ's second coming which assured him of a share in the final event.[20] But whether Dr. Selwyn carries us with him, or not, in this interpretation of the original sense of ὁ καὶ τῆς μελλούσης ἀποκαλύπτεσθαι δόξης κοινωνός, there is every reason to believe that Second Peter read it that way.[21] That 1 Pet. 5:1 should then come to his mind inducing him to mention the transfiguration whilst developing the thought of 1 Pet. 1:10–12 in 2 Pet. 1:12–21 is natural enough, in view of the later writer's concern in 1:12–21 to justify belief in the parousia. The parallelism of wording between 1 Pet. 1:11 and 1 Pet. 5:1 may also have helped in the recall of the second passage.

The discussion of the relationship between 1 Pet. 1:10–12 and 2 Pet. 1:12–21 must end there; and is it too much to claim that it has again shown 2 Peter continuing to develop thought and argument which spring directly out of the former epistle, this time out of 1 Pet. 1:10–12 in particular, supplemented by 1 Pet. 5:1? If there is weight in the case which we have also presented for tracing much of the substance of 2 Pet. 1:2–11 to 1 Pet. 1:2–9, then it is now possible to conclude that the structure of the first chapter of 2 Peter in its framework and sequence of thought lies in very real debt to the way in which the writer of the second epistle read 1 Pet. 1:2–12, not forgetting his more detailed explication of 1 Pet. 5:1 in 2 Pet. 1:16–18.

Immediately after 1 Pet. 1:10–12, 1 Peter begins to exhort his readers to abandon former lusts and live holy lives in obedience to the truth. At the close of chapter one, 2 Peter does the same; but now 1 Peter's message ceases to have enough relevance for him. Unlike 1 Peter, the author of the second epistle has readers to save from a dangerous coterie of libertine, false teachers existing within the fellowship of the Church itself. He must therefore have material more apposite to the task on hand—sterner, even vehement material. He therefore turns to Jude.

It would be valuable at this point to embark on a study of the possible influence of 1 Peter on 2 Peter's use of Jude. We shall, however, pass by this question to examine as our last line of inquiry a verse connected with passages already discussed. It will be:

2 Peter 1:14. The principal exegetical problem in this verse is the reference of the words καθὼς καὶ ὁ Κύριος ἡμῶν Ἰησοῦς Χριστὸς ἐδήλωσέ μοι. To what revelation, or special instruction, given by Jesus Christ to Peter, does the writer of 2 Peter here allude?

Most expositors suggest that he was looking back to John 21:18 f. (cf. 13:36), or some other version of the same tradition. Some, like Spitta, prefer the theory of dependence upon the tradition lying behind the *Quo Vadis* legend in the Acts of Peter.[22] Others think that all traces of the occasion of the disclosure in question have now been lost.[23] One should, however, resort to the second and third hypotheses only if John 21:18 proves an improbable source and no other likely solution is in sight.

Taking the wording of John 21:18 f. in itself, it is difficult to feel the strength of the objection that, because it seems to prophesy a violent martyr-death for Peter in old age, it is unfitting as the origin of what is said in 2 Pet. 1:14.[24] This contention appears to underrate two possibilities. First of all, the tradition that the apostle Peter suffered martyrdom was widely diffused in the early Church by A.D. 140/50—the date frequently assigned to 2 Peter.[25] This surely implies that Second Peter knew the tradition; and therefore, although 1:14 speaks less explicitly of violent death than John 21:18 f. does, it will none the less have been a reference to the apostle's martyrdom. Secondly, although in 2 Pet. 1:14 'Peter' does not describe himself as old (cf. John 21:18), he was probably writing as though he were a Peter of old age.[26] From such a standpoint, it would be logical enough for him to say that his death was coming ταχινή and to mean thereby that, when it came, it would be a fulfilment of John 21:18. Given these legitimate presuppositions, John 21:18 f. seems to provide all that is required by 2 Pet. 1:14, as Chase thought.[27]

But the case against John 21:18 f. as the passage recalled by 2 Pet. 1:14, could perhaps be more strongly presented on other grounds. First, 2 Peter differs from the Fourth Gospel so radically in outlook and teaching—in its eschatology, for instance—as to make it questionable whether Second Peter is likely to have drawn on the Fourth Gospel. Then again, in the immediate context of 1:14, the transfiguration of Jesus finds mention (17 f.). The author is here employing some form of Gospel tradition, but obviously it is not the Fourth Gospel to which he turned, since the Fourth Gospel does not report the transfiguration. These points scarcely rule out the possibility that 2 Pet. 1:14 is indebted to John 21:1 8f. Yet they do suggest the need of searching elsewhere to try to find a communication to Peter resembling that of which 2 Pet. 1:14 speaks, but less liable to objection as a source than John 21:18 f.

The first step must be a fuller clarification of the meaning and implications of 2 Pet. 1:14. What exactly does the verse say? And what does it show by implication to have been in the mind of 2 Peter, as he wrote it? Some additional points, though small ones, may have their significance. First of all, whilst δηλοῦν could denote a divine revelation of an unusual nature, granted on a special occasion, it does not necessarily do so. It was commonly used for 'inform', 'make clear to', or 'explain' in the ordinary senses. Thus 1:14 need not refer to some unique, revelatory event. Further, as suggested above, 2 Peter must have written in awareness of the tradition that Peter suffered martyrdom, so that the verse was intended as an allusion to the martyrdom. But it should then be recalled that the tradition also reported that Peter was put to death during a period of persecution, when many of the faithful perished.[28] So 2 Peter is likely to have been thinking of that, as well. It may further be worth mention that 2 Pet. 1:15 terms Peter's death an ἔξοδος—a word which appears in Luke's transfiguration narrative (9:31), as a designation of the approaching 'martyrdom' of Jesus.[29] Finally, in 1:14, 2 Peter writes ταχινή ἐστιν ἡ ἀπόθεσις τοῦ σκηνώματός μου. It is agreed that in itself ταχινή means 'soon' or 'sudden', or both. Which connotation operates in 2 Pet. 1:14? Most commentators seem to prefer 'soon', whilst conceding that both senses may be present. Now ταχινή occurs in the NT only in 2 Pet. 1:14 and 2:1. Its use in 2:1 should therefore be considered. In 2:1 it describes the ἀπωλεία which is to befall the false teachers. But in the rest of the epistle it is the suddenness rather than the imminence of ἀπωλεία which receives emphasis. The destruction will not occur until the day of judgment (3:7), and although the appearance of mockers of the parousia is a sign of 'the last days' (3:3), the inbreaking of the day itself is to be sudden (3:10; cf. 3:4) rather than instant (cf. 3:4, 8 f.). Thus in 2:1 at least, ταχινή seems to describe catastrophic doom which, when it comes, will break upon the 'false teachers' quite unexpectedly, that is, suddenly, rather than swiftly or without delay. Though 'soon' was probably a secondary meaning, ταχινή could therefore have been used with the same two primary and secondary senses in 1:14. If so, it would be an apt enough adjective to describe death in a wave of persecution.

Summing up, there is good reason to conclude that 2 Pet. 1:14 was 2 Peter's way of saying that Peter's decease would shortly come in the manner described in the tradition with which the pseudo-Petrine author was familiar: it would be a sudden and violent martyr-death in an approaching time of persecution. This fate the Lord Jesus Christ had made clear at some time to the mind of Peter. It is thus the surviving source (if there is one) of 2 Pet. 1:14, written in this sense, which we have to track down. It still leaves John 21:18 f. in the picture; but is an alternative with a better claim now coming into view?

If the investigations in the foregoing sections of this essay have yielded acceptable results, it is now possible to approach the present question from at least the following established, or probable positions: 2 Pet. 3:1 does allude to 1 Peter; 2 Peter writes under a measure of debt to the contents of 1 Peter; and in 2 Pet. 1:12–21 his mind was running strongly on 1 Peter. Then did it jump elsewhere for what he writes in 1:14? It would be quite improbable, if there is anything in 1 Peter at all corresponding to the remarks in 2 Pet. 1:14. And in pursuing this question further, may we remind ourselves again that it is not only the original meaning of passages in 1 Peter which must be seen, but also the way in which 2 Peter is likely to have understood them? For our immediate purpose, the latter is, to be sure, the more important question. The pertinent passage in 1 Peter is 1 Pet. 5:1 and its context. 1 Pet. 5:1 reads πρεσβυτέρους οὖν ἐν ὑμῖν παρακαλῶ ὁ συμπρεσβύτερος καὶ μάρτυς τῶν τοῦ Χριστοῦ παθημάτων, ὁ καὶ τῆς μελλούσης ἀποκαλύπτεσθαι δόξης κοινωνός.   From ὁ συμπρεσβύτερος to the end of the verse, there is mention of three aspects of Peter's standing and destiny: he is συμπρεσβύτερος, μάρτυς, and κοινωνός of glory to be revealed. Beyond this, general agreement about the precise meaning of the three designations ceases. Shall we, then, re-examine them?

Whether 1 Peter was written by the apostle, or someone else, why was he styled συμπρεσβύτερος? At the beginning of 5:1, πρεσβύτερος describes those who exercised local, pastoral office in the Church. Would a leading apostle like Peter have adopted a similar designation for himself? Commentators have felt the difficulty, and modesty on the apostle's part is a commonly offered explanation. But without entering upon a discussion of the extent to which πρεσβύτερος is here used as a technical term for an established, ecclesiastical office, it will not raise dissent to say that the connotation 'elderly' or 'senior in years' is included in its sense. The πρεσβύτεροι in the early Christian churches will, more often than not, have been elderly men, and 5:5 shows that this aspect of the meaning of the word plays its part in 5:1. This being so, why does the designation of Peter as συμπρεσβύτερος cause surprise? It could well have been an elderly Peter who was writing —or alleged to be—and who, as Moffatt has remarked, 'plays on the double sense of the term'.[30] But that does not necessarily mean, as Moffatt seems to imply, that the writer carried over both senses of πρεσβύτερος with more or less equal weight into συμπρεσβύτερος. It may well have been in years rather than in office that, by the use of this word, he put himself—or was put—alongside those addressed as πρεσβύτεροι. Were it so, no further explanation of the language seems wanted, since there is nothing unusual about the self-alignment: συμπρεσβύτερος is another way of saying that an elderly Peter writes, and Second Peter could have read it so.[31]

The elderly apostle, however, is also μάρτυς τῶν τοῦ Χριστοῦ παθημάτων. What is to be understood by that? It is generally translated 'witness of the sufferings of Christ' and has been held to refer to Peter's role as both an eye-witness of the passion of his

Lord and a preacher of Christ crucified. But some recent expositors, like Windisch, have observed that there is probably more to the meaning of μάρτυς τῶν τοῦ Χριστοῦ παθημάτων than this: it may well include a reference to the share which Peter himself had in Christ's suffering and death, especially if 1 Peter was written at a time when μάρτυς had begun to mean 'martyr' as well as 'witness'.[32] This strikes a line of interpretation which well befits the following clause: the apostle is to suffer and die, as Christ did, and will in consequence participate in Christ's heavenly glory. Much the same is said of other Christians in 4:13, and this theme of suffering (whether of Christ or Christians) issuing in heavenly glory is prominent throughout 1 Peter.[33] The lot, therefore, which this epistle elsewhere attributes to Christ and regards as possible for Christians in general is mentioned in 5:1 as the apostle's own appointed destiny. That this is the sense which Second Peter is likely to have attached to the passage can scarcely be denied, writing, as he did, fully acquainted with the tradition concerning Peter's martyrdom and also at a time when μάρτυς was being commonly used with the meaning 'martyr'—a connotation widely current by the middle of the second century.[34]

There remains the last clause of 5:1. It again, apparently, refers in part to Peter's standing whilst yet alive: ὁ καὶ τῆς μελλούσης ἀποκαλύπτεσθαι δόξης κοινωνός. The words have been discussed above on p. 43. 'The glory that shall be revealed' is the celestial glory of Christ to be manifested at the parousia and enjoyed by Christians in heaven thereafter; but just as the ostensibly still living apostle is already μάρτυς (presumably because the suffering to which he has been appointed had already begun), so is he also κοινωνός of Christ's parousia glory. This time, however, the collocation of present state and future lot is less straightforward. The difficulty seems to have escaped the eye of some expositors, or to have been regarded as insignificant. Others have treated the clause as a pseudo-Petrine author's allusion to an already accomplished entry of the martyred Peter into the initial stages of his heavenly reward, after the manner indicated in 1 Clem. 5:4—the consummation of his bliss being held in reserve until the parousia.[35] But is there not a more attractive explanation in the direction taken by Dr. E. G. Selwyn, and already mentioned (p. 43)? In the early Church the transfiguration was sometimes interpreted as a foreshadowing of the parousia. Peter and the other two disciples who were there, were thus granted an anticipatory experience of Christ's parousia glory. This privilege, then, could well be said to have constituted Peter forthwith κοινωνός of Christ's future heavenly glory, whilst also confirming his future participation in its fuller manifestation at the parousia. To 2 Peter, who regarded the transfiguration as an anticipatory portrayal of the parousia, this is certainly likely to have been the meaning of ὁ καὶ τῆς μελλούσης ἀποκαλύπτεσθαι δόξης κοινωνός; and 2 Pet. 1:16–18 could well have been written as a fuller explication of the clause.

So much for the exposition of 1 Pet. 5:1, but before gathering up results, let not the context of the verse be overlooked. It expounds the apostle's view of the contemporary situation, which from 4:7 onwards is described as one of crisis and impending eschatological fulfilment. The woes of the last days have begun (4:7), manifesting themselves in the πύρωσις which has already engulfed the readers (4:12). This is the first phase of the inbreaking of God's final judgment—a judgment appointed to descend first and immediately upon the members of the household of God (4:17), who must therefore live in expectation of treading at any moment the path through suffering to eternal glory (4:19; 5:10, etc.).

Shall we now draw together the principal conclusions to which the examination of 1 Pet. 5:1 and its context points, when one tries to read the passage through the eyes of 2 Peter? He knew the tradition that Peter died a martyr's death in a period of persecution. He also had a version of the transfiguration which related it to the parousia. Our argument, then, seems to show that when this pseudo-Petrine writer studied the former epistle in Peter's name, he saw in 1 Pet. 5:1 a Peter, already advanced in years, who knew that he was to perish as a martyr. This he understood as the apostle's God-appointed road to that fuller share in Christ's celestial glory of which he had already been granted a token participation at the transfiguration. From the immediate context of 1 Pet. 5:1, which warned of the near approach of the End, 2 Peter could also have deduced that the apostle anticipated the early realization of his martyr destiny, and as a part of a general persecution. That is, the πύρωσις enveloping Christians would be one which Peter himself would not survive, being old and already appointed a μάρτυς ('martyr'), and κοινωνός of future glory. All this, as

E

2 Peter saw it, will also have been written by the apostle under the revealing guidance of the Holy Spirit; or the Spirit of Jesus Christ (cf. 2 Pet. 1:21; 3:15 f.)

Is it then, necessary to look further afield for the source of the words of 2 Pet. 1:14? 1 Pet. 5:1 and its context seem to offer details corresponding sufficiently closely to the meaning of 2 Pet. 1:14 as expounded above (pp. 45–6) to have a good claim to be their origin.

But one final word, lest we end the discussion of this matter prematurely. If it has been substantiated that the immediate source of 2 Pet. 1:14 is 1 Pet. 5:1 and the preceding verses in 4:7–19, is this section of First Peter necessarily the ultimate source? It was said earlier in the discussion that one of the reasons against John 21:18 f. as the origin of 2 Pet. 1:14 was 2 Peter's obvious use of some form of Synoptic, rather than Johannine, tradition in 1:16–18, that is, in the immediate context of 1:14. And what effort by the apostle is meant in 2 Pet. 1:15? Was it St. Mark's Gospel, as some suppose? Were it possible to be sure, it would be additional evidence that at this point and its context the mind of 2 Peter is not reverting to St. John. It is, of course, true that his description of the transfiguration is not exactly parallel to any one of the Synoptic versions, but the divergences are not so great as to require the hypothesis of some non-synoptic source. They are quite intelligible, if he was trusting to his memory of the Synoptics.[36]

Now if, as he writes, he recalls those sections of the Synoptic Gospels which record the transfiguration, is he oblivious of the topically related material which immediately precedes the transfiguration in all of them? In Matthew, Mark and Luke, the transfiguration is narrated as an event closely knit with the preceding teaching about discipleship and Peter's confession of Christ. For our purpose, and using Matthew and Mark, the significant points are as follows. From Caesarea Philippi to the transfiguration, Peter plays a prominent part in the sequence of events. He is rebuked for questioning the necessity of the suffering and death of the Son of man. Jesus then shows his disciples (and Peter in particular, we might say) that they must take up their cross, and that it is the disciple who in this way loses his life, who will not be disowned, but rewarded by the Son of man when he comes with the angels in his parousia glory. 'And after six days' on a 'high mountain', Peter—accompanied by James and John—has the experience which in 2 Peter's thought constituted him forthwith a κοινωνός of Christ's heavenly glory.

Put all this alongside what Second Peter found in First Peter, and suppose that Second Peter read the Synoptic passages in the light of First Peter, what more is necessary, or what more appropriate material must the investigator be asked to produce in order to reveal in its entirety the source of 2 Pet. 1:14? The theory propounded here has the further advantage of harmonizing with the fact that in the verses immediately adjoining 2 Pet. 1:14, the mind of 2 Peter was running on the Synoptics and on 1 Peter: in 2 Pet. 1:16–18, and perhaps in 1:15, on the Synoptics; and in 2 Pet. 1:12 f., as shown earlier in this investigation, on 1 Peter.

Thus our final conclusion is that when the antecedent line of 2 Pet. 1:14 is fully traced, it is found to run through 1 Pet. 5:1 and its context (especially 1 Pet. 4:7–19) back to the Synoptics—probably to St. Matthew's or St. Mark's account (or a mixture of both) of the martyr-teaching of Jesus, given to Peter and other disciples between Peter's confession near Caesarea Philippi and the transfiguration of Christ.

NOTES

[1] In *The Epistle of St. Jude and the Second Epistle of St. Peter* (1907), 1–15, J. B. Mayor sets out the Greek texts of Jude and 2 Pet. in parallel columns, clearly revealing the closeness of the connection between them.

[2] Similarly Mayor, *op. cit.*, xiii.

[3] Spitta and Zahn were notable exceptions. Maintaining that 2 Pet. 3:1 f. gives an inappropriate description of 1 Peter, they suggested that the passage refers to some other Petrine epistle now lost.

[4] *Die Briefe Petri und Judä* (1912), 254.

[5] *Die Katholischen Briefe*, 3rd edn. (umgearb. H. Preisker, HNT, 1951), 99.

[6] *Op. cit.*, cxiv. Cf. J. Moffatt, *Introduction to the Literature of the N.T.* (1912), 364.

[7] *Epistles of St. Peter and St. Jude* (ICC, 2nd edn., 1902), 232 and 234.

[8] *Op. cit.*, 224–36.

[9] *Op. cit.*, ch. IV, lxviii–cv. Cf. Chase, 'Peter, the Second Epistle of', HDB, iii, 812–14; W. H. Bennett, *The General Epistles* (Cent. B.), 56–8; Bigg, *op. cit.*, 224–36.

[10] The extent to which the polemic against both libertinism and the scoffing of the parousia is interwoven throughout the epistle and also a passage like 3:3 favour the theory that both dangers come from the same group of reprobates.

[11] In addition to 3:1 f., *vide* 3:15 f., 1:12–21.

[12] For a fuller explanation of this interpretation of 2 Pet. 1:16–18, may I refer to my treatment of the passage in *St. Mark and the Transfiguration Story* (1942), 43–46? I have also dealt with this passage and others used in this article in the new edition of *Peake's Commentary on the Bible* (sections 894–97 and 904–05) to be published by Nelson.

[13] For ὑπογραμμός used of Jesus Christ, see also 1 Clem. 16:17, 33:8.

[14] In 1 Pet. 1:10–12, a clear distinction is made between prophets of a bygone age and a new era which begins with those who first proclaimed the Christian gospel. This implies that the prophets of 1:10 are the OT prophets, as most commentators maintain, not Christian prophets. That the OT prophets should be guided by 'the Spirit of Christ' is not a difficulty in the light of the christology of the early Christian church.

[15] R. Knopf, *op. cit.* (in footnote 4), 37 cites parallels from Dan. 3:98 (31) LXX and Theodotion; 4:34 LXX; 6:25 Theodotion. *Vide* also HRCS 1145.

[16] *Op. cit.*, 260.

[17] On 2 Pet. 1:5 and James, cf. Bennett, *The General Epistles* (Cent. B.), 262, and Wand, *The General Epistles of St. Peter and St. Jude* (1934), 154. See also the latter's comment on 2 Pet. 1:8 (p. 155).

[18] Cf. E. G. Selwyn, *The First Epistle of St. Peter* (1949), 136 f., F. L. Cross, *1 Peter: A Paschal Liturgy* (1954), 21 f. See also the discussion of μάρτυς τῶν τοῦ χριστοῦ παθημάτων (5:1) on pp. 47 f. of this essay.

[19] For the association of the transfiguration and the parousia in the Apocalypse of Peter, may I again refer to my *St. Mark and the Transfiguration Story* (30–40)? But the view that the Apocalypse of Peter was written before 2 Peter, seems to me improbable, although it was held by Harnack and looked upon as possible by Chase (HDB iii, 814–16).

[20] E. G. Selwyn, *op. cit.*, 228 f.

[21] Cf. J. A. T. Robinson, *Jesus and His Coming* (1957), 133 and 136.

[22] *Vide* Vercelli Acts of Peter XXXV, in M. R. James, *Apocryphal N.T.*, 333.

[23] E.g. Windisch, *op. cit.* (note 5), 88; J. Moffatt, *The General Epistles* (Moffatt NT Comm. 1928), 184.

[24] Cf. Mayor, *op. cit.* (note 1), 101 f.

[25] For the early development and spread of the tradition of Peter's martyrdom, attested in John 21:18 f., cf. also Rev. 11:3–13 (? *vide* J. Munck, *Petrus u. Paulus in der Offenbarung Johannes*, 1950); 1 Clem. 5:1–6:1; Ignat., *Rom.* 4:3; Acts of Peter XXXV–XL. *Vide* also O. Cullmann, *Petrus*, 73–169.

[26] Cf. the exegesis of συμπρεσβύτερος in 1 Pet. 5:1 as given below p. 47.

[27] HDB iii, 809.

[28] So, for instance, as early as 1 Clem. 5–6.

[29] Cf. the reference to Peter's death as an ἔξοδος by Irenaeus (*Adv. Haer.* III, i, 1, in Eus. HE, V, viii. 2 f.).

[30] *The General Epistles*, 161.

[31] Assuming that the following μάρτυς τῶν τοῦ Χριστοῦ παθημάτων in 5:1 includes a reference to Peter's sufferings as a Christian (as suggested on p. 42), the collocation of πρεσβύτερος and suffering recalls a like association of πρεσβύτης and Christian suffering in Philem. 9.

[32] Cf. Windisch, *op. cit.* (note 5), 79; Wand, *op. cit.* (note 17), 122; F. W. Beare, *The First Epistle of Peter* (1947), 172; TWNT iv, 498–99; O. Cullmann,

Petrus (1952), 92 etc. Knopf, *op. cit.* (note 4), suggested that μάρτυς τῶν του Χριστοῦ παθημάτων might be a prophecy *ex eventu* of Peter's death.

[33] In addition to 5:1 and 4:12 f., *vide* 1:6 f., 11, 3:18–22, 4:19, and 5:9–10. Cf., too, Selwyn, *op. cit.* (note 18), 228.

[34] Cf. R. P. Casey, *Beginnings of Christianity* v, 30–7; TWNT iv, 512.

[35] Cf. Knopf, *op. cit.* (note 4), 188 f.; Windisch, *op. cit.* (note 5), 79.

[36] Three points would favour the view that 2 Peter drew on Matthew's narrative of the transfiguration: (i) the words of the heavenly voice in 2 Pet. 1:17; (ii) the reference to the disciples hearing the voice, cf. Matt. 17:6; (iii) a church leader who, around the middle of the second century, writes in the name and under the authority of Peter might well have had a preference for the Gospel which assigned Peter a leading place in the Church.

At the same time, the importance of the tradition linking St. Mark's Gospel with Peter must not be set on one side.

THE TERM *GOSPEL* AND ITS COGNATES
IN THE PALESTINIAN SYRIAC

by

J. W. BOWMAN

THERE is at present among biblical theologians perhaps more lively interest in a subject that concerned the Anti-judaic Gnostic Marcion in the second century and St. Augustine in the fourth and fifth than in any other that could be named. This is the problem of *continuity* in the divine revelation and in redemptive history (*Heilsgeschichte*). Although this problem obviously has its philosophical aspects, as for example in the investigation of the possible ontological reference of 'time' and 'history', it is a notable fact that present interest in the subject as it relates to the Christian Faith generally and in the development of a solution for it is largely on the part of biblical scholars rather than of systematic theologians or even of philosophers of history. Perhaps this phenomenon is symptomatic of a recapturing by biblical theologians of the centre of the theological stage—a position from which during the first half of the century they appear to have been driven. However this may be, at all events the endeavour to set forth the divine revelation and redemption in terms of the time-process and of history is one of the significant undertakings of biblical scholarship at the moment.

At one pole in the present discussion stands Rudolf Bultmann with his wish to *demythologize* the New Testament (an endeavour which opponents of his views fear will result in dehistorizing as well, and this, in spite of Bultmann's distinction between the terms *geschichtlich* and *historisch*), and as representative of the other extreme one may mention Oscar Cullmann, for whom redemptive history (*Heilsgeschichte*) or revelational history (*Offenbarungsgeschichte*)—and he would be understood as including in these terms both the 'framework' and inner 'kernel' of the history involved—'is the heart of all New Testament theology'. The interest aroused and the keen championing of one or other side in this debate on the part of biblical theologians is sufficient evidence of the fertile soil into which the seeds of the discussion have been cast.[1] This question of redemptive history and of the continuity between the *old* and the *new*, between 'chosen people of God' and Church, between Judaism and Christianity was already an old one in Marcion's day. Essentially it was the problem which drew forth such bitter antagonism against the apostle Paul and his preaching (*kerygma*) from the side of the Judaizing element in the early Jewish Christian community and, if we are to accept at its face value a passage like Mark 2:18–22, it was this same question of continuity which on the occasion(s) indicated was a subject of concern for Jesus and his Pharisaic opponents.

Believing as he does that the entire message of Scripture is rightly apprehended only when considered as embraced within the category of *redemption or revelation history*, the present writer has elsewhere endeavoured to demonstrate that in the New Testament itself there lie side by side three distinct traditions which separately (and jointly) give evidence of the Church's interpretation of the Old and New Testament historical data in accordance with this thesis.[2] These are: (*a*) the tradition of a 'Herald-Christology' in the Synoptic Gospels deriving from such passages as Isa. 40:9; 52:7; and Nahum 1:15, (*b*) the proclamation of the *gospel* in terms of the 'rest of God' promised respectively through Joshua, David, and Jesus Christ according to the author of *Hebrews*, and (*c*) Paul's philosophy of history as found in Gal. 3, wherein he finds promise in Abraham and fulfilment in Jesus Christ. Each of these traditions selects for its purposes a different point of departure or *terminus a quo* (the *herald* of Deutero-Isaiah in the Synoptics, Joshua in *Hebrews*, and Abraham in Paul), but discloses the united belief of the Church in the same event of fulfilment—viz. the redemptive activity of Jesus Christ. And each tradition develops between the two points chosen as *termini a quo* and *ad quem* respectively a 'yardstick' intended to serve as a norm for understanding God's dealing with man for his redemption. It is argued that in this diversity of selected materials there is to be seen an underlying unity of faith in the God of history and in the redemption-revelation events through which His purpose relative to man is achieved.

In the present study my interest concerns the proper definitive term (*gospel*) applied to this redemption-revelation activity of God in the three early traditions to which reference has just been made. And my hope is merely that the study may bring forward a small bit of evidence serving to bridge a gap in the continuity from the Old to the New Testament at this point. For it would appear that hitherto—with the single exception of the 'missing link' referred to—New Testament scholarship has succeeded in exhibiting satisfactorily all the elements of the argument in favour of applying the term 'gospel' to God's activity throughout history on behalf of man's salvation.

We shall first review the evidence for the use of the terms 'gospel' and 'to preach the gospel' in the technical sense here intended as this has been previously collected by others and shall then supply the 'missing link' at the proper point in the chain. It will be convenient to begin with Gerhard Friedrich's exhaustive summary in his article devoted to εὐαγγελίζεσθαι and its cognates in TWNT.[3] In this article Friedrich arrives at some significant results relative to the usage of these terms in the Hebrew-Greek Scriptures which may be presented in brief as follows—

(1) for the use of the verb εὐαγγελίζεσθαι:

(*a*) the Hebrew verb *biśśēr* behind the Greek derives from a stem which, as comparison with the cognate languages indicates, etymologically conveys the sense of *glad* or *good* tidings (*Freude*).[4] As employed in the OT, then, this verb acquires, *first*, a cultic connotation, as in 1 Sam. 31:9 where it is employed in announcing the 'glad news' (*die freudige Botschaft*) relative to the defeat and death of Saul at the pagan shrines of the Philistines; *then*, a more general sense, as in Ps. 40:10; 68:12; and *finally*, in Isa. 52:7 where the substantival participle *mᵉbhaśśēr* occurs, the specifically eschatological reference to the 'glad tidings' that God had begun His reign in Zion. From this and the like evidence Friedrich concludes that 'für das Vorverständnis des nt.lichen Euangelion begriffes ist Deuterojesaja und die von ihm beeinflusste Literatur am wichtigsten' (p. 706, lines 10 f.).[5]

(*b*) The use of the Greek verb by contrast, including that to be found in secular literature, in the LXX, and in Philo and Josephus, makes no significant contribution from a religious point of view, nor does the Greek verb εὐαγγελίζεσθαι ever attain to the wealth of religious meaning of its Hebrew equivalent as noted above. Friedrich, indeed, remarks—'Dadurch wird deutlich, dass die

LXX nicht mehr verstanden hat, was Deuterojesaja mit dem kommenden Freudenboten gemeint hat,' [6] and again, 'Bei Philo wie bei Josephus findet sich nirgendwo der Gedanke an den Freudenboten aus Deuterojesaja. Das ist auch nicht verwunderlich. Sie haben kein Geschichtsverständnis, sie kennen keine Heilsgeschichte, keine wahre Eschatologie'.[7]

(c) Palestinian Judaism, however, kept alive—as Hellenistic Judaism represented by LXX, Philo, and Josephus did not—the Deutero-Isaiah connotation of the verb *bissēr* and particularly the eschatological reference to be found in its employment of the substantival participle *mᵉbhassēr*.[8]

(2) For employing the noun εὐαγγέλιον:

(a) The Hebrew noun *bᵉśōrāh*, unlike its related verb, had no religious connotation in the OT; so that Friedrich can conclude his study at this point with the unequivocal statement—'Im AT wird *bᵉśōrāh* nur profan gebraucht. Ein religiöser Sprachgebrauch des Substantivs fehlt vollkommen.' [9]

(b) As for the Greek, εὐαγγέλιον, -ία was employed in a religious context in Emperor Worship; as for example, for the announcement made at an emperor's birth, at his enthronement, and on the occasion of other important events during his life and reign.[10] On the other hand, neither LXX, Philo, nor Josephus employs the noun in a significant manner for religious purposes. In this respect their usage is exactly in accord with their failure with reference to the Greek verb.

(c) Again, however, it is to be noted that Palestinian Judaism now supplied a religious usage and connotation to the noun just as it had kept alive that of the verb, though it appears that the eschatological reference is never found in the noun as in the verb and its participle.[11] (But cf. p. 62 below.)

At this point, Friedrich turns to a study of the Greek terms in the New Testament and his conclusions essentially follow those already arrived at by George Milligan[12] and Millar Burrows[13] in independent studies. This is to the general effect that the NT usage of the Greek terms (εὐαγγέλιον and εὐαγγελίζεσθαι) derives from the developed religious connotation of the Hebrew verb and particularly its participle in Deutero-Isaiah. Thus, with reference to Isa. 61:1, Milligan remarks that this passage 'from our Lord's own use of it in Luke iv:18 f. may be said to have set the stamp upon εὐαγγελίζομαι as the most fitting term to describe the true character of the message of the new Messianic King' (p. 142). Millar Burrows in somewhat similar fashion concludes relative to Isa. 40:9, 52:7, 60:6, and 61:1—'We may be quite sure that in these four passages from the Second Isaiah is to be found the main source for the Christian use of the term "gospel" ' (p. 22).

Friedrich agrees that through their use of the verb (εὐαγγελίζεσθαι) the Evangelists not only indicate Jesus to be the 'herald' of the *erwarteten Endzeit* (Matt. 4:23), but also represent him as claiming as much himself (Matt. 11:5 = Luke 7:22; Luke 4:18, 43, 16:16). He is less certain that Jesus employed the noun (or its Aramaic equivalent) to describe the nature of his message, holding that this question is bound up with the problem of Jesus' 'messianic consciousness'.[14] I have already discussed Friedrich's argument at this point in a previous publication[15] and shall not go over the ground again except to say that

it appears to me that the Marcan tradition as exhibited in these five passages [see below, note 14] is more likely than not to be authentic and so from our Lord's lips, if for no other reason than that *they appear to reflect an early period when the gospel was still something that Jesus heralded rather than something that he was himself.* It is admitted on all hands that in the later Church the latter meaning attached to the word 'gospel' and it seems inconceivable, therefore, that the five passages in Mark which represent Jesus as merely the gospel's Herald, rather than its embodiment, should be the creation of that later Church.

For our present purpose it is relevant now to turn to a summary of the evidence for the Syriac equivalents of these terms which we have been discussing. And it is at once rather startling to discover that throughout the long period represented by the translation from the original Greek into successively the Old Syriac (Sinaitic and Curetonian), the Peshitta, and the Harkleian versions, at least that is from the second to the seventh century, the Christian Syriac-speaking peoples consistently employed for the terms 'gospel' and 'to preach the gospel' (i.e. for εὐαγγέλιον and εὐαγγελίζεσθαι, wherever they occur in the NT text), s*bhartā* and s*bhar*— words whose etymological meaning is 'to think, hold as true, be convinced, believe, suppose', and the like.[16] The only exceptions to this rule apparently concern the use of the term 'Gospel' in the title to the works of the Evangelists and at Mark 1:1, in both of which cases the Syriac simply transliterates the Greek to read *euangeliōn*.

The evidence for these statements may be conveniently tabulated as follows:[16]

(1) For the noun (εὐαγγέλιον), *Codex Sinaitic* reads *s*ᵉ*bhartā*[17] in Matt. 4:23, 9:35, 24:14, 26:13; Mark 1:14, 15, 8:35, 10:29, 13:10, 14:9. *Codex Curetonian* reads the same at Matt. 4:23 and is lacking elsewhere; the *Peshitta* employs the same noun everywhere with the exception of Mark 1:1, where *euangeliōn* occurs;[18]

(2) For the verb (εὐαγγελίζεσθαι), *Codex Sinaitic* has *s*ᵉ*bhar* in some one of its forms at Luke 2:10, 3:18, 4:18, 43, 8:1, 9:6, 16:16, 20:1, being lacking elsewhere; similarly, *Codex Curetonian* at Matt. 11:5; Luke 8:1, 9:6, 20:1, where alone the codex is complete; the *Peshitta* also has the same verb in one form or other in all the passages cited; the *Harkleian* has it at Luke 4:18 and 4:43.[19]

(3) For εὐαγγελιστής, found only in Acts 21:8, Eph. 4:11, and 2 Tim. 4:5 in the NT—in all of which passages the *Old Syriac* is, of course, lacking—the *Peshitta* employs *m*ᵉ*sabb*ᵉ*rānā*.[20]

For the OT the *Old Syriac* is lacking, but the evidence from the *Peshitta* confirms that for the NT relative to the proper Syriac equivalents for derivatives of εὐαγγελίζεσθαι—and as may now be added, for those of *bāśar* as well. The evidence for this statement is as follows:

(1) For the verb *biśśēr* (LXX, εὐαγγελίζεσθαι), the *Peshitta* employs some form of *s*ᵉ*bhr* in every OT passage concerned. These are—1 Sam. 4:17, 31:9; 2 Sam. 1:20, 4:10, 18:19, 20(bis), 18:31; 1 Kings 1:42; 1 Chron. 10:9, 16:23; Ps. 40:9, 68:11 (noun), 96:2; Isa. 40:9(bis), 52:7(bis), 60:6, 61:1; Nahum 1:15; Jer. 20:15.[21]

(2) For the noun *b*ᵉ*śōrāh* (LXX, εὐαγγέλιον, -ία), the *Peshitta* again has *s*ᵉ*bhartā* in all passages concerned—viz. at 2 Sam. 4:10, 18:22, 25, 27; 2 Kings 7:9.[22]

The complete uniformity of this evidence is impressive and it is, of course, on this basis that the *Thesaurus Syriacus* of R. Payne Smith (2 vols., 1879), together with Mrs. Margoliouth's smaller work (*A Compendious Syriac Dictionary*, 1903) founded upon the larger one, provides *s*ᵉ*bhartā* and *s*ᵉ*bhar* respectively as the normal Syriac equivalents for 'gospel' and 'to preach the gospel'. This phenomenon raises a problem of real interest for its own sake—viz. why the Syriac either never developed a term (noun and verb) with the root meaning of 'joy' and hallowed by long usage in the cognate languages of Hebrew, Accadian, and Arabic to designate 'glad tidings' of both a secular and religious nature, or if it did so, then abandoned it for purposes of designating the distinctive message of the Scriptures and chose instead a word with the etymological sense of 'to show a bright face, be pleasant, think, suppose, hope', and the like.[23] But whatever be the reason for this phenomenon, the fact remains that the Syriac language from the second century forward fails to supply us with the link between the OT and LXX, on the one hand, and the Greek of the NT, on the other, as far as the proper terms to be employed for 'gospel' and its cognates are concerned. For reasons of its own, the Syriac rejected the stem *bsr* (both verb and noun) to designate the central message of Scripture (or at any rate, its eschatological aspect as found in Deutero-Isaiah), and chose instead terms derived from the stem *śbhr* (Heb.; Aram. *sbhr*) to serve this purpose.

In the light of the foregoing, it is striking to find that the Christian Palestinian Syriac (or Aramaic) is as uniform in its retention of the noun and verb from the stem *bsr* (*b^e sōrā*, *bsr*) in all places where the prophetic eschatological hope and the distinctively Christian gospel are had in mind as all other types of Syriac have been in abandoning them. There is no exception to this surprising phenomenon as far as I have been able to discover in any extant manuscript of the Palestinian Syriac for those parts of OT and NT that have been preserved. It is true that the Palestinian Syriac is known to us only in the form of lectionaries, so far at all events as a continuous text is concerned, and that lacunae, therefore, are present and these of an extensive sort. No manuscript of the Palestinian Syriac extant contains 2 Sam. 4:10, 18:20, 22, 25, 27; 2 Kings 7:9; Mark 1:14, 15, 10:29, 13:10, or 14:9, where the Hebrew employs *b^e sōrāh* and LXX and NT respectively εὐαγγέλιον, -ία; nor 1 Sam. 4:17, 31:9; 2 Sam. 4:10, 18:19, 20, 26, 31; 1 Kings 1:42; 1 Chron. 10:9, 16:23; Ps. 40(39):9, 68(67):11, 96(95):2; Isa. 52:7; Nahum 1:5(2:1); Jer. 20:15, 51(28):10; Luke 3:18, 4:43; or 16:16, where the Hebrew has *biśśēr* and LXX and NT respectively εὐαγγελίζεσθαι. The presence of these lacunae is somewhat disconcerting, to be sure, though fortunately the passages extant are found at strategic points in both OT and NT text, sufficiently so indeed for us to arrive at a definitive conclusion in the matter.

The evidence upon which this statement is based follows—

(1) Translating the noun εὐαγγέλιον, the Palestinian Syriac employs *bsōrā* in *Codex Climaci Rescriptus* at Mark 1:1; Rom. 15:16, 19; 1 Cor. 4:15, 15:1; Gal. 1:6, 7, 11 (*bsrā*); Phil. 2:22; 1 Thess. 1:5;

2 Thess. 1:8; 2 Tim. 1:10; Philem. 13: in *Pal. Syriac Lect. No. VI* at Rom. 1:1; 1 Cor. 15:1; Eph. 1:13; and 2 Tim. 2:8; in *Pal. Syriac Lect. of the Gospels:* (a) its *Codex A* at Matt. 4:23(bis), 9:35, 24:14, 26:13(bis); Mark 1:1, 8:35; (b) its *Codex B* at Matt. 4:23(bis), 9:35, 24:14(bis), 26:13(bis); Mark 1:1, 8:35; (c) its *Codex C* at Matt. 4:23(bis), 9:35, 26:13(bis); Mark 1:1, 8:35:

(2) Translating the verb εὐαγγελίζεσθαι, the Palestinian Syriac similarly has *bsr* in some one of its forms in *Codex Climaci Rescriptus* at Rom. 15:20; 1 Cor. 1:17, 15:1, 2; Gal. 1:8, 9, 11, 16, 23; in *Pal. Syriac Lect. VI* at Isa. 40:9(bis), 60:6, 61:1; Joel 2:32; 1 Cor. 15:1, 2; Eph. 2:17; in *Pal. Syriac Lect. of the Gospels:* (a) its *Codex A* at Matt. 11:5; Luke 1:19, 2:10, 3:18, 4:18, 7:22, 8:1, 9:6, 20:1; (b) its *Codex B* at Matt. 11:5; Luke 1:19, 2:10, 3:18, 4:18, 8:1, 9:6, 20:1; (c) its *Codex C* at Matt. 11:5; Luke 1:19, 2:10, 4:18, 7:22, 8:1, 9:6, 20:1.[24]

In addition to the above, Friedrich Schulthess is authority for the following evidence to which I have not had access: (a) for the presence of the noun (*bsōrā*) in *Codices Damasceni* at Rom. 1:16; Phil. 1:27(bis), 4:3, 15; in the *Taylor-Schechter palimpsest fragments* at 2 Cor. 4:3; in *Biblical Fragments* edited by J. Rendel Harris at Gal. 2:5, 14; in *Anecdota Syriaca* edited by J. P. N. Land at Matt. 9:35, 24:14; (b) for the presence of the verb (*bsr*) in one or other of its forms in *Codices Damasceni* at Luke 20:1; Rom. 1:14 f.; Heb. 4:2; in the *Taylor-Schechter frag.* at 1 Thess. 3:6; in *Anecdota Syriaca* at Isa. 40:9; Luke 4:43, 7:22; Acts 14:7.[25]

A review of the above evidence appears to leave no doubt that the terms adopted by the Christian Palestinian Syriac (Aramaic) as the exclusive technical terminology for 'gospel' and 'to preach the gospel' were respectively *bsōrā* and *bsr*. And equally it appears clear that this same Aramaic simply took over these terms from the Hebrew of OT, making the slight change in spelling and vocalization required to clothe them in an Aramaic dress. And since this is so, we appear to have found in the Palestinian Syriac the 'missing link' between the OT Hebrew *beśōrāh* and *biśśer*, on the one hand, and the adoption by the NT Scriptures of the terms εὐαγγέλιον and εὐαγγελίζεσθαι as their proper equivalents, on the other—in accord with the thesis of Friedrich, Milligan, and Burrows above outlined. That is to say, it would appear to have been the Christian Palestinian Syriac which preserved the traditional Galilean Aramaic at this point. It would have been natural for

Jesus, for example, to employ *bsr* and *bsōrā* for the distinctive NT gospel message and its proclamation, because it was these words which he had been accustomed to use in his native Aramaic in quoting or paraphrasing from Deutero-Isaiah or the Psalms such passages as referred to the eschatological hope of his people and because he believed that hope now to be fulfilled in his own ministry.[26]

There is a degree to which the Jewish Aramaic of Jonathan bar Uzziel's Targum on Isaiah[27] may be employed as contributory evidence for the above conclusions, so far at any rate as those passages are concerned which C. H. Dodd labels as 'primary sources' for the catena of testimony passages employed by Jesus and the early Church—e.g. Isa. 41:7, 53:1, 61:1. Though this Targum, like that of Onkelos on the Penteteuch, in its present form exhibits 'traces of Babylonian Aramaic influence' and, therefore, as Matthew Black has pointed out, it is to be 'regarded as a secondary authority only for the language of Jesus',[28] yet it is just at this point in our present argument where such 'secondary authority' is of contributory value and surely may be legitimately employed. For in the passages above cited, the Targum adopts the verb *bsr* in Isa. 41:27, and—contrary to the Hebrew use of the noun for 'profane' purposes only (cf. Friedrich above)—the noun in 53:1 (*lbhsōrt·ıā*) and 61:1 (*lbhsrā*). It seems clear that the coincidence of evidence between the Christian Palestinian Syriac and the Jewish Aramaic of the Targum at this point, when viewed conjointly with the clear abandonment of the stem in favour of another by the later Christian Syriac versions, can be accounted for in no other way than to suppose that here is to be seen the 'missing link' between OT (Hebrew and LXX) and NT Greek usages. The alternative suggestion would be to suppose that the Palestinian Syriac and the Targumic Aramaic, representing later (rather than earlier) usage than the bulk of the Syriac versions (Old Syriac, Peshitta, and Harkleian), rejuvenated a Semitic stem and its derivatives which had been employed in OT Hebrew but long since abandoned by Christian Syriac. This, though admittedly possible, does not commend itself as likely.

The discontinuity which we have remarked relative to the use of the gospel words as between the OT (Hebrew and LXX) and the Greek NT, on the one hand, and all the Syriac versions exclusive of the Palestinian, on the other, appears the more striking

when viewed in the context of the like history of κηρύσσειν and
its cognates (Hebrew *qārā, zāʿaq*, and the like). Here there is unbroken continuity throughout, in spite of Friedrich's acute observation that in the LXX the verb κηρύσσειν, 'contrary to all
expectation' is seldom found as the proper term to give expression
to the content of the prophetic message;[29] and, I might add, there
is even less evidence for the use of the noun κήρυγμα in the LXX.[30]
In fact, even in the NT—in spite of the publicity given to the term
'kerygma' in the theological literature of the present day, the noun
κήρυγμα as applied to the Christian message is exclusively a Pauline
word, being found only in Rom. 16:25; 1 Cor. 1:21, 2:4, 15:14;
2 Tim. 4:17, and Titus 1:3.[31] The verb κηρύσσειν is more commonly used in the technical sense in the NT, but even here a defining phrase such as τὸ εὐαγγέλιον τοῦ θεοῦ, τὸ εὐαγγέλιον τῆς
βασιλείας, τὸν Χριστόν, and the like is generally required to complete its meaning.[32] It is all the more striking, therefore, that continuity in the traditional use of these terms should be discovered
throughout the Hebrew, Aramaic, Syriac, and Greek texts for OT
and NT. The evidence for this continuity in the Syriac tradition
follows:

(1) For the verb *krz*: the Palestinian Syriac has it in one or
another of its manuscripts, thus—in the *Pal. Syriac Lect. VI*, at Isa.
61:1 (for *qārā*); Joel 1:14(do.), 2:1 (*rūʿa*—Hiph.); 2:15 and 3:9
(*qārā*); Jonah 1:2, 3:2, 4, 5 (do.), 3:7 (*zāʿaq*—Hiph.); Zech. 9:9
(*rūʿa*—Hiph.); Matt. 3:1, 4:17, 23; Rom. 10:8; 1 Cor. 1:23, 15:11;
1 Tim. 3:16: in *Codex Climaci Rescriptus*, Prov. 1:21; Matt. 3:1,
4:17, 23; Mark 1:4, 7; in the *Pal. Syriac Lect. of the Gospels*: (a)
Codex A has it at Matt. 3:1, 4:17, 23, 9:35, 10:7, 11:1, 24:14, 26:13,
Mark 1:4, 7, 38, 39, 7:36, 16:15, 20; Luke 3:3, 4:18, 19, 8:1, 39,
9:2, 12:3, 24:47; (b) *Codex B* has it in all the same places except
Mark 16:15 which this codex lacks; (c) *Codex C* also has it in the
same passages with the like exception; the *Old Syriac* also employs
the verb in its two manuscripts, thus—in the *Sinaitic*, at Matt. 3:1,
4:17, 23, 9:35, 10:7, 11:1, 24:14, 26:13; Mark 1:38, 39, 7:36; Luke
3:3, 4:18, 19, 8:39, 9:2, 12:3, 24:47; in the *Curetonian*, at Matt. 3:1,
4:17, 23, 11:1; Mark 16:20; Luke 3:3, 8:39, 9:2, 12:3; the *Peshitta*
employs the verb in some form in every NT passage listed without exception, but in the OT it generally employs rather some form
of the verb *qrā*, as at Isa. 61:1, Joel 1:14, etc.; and in both respects
the *Modern Syriac* generally follows the custom of the Peshitta.

(2) For the noun *akrzūthā, krūzūthā* there is little evidence extant, as follows: in the *Pal. Syriac Lect. VI* Jonah 3:2 reads *akrzūthā* for *qᵉrīāh* and the spelling occurs at 1 Cor. 1:21; *Codex A* of the *Pal. Syriac Lect. of the Gospels* reads *akrzūthā* at Luke 11:32; no evidence exists for the Old Syriac readings in any passage where the Greek employs *κήρυγμα*; the *Peshitta* has *krūzūthā* at Jonah 3:2, Luke 11:32, and 1 Cor. 1:21; and the Modern Syriac, at Luke 11:32 reads *bᵉkārōzūtheh*.

In the light of the above discussion certain results appear to emerge, viz.—(a) it may be taken as established that Christian Palestinian Syriac (Aramaic), departing as it does radically from the Syriac tradition as otherwise known to us in the use of the *terms* for 'gospel' and 'to preach the gospel', has perpetuated for these terms the proper Aramaic terminology of the first Christian century and so furnished us with the evidence (hitherto lacking) for the manner of their transmission from OT Hebrew to NT Greek—a transition facilitated by reason of the fact that the Hebrew and Aramaic words were derived from the same Semitic stem; (b) since, as Friedrich has shown, the Greek tradition (LXX, Philo, and Josephus particularly) failed to apprehend the significance of the Hebrew *verb biśśēr* when employed in the religious (eschatological) sense, it seems certain that the transfer of *ideas* (as well as of *terms*) from OT to NT followed the path represented by the steps: *Hebrew → Galilean Aramaic → NT Greek*; (c) the *noun*, as Friedrich suggests and as is obvious, is essentially contained in the *verb* in all the languages involved, but neither the Hebrew nor LXX (nor for that matter, Philo and Josephus) made anything of this fact; rather so far as our evidence is complete, it would appear that Jewish and following it Christian Aramaic first employed the *noun* to mean 'gospel' in the technical sense; so that again the *idea* of a gospel must have followed the path designated by the steps: Hebrew *verb → Galilean Aramaic verb and noun →* NT Greek *verb* and *noun*; (d) it would have been natural, therefore, for Jesus along with the rest of the Jewish Aramaic-speaking community and the early Jewish Church in the days before the development of the Hellenistic mission to have employed both *verb* and *noun* for the prophetic eschatological hope and its fulfilment; (e) and it appears, finally, that the study has contributed in a small way to furthering the thesis of Friedrich Schulthess, A. J. Wensinck, Agnes Smith Lewis, Matthew Black and others like-

minded relative to the importance of the Christian Palestinian
Syriac (Aramaic) and the documents witnessing to it as contribu-
ting to our knowledge of the Galilean Aramaic spoken by Jesus
and his associates.[33]

The study has also raised the problem relating to the complete
abandonment of the Aramaic terms involved, in the later Syriac.
It would appear either: (*a*) that the Palestinian Syriac (Aramaic)
translation from the Greek NT was too late to have influenced the
other Syriac translations (including the Old Syriac and the
Peshitta), or else, if early, was unknown to their translators, or
(*b*) that the stem *bsr* never existed in Syriac other than in the form
of the Christian Palestinian which is really Aramaic, and hence
was abandoned in translation in favour of the stem *sbhr* which is
found in all three languages (Hebrew, Aramaic, and Syriac), or
(*c*) that, though the stem was available in Syriac to the translators
of the Bible, it was abandoned for some reason quite unknown to
us. It is tempting to accept the third possibility and to suggest
tentatively that it was the apocalyptic interest of the second-
century Church that led it to abandon a stem (*bsr*) with its intrinsic
stress on the *gladsome element* in the Christian gospel because of
what had already occurred through Jesus Christ (*and lay, therefore,
in the past*), and in its place to employ the stem *sbhr* (a stem so like
the other as to suggest its formation by metathesis, were there not
good evidence for its independent existence in the cognate languages, Hebrew and Aramaic—including Christian Palestinian
Aramaic), with its reference to *the future eschatological hope*.

NOTES

[1] Cf. Rudolf Bultmann, 'New Testament and Mythology' in *Kerygma and
Myth: A Theological Debate*, edited by Hans Werner Bartsch and translated by
Reginald H. Fuller (1953), 1 to 44, and for a characteristic application of his
views, *Theology of the New Testament* (1951), i, 26 ff.; for Cullmann's position,
cf. his *Christ and Time* (1950), 13, 26 f. (esp. note 10).
[2] Cf. his *Prophetic Realism and the Gospel* (1955), 51–78.
[3] TWNT, ii, 705–35.
[4] Marcus Jastrow agrees with Friedrich's conclusions, so far at all events as
both Mishnaic (Talmudic) Hebrew and Aramaic are concerned; cf. his *A Dictionary of the Targumim, The Talmud Babli and Yerushalmi, and the Midrashic
Literature* (1903), i, 199, col. 2.
[5] Cf. also Ps. 96:2 ff. and its 'Gedankenwelt Deuterojesajas' (p. 707, lines 4 ff.).
Note that at Isa. 61:1 the prophet is the 'herald'.
[6] Cf. p. 710, lines 28–30.

F

[7] Cf. pp. 711 f., lines 40 ff.

[8] Cf. p. 712, lines 24–7. Friedrich's words are—'Von grösster Bedeutung ist es, dass in palästinischen Judentum die Anschauung vom Freudenboten aus Deuterojesaja lebendig geblieben ist. Es kommt der *mᵉbhaśśēr*, und die messianische Zeit bricht an. Er verkündet die Erlösung Israels, bringt Friede und Heil in die Welt'. Cf. also pp. 713 f., lines 38 ff., to the effect that'Die Erwartung des *mᵉbhaśśēr* aus dem AT ist zur Zeit Jesu lebendig gewesen . . . Der Freudenbote kommt. Er kann der Messias sein, er braucht es aber nicht zu sein, er kann ein Ungenannter sein . . . Alle Menschen von Adam an hören die Stimme des Freudenboten: das Heil ist da, die neue Zeit, die Freudenzeit, ist angebrochen.'

[9] Cf. p. 719, lines 17 f.

[10] Cf. pp. 721 f.

[11] It will be worth while to quote at length from Friedrich's conclusions at this point, as follows—'Dass auch das nt.liche εὐαγγέλιον aus der jüdischen und nicht aus der griechischen Welt herzuleiten ist, dafür sprechen schon die Beziehungen von Verb und Substantiv zueinander (*bśrh bśr* . . .). . . . Das Verb *bśr* hat sich im Substantiv εὐαγγὲλιον erhalten [i.e. in NT usage], und dieses weist uns deutlich nicht nach Griechenland, sondern nach Palästina' (p. 723, lines 38 ff.).

[12] Cf. his *St. Paul's Epistles to the Thessalonians* (1908), Note E, pp. 141–4, art. 'On the history of εὐαγγέλιον, εὐαγγελίζεσθαι'.

[13] Cf. art. on 'The Origin of the Term "Gospel" ', in JBL 44 (1925), 21–33.

[14] Cf. pp. 724 f. The noun is placed on Jesus' lips only in Mark's Gospel (1:15, 8:35, 10:29, 13:10, 14:9). Friedrich dismisses the first three of these because they fail to appear in the parallel Synoptic passages (in Matthew and Luke); 13:10 because it contains a reference to the Gentile mission of the Church, and 14:9 because it does not present a unified thought when taken in conjunction with vs. 3 ff.

[15] Cf. my *Prophetic Realism and the Gospel* (1955), 64–8.

[16] This summary tabulation includes every case in which εὐαγγέλιον, εὐαγγελίζεσθαι, and εὐαγγελιστής occur in the Greek NT as listed in MGC.

[17] I.e. either in the emphatic form as listed or in an inflected form.

[18] Modern Syriac, too, employs *euangelion* at Mark 1:1 and in Rom. 1:16; elsewhere generally *mashḥadhtā* (from *shᵉhadh*).

[19] Modern Syriac employs the verb *shᵉḥad* in all these passages.

[20] Modern Syriac has *euāngālestā* at Acts 21:8, thus exhibiting the influence of the older idiom, but at Eph. 4:11 and 2 Tim. 4:5 it reads *mashḥedhānē*.

[21] Modern Syriac again employs *shᵉhadh* regularly here.

[22] Modern Syriac has *shehdā* here throughout. In compiling the above I have employed for the OT references both Solomon Mandelkern's 'Veteris Testamenti Concordantiae Hebraicae atque Chaldaicae' (1925), and HRCS; and for the Syriac, Bensly, Harris, and Burkitt, *The Four Gospels in Syriac transcribed from the Sinaitic Palimpsest* (1894), Agnes Smith Lewis's *Some Pages of the Four Gospels retranscribed from the Sinaitic Palimpsest with a Translation of the Whole Text* (1896), Wm. Cureton's *Remains of a Very Ancient Recension of the Four Gospels in Syriac* (1858), together with the usual Peshitta and Modern Syriac texts. For the Harkleian I have at hand only the relevant pages in W. H. P. Hatch's *An Album of Dated Syriac Manuscripts* (1946).

[23] Cf. *Thesaurus Syriacus* of R. Payne Smith (1879) and Mrs. Margoliouth's smaller recension of this work; also Jastrow, *op. cit.*

[24] Cf. in order of the evidence presented—*Codex Climaci Rescriptus*, transcribed and edited by Agnes Smith Lewis (1909), *A Palestinian Syriac Lectionary*, *Studia Sinaitica* No. VI, edited by Agnes Smith Lewis (1897) and the Supplement to the same (1907), *The Palestinian Syriac Lectionary of the Gospels*, re-edited by Agnes Smith Lewis and Margaret Dunlop Gibson (1899). I can discover in the Palestinian Syriac but one passage in which an equivalent for εὐαγγελιστής occurs, viz. at Acts 21:8, where *Codex Climaci Rescriptus* reads *mbhsrnā*. Schulthess cites the same form from 'The Liturgy of the Nile', 695:6 (edit. by G. Margoliouth, 1896).

[25] Cf. Friedrich Schulthess, *Lexicon Syropalaestinum* (1903), art. *bsr* III, 28 f. This evidence for the Christian Palestinian usage may be supplemented for Jewish Aramaic from Jastrow, *op. cit.*, arts. *beśr*, *besr* I, 199; *besōrāh* and *beś(s)ōrtā*, 198.

[26] Cf. C. H. Dodd, *According to the Scriptures* (1953), 108–10, on this general theme.

[27] Cf. the passages cited in J. F. Stenning's *The Targum of Isaiah* (1949), *in loc.*

[28] Cf. Matthew Black, *An Aramaic Approach to the Gospels and Acts* (1954), 17 ff. I should perhaps have remarked above that the presence of *sbhrtî* at Mark 16:15 in *Codex A* of the *Palestinian Syriac Lectionary of the Gospels* does not constitute an exception to the rule that the Pal.Syr. never employs the stem *sbhr* for 'gospel' or 'to preach the gospel'. As Schulthess says *ad loc*, this is merely *vox syriaca* in an interpolation into the true text.

[29] Cf. TWNT iii, 682–717, on κηρύσσειν and its cognates, particularly p. 699, lines 25 f. and p. 700, lines 28 ff.

[30] The LXX usage of these words follows: (a) κήρυγμα, at 2 Chron. 30:5 (*qōl*) 1 Esdras 9:3; Prov. 9:3; Jonah 3:2 (*qeriāh*): (b) κῆρυξ for *kārōz*, at Gen. 41:43; Ecclus. 20:15; Dan. 3:4 (LXX); Dan. 3:4 (Theod.); 4 Macc. 6:4: (c) κηρύσσειν, at Gen. 41:43 (*qārā*); Exod. 32:5 (do.), 36:6 (*he 'aebhir qōl*); 2 Kings 10:20 (*qārā*); 2 Chron. 20:3 (do.), 24:9 (*nāthan qōl*), 36:22 (do.); 1 Esdras 2:2; Esther 6:9 (*qārā*), 6:11 (do.); Prob. 1:21 (do.), 8:1 (do.); Hos. 5:8 (*rū'a*—Hiph.); Mic. 3:5 (*qārā*); Joel 1:14 (do.), 2:1 (*rū'a*—Hiph.), 2:15 (*qārā*), 3(4):9 (do.); Jonah 1:2 (do.), 3:2 (do.), 3:4 (do.) 3:5 (do.), 3:7 (*zā'aq*—Hiph.); Zeph. 3:14 (*rū'a*—Hiph.); Zech. 9:9 (*qārā*); Isa. 61:1 (do.); Dan. 3:4 (LXX *qera*); Dan. 5:29 (Theod. *eraz*—Aph.); 1 Macc. 5:49, 10:63 f.—cf. HRCS.

[31] Cf. MGC. The only other appearance of the noun in the NT is at Matt. 12:41 = Luke 11:31 ('Q'), and here it relates to the preaching of Jonah rather than to that of Jesus.

[32] Cf. MGC.

[33] The name of Paul Kahle should, of course, be added to the above list. The Rev. T. W. McNeil has called my attention to the occurrence of the verb *beśr* at Lev. 22:27 in the Palestinian Pentateuch Targum edited by Kahle under the title *Masoreten des Westens* in *Texte und Untersuchungen zur Vormasoretischen Grammatik des Hebräischen*, IV, ii (1930).

ZUR FRAGE NACH DEN QUELLEN DER APOSTELGESCHICHTE

von

R. BULTMANN

IN seinem 1956 erschienenen Kommentar zu den Acta Apostolorum gibt Ernst Haenchen einen lehrreichen Ueberblick über die historischkritische Erforschung der Acta: der Epoche der „Tendenzkritik", die mit Joh. Weiss verstummt, folgt die Epoche der „Quellenkritik", die ihren Höhepunkt mit Wellhausen erreicht hat, die aber immer noch die Forschung beschäftigt. Ist sie auch noch nicht erledigt, so ist sie doch in den Hintergrund gedrängt worden durch die stil- und formgeschichtliche Arbeitsweise, die wesentliche Anstösse durch P. Wendland und Ed. Norden empfangen hatte und dann von M. Dibelius weitergeführt wurde. Das Verdienst Haenchens ist es, in seinem Kommentar diese Betrachtungsweise für die Interpretation der gesamten Acta durchgeführt äu haben.[1] Für ihn sind die Acta nicht in erster Linie das Werk eines Historikers, das auf seinen Quellenwert befragt werden müsste. Sie müssen vielmehr als eine Komposition des Autors gewürdigt werden, in der dessen Theologie, — oder wohl besser: die in seiner Theologie begründete Auffassung der urchristlichen Geschichte ihren Ausdruck findet, einer Geschichte, in der sich das Verhältnis des christlichen Glaubens zum Judentum und zum römischen Staat erkennen lässt.

Abschnitt für Abschnitt unterwirft Haenchen die Behandlung des betreffenden Stückes durch die historische Kritik und ihre Quellenanalyse seinerseits einer Kritik, die durchweg die Unhaltbarkeit der Hypothesen jener Kritik aufzeigt, ihr aber vor allem — und zwar mit Recht — den Vorwurf macht, dass sie nicht zuerst den Versuch gemacht hat, den betreffenden Abschnitt als eine Einheit aus der schriftstellerischen Absicht des Autors der Acta zu verstehen. Wenn diese erkannt ist, so erledigen sich vielfach die Anstösse, die die frühere Forschung zu quellenkritischen Analysen veranlasst haben. Die Geschichtsschreibung des Autors enthält „nach unseren Begriffen ein dichterisches Element, und wir tun Lukas Unrecht, wenn wir sein freies Gestalten leugnen und es zu protokollarischer Genauigkeit verfälschen" (S. 118).[2] Natürlich meint Haenchen nicht, dass die Darstellung des „Lukas" reine Dichtung sei. Selbstverständlich hat „Lukas" seine Darstellung aufgrund der ihm überkommenen Tradition, die auch eine schriftliche sein konnte, entworfen. Infolgedessen schliesst die Erklärung eines Abschnitts aus der Absicht des Autors (bzw. aus seiner Geschichts-Auffassung) eine Analyse des betreffenden Abschnitts nicht aus. Nur darf die Analyse nicht vollzogen werden, ohne dass zuvor die Absicht des Autors bzw. die Sinneinheit des betreffenden Abschnitts erkannt ist. Da nun die Absicht des Autors gerade auch dann deutlich werden kann, wenn man sieht, über welche Tradition er verfügt und wie er sie gestaltet, so besteht freilich zwischen der exegetischen Frage nach der Sinneinheit und der analytischen Frage nach der benutzten Tradition eine Wechselwirkung. Die Ausbalancierung beider Fragen ist eine Sache des exegetischen Taktes, und in dieser Hinsicht dürfte Haenchens Interpretation meist das Richtige treffen.

Die Analyse hat jetzt auch einen anderen Sinn gewonnen als früher. Sie dient dem Verständnis des Textes der Acta, so wie dieser uns vorliegt, und d. h. dem Verständnis der Komposition und ihren theologischen Motiven. Die Interpretation will also nicht hinter den Text zurückfragen und zur Erkenntnis historischer Vorgänge durchstossen, die zeitlich vor dem Texte liegen. Sie legt es nicht von vornherein darauf ab, Quellen — und zwar schriftliche, möglichst durchlaufende, umfassende Quellen — herauszuarbeiten, auf die man sich verlassen kann als auf historische Dokumente für die Rekonstruktion der Geschichte des Urchristentums. Eben diese Absicht leitete durchweg die quellenkritische Forschung, die sich die Arbeit des Autors wesentlich als die Kombination von Quellen vorstellte. Dagegen richtet sich Haenchens berechtigte Kritik.

Indessen darf man nicht verkennen, dass die Fragestellung der quellenkritischen Forschung auch ihr Recht hatte und in gewisser Weise auch von den Acta selbst herausgefordert wird. Denn unbeschadet ihrer theologischen Tendenz wollen die Acta doch auch ein Bild entwerfen, wenn auch nicht vom Urchristentum überhaupt, so doch von wichtigen Momenten und Vorgängen seiner

Geschichte. Herausgefordert wird die kritische Fragestellung besonders auch dann, wenn sich parallele oder konkurrierende Angaben oder Berichte in den paulinischen Briefen finden, also z. B. durch das Verhältnis von Act. 15 zu Gal. 2. Auch Haenchen denkt ja nicht daran, die Diskussion darüber abzuschneiden und ein Urteil über geschichtlich oder ungeschichtlich zu vermeiden. Aber die kritische Fragestellung wird erst fruchtbar, wenn zuvor die Texte unter der Frage nach ihrer Sinneinheit als Komposition des Autors verstanden sind. Gerade dann kann ein Urteil über den historischen Wert oder Unwert eines Berichtes gewonnen werden.

Die Frage nach der Einheit und dem Sinn eines Abschnitts ist nun nicht zu trennen von der Frage nach seiner Stellung im Zusammenhang der ganzen Acta. Denn „Lukas hat nicht nur aus allen möglichen Traditionsstücken jene grossen lebendigen Einzelszenen gestaltet . . ., sondern darüber hinaus die Szenenfolge der Apg selber: er hat ein Geschichtswerk geschaffen". Die dem einzelnen Abschnitt im Zusammenhang der ganzen sinnvollen Komposition angewiesene Stellung bestimmt ja auch seinen Sinn. Das ist von Haenchen z. B. ausgezeichnet klar gemacht durch die Interpretation der drei Berichte von der Bekehrung des Paulus.[3] Dass in ihnen Tradition verwendet ist, versteht sich von selbst. Aber wie sie jeweils in c. 9, c. 22 und c. 24 gestaltet ist, das ist durch den jeweiligen Zusammenhang in der Komposition des Ganzen bestimmt. Damit sind alle Versuche, diesen oder jenen der drei Berichte mittels psychologischer Deutung als den historisch zuverlässigsten den anderen vorzuziehen, erledigt.

Ich habe nun meinerseits doch einige kritische Fragen an Haenchens grossen Kommentar zu richten, unbeschadet meiner grundsätzlichen Zustimmung zu seiner Methode und unbeschadet der Dankbarkeit für die reiche Belehrung, die ich aus dem Kommentar geschöpft habe. Ich möchte fragen: (1) Ist die Analyse, die in Wechselwirkung mit der Interpretation der Sinneinheit steht, immer in den Blick gefasst worden, und ist sie nicht manchmal zurückgedrängt worden zu Gunsten der Frage nach der Sinneinheit, so dass sogar die Sinneinheit als ein Kriterium gegen die Benutzung einer Quelle geltend gemacht wird? (2) Macht sich Haenchen die Frage nach schriftlichen Quellen nicht zu leicht? Begnügt er sich nicht oft zu schnell mit dem einfachen Hinweis, dass hier oder dort „Tradition" vorliege, ohne genauer zu fragen, welcher Art diese Tradition sei? Ad (1) Als Beispiel wähle ich Haenchens Interpretation von Act. 15:1-35. Wie Dibelius[4] zeigt Haenchen, dass sich der Text ohne Quellenscheidung verstehen lässt, und macht den Aufbau und die Geschlossenheit der lukanischen Komposition deutlich (S. 407). Der Autor schrieb nicht als Historiker, sondern wollte „mit seiner Erzählung seiner Generation die Gewissheit vermitteln . . ., dass ihr Heidenchristentum in Ordnung war, von Gott und den verantwortlichen Menschen gebilligt" (S. 402). Auch die Bedeutung von Act. 15 innerhalb des Ganzen der Acta ist einleuchtend charakterisiert: Act. 15 bezeichnet den Wendepunkt in der Geschichte, den Uebergang von Jerusalem als dem Mittelpunkt der Frühgeschichte auf den neuen grossen Schauplatz der christlichen Mission (S. 407 ff.).

Aber ist damit die Frage nach den Quellen, die der Autor für seine Komposition benutzte, wirklich erledigt? Haenchen geht an einem Punkte noch über Dibelius hinaus, nämlich das Aposteldekret betreffend. Nach Dibelius scheint der Autor das „Dokument der vier Klauseln" wirklich gekannt zu haben. Nach Haenchen hat es ein solches Dokument nie gegeben. Es ist eine Bildung des Autors, der wusste, dass die vier Forderungen, die nach alttestamentlich-jüdischer Vorstellung für die unter den Juden lebenden Heiden galten, auch zu seiner Zeit bei den Heidenchristen in Geltung standen, und zwar als „eine lebendige Tradition", die man wahrscheinlich schon damals auf die Apostel zurückführte. Nun, wenn Dibelius Haenchen gegenüber Recht haben sollte, und wenn das Dekret wirklich (als Beschluss der jerusalemer Gemeinde) existiert hätte und der Autor es seiner Erzählung eingegliedert hätte, — was wäre damit geändert an Haenchens Charakteristik des Aufbaus und der Geschlossenheit des Berichtes? Nicht das Mindeste! Diese Geschlossenheit kann also kein Kriterium dafür sein, dass der Autor nicht einen überlieferten Text, ein Stück „Quelle" seiner Komposition eingegliedert hat.

Es ist aber wahrscheinlich, dass das Dekret wirklich ein dem Autor überlieferter Text war. Nach Dibelius ist dafür beweisend „die Adressierung lediglich nach Antiochien, Syrien und Kilikien".[5] In der Tat! Wie konnte der Autor auf diese einschränkende Adresse verfallen, wenn er das Dekret als ein uneingeschränktes verstand, was nach Haenchen der Fall war.

Aber dann erheben sich sofort andere Fragen, die zwar das Bild der geschlossenen Komposition nicht zerstören, die aber die Arbeitsweise des Autors in neuem Lichte erscheinen lassen. Wo und wann ist das Dekret beschlossen worden? Es wird kein Zweifel sein können: in Jerusalem, von der dortigen Gemeinde, mögen nun ursprünglich als die Absender nur die ἀδελφοί genannt gewesen sein, und mag (οἱ) ἀπόστολοι καὶ οἱ πρεσβύτεροι 15:23 redaktioneller Zusatz des Autors sein. Aber wann? Dibelius und Haenchen sind in gleicher Weise der Meinung (und ich glaube: mit Recht), dass das nicht auf dem Konvent geschehen sein kann, von dem Gal. 2 berichtet. Früher selbstverständlich nicht; also später. Von Weizsäcker stammt bekanntlich die von Vielen aufgenommene Hypothese, dass das Dekret „auf Grund des antiochenischen Zwischenfalles (Gal. 2:11 ff.) ohne Mitwirkung des Paulus beschlossen worden sei" (Haenchen S. 415). Es sagt ja in der Tat nichts von der Beschneidung, die beim Konvent von Gal. 2 die aktuelle Frage war; seine Bestimmungen wollen offenbar das Zusammenleben in gemischten Gemeinden ermöglichen. Die Ablehnung dieser Hypothese durch Haenchen scheint mir nicht durchschlagend zu sein. Er meint, sie leide daran, dass sie nicht die lukanische Darstellung selbst gründlich und genau nach ihrem eigenen Sinn befragt habe (S. 415). Nun, diese Aufgabe hat Haenchen zwar überzeugend gelöst; aber ist damit die Hypothese widerlegt? Nicht im Mindesten! Denn mag das Dekret, so wie es in Act. 15 erscheint, sich der Komposition des Autors noch so glatt einordnen und an seinem Platze verständlich sein, so ist doch die Geschlossenheit der Komposition kein Kriterium dafür, dass der Autor nicht einen überlieferten Text verarbeitet hat.

Für die Bestätigung jener Hypothese wird oft angeführt, dass das Dekret dem Paulus Act. 21:25 als etwas Neues (und dann natürlich aufgrund einer in c. 21 benutzten Quelle) mitgeteilt wird. Auch mit diesem Argument scheint mir Haenchen zu schnell fertig zu werden. Dort richte sich das Dekret — wie Haenchen nach Loisy urteilt — gar nicht an Paulus, sondern an die Leser. Aber hätte der Autor dann nicht ein οἶσθα (γὰρ) ὅτι eingefügt wie das ὑμεῖς οἴδατε 10:37 oder das ἐπίστασθε 15:7?

Aber wie dem auch sei! Ausser der Möglichkeit, dass der Autor das Dekret — historisch gesehen: fälschlich — in einer Verhandlung der Jerusalemer mit Paulus und Barnabas untergebracht hat, kommt noch eine andere Möglichkeit in Frage. Wie wäre es, wenn der Autor eine Tradition, ja, eine schriftliche Quelle, benutzt hätte, die von einer Verhandlung in Jerusalem berichtete, deren Ergebnis das Dekret war? In diesem Falle hätte er nicht das Dekret von sich aus in eine (von ihm frei benutzte) Tradition eingefügt, sondern er hätte jene Verhandlung, bei der Paulus und Barnabas nicht zugegen waren, dadurch umgestaltet, dass er Paulus und Barnabas einführte. Mit anderen Worten, die Verse bzw. Worte in Act. 15:1-35, die von diesen beiden reden, wären von ihm in seine Quelle eingefügt worden, wie ja auch sonst schon z. B. von Bousset vermutet worden ist.[6] Ich halte das für wahrscheinlich. So würde es sich auch erklären, warum nach V. 1 in V. 5 noch einmal der Einspruch gegen die Gesetzesfreiheit der Heidenchristen erhoben wird. Jedenfalls ist Haenchens Erklärung (von V. 4) dafür, dass Paulus und Barnabas in Jerusalem nicht sogleich ihren Auftrag ausführen, sondern vielmehr von ihrer Mission erzählen, nicht überzeugend. Er meint, der Fall wäre dann zu schnell erledigt gewesen; es sei dem Autor aber an einer eindrucksvolle Szene gelegen. „Deshalb kommt es besonders darauf an, das entscheidende Ereignis, die endgültige Billigung der gesetzesfreien Heidenmission, in einer unvergesslichen Szene den Lesern einzuprägen" (S. 404). Aber es ist nicht einzusehen, warum der Autor, um das zu erreichen, nicht auf V. 3 gleich V. 6 hätte folgen lassen können.[7]

Aber worauf es mir hier ankommt, ist das Methodische: an dem Bilde der Komposition, das Haenchen entwirft, ändert sich nichts, wenn der Autor eine Quelle benutzt hat, die nicht von Paulus und Barnabas erzählte. Nur seine Arbeitsweise wäre deutlicher geworden, und seine Fähigkeit, eine einheitliche Komposition auf Grund des ihm zur Verfügung stehenden Materials zu entwerfen wäre noch glänzender erwiesen. Wenn z. B. V. 12 als ein Einschub in die Quelle gelten müsste, so wäre damit doch der Auffassung Haenchens, dass dieser Vers „eine wichtige Aufgabe im Rahmen der lukanischen Erzählung" hat (S. 405), nicht widersprochen.

Einige kleinere Beispiele mögen noch hinzugefügt werden. Würde etwa Haenchens Interpretation von Act. 1:15-26 modifiziert werden, wenn V. 18 ein Einschub in eine Quelle ist? Keineswegs! Auch dann bliebe das Urteil bestehen, dass man nach solcher Ausscheidung nicht eine historisch „gute Ueberlieferung" vor sich hat.

Würde die Interpretation von c. 2 hinfällig werden, wenn man annimmt, dass in der Petrusrede die Verse 14-21, 24-31, 33-5 in einen Quellenbericht eingefügt sind? Keineswegs! Die Einheit der lukanischen Komposition wäre damit nicht angefochten. Aehnlich ist über 4:32; 5:12b-14; 6:12b-14a zu urteilen. Aber ich will diesen Gesichtspunkt nicht weiter verfolgen. Worauf es mir ankommt, ist, zu betonen, dass mit dem Nachweis der Einheit einer Komposition nicht über die etwaige Verwendung von Quellen entschieden ist, — so sehr ich Haenchen darin Recht gebe, dass die primäre Aufgabe der Exegese die Klarstellung der Komposition sein muss.

Ad (2) Haenchen ist gewiss mit Recht der Meinung, dass es vor den Acta keine „Apostelgeschichten" gegeben hat; an solchen konnte die apostolische Zeit kein Interesse haben. „Eine ‚Apostelgeschichte' wie die lukanische konnte erst in einer neuen Generation geschrieben werden" (S. 87). Aber es gab freilich Ueberlieferung aus der apostolischen Zeit, auf die Lukas für sein Werk angewiesen war. Doch in welcher Form gelangten sie an „Lukas"? Als mündliche oder schon als schriftliche Tradition? Man vermisst bei Haenchen eine zusammenhängende Untersuchung dieser Frage. Der auffallend kurze Abschnitt „Die in der Apg. benutzte Tradition" (S. 95 f.) geht auf die Frage nicht ausdrücklich ein, sondern spricht nur unbestimmt von Traditionen. Wenn Haenchen sagt, dass es für den zweiten Teil der Acta erheblich günstiger stehe als für den ersten, weil der Autor ein Itinerar der paulinischen Reisen benutzen konnte, so scheint Haenchen im Uebrigen nur mit mündlicher Tradition zu rechnen, und diese Vermutung wird bestätigt durch die im Kommentar gebenen Kompositions-Analysen.

Aber ist diese Anschauung haltbar? Ist es z. B. denkbar, dass Namenlisten wie Act. 6:5, 13:1, 20:4 in mündlicher Tradition weitergegeben wurden? Gewiss pflegen in mündlicher Tradition Namen zuzuwachsen, aber doch nur dann, wenn ein novellistisches Interesse für bestimmte Personen vorliegt wie z. B. für den Centurio am Kreuz. Davon kann in den genannten Fällen ja keine Rede sein, und für 20:4 speziell ist anzunehmen, dass die Angabe aus dem Itinerar stammt.

Aber weiter! Haenchen bestreitet nicht, dass der Autor eine Gemeindeüberlieferung über die Bekehrung des Paulus benutzt hat (S. 284). Wenn er nun sagt, dass wir sie „nicht im Wortlaut

wiederherstellen können" — wie denkt er sich dann den Vorgang
des Ueberlieferns? War der Wortlaut in der Ueberlieferung so
fest geprägt, dass man eine Geschichte wie die der Bekehrung des
Paulus sozusagen auswendig lernen konnte? Sonst hätte doch die
Reflexion auf eine Wiederherstellung des Wortlauts keinen Sinn!
Die Geschichte von der Befreiung des Petrus (12:7–17) hat der
Autor nach Haenchen der Tradition entnommen und sie nur ein
wenig retouchiert (S. 339–42). Ist es denkbar, dass sie in der mündlichen Tradition so fest geprägt war, dass man die Retouchen des
Autors abtrennen kann? Das Gleiche gilt für 19:13–17 (S. 506 f.).
Wenn es zutrifft; „Lukas hat hier einen seinem Zweck fremden
Stoff verwendet, den er trotz aller darauf verwendeten Bemühung
nicht ganz hat einschmelzen können", so kann ich mir das nicht
anders vorstellen, als dass der Autor einen schriftlichen Text
bearbeitet hat. Und kann er zur Aufnahme dieses „seinem Zweck
fremden Stoffes" anders veranlasst worden sein als dadurch, dass
er ihn im Zusammenhang einer schriftlichen Quelle fand, die er
in c. 19 überhaupt zu Grunde legte? Gewiss; man kann sagen: der
Autor hätte dieses Stück der Quelle weglassen können. Aber das
konnte er doch erst recht tun, wenn er es nur aus mündlicher
Ueberlieferung kannte.

Dass die Geschichte vom Aufruhr des Demetrius 19:23–40 nur
auf der mündlichen Tradition von einem θόϱυβος stammt, der der
Abreise des Paulus aus Ephesus vorausgegangen war (S. 518), ist
mir recht zweifelhaft. Traut Haenchen hier nicht der kompositor-
ischen Phantasie des Autors reichlich viel zu? Es scheint mir doch
eine Verlegenheitsauskunft zu sein, wenn er die Gestalt des
Demetrius darauf zurückführt, dass die Erinnerung an einen in-
schriftlich bezeugten νεωποιὸς ἐπώνυμος namens Demetrius bei
der Christen fortgelebt habe, und wenn er die Gestalt des Alexander auf einen 1 Tim. 1:20; 2 Tim. 4:14 bezeugten Gegner des
Paulus zurückführt.

Zu Act. 21:27–36 (die Verhaftung des Paulus) sagt Haenchen,
dass der Autor dem „nüchternen Bericht" auf seine Weise „einige
Lichter aufgesetzt" habe, und zwar meint er in diesem Falle, dass
der Bericht einer schriftlichen Quelle (nach S. 548 dem Itinerar)
entnommen sei. Wohl mit Recht! Aber warum soll man in den
anderen genannten Fällen anders urteilen?

Die Geschichte von der Erweckung des Eutychos (20:7–12) ist
gewiss, wie Haenchen urteilt, in das Itinerar eingefügt und durch

Einbringung des „Wir" mit ihm verklammert. Ob die Geschichte einer schriftlichen Quelle entnommen ist, kann man wenigstens fragen; die auffällige Erwähnung der Lampen (V. 8) scheint dafür zu sprechen.[8] Wenn der Autor in den Bericht von Apollos (18:24–28) „eine Art Bremse eingesetzt" hat (S. 496), indem er in V. 25 die Worte ἐπιστάμενος μόνον τὸ βάπτισμα Ἰωάννου und dazu V. 26 einfügte,[9] so doch wohl in eine schriftliche Quelle. Leider äussert sich Haenchen nicht dazu. Anders kann es doch auch nicht sein, wenn in 18:18–23 die Verse 19b–21a als „Einschub" gelten (S. 489), doch wohl in eine schriftliche Quelle, über die wir von Haenchen auch nichts Genaueres erfahren.

Die einzige schriftliche Quelle, mit der Haenchen rechnet, ist das „Itinerar". Leider gibt er keine Zusammenfassende Darstellung, wo er sie findet und wie etwa ihr Zusammenhang zu denken ist. Dass der Autor den Text des Itinerars nicht „sklavisch übernommen, sondern zu einem neuen Ganzen verarbeitet hat" (S. 483), ist zweifellos richtig; ebenso, dass es deshalb nicht immer möglich ist, den Text von der lukanischen Bearbeitung zu unterscheiden. Auch ist es richtig, was schon Dibelius bemerkte, dass der Autor, um den Bericht des Itinerars mit anderer Tradition zu verklammern, das „Wir" des Itinerars in umgebende bzw. nachfolgende Stücke einfügte, was offenbar 16:16 f., 20:7–12 und wohl auch 21:10–14 der Fall ist.

Das hindert jedoch nicht, dass man mit einiger Wahrscheinlichkeit feststellen kann, welchen Abschnitten das Itinerar, das im Wir-Stil berichtete, zu Grunde liegt. Nach Haenchen gehört dazu wohl auch der Bericht über das Eintreffen des Paulus in Jerusalem (21:15 ff.) und über die „entscheidungsschwere Zeit bis zur Verhaftung" (S. 548). Haenchen ist auch geneigt, den Bericht über die Seefahrt nach Rom und den Schiffbruch (27:1–44)[10] auf einen Fahrtgenossen des Paulus zurückzuführen, während Dibelius (nach Wellhausen) der Meinung war, „dass dem Fahrtbericht eine ‚profane' Darstellung von Fahrt und Schiffbruch als Vorbild, Modell oder Quelle gedient hat, in die der Verf. ein paar kleine Nachrichten über Paulus . . . einfügt".[11] Mir ist das wahrscheinlicher; denn wenn der Bericht von einem Fahrtgenossen des Paulus stammte, so wäre es doch schwer zu begreifen, dass er gar nicht von Paulus redet. Die von Paulus handelnden Stellen sind ja, wie auch Haenchen annimmt, in den zu Grunde liegenden Bericht eingefügt.

Aber mag das dahingestellt bleiben. Mag das Itinerar mit der Verhaftung in Jerusalem oder mit der Romreise geendet haben, — wo haben wir seinen Anfang zu suchen? Das „Wir", das mit 16:10 einsetzt, ist zwar ein Indizium der Quelle; aber weder können alle das „Wir" enthaltenden Sätze zu dieser Quelle gerechnet werden, wie vorhin schon gesagt wurde, noch ist das Fehlen des „Wir" ein Beweis dafür, dass die Quelle nicht vorliegt. Wie der Autor ein „Wir" einsetzen konnte, so konnte er es auch tilgen. Es ist also durchaus möglich, dass die mit 16:10 einsetzende Quelle schon im Vorausgehenden zu Grunde liegt.

Ein Fall, in dem der Autor das „Wir" getilgt hat, scheint mir 13:2 voräuliegen. Nach V. 1 müssten als Subjekt des λειτουργ-ούντων δὲ αὐτῶν die in V. 1 genannten προφῆται καὶ διδάσκαλοι gedacht werden, die dann in V. 2 vom πνεῦμα angeredet werden: ἀφορίσατε δή μοι κτλ Sie wären es dann auch, die in V. 3 den Barnabas und Saulus nach Fasten, Gebet und Handauflegung aus-senden, — sie, aber abzüglich des Barnabas und Saulus. Wie diese nicht das Subjekt in V. 3 sein können, so doch auch nicht die in dem ἀφορίσατε V. 2 Angeredeten, wie es zufolge dem λειτουργούν-των δὲ αὐτῶν κτλ doch sein müsste. Die Schwierigkeit verschwin-det, wenn man statt des λειτουργούντων δὲ αὐτῶν liest λειτουργ-ούντων δὲ ἡμῶν. Dann ist in V. 2 die Gemeinde als Subjekt ge-dacht; sie wird angeredet und sie entsendet die vom πνεῦμα Auserwählten.

Ist diese Vermutung richtig, so wäre die Quelle als eine anti-ochenische zu bezeichnen, und es wäre dann zu fragen, ob und wieweit wir sie auch als die Grundlage des vorausgehenden Be-richts annehmen dürfen. Nun, jedenfalls nur soweit in diesem Bericht von Antiochien direkt oder indirekt die Rede ist. Rech-nen wir nach rückwärts, so käme 12:25 in Betracht, wo die Rück-kehr des Paulus und Barnabas von Jerusalem nach Antiochien erzählt wird; damit aber auch 11:27–30, wo ihre Reise von Anti-ochien nach Jerusalem berichtet wird. Ich wundere mich, dass Haenchen über die Lesart des „westlichen" Textes in 11:28 so schnell hinweggeht.[12] Sie scheint mir zu den wenigen ursprüng-lichen Lesarten von D zu gehören; denn die Einbringung des „Wir" scheint mir als spätere redaktionelle Arbeit nicht ver-ständlich zu sein. Dann würde also 11:27–30 auch ein Stück der antiochenischen Quelle sein.[13]

Geht man weiter nach rückwärts, so dürfte es sehr

wahrscheinlich sein, dass der Hauptbestand von 11:19–26 auch aus dieser Quelle stammt. Der Autor hat sie freilich redigiert, vor allem dadurch, dass er den Barnabas von Jerusalem nach Antiochien als Inspektor geschickt werden lässt. Act. 11:19 dürfte nun aber die Wiederaufnahme von 8:4 sein. Denn dass 11:19 ff. ein „lukanisches Summarium" sei, davon kann mich Haenchen nicht überzeugen (S. 320). Mir scheint vielmehr, dass 8:4a ein abgebrochener Satz ist; das οἱ μὲν οὖν διασπαρέντες διῆλθον fordert unbedingt die Angabe des Zieles. Der absolute Gebrauch von διέρχεσθαι 10:38, 17:23 scheint mir keine Analogie zu sein, weil an diesen Stellen ein Ausgangspunkt des διέρχεσθαι nicht in Frage kommt, wie er 8:4 zwar nicht ausdrücklich genannt, aber vorausgesetzt ist. Der in 8:4a abgebrochene Satz wird in 11:19 wieder aufgenommen und durch ἕως Φοινίκης κτλ. zu Ende geführt, wobei natürlich das ἀπὸ τῆς θλίψεως . . . ἐπὶ Στεφάνῳ eine redaktionelle Einfügung des Autors ist.

Nun setzt 8:4 die Geschichte vom Fall des Stephanus voraus und diese wiederum den Bericht von den Hellenisten in Jerusalem. Ich bin nun keineswegs der Meinung, dass 6:1–8:4 einfach der antiochenischen Quelle entnommen ist, sondern gebe der Analyse Haenchens, dieses Stück betreffend, durchaus Recht. Nur dass ich allerdings glaube, dass der Autor diese Quelle in 6:1–8:4 als Grundlage verwendet hat. Ein Indizium dafür dürfte doch die Namenliste 6:5 sein. Im übrigen verzichte ich auf eine literarkritische Analyse und bemerke nur, dass 6:12b (καὶ ἐπιστάντες κτλ.) bis 15 ein Einschub ist in eine, vom Autor freilich redigierte Quelle; ebenso natürlich 7:1–53.

Ich glaube also, an einer antiochenischen Quelle, wie einst Harnack und dann J. Jeremias sie angenommen und zu rekonstruieren versucht haben,[14] festhalten zu müssen, freilich mit den angedeuteten Modifikationen,[15] Ich glaube zudem, dass sie im Wir-Stil geschrieben war. Man könnte sie als die Annalen oder als die Chronik der antiochenischen Gemeinde bezeichnen.

Ich halte es auch für wahrscheinlich, dass dem Bericht über die sogenannte erste Missionsreise des Paulus c. 13–14 ein Itinerar im Wir-Stil zu Grunde liegt. Es lässt sich freilich nicht beweisen; aber jedenfalls darf man m. E. nicht sagen, dass von einem Itinerar nichts zu spüren sei (S. 366). Die Verse 13:3 f., 13 f., 43 f., 48 f. (auch 52?) machen durchaus den Eindruck aus einem Itinerar zu stammen (wieviel von 13:4–12 lasse ich dahingestellt). Ebenso

14:1–6 (wo V. 3 wohl auf die Redaktion des Autors zurückgehen wird); dafür spricht der dem Autor sonst fremde Gebrauch von ἀπόστολος (V. 4). Da sich dieser auch in V. 14 findet, wird auch der Einschub 14:8–20 aus einer schriftlichen Quelle geschöpft sein. Die ursprüngliche Fortsetzung von 14:1–6 dürfte 14:21–6 sein. Ueber diese Probleme scheint mir Haenchen zu schnell hinweg zu gehen.

Wie dem auch sei! Die Hauptfrage dürfte die nach dem Verhältnis des von c. 16 an zu Grunde liegenden Itinerars zu der „antiochenischen" Quelle sein. Dass beide Quellen eine literarisch Einheit gebildet haben, ist nicht gerade wahrscheinlich. Eher dürfte man vermuten, dass der oder die Reisebegleiter des Paulus (es können ja durchaus mehrere nacheinander gewesen sein) aus der antiochenischen Gemeinde stammten. Im Archiv der Gemeinde hätte dann der Autor, der vielleicht selbst Antiochener war, sowohl die „antiochenische" Quelle wie das Itinerar benutzen können.

ANMERKUNGEN

[1] Vgl. dazu auch E. Haenchen, „Tradition und Komposition in der Apostelgeschichte", *Zeitschr. f. Theologie u. Kirche* 52 (1955), S. 205–25.

[2] S. dazu auch a. a. O. (Anm. 1) S. 210: „. . . dass Lukas kein Historiker in dem Sinne war und sein wollte, in dem wir diesen Begriff fassen, und dass deshalb die Komposition als das freie, nur vom kirchlichen Gesamtbild der Vergangenheit gelenkte Entwerfen von Szenen in der Apg eine Rolle spielt, wie wir sie heute nur in geschichtliclen Romanen zulassen."

[3] S. dazu a. a. O. (Anm.1) S. 217: „Lukas hat also nicht zwei oder drei Berichte von der Bekehrung des Paulus benutzt, sondern jene eine Tradition, die ihm bekannt war. Er hat sie — das gehört mit zu seiner Kompositionsarbeit — in Kap. 9, 22 und 26 durch Kürzung, Ergänzung und Aenderung jeweils zum Bestandteil einer grösseren Einheit und damit einem Ziel dienstbar gemacht, an das die volkstümlichen Erzähler vor Lukas noch nicht gedacht hatten."

[4] Martin Dibelius, *Aufsätze zur Apostelgeschichte*, 3. Aufl. (1957), S. 89.

[5] A. a. O. S. 89.

[6] Die Sätze, in denen von Paulus und Barnabas die Rede ist, lassen sich leicht herausheben: V. 2 (es würde genügen: ἔταξαν ἀναβαίνειν τινὰς ἐξ αὐτῶν πρὸς κτλ), 3–5, 12; das σὺν τῷ Παύλῳ καὶ Βαρναβᾷ in V. 22; V. 25 f. — Vgl. W. Bousset, ZNTW 14 (1913), S. 156–62.

[7] Auch die Frage nach dem Verhältnis der 11:30 erzählten Reise des Paulus und Barnabas von Antiochien nach Jerusalem zu der Reise von 15:1 ff. würde dann eine Antwort finden. Die Reise von 11:30 ist mit der von Gal. 2:1 ff. identisch. Dass Paulus und Barnabas nach 11:30 eine Unterstützung nach Jerusalem bringen, steht doch in keinen Widerspruch zu Gal. 2:1 ff.

[8] Haenchen, *Komm.*, S. 524, 2; M. Dibelius, a. a. O., S. 23, 1.

⁹ Ich glaube, dass nur der Schluss von V. 25 (ἐπιστάμενος κτλ.) eingefügt ist. Vgl. meine *Geschichte der synopt. Tradition*, 3. Aufl., S. 263 (Anm. 2 zu S. 262) und E. Käsemann, *Zeitschr. f. Theol. u. Kirche* 49 (1952), S. 151.

¹⁰ Vgl. dazu auch Haenschen, *Zeitschr. f. Theol. u. Kirche* 52 (1955), S. 22, 1.

¹¹ Dibelius a. a. O. S. 174, auch S. 180.

¹² S. 324, A. 6. In dem Abschnitt über den Text der Acta (S. 41–50) ist die Lesart nicht erwähnt. Auch in Haenschens Aufsatz, „Zum Text der Apostelgeschichte", *Zeitschr. f. Theol. u. Kirche* 54 (1957), ist diese Frage nicht diskutiert.

¹³ Diese Vermutungen würden sich höchstens modifizieren, wenn man 11:30, 12:25 der antiochenischen Quelle abspricht, wie Joachim Jeremias (ZNTW 36 (1935), S. 218) es tut. Es würden dann 11:27–29 übrig bleiben. Ich sehe aber keinen zwingenden Grund 11:30, 12:25 auszuschalten.

¹⁴ Ad. Harnack, *Die Apostelgeschichte* (1908), S. 169 ff.; J. Jeremias, ZNTW 36 (1937), S. 213–20.

¹⁵ Dass z. B. 9:1–30 zu ihr gehört haben sollte, halte ich für unmöglich.

Ο ΛΟΓΟΣ ΤΟΥ ΘΕΟΥ DANS L'ÉPÎTRE AUX HÉBREUX

par

H. CLAVIER

L'EXPRESSION Ὁ λόγος τοῦ Θεοῦ ne se rencontre que deux fois dans l'épître aux Hébreux.[1] La grande majorité des interprètes ne voient aucune relation entre ces deux textes dans leurs contextes, et la notion du Logos éternel, incarné en Christ. Il s'agirait seulement de la parole de Dieu au sens biblique le plus ordinaire, avec l'une ou l'autre de ses connotations les plus courantes: voix de Dieu,[2] révélation divine ou message divin,[3] enseignement ou prédication de ce message.[4]

Si l'on était sensible à l'allure personnelle de cette parole de Dieu dans le premier de ces deux textes, il suffirait de se dire qu'il s'agit là d'un procédé classique de rhétorique ou de poétique.[5] Le cas du second texte est encore plus simple, puisqu'aucune personnification de la parole de Dieu n'y est apparente.[6]

Avant tout examen de thèses divergentes, il sera bon de prendre un aperçu de la complexité des problèmes, ne fût-ce que pour une mise en garde contre certaines simplifications.

La principale difficulté surgie de l'épître elle-même, considérée in abstracto, en attendant d'être située dans son cadre et dans son milieu, c'est l'usage des termes synonymes ῥῆμα ou ῥῆμα Θεοῦ, dans des contextes qui ne permettent guère de leur refuser tout sens théologique.[7] Faudrait-il en induire que l'auteur a délibérément réservé ce sens à ces termes plutôt qu'à λόγος τοῦ Θεοῦ qui le comportait plus souvent de son temps? Serait-ce pour faire pièce aux usages métaphysiques ou pré-gnostiques de cette expression qu'il l'aurait ramenée à son acception biblique ordinaire, en se servant de ῥῆμα pour les besoins théologiques? Un examen attentif des quatre textes où apparaît ce terme ne confirme pas cette hypothèse, car si deux d'entre eux étaient utilisables à cet effet,[8] les deux autres nous reconduiraient indubitablement aux acceptions les

G

plus courantes,[9] celles que l'on voudrait attribuer à ὁ λόγος τοῦ Θεοῦ dans cette épître, en dehors de toute connotation métaphysique ou christologique.

Quelques remarques schématiques sur les rapports de fond entre λόγος et ῥῆμα aideront à mieux poser les problèmes qui surgissent de leurs utilisations religieuses, jusqu'à celles que s'est approprié dans un nouveau contexte, l'auteur de l'épître aux Hébreux.

Aux origines étymologiques, λόγος exprime les notions de groupement, de collection, avec choix. Au cours de ses ramifications sémantiques, il gardera toujours quelque chose de ces acceptions primitives; il oscillera souvent entre le rassemblement et la sélection, avec son facteur de discrimination et de distinction.[10] Ainsi, quand on en viendra au groupement de faits à conter, par où λόγος va rencontrer ῥῆμα et la notion de parole exprimée que ce terme signifie dès le début, il en sera de même.[11]

Ῥῆμα serait donc le terme propre, beaucoup plus que λόγος, pour désigner une expression audible, un mot prononcé, un nom, une parole articulée. Mais il est dans la nature même de ῥῆμα d'exercer une détermination dans l'indéterminé, une définition dans l'indéfini, une précision qui suppose une distinction, par où ῥῆμα, suivant la marche inverse de λόγος, va pour ainsi dire à sa rencontre et se prépare à interférer avec lui dans le langage philosophique et religieux.[12] Nul exemple n'est plus probant que celui offert par la LXX dans sa traduction de l'hébreu DBR où le caractère objectif et dynamique de l'expression verbale, surtout quand elle vient de Dieu, est beaucoup plus marqué même que dans ῥῆμα, son correspondant naturel.[13] Or, il se trouve que λόγος intervient dès la traduction du Pentateuque, et que son emploi ne cesse de croître, jusqu'à prédominer considérablement dans les écrits prophétiques, et plus tard, dans les apocryphes.[14] Cet usage croissant de λόγος pour traduire DBR peut marquer le passage des livres historiques, et du style historique, à d'autres genres littéraires; mais son importance doit aussi répondre à l'hellénisation plus grande des livres traduits les derniers ou de ceux qui ont été écrits directement en grec. De toutes façons, il y a eu interpénétration du génie des deux langues. Plus encore que de son voisinage avec ῥῆμα, λόγος tirera de DBR, en le traduisant, un dynamisme plus fort.[15] Cela devient évident quand il s'agit d'une parole divine, de la parole de Dieu.[16]

Sur le tracé normal de son développement sémantique à travers

la pensée grecque,[17] λόγος porte l'accent tantôt des rapproche-
ments, tantôt des distinctions logiques.[18] C'est une dialectique où
le Verbe pensé l'emporte sur le Verbe parlé.[19] Quand ce Verbe
devient créateur, c'est moins en étant prononcé que par l'idée
qu'il exprime.[20] Il serait apparenté à νοῦς plutôt qu'à ῥῆμα.[21] Cette
prédominance logique et rationnelle caractérise le classicisme grec.

Il en va autrement chez les peuples incultes[22] ou chez ceux de
culture orientale, tels que les Suméro-Babyloniens[23] ou les
Egyptiens.[24] Le miracle du langage articulé, la puissance de la
parole prononcée, la magie du mot qui ordonne et qui crée dans
le chaos des choses et des notions confuses y sont au premier
plan.[25]

L'Hellénisme post-classique, et notamment l'alexandrin, associe
plus au moins heureusement ces tendances divergentes. La LXX
en est un témoin. Le plus remarquable est Philon. Tout semble
avoir été dit sur lui et sur la complexité de son Logos, alimenté
par des sources variées.[26] La juive était déjà pénétrée d'hellénisme.[27] On pourrait être tenté de réserver à cet hellénisme
toute la logique du logos, en attribuant à l'Orient ce qui s'y
mêlerait d'irrationnel. Ce serait une vue simpliste des choses; car
si le Logos grec est essentiellement noétique, les écrits sapientiaux
de l'Orient ne sont pas absolument dépourvus de ce trait avant
leur contact avec lui.[28] Si l'originalité de Philon n'est pas grande,
elle est pourtant réelle par le dosage particulier des éléments qu'il
synthétise ou syncrétise dans son Logos.[29] Elle nous semble
ressortir principalement d'une notion que ses historiens ou commentateurs n'ont certes pas ignorée,[30] mais à laquelle ils ont rarement attribué la valeur qu'elle mérite: la notion du λόγος τομεύς.[31]
Son importance pour nous s'accroît du fait qu'elle constitue un
parallèle évident, et généralement reconnu, au λόγος τομώτερος
de notre premier texte: Hébreux 4:12.[32] Sans doute, comme
Philon lui-même l'atteste, on peut faire remonter cette notion
jusqu'à Héraclite.[33] Mais celui-ci, déjà, par son identité des contraires,[34] faisait perdre au Logos le pouvoir de maintenir les intervalles et de conjurer ainsi la tentation du monisme panthéistique.
Le stoïcisme que connaissait Philon cédait entièrement à ce risque.[35]
On peut estimer à bon droit que son judaïsme a joué dans la mise
au point de cette remarquable fonction du Logos qui pensé, aussi
bien que parlé, demeure indéfectiblement l'agent suprême et le
juge souverain des discriminations et des distinctions logiques,

naturelles ou morales.[36] L'image du couteau ou du glaive se trouvait déjà dans la Bible, pour marquer la séparation, la préservation, le jugement ou le châtiment.[37] Elle est appliquée à la bouche du Serviteur de l'Eternel[38] dont la parole est, de ce fait, ῥῆμα τόμον ou λόγος τομεύς. Philon n'en ignorait rien, et les échos bibliques sont encore perceptibles là même où, sur les traces de ses maîtres grecs, il esquisse ou détaille une métaphysique du Logos. La complexité même de son éclectisme lui a permis de rayonner dans des milieux variés, à une époque où la pensée n'avait plus l'exigence des grands classiques d'autrefois.[39]

L'éclectisme, favorisé par l'allégorie qui faisait dire à peu près tout à tout,[40] sévissait à l'époque un peu partout.[41] Le λόγος τομεύς aurait dû en préserver Philon; mais il s'en montra incapable. Sans doute fallait-il pour cela un λόγος τομώτερος que connaissait l'auteur de l'épître aux Hébreux, mais auquel il n'a pas été absolument fidèle, habitué qu'il était sans doute aux jeux alexandrins, ou rabbiniques.[42] Il se peut qu'il l'ait été aux uns comme aux autres, qui se ressemblaient.[43] Les sens multiples qu'un terme avait pu acquérir au cours de ses développements sémantiques donnaient lieu à des variations imprévues sur le même thème apparent. Quand l'allégorie s'en mêlait, le terrain s'élargissait indéfiniment. Les règles du jeu durent être établies pour que l'on pût s'y reconnaître tant soit peu. La scolastique en hérita.[44] Toutes les gnoses avant elle s'y étaient complues.[45]

Il n'est pas inutile de bien se rendre compte de cette mentalité d'une époque pour mesurer la relative, mais très réelle sobriété des écrits du Nouveau Testament qui auraient pu céder à la tentation générale et entrer dans le jeu. Les plus menacés furent les écrits johanniques.[46] Parmi les écrits pauliniens et deutéro-pauliniens qui le furent aussi,[47] l'épître aux Hébreux figure en première ligne.[48] Il se peut que les exégètes mentionnés, qui voient dans le Logos de Dieu suivant l'épître aux Hébreux, les acceptions déjà variées de voix, révélation, message, enseignement de Dieu,[49] aient à la fois raison et tort: raison de distinguer telle ou telle de ces nuances, tort de ne pas lui ou leur en associer d'autres, de genre différent: métaphysique, théologique, christologique. Inversement, les exégètes qui discernent ce genre d'acceptions ont peut-être raison de le faire, mais tort de ne pas reconnaître que d'autres, plus ordinaires, y sont également associées. Mais il convient de préciser sur les textes mêmes.

Si l'on reprend d'abord Hébreux 4:12, dans cette perspective élargie, on s'aperçoit que son exégète le plus perspicace a sans doute été Origène. Il peut sembler paradoxal de le supposer, puisque le Commentaire d'Origène sur l'épître aux Hébreux est justement de ceux qui se sont perdus. Mais dans les œuvres du grand Alexandrin qui nous ont été conservées, soit dans le texte grec original, soit dans leur traduction latine, figurent au moins sept citations de ce passage.[50] Cette abondance relative, en dehors du Commentaire lui-même, témoignerait déjà d'un intérêt particulier. En outre, situées dans leurs contextes, ces citations permettent de se rendre compte de la pensée d'Origène qui va de l'interprétation ordinaire à l'interprétation théologique, suivant les cas.[51] On pourrait assurément en conclure que rompu aux méthodes alexandrines, dont il fut le plus brillant représentant, le grand exégète n'a pas hésité à « solliciter doucement les textes »[52] dans un sens ou dans l'autre, selon les besoins de son raisonnement. N'a-t-il pas pratiqué souvent l'allégorie?[53] Mais il n'y a pas trace d'allégorie dans l'usage de ces citations. On n'y voit rien qui suggère l'emploi de ces espèces de grilles exégétiques avec lesquelles certains Alexandrins et Scolastiques déformèrent systématiquement l'Ecriture.[54] Il paraît donc beaucoup plus probable que devant ce texte, comme heureusement devant beaucoup d'autres,[55] Origène a magistralement calqué sa pensée sur celle de l'auteur sacré, qui était lui-même, en quelque manière, un Alexandrin mesuré. Chaque utilisation de ce texte peut être examinée en soi pour souligner ensuite une divergence d'interprétation de l'une à l'autre. Mais s'en tenir là ne serait conforme ni à l'esprit d'Origène, ni à l'esprit du texte qui n'a pas été conçu ni écrit dans cette mentalité de stricte analyse à laquelle parfois les arbres masquent la forêt. Il semble donc préférable, en l'occurrence, de faire succéder la synthèse à l'analyse, et légitime de supposer que le plus génial, apparemment, des exégètes patristiques tentait lui-même cet amalgame des sens et des nuances sur lesquels joue l'auteur, dans son Commentaire perdu.

Quelques modernes, sans l'avoir exprimé nettement, ont eu l'intuition de cette complexité, et tout en se rattachant à l'exégèse courante, ont admis implicitement d'autres résonances.[56] Holtzmann est sans doute l'un de ceux qui sont allés le plus loin sur cette voie;[57] mais néanmoins, il ne croit pas pouvoir admettre une référence à Christ,[58] comme le faisait manifestement Origène. Il est curieux qu'en rapprochant Hb. 4:12, 13 et Jean 12:48,[59] il ne se soit pas rendu compte que le même jeu sur le terme λόγος ait pu se jouer de part et d'autre.[60] De même, quand il constate l'analogie d'Apoc. 19:13 avec notre texte,[61] on est surpris qu'il hésite à reconnaître d'un côté comme de l'autre, ce jeu des sens multiples où la personne du Christ est impliquée.[62] Ne l'était-elle pas déjà sous le terme ῥῆμα, pourtant moins favorable à cet effet?[63]

Si maintenant l'on passe au second texte: Hébreux 13:7, il attire beaucoup moins l'attention. Il ne semble pas qu'aucun auteur moderne ait vu dans τὸν λόγον τοῦ Θεοῦ autre chose que le message biblique.[64] Quant à Origène, la perte de son commentaire ne peut être suppléée ici par des citations. Mais il est peu vraisemblable que sa perspicacité aît été mise en défaut devant le hiatus que crée ce sens exclusif et qui ne manque pas d'embarrasser les commentateurs.[65] En effet, l'admirable verset 8 nous transporte alors brusquement, et sans transition, sur un plan différent, et d'une tout autre élévation.[66] Il en va autrement si l'on perçoit au verset 7 le même jeu subtil qu'en 4:12. Le premier sens qui s'offre à nos pensées analytiques est sans doute celui du message divin, enseigné ou prêché; mais en quoi ce sens apparent, et certain, pouvait-il empêcher un esprit d'une autre formation, l'esprit alexandrin, de sous-entendre, en même temps, le *logos* éternel qui remplit ce message et l'anime? Et qui, sur cette pente, aurait pu retenir l'Alexandrin juif et chrétien de monter jusqu'au point culminant de cette révélation qui, pour lui, ne pouvait être que Jésus-Christ, le même, hier, aujourd'hui, éternellement?

Il semble donc, pour conclure, que devant un écrit comme l'épître aux Hébreux, dont l'inspiration judéo-alexandrine n'est guère contestable, et rarement contestée, l'exégète doive dépouiller cette rigueur qui l'oriente, en bon philologue, vers la recherche d'un sens exclusif. Il doit se faire historien pour connaître les subtilités du langage de l'époque et du milieu où vivait l'auteur. Il doit entrer dans son jeu sans en être dupe, afin de ne rien perdre, dans son commentaire, du trésor qui peut être enfermé dans un mot riche de sens, tel que λόγος, et dans cette expression, la plus précieuse de toutes: Ὁ λόγος τοῦ Θεοῦ.

NOTES

[1] Le premier texte, en Heb. 4:12, se présente ainsi: Ζῶν γὰρ ὁ λόγος τοῦ Θεοῦ καὶ ἐνεργὴς καὶ τομώτερος ὑπὲρ πᾶσαν μάχαιραν δίστομον καὶ διϊκνούμενος ἄχρι

μερισμοῦ ψυχῆς καὶ πνεύματος, ἁρμῶν τε καὶ μυελῶν, καὶ κριτικὸς ἐνθυμήσεων καὶ ἐννοιῶν καρδίας ·

Le second texte, en Heb. 13:7, est le suivant: Μνημονεύετε τῶν ἡγουμένων ὑμῶν οἵτινες ἐλάλησαν ὑμῖν τὸν λόγον τοῦ Θεοῦ, ὧν ἀναθεωροῦντες τὴν ἔκβασιν τῆς ἀναστροφῆς μιμεῖσθε τὴν πίστιν.

Les problèmes de critique du texte sont minimes, surtout en ce qui touche Heb. 13:7, où la seule variante (προηγουμένων au lieu de ἡγουμένων, en D) est manifestement postérieure et intentionnelle. Peu importante aussi est, en Heb. 4:12, la question du ἐναργής de B, et, partiellement, de Jérôme, au lieu de ἐνεργής. Cette variante isolée aurait-elle été inspirée par le fait que le terme ἐνεργής est rare comparativement à ἐνεργός, dans le classique? Mais nous n'y sommes plus, et la forme ἐνεργός n'apparaît même pas dans le N.T., tandis que ἐνεργής s'y retrouve, sans variante, en 1 Cor. 16:9 et Philem. 6. Il eût d'ailleurs été aussi facile de transformer le η en ο que le ε en α. Quant au sens introduit par ἐναργής, celui de clarté, on ne voit pas que, dans ce texte et ce contexte, il soit préférable à celui de vigueur où d'efficacité, sans compter que ἐναργής serait un hapax, puisqu'on ne le trouve nulle part ailleurs dans le N.T. — Le remplacement de πνεύματος par σώματος présenterait plus d'intérêt s'il n'était aussi rare, aussi tardif, et peut-être calqué sur Matt. 10:28.

Les problèmes de signification, notamment celui de l'expression ἄχρι μερισμοῦ ψυχῆς καὶ πνεύματος, se poseront avec celui du sens de λόγος dans ce texte et dans ce contexte.

² Ainsi, pour Eugène Ménégoz, *La Théologie de l'Epître aux Hébreux* (1894), 199, « Le λόγος τοῦ Θεοῦ, c'est la « voix de Dieu », dont l'auteur vient de dire: « Aujourd'hui, si vous entendez *sa voix* (ἐὰν τῆς φωνῆς αὐτοῦ ἀκούσητε), n'endurcissez pas vos coeurs » (ch. 3, 7; 4, 7, 8; comp. Luc 8,11). Et il continue en exhortant ses lecteurs: « Hâtons-nous donc d'obéir, car la parole de Dieu est vivante, puissante, énergique.» Dans sa pensée, la parole de Dieu se confond si bien avec Dieu lui-même, qu'il passe, sans transition, d'une idée à l'autre, et que, dans sa phrase finale (v. 13), le pronom αὐτοῦ ne se rapporte plus à λόγος, mais à Θεοῦ: « Nulle créature n'est cachée devant *lui* (devant Dieu), mais tout est à découvert à *ses* yeux.» Dans tout ce passage, il n'est question que de Dieu et de sa parole, et non du Fils de Dieu.»

On notera que le verset 13 peut s'entendre autrement, qu'il est plus naturel de mettre en relation directe αὐτοῦ avec λόγος, et, incidemment, que τραχηλίζειν est de traduction délicate. Il semble abusif de fondre dans l'expression « à découvert »: γυμνά et τετραχηλισμένα. Il y a une gradation du 1er au 2d terme qui accentue l'impossibilité d'une défense quelconque devant le logos de Dieu. A l'image de la nudité s'ajoute celle de la situation désespérée du lutteur saisi au cou, peut-être du rétiaire vaincu, la tête rabattue en arrière, la gorge offerte au glaive. Il est à la merci de son adversaire. Les remarques intéressantes de Jean Héring, *Commentaire* (1955), 46, 47, mettent en relief le sens fort de τραχηλίζω, mais n'indiquent pas cette relation entre les deux termes, ni cette gradation.

L'interprétation que Ménégoz donne du verset 12 s'apparente à celle d'Edouard Reuss, *La Bible, les Epîtres Catholiques* (1878), 48, 49.

³ Telle est l'interprétation de Otto Michel, *Der Brief an die Hebräer* (1936), 51–54. La parole de Dieu est, tour à tour, ἐπαγγελία (4:1), ὅρκος (6:16), ὁρκομοσία (7:20), παράκλησις (12:5). « Ausserhalb dieses Wortes Gottes kennt

der Hb keine Offenbarung, ausserhalb dieses Wortes kennt der Hb auch keine
Schriftauffassung. . . . Wort Gottes, Schrift, Gnadenzeit, Heil und Gericht sind
Begriffe, die aufeinander hinweisen und einander bedingen » (53 *in fine*).

Quant à l'image évoquée par τετραχηλισμένα, au verset 13, elle serait celle de
la victime offerte sans défense possible, au sacrifice: « Der Ausdruck « den Hals
zurückgebogen » kennzeichnet die Wehrlosigkeit des Opfers, das keine Gegen-
wirkung veranlassen kann » (53).

Sans faire une exégèse aussi approfondie de Heb. 4:12, Jules Lebreton, *Histoire
du Dogme de la Trinité* (1927), i, 626, déclare: « Au contraire (de Philon), l'auteur
de l'épître aux Hébreux ne parle pas ici du Verbe ni du Fils de Dieu, mais de la
parole révélatrice.»

[4] Ainsi, Calvin, *Comment. in loc.*, déclare: « Il faut noter que l'Apostre parle
yci de la parole de Dieu, laquelle nous est apportée par le ministère des hommes
... cela n'empesche point que le S. Esprit ne desploye sa vertu en la parole
preschée.» Un point de vue semblable est présenté pour notre texte et quelques
autres, par Ethelbert Stauffer, *New Testament Theology* (1955), p. 195.

[5] C'est ce qu'affirme Paul Feine, *Theologie des N.T.*, 7 te. Aufl. (1936), 391:
« Hier liegt aber nur eine poetische Personifikation des Wortes auch als richt-
enden Wortes vor.»

D'après Hans Windisch, *Der Hebräerbrief* (1913), 37, cette personnification
d'apparence presque hypostatique (fast hypostatisch angeschaut), n'est cependant pas en relation avec le Fils.

[6] Aussi, les exégètes et théologiens cités jusqu'ici y ont-ils vu la parole de Dieu
enseignée ou prêchée. Ainsi, Calvin, *ad loc.*; Reuss, 102; Ménégoz, 177; Windisch, 105; Michel, 222; Héring, 123, s'accordent-ils sur ce point. La plupart
précisent qu'il s'agit de la prédication ou de l'enseignement de l'Evangile. Par
contre, Gerhard Kittel, TWNT, iv, 113, reste indécis: « Auch ob Hb 13, 7 die
Vorsteher das at.liche oder das nt.liche « Wort » oder beides in einem gesagt
und gelehrt haben, ist schwerlich auszumachen.»

[7] Le premier de ces contextes, dont nul ne met en doute le caractère théologique, est le prologue même de l'épître. C'est dans son cadre que se situe, au
verset 3, un « φέρων τε τὰ πάντα τῷ ῥήματι τῆς δυνάμεως αὐτοῦ » qui, sans conteste, se rapporte au Fils, et même, selon la plupart des exégètes, au Fils pré-
existant. Charles Bruston, *La Notion du Fils de Dieu dans l'Epître aux Hébreux*
(1907), 7–11, admet que le terme φέρων appuierait fortement cette opinion, s'il
était universellement attesté. Mais, après en avoir contesté la logique, il fait
appel, ce qui pourrait être plus convaincant, à la leçon φανερῶν en B, leçon
attestée par Sérapion, d'après TU (1899), et il écarte entièrement de tout le
passage, la notion de préexistence. On peut cependant estimer que cette notion
est trop profondément enracinée dans ces versets et notamment en 2, pour
pouvoir être ainsi extirpée. Un φανερῶν, même étendu, ce qui est purement
conjectural, à un parallèle philonien (*Rer. div. haer.* § 7), n'y changerait rien.
Il se peut, comme le suggère Michel, *op. cit.* 23, n. 2, que la notion de φῶς, telle
que nous la connaissons par le prologue johannique, ait eu sa place dans un
schéma christologique tripartite: création, conservation, illumination du monde.
La variante φανερῶν introduirait, ou rétablirait, la troisième partie dans notre
texte. Mais ne serait-ce pas au détriment de la seconde? Il ne semble pas y avoir
de raisons suffisantes pour préférer cette leçon relativement isolée à l'autre. C'est

bien, d'ailleurs, l'opinion de Michel, *ibid.* Jean Chrysostome, Εἰς τὴν πρὸς Ἑβραίους Ἐπιστ. (éd. Paris, 1838), 20, 21, ne connaît pas d'autre leçon. Il commente φέρων à la lumière du prologue johannique. Le Logos n'est pas seulement créateur; il soutient également le poids du monde (τὸν ὄγκον τῆς κτίσεως), ce qui n'est pas de moindre importance (*ibid.* et 24, 25). Le nom dont il hérite, au verset 4, est celui de Fils, tel qu'il s'attache à son incarnation, et non celui de Logos, qu'il a dès l'origine, et toujours (ibid. et 12, 13, 28, 29). Chrysostome se rend compte des amphibologies qui peuvent surgir de ce passage d'un plan à l'autre: Οὕτω καὶ περὶ τοῦ χριστοῦ, ποτὲ μὲν ἀπὸ τοῦ ἐλάττονος, ποτὲ δὲ ἀπὸ τοῦ κρείττονος διαλέγεται (*ibid.* 13). Son exégèse implique l'équivalence des deux termes ῥῆμα et λόγος.

Cette équivalence est également admise par Michel, *op. cit.*, 162, n. 2, à propos du second passage à mentionner: Heb. 11:3: πίστει νοοῦμεν κατηρτίσθαι τοὺς αἰῶνας ῥήματι θεοῦ; mais il exclut toute influence étrangère à l'A.T. Lebreton, *op. cit.*, i, 453, voit ce texte et le précédent dans une perspective plus large (*ibid.*, 445-8). Windisch, *op. cit.*, 13, 91, mentionne de nombreux parallèles. Rudolf Bultmann, *Theol. d. N.T.* 2 te. Aufl. (1954), 131, fait appel au contexte historique pour éclairer les textes qui affirment ou suggèrent le rôle cosmique du Christ.

[8] Heb. 1:3 et 11:3.

[9] Heb. 6:5 et 12:19. Sur divers sens de ῥῆμα, cf. Kittel, *art. cit.*, 117.

[10] Cf. Debrunner, *Die Vokabeln* λέγω, λόγος, ῥῆμα, λαλέω *im Griechentum*, in TWNT, iv, 69-76, et Kleinknecht, *Der Logos in Griechentum und Hellenismus*, *ibid.*, 76-89.

[11] Cf. Debrunner, *art. cit.*, 74, 75.

[12] La fonction tour à tour médiatrice, ordonnatrice, et quasi créatrice du langage a inspiré de belles pages au philosophe Louis Lavelle, *La Parole et l'Ecriture* (1942), 15-18, 32-4, 103-8, etc.

[13] Cf. Procksch, 'Wort Gottes im A.T.', in TWNT iv, 91; A. Robert, 'La Parole divine dans l'A.T.', *Dic. d. l. Bible*, Suppl. (1952), v, 442.

[14] Cf. Procksch, *art. cit.*, 91, et HRCS ii, 881-7, 1249-51.

[15] Cf. Procksch, *art. cit.*, 91; A. Robert, *art. cit.*, 442.

[16] *Ibid.*, et R. Bultmann, *Das Evang. d. Johannes*, 11 te. Aufl. (1950), 7-8.

[17] Cf. Anathon Aall, *Geschichte d. Logosidee in der griech. Philo.* (1896); Debrunner, *art. cit.*; Kleinknecht, *art. cit.*; Brice Parain, *Essai sur le Logos platonicien* (1942); W. R. Inge, 'Logos', ERE viii, 134-5.

[18] Déjà, sans doute, chez Héraclite qui insiste, d'une part, sur les oppositions, jusqu'à dire: πόλεμος πάντων μέν πατήρ ἐστι, et, d'autre part, sur les accords profonds, jusqu'à l'identité même des contraires si l'on en croit Aristote. Cf. A. Aall, *op. cit.*, 33, 50, 52, 55-56; B. Parain, *op. cit.*, 20-22; Emile Bréhier, *Hist. de la Philo.* (1938), i, 56-9.

[19] Cf. Kleinknecht, *art. cit.*, A. Aall, *op. cit.*, *passim*; Inge, *art. cit.*

[20] Cf. B. Parain, *op. cit.*, 159 s.; A. Aall, *op. cit.*, 69-71.

[21] Cf. Kleinknecht, *art. cit.*, 80, 81.

[22] Cf. G. Foucart, « Names » (Primitive), ERE, ix, 132, 133, 135, 136.

[23] Cf. S. Langdon, « Word » (Sumerian and Babylonian); ERE, xii, 749-52; Ch. F. Jean, *Le Milieu biblique avant J.C.* (1936), iii, 160, 161, 204-7, 656; S. N. Kramer, *L'Histoire commence à Sumer* (1957), 125; Tournay, 'Logos' (babylonien), *Dic. Bibl.* Suppl. *op. cit.*, 426, s.

²⁴ Cf. Jacques Vandier, *La Religion Egyptienne* (1944), 35, 62, 63; C. Desroches — Noblecourt, *Les Religions Egyptiennes* (1948), in *Hist. Gén. des Relig.*, i, 214, 248, 252, 253; A. Barucq, 'Logos' (égyptien), *Dic. Bibl.*, *Suppl.*, *op. cit.*, 434, s.

²⁵ *Ibid.*, et Lavelle, *op. cit.*, 94.

²⁶ Cf. notamment, Emile Bréhier, *Les Idées philosophiques et religieuses de Philon d'Alexandrie* (1907), 83–111; Lebreton, *op. cit.*, i, 75–84; J. Starcky, 'Logos' (Philon), in *Dic. Bibl.*, *Suppl.*, *op. cit.*, v, 473–5; Aall, *op. cit.*, 168–231; Kleinknecht, *art. cit.*, 86–8; Jean d'Alma, *Philon d'Alexandrie et le 4e Evangile* (1910), 13–52; Jean Réville, *Le Logos d'après Philon* (1877).

²⁷ Et cela, en proportions variées, de la Diaspora jusqu'au coeur de la Palestine, à Jérusalem. C'est un fait presque universellement reconnu. Cf., entre autres, G. Kittel, *Urchristentum, Spätjudentum, Hellenismus* (1926), 11 s.; J. Bonsirven, *Le Judaïsme palestinien* (1934), i, 36–40, 284, 285; ii, 11, 70 s., 310 s., 386; Ch. Guignebert, *Le Monde juif vers le temps de Jésus* (1935), 261 s., 309–311; W. D. Davies, *Paul and Rabbinic Judaism* (1948), 5 s., 8, 14; Saul Lieberman, *Hellenism in Jewish Palestine* (1950); H. Clavier, *Η ΣΥΝΕΙΔΗΣΙΣ, Une pierre de touche de l'Hellénisme Paulinien* (1953), 3–5.

²⁸ Cf. notamment, le parallélisme entre les fonctions du λόγος et celles de la 'HoKhMah dans les écrits sapientiaux. Cf. Davies, *op. cit.*, 151; Bultmann, *D. Ev. d. Joh.*, *op. cit.*, 9; Kittel, TWNT, iv, 135–7; Lebreton, *op. cit.*, i, 122–33.

²⁹ Cf. Bréhier, *Philon. op. cit.*, 110, 111, *et supra, n.* 26.

³⁰ Cf. Bréhier, *op. cit.*, 86–9; Aall, *op. cit.*, 223; Lebreton, *op. cit.*, i, 229, 230.

³¹ Le terme de τομεύς = coupeur, trancheur, diviseur, appliqué au λόγος, se rencontre six fois dans le traité sur l'Héritier des choses divines, dont le titre complet montre l'importance que Philon attache à cette notion: Περὶ τοῦ τίς ὁ τῶν θείων ἐστὶν κληρονόμος καὶ περὶ τῆς εἰς τὰ ἴσα καὶ ἐναντία τομῆς. Cf. *Phil. Alex. Op.*, éd. P. Wendland (1898), iii, 30, 31, 32, 38, 49, 51 (§§ 130, 131, 140, 165, 215, 225). La notion même est exprimée plus souvent encore par le verbe τέμνειν et par le substantif τομή, non seulement dans ce traité, mais dans d'autres. Par contre, l'adjectif τομός, employé, au comparatif, en Heb. 4:12, paraît absent chez Philon. Il est toutefois évident que τομεύς en est un synonyme très proche.

³² Cf. Windisch, *op. cit.*, 36, 37; Ménégoz, *op. cit.*, 199, 200; Michel, *op. cit.*, 51–2; Kittel, *op. cit.*, 113; Lebreton, *op. cit.*, i, 625, 626. Le texte philonien qui présente, sans doute, le meilleur parallèle se trouve dans le traité susmentionné: Περὶ τοῦ τίς ὁ τ. θ. κληρονόμος, *ed. cit.*, 30, 31 (§§ 130–2). Le Logos y est comparé à un tranchet sans cesse aiguisé pour remplir son office permanent de séparation, de coupure ou de distinction (τῷ τομεῖ . . . λόγῳ, ὃς εἰς τὴν ὀξυτάτην ἀκονηθεὶς ἀκμὴν διαιρῶν οὐδέποτε λήγει). Il pénètre ainsi jusqu'à l'impénétrable, jusqu'à l'indivisible, et partage ce qui semble ne point avoir de parties (μέχρι τῶν ἀτόμων καὶ λεγομένων ἀμερῶν διεξέλθη). Il tranche en plein milieu de chacune des facultés humaines; il sépare dans l'âme ce qui est raisonnable de ce qui ne l'est pas, dans la parole ce qui est vrai de ce qui est faux, dans l'expérience sensible ce qui atteint l'intelligence de ce qui est inintelligible (ἕκαστον οὖν τῶν τριῶν διεῖλε μέσον. τὴν μὲν ψυχὴν εἰς λογικὸν καὶ ἄλογον, τὸν δὲ λόγον εἰς ἀληθές τε καὶ ψεῦδος, τὴν δὲ αἴσθησιν εἰς καταληπτικὴν φαντασίαν καὶ ἀκατάληπτον ·) Dans ce texte, la fonction du Logos n'est pas seulement de marquer

ou de maintenir les frontières naturelles entre les facultés, mais d'établir en chacune d'elles une distinction, une discrimination entre ce qui est valable et ce qui ne l'est pas. Il en serait de même en Heb. 4:12, où il ne s'agirait donc pas du tracé d'une ligne de démarcation entre l'âme et l'esprit, les jointures et les moelles (?) (μερισμοῦ ψυχῆς καὶ πνεύματος, ἁρμῶν τε καὶ μυελῶν). Μερισμός, avec le sens actif habituel des substantifs verbaux en μος, signifierait non le résultat d'un partage déjà effectué (μέρισμα), mais l'acte de l'établir à l'intérieur même de l'objet ou des objets visés: ici, l'âme, l'esprit, les jointures et les moelles. Cette nuance a été saisie par Calvin, *Comment. ad loc.*, par O. Michel, *op. cit.*, 52, par Héring, *op. cit.*, 46; ce dernier prend « jointures et moelle » au sens figuré psychique. Cf. *infra*, note 51.

[33] Philon la fait même remonter plus haut: jusqu'à Moïse, en passant par Héraclite (*op. cit.*, 48 (§ 214) « ce qui revient au même », comme l'observe avec humour Bréhier, *op. cit.*, 87, n. 1.

[34] Cf. *supra*, note 18.

[35] Cf. Aall, *op. cit.*, 157 s.

[36] C'est le *Logos* qui a tiré l'univers organisé du chaos, et qui l'empêche d'y retomber, en maintenant les intervalles et les distinctions nécessaires. Son rôle cosmologique est ainsi longuement traité dans « L'Héritier des choses divines », tel que nous le possédons. Mais il semble que ce soit une suite qui fut peut-être précédée d'un exposé de cette fonction du *Logos* dans le domaine de l'anthropologie et de la psychologie. Cf. Bréhier, *op. cit.*, 87, n. 2.

[37] Cf. notamment, Gen. 3:24; 1 Chron. 21:16, 27; Job 19:29; Ps. 7:13, 17:13; Ezek. 21:8, 14 s.

[38] Isa. 49:2. Comp. Job 5:15; Ps. 57:5, 64:4; Rev. 2:16, 19:15 21. Cf. aussi: τὴν μάχαιραν τοῦ πνεύματος, ὅ ἔστιν ῥῆμα Θεοῦ, en Eph. 6:17, et comp. Sap. Sal. 7:22-4, où la Sagesse et l'Esprit sont associés (cf. Sap. Sal. 1:6, 7). Cf. Bréhier, *op. cit.*, 115-20.

[39] Cf. Bréhier, *op. cit.*, 97-100, 110, 156-61, 238.

[40] Cf. Bréhier, *op. cit.*, 35-37; J. Geffcken, « Allegory », ERE, i, 327.

[41] Cf. Bréhier, *op. cit.*, 35-61; Lebreton, *op. cit.*, i, 33-43, 69-74, 91, 179-84; Geffcken, *art. cit.*; H. Pinard de la Boullaye, *L'Etude comparée des Religions* (1931), i, 30, 50, 53; Friedrich Büchsel, ἀλληγορέω, TWNT, i, 260-4. Fr. Torm *Hermeneutik d. N.T.* (1930), 213-16.

[42] Il était lui-même, vraisemblablement, un Alexandrin.

[43] Sur les ressemblances et les différences, cf. Ménégoz, *op. cit.*, 215-17; Bréhier, *op. cit.*, 35-61; J. Bonsirven, *Le Judaïsme palestinien* (1934), i, 298, 299.

[44] Cf. G. Heinrici, *Hermeneutik* (*Realencykl. f. protest. Theol. u. Kirche*, ed. Hauck), vii, 733, 734, F. Torm, *op. cit.*, 33, 217.

[45] Cf. Pinard de la Boullaye, *op. cit.*, i, 76-80; Lebreton, *op. cit.*, II, 116-19; Torm, *op. cit.*, 236.

[46] Cf. C. H. Dodd, *The Interpretation of the Fourth Gospel* (1953), 133-43.

[47] Cf. W. D. Davies, *Paul and Rabbinic Judaïsm* (1948), 11, 28, 30, 96, 146; Büchsel, *art. cit.*, 263, 264; Torm, *op. cit.*, 219-29, différencie la typologie paulinienne.

[48] Cf. R. Bultmann, *Th. d. N.T.*, *op. cit.*, 110, 476.

[49] Cf. *supra*, notes 2-6.

[50] Cf. Origenis *Opera Omnia*, ed. E. Lommatzsch (1835-1846), v, 276 (Com-

ment. 1 Thess. 4:15); vii, 141 (Comment. Rom. 8:31); i, vii, 307 (Comment. Rom. 12:6); viii, 159 (In Gen. Hom. 3); ix, 443 (In Lev. Hom. 16); xx, 253 (Ad Martyr. 15, Mark 10:30); xx, 286 (Ad Martyr. 37).

[51] Il semble même que l'interprétation théologique ne soit jamais absente. C'est elle qui prévaut dans le premier texte mentionné (v, 276), où la Parole et le Christ sont identifiés: « vivunt in eo, qui vita est, et vivit in iis Christus, de quo scriptum est: « vivens (Heb. 4:12) est sermo Dei, et efficax », qui est (1 Cor. 1:24) Dei virtus Deique sapientia.»

Dans le second texte (vii, 141), la Parole est identifiée à l'Esprit: « Habeo enim fortiorem mecum gladium (Eph. 6:17), Spiritus, quod est verbum Dei, et mecum est « vivens (Heb. 4:12) et efficax sermo Dei », qui est penetrabilior omni gladio utrinque acuto.»

Dans le troisième texte (vii, 307), il pourrait s'agir de la parole de Dieu au sens ordinaire; mais son acuité est mise en parallèle avec celle de l'Esprit (1 Cor. 2:10), « penetrans usque ad divisionem animae et spiritus, compagum quoque ac medullarum ». Origène adopterait ici pour μερισμός le sens de limite entre et non celui de coupure au milieu (cf. *supra*, note 32). Il en serait de même dans le quatrième texte et dans le cinquième (viii, 159; ix, 443). Toutefois, il s'agit de fragments traduits en latin. Les sixième et septième textes (xx, 253, 286) qui sont dans la langue originale, en grec, suggèrent plutôt l'autre interprétation. Le septième qui cite intégralement Heb. 4:12, suivant la leçon habituelle, commente ainsi: οὗτος (ὁ λογος τ.Θ.) μάλιστα νῦν εἰρήνην (Philip 4:7) μὲν τὴν ὑπερέχουσαν πάντα νοῦν, ἣν ἀφῆκε (Joan. 14:27) τοῖς ἀποστόλοις ἑαυτοῦ, βραβεύει ταῖς ψυχαῖς ἡμῶν · μάχαιραν δὲ ἔβαλε μεταξὺ τῆς τοῦ χοϊκοῦ (1 Cor. 15:49) εἰκόνος, καὶ τοῦ ἐπουρανίου · ἵν᾽ ἐπὶ τοῦ παρόντος τὸν ἐπουράνιον ἡμῶν παραλαβὼν, ὕστερον ἀξίους γενομένους τοῦ μὴ διχοτομηθῆναι (Luc. 12:46) ἡμᾶς, ἐξ ὅλων ποιήσῃ ἐπουρανίους.

Dans ce dernier texte, ainsi qu'on le voit, le Logos est identifié avec Jésus Christ. Il en est de même dans le sixième qui fait également partie de l'Exhortation au martyre. Le glaive acéré du Logos vivant permet à ceux qui l'ont reçu de trancher tous les liens, et de rejoindre en un vol d'aigle celui qui marche devant eux.

Le cinquième texte est encore plus explicite sur cette identité: « nos docet, qui sit hic gladius (Heb. 4:12)... Sermo namque Dei est, qui prosternit omnes inimicos et ponit eos sub pedibus suis, ut subditus fiat omnis mundus Deo (Heb. 2:8; 1 Cor. 15:25; Eph. 1:22).»

[52] Le mot et le conseil (!) sont de Renan, *Vie de Jésus*, 11e éd. (1864), LVI.

[53] Cf. Pinard de la Boullaye, *op. cit.*, i, 53, 80, 558; Lebreton, *op. cit.*, ii, 115-17; A. Puech, *Hist. de la Litt. Grecque Chrétienne* (1928), ii, 381-6; Fr. Torm, *Hermeneutik d. N.T.* (1930), 32, 237.

[54] Cf. *supra*, n. 44.

[55] Cf. *supra*, n. 53, et, à propos de Matt. 16:18, H. Clavier, Πέτρος καὶ πέτρα, in *Neutest. Stud. f. R. Bultmann* (1954), 94, 95, 106.

[56] Cf. E. Ménégoz, *op. cit.*, 200, 203, 205; Windisch, *op. cit.*, 37; Starcky, *art. cit.*, 484, 485; Héring, *op. cit.*, 123.

[57] Cf. H. J. Holtzmann, *Lehrbuch d. Neutest. Theol.*, 2te Aufl. (1911), i, 548, ii, 3, 334, 446.

[58] *Ibid.*, ii, 334, 446.

[59] *Ibid.*, 446.

[60] Holtzmann admet implicitement ce jeu en ce qui concerne Jean. Bien que le Christ lui-même soit censé parler de *logos* en 12:48, ce qui, en apparence, exclut l'identité de ce *logos* et de lui-même, dans la réalité, ce serait bien ce que l'auteur suggère.

[61] Cf. Holtzmann, *op. cit.*, i, 547, 548.

[62] Il semble pourtant l'admettre ici (548), contrairement à ce qu'il affirme ailleurs. Il écrit, en effet, dans ce passage: « Das plötzliche Auftreten des Schlagwortes einer neuen Theologie überrascht, kann aber doch nicht wirklich befremden, weil ein frühes Eindringen alexandrinischer Denk- und Ausdrucksweise durch die ephesinische Wirksamkeit des Apollos und die Theologie von Hbr wahrscheinlich genug ist. » Cf., par contre, Lebreton, *op. cit.*, i, 470.

[63] Cf. *supra*, n. 7. Sur le jeu du double sens, cf. H. Clavier, *art. cit.*, 105-7.

[64] Cf. *supra*, n. 1, 6.

[65] Ainsi, Héring, *op. cit.*, 123 trouve que ce verset 8 « se rattache mal à ce qui précède, ainsi qu'à la suite. » Nous serions « en présence de quelque chose comme une formule liturgique, qui doit terminer la première section de cette exhortation, laquelle devait peut-être primitivement clôre l'épître ». Reuss, *op. cit.*, 102, y voyait « une espèce de devise qui résume la pensée chrétienne ».

[66] Ἰησοῦς Χριστὸς ἐχθὲς καὶ σήμερον ὁ αὐτὸς καὶ εἰς τοὺς αἰῶνας.

L'APÔTRE PIERRE INSTRUMENT DU DIABLE ET INSTRUMENT DE DIEU.

LA PLACE DE MATT. 16:16–19 DANS LA TRADITION PRIMITIVE

par

O. CULLMANN

EN 1942, un exégète catholique[1] pouvait constater un « consensus nouveau » parmi les critiques protestants dont la majorité se prononçait alors, à la suite des travaux de F. Kattenbusch[2] et de K. L. Schmidt[3], en faveur de l'authenticité du texte si controversé Matt. 16:16–19 sur Pierre, roc de l'église. Mais, au moment où nous avons publié notre livre sur « S. Pierre »,[4] nous avons déjà noté, en nous basant sur une statistique établie par A. Oepke[5] que le nombre des exégètes affirmant l'inauthenticité était devenu à peu près égal à celui des partisans de l'authenticité. Depuis lors, la proportion s'est nettement déplacée encore dans le sens d'un retour à la thèse de l'inauthenticité, comme le prouvent les comptes rendus protestants de notre ouvrage dans lequel nous avons expliqué ces logia comme des paroles de Jésus. Déjà dans notre livre, nous avons pris comme point de départ de l'argumentation l'examen du *cadre littéraire* de la péricope. Nous avons essayé de montrer que le récit auquel, dans l'évangile selon Matthieu, se trouvent liées les paroles controversées Matt. 16:16–19, c'est-à-dire la scène qui s'est passée à Césarée de Philippe et que rapportent aussi Marc (8:27–33) et Luc (9:18–22) n'est certainement pas leur cadre primitif, et nous avons soulevé la question de savoir quelle pouvait bien être la place primitive de ce morceau. Nous avons indiqué les arguments qui paraissent parler en faveur de l'entretien de Jésus avec ses disciples lors du dernier repas où, dans Luc 22:31–34, nous lisons effectivement une parole analogue adressée à Pierre.[6]

Nous regrettons que, à la différence de la plupart des critiques catholiques, les exégètes protestants, préoccupés trop exclusivement à soutenir contre nous l'inauthenticité de la promesse faite par Jésus à Pierre, n'aient, en général, même pas pris en considération la thèse que nous avons proposée concernant son cadre primitif.

Il nous paraît cependant que même lorsqu'on conteste l'authenticité de ces logia, solution dont nous continuons à penser qu'elle ne s'impose pas, la question de la place primitive qu'occupe ce morceau dans la tradition antérieure à son utilisation par Matthieu, devrait être posée tout de même. Il faut même dire qu'il faut la soulever surtout dans ce cas. En effet, si vraiment il ne s'agit pas d'un dialogue historique, il faut en indiquer l'origine, et la première question à résoudre est alors également celle de son cadre. Il est vrai qu'à l'origine la tradition orale n'a transmis que des récits et des paroles isolés. Mais K. L. Schmidt qui a soutenu cette thèse avec une vigueur particulière,[7] a lui-même posé le problème du cadre primitif pour ces versets Matt. 16:16–19.[8] Car la façon dont ils sont rattachés au début du récit de Marc 8:27–33 prouve que dès avant d'avoir été insérés par Matthieu à cet endroit de son évangile, ils doivent avoir été encadrés d'un récit complet qui cependant n'était sûrement pas celui de Marc 8:27–33, la scène de Césarée de Philippe. En effet, il manque le complément du verbe ἀπεκάλυψε. Le pronom « cela » qu' ajoutent les traductions modernes: « . . . mon père céleste t'a révélé cela » n'est pas dans le texte grec. Cette omission nous permet de supposer que cette réplique de Jésus se rapporte, dans la tradition antérieure, à une autre déclaration de Pierre.

K. L. Schmidt avait pensé, mais sans approfondir la question, que le dialogue avait appartenu d'abord à un cadre différent, mais quand-même analogue à celui de l'événement de Césarée de Philippe.[9] Nous allons examiner de plus près si tel est vraiment le cas.

La question telle que nous la posons n'existerait pas, si les paroles controversées avaient été interpolées beaucoup plus tard par des partisans du primat du siège de Rome dans le texte de Matthieu dans lequel elles auraient manqué primitivement. Dans ce cas, il s'agirait d'un problème d'histoire du texte. Cette opinion[10] qui trouve encore des défenseurs semble cependant être abandonnée aujourd'hui par la plupart des défenseurs de l'inauthenticité eux-mêmes.[11] Ainsi Bultmann qui soutient énergiquement l'origine secondaire des logia en question, en relève pourtant le caractère sémitique, donc l'âge relativement ancien. S'il s'agit d'une tradition antérieure à Matthieu et si l'évangéliste lui-même l'a tirée d'un autre contexte, il faut se demander quel est ce contexte.

Nous allons donc d'abord indiquer les raisons pour lesquelles le récit Marc 8:27–33 ne saurait être le cadre primitif de Matt. 16:16–19; en second lieu, nous devons examiner de près, en nous basant sur les autres évangiles, les traces d'un contexte différent; enfin, en troisième lieu, nous essaierons de préciser le motif qui a déterminé Matthieu à insérer la tradition en question dans le récit Marc 8:27–33.

I

Quant au premier point nous pourrons être bref. Dans notre livre sur S. Pierre[12], nous nous sommes efforcés de montrer que le but, la « pointe » même du récit Marc 8:27–33, qui forme une unité,[13] réside justement dans le blâme et l'ordre que Jésus est obligé d'adresser à Pierre à cause de sa fausse conception (politique) du rôle du Messie. Le sens de cette péricope est donc tout à fait parallèle à celui du récit de la tentation de Jésus dans le désert. Elle se termine d'une façon toute analogue par les paroles extrêmement sévères de Jésus: « Arrière de moi, Satan!». Cette fois-ci, le diable qui déjà après le baptême avait voulu suggérer à Jésus d'assumer le rôle d'un Messie politique qui dominerait sur les royaumes de ce monde, s'est servi de Pierre. L'apôtre qui dit « tu es le Messie » est ici l'instrument du diable. Il est absolument inconcevable que dans le récit qu'on appelle à tort celui de la « confession de Pierre » et qui, en réalité, rapporte la « tentation de Jésus par Pierre, instrument de Satan », Jésus ait dit à l'apôtre: c'est Dieu lui-même qui t'a inspiré! Car au moment même où Pierre a fait la déclaration « tu es le Messie », il devait, d'après le récit de *Marc*, déjà avoir la *conception diabolique* du rôle politique du Messie, celle que la majorité des Juifs partageaient et qui excluait sa souffrance.[14] Dans le récit de Césarée de Philippe (Marc 8:27–33), Pierre est l'instrument du diable, dans celui de Matt. 16:16–19, il est l'instrument de Dieu. Primitivement, il s'agit de deux récits entièrement différents. Seul le deuxième est une « confession de Pierre ».

2

Quel est alors le cadre primitif de ce récit Matt. 16:16–19? Nous avons vu que K. L. Schmidt avait émis l'hypothèse qu'il devait s'agir d'un cadre analogue à celui du récit tout différent aussi selon lui, de Marc 8:27-33. En réalité, l'analogie réside seulement dans le fait qu'il s'agit de part et d'autre du problème christologique. Mais pouvons-nous préciser les circonstances de la vie de Jésus dans lesquelles une tradition antérieure à l'evangile selon Matthieu aurait situé les paroles que nous lisons actuellement dans Matt. 16:16-19? On a pensé à un récit d'apparition de Jésus ressuscité à Pierre dont nous trouverions les traces dans Jean 21:15 ss. Ce récit aurait été rejeté, après coup, dans la vie de Jésus.[15] Il est certain qu'il existe un lien entre le dialogue Jean 21:15 ss et Matt. 16:16-19, et nous en ferons état nous-même dans l'explication que nous proposerons. Il ne faut pas exclure, d'autre part, a priori la possibilité qu'un récit d'apparition ait été « antédaté » de cette façon-là. Mais il faudrait réserver les explications de ce genre aux cas où elles s'imposent, c'est-à-dire où une situation de la vie historique de Jésus ne peut pas entrer en ligne de compte. Ce cas ne se présente pas ici. D'autre part, le dialogue Jean 21:15 ss. appartient, sous sa forme actuelle, à une tradition assez tardive de sorte qu'il faut se demander si elle ne présuppose pas, vice-versa, un récit de la vie de Jésus qu'elle a pour but de placer dans la perspective nouvelle du Christ ressuscité.

Nous avons rendu attentif au fait que Luc rapporte une parole analogue à Matt. 16:18-19, quoique différente quant à la forme,[16] dans le cadre du dernier repas de Jésus ou en tout cas des entretiens qui suivent ce repas. Dans ces « discours d'adieux » de Luc, Jésus envisage la situation dans laquelle les disciples se trouveront après sa mort, et il adresse à Pierre ces paroles (chap. 22:31 ss.) qui ne représentent, en ce qui concerne le rôle particulier assigné à l'apôtre, qu'une variante de Matt. 16:16-19 bien que Matthieu, conformément à sa méthode littéraire générale, ait groupé à cet endroit plusieurs logia qui expriment la même tendance et qui manquent dans Luc 22:31 ss.: « Simon, Simon, voici que Satan a demandé à vous cribler comme le blé. Mais moi j'ai prié pour que ta foi ne défaille point, et toi, une fois que tu seras converti, fortifie tes frères. Alors Pierre lui dit: Seigneur, je suis prêt à aller avec toi et en prison et à la mort. Jésus dit: Je te dis, Pierre, tu auras trois fois nié de me connaître avant que le coq ne chante aujourd'hui ».

Le v. 32 est parallèle à Matt. 16:18. Pierre est appelé à remplir une mission particulière à l'égard de ses frères. A la place de la promesse que « les portes de l'enfer ne prévaudront pas contre

H

le qehal », la communauté que Jésus va bâtir, il y a ici la prière de
Jésus pour que la foi de Pierre ne défaille pas vis-à-vis des assauts
de Satan dirigés contre tous les disciples. Le rapport est manifeste.
A la place de la confession christologique, il y a ici de la part de
l'apôtre une promesse solennelle de fidélité: de suivre le maître
en prison et jusqu'à la mort. Là encore, il y a analogie, la promesse
présupposant la conviction christologique, d'autant plus que dans
un texte parallèle de l'évangile johannique que nous examinerons
tout à l'heure, promesse et confession sont effectivement réunies.
Dans Matt. 16:16 ss., il manque un élément que nous trouvons
dans Luc 22:33: la prédiction du reniement de Pierre. Mais on peut
montrer que ce trait appartient très probablement au cadre primitif du récit utilisé par Matthieu. En effet, le dialogue entre Jésus
ressuscité et Pierre dans Jean 21:15 qui reprend, nous l'avons dit,
le thème d'un récit de la vie de Jésus réunit la prédiction de la
future fonction « pais mes brebis » et du martyre de Pierre avec
la triple confession de l'apôtre: Je t'aime, qui renvoie certainement
à son triple reniement. Nous comprenons aussi pourquoi Matthieu a dû omettre ici cette prédiction du reniement qui dans le
contexte primitif dont il s'est servi était probablement liée à celle
de sa future mission: c'est parce qu'il a placé toute la scène à un
moment antérieur, à savoir à Césarée de Philippe, et qu'il a voulu,
de propos délibéré, comme nous allons voir dans la troisième
partie du présent travail, atténuer par la combinaison des deux
récits si différents l'impression fâcheuse de la terrible accusation
lancée par Jésus contre Pierre: « Arrière de moi, Satan! ». Selon une
tradition plus ancienne, c'est donc après le dernier repas qu'à la
suite d'une déclaration de Pierre, Jésus a prédit à l'apôtre en même
temps sa grande tâche à accomplir et son reniement.[17]

Nos études christologiques nous ont amenés à trouver une confirmation frappante de notre manière de voir et à préciser en même
temps le motif qui a décidé Matthieu à insérer le morceau dans le
récit de Césarée de Philippe dont la signification est radicalement
différente.

Il est à remarquer que le *titre* conféré par Pierre à Jésus n'est pas
le même dans les trois récits parallèles. Marc dit seulement: tu es
le Messie (Luc avec une légère variante: le Messie de Dieu), Matthieu par contre: tu es le Messie, *le fils de Dieu*. « Fils de Dieu » n'est
pas un attribut du Messie.[18] Il y a donc dans Matthieu réunion de
deux confessions assez différentes dont l'origine n'est pas la même,

et dont l'une n'est nullement une précision de l'autre, comme nous sommes tentés de le croire en nous basant précisément sur ce passage de Matthieu. Dans Marc, il n'est question que du Messie, et si nous tenons compte du sens du récit de Marc selon lequel Pierre doit se faire traiter de Satan précisément à cause de sa fausse conception du Messie, il faut même dire qu'entre cette confession du Messie et celle du fils de Dieu il n'y a pas seulement différence, mais opposition. Car l'accomplissement du rôle de fils de Dieu, considéré comme le secret de Jésus, implique dans les synoptiques d'une part l'obéissance, d'autre part la conscience de l'unité complète de volonté entre Jésus et Dieu.[19] Dans Marc 8:27–33, c'est le diable qui parle par Pierre; dans Matt. 16:16–19, au contraire, Pierre entre dans le secret le plus intime de Jésus, mystère que nul ne peut lui avoir révélé sinon Dieu lui-même qui est seul à le connaître. Effectivement, nous lisons dans Matthieu, au v. 17: « ce n'est pas la chair et le sang qui t'ont donné la révélation, mais mon père qui est dans les cieux.» C'est là l'idée relative à la connaissance du fils de Dieu que nous trouvons dans un autre logion rapporté par Matthieu et Luc: « ...personne ne connaît le Fils si ce n'est le Père, et personne ne connaît le Père si ce n'est le Fils et celui à qui il veut le révéler» (Matt. 11:27; Luc 10:22).[20]

La conclusion s'impose: il n'y a pas seulement deux titres christologiques qui ont été combinés ici par Matthieu, mais deux récits: dans l'un, Pierre appelle Jésus « Messie », mais il l'entend au sens politique. L'apôtre tentateur est repoussé de la façon la plus violente par Jésus: « Arrière de moi, Satan!». Dans l'autre, au contraire, Pierre appelle Jésus « fils de Dieu ». Jésus lui répond que c'est le Père qui lui a révélé ce secret. Nous trouvons confirmé que les deux récits n'ont primitivement rien à voir l'un avec l'autre. Si précédemment nous avons constaté que leur cadre extérieur et leur sens est tout à fait différent dans les deux cas, nous voyons maintenant que *le point de depart* l'est également. Nous nous rappelons que dans Matthieu 16:17 le complément du verbe ἀπεκάλυψε manque, que l'objet de la révélation n'est pas indiqué. A présent nous en comprenons la raison: c'est que la révélation divine ne se rapporte pas à l'affirmation: tu es le Messie, mais seulement à la deuxième partie de la déclaration de Pierre: tu es le fils de Dieu.

Nous avons dit que le récit de Marc, loin de rapporter une « confession de Pierre », est en réalité le récit d'une deuxième tentation messianique de Jésus. Nous constatons à présent que

l'appellation « confession de Pierre » peut s'appliquer par contre
parfaitement à l'autre récit. Seulement l'objet de la confession n'y
est pas le Messie, mais le fils de Dieu, et ce récit fait très probablement partie des entretiens de Jésus avec les siens après le dernier
repas.

Pour cette dernière supposition, nous nous sommes basés
jusqu'ici sur Luc 22:31–34 qui contient une promesse parallèle à
celle de Matt. 16:18. Mais nous avons vu que si Pierre s'y déclare
prêt à suivre Jésus partout, il y manque une confession pro prement
dite analogue à celle de Matt. 16:16. Nous avons dit que cette considération ne saurait infirmer notre thèse selon laquelle il s'agit
d'un parallèle de sorte que le cadre du logion de Matt. 16:16–19
peut être celui de Luc 22:31 ss. Nous trouvons une confirmation
frappante de notre explication, en ce qui concerne ce point, dans
Jean 6:66–71, passage que déjà B. Weiss[21] et d'autres après lui ont
rapproché de Matt. 16:16–19: « A partir de ce moment-là, beaucoup de ses disciples se retirèrent et n'allaient plus avec lui. Jésus
dit aux douze: Ne voulez-vous pas vous en aller vous aussi? Simon
Pierre lui répondit: Seigneur, à qui irions-nous? Tu as des paroles
de vie. Nous sommes arrivés à la foi et à la connaissance que *tu es
le Saint de Dieu*. Jésus lui répondit: Ne vous ai-je pas choisis vous
les douze, et l'un d'entre vous est un diable … ».

On a fait remarquer avec raison que ce passage rapporte la confession de Pierre sous la forme johannique. Mais nous pensons
que là comme souvent le quatrième évangéliste se base sur une
tradition fort ancienne dont nous trouvons les traces chez Luc qui
si fréquemment s'accorde avec l'évangile johannique, précisément
dans Luc 22:31–33. En effet, il y a dans Jean 6, 66 ss. comme chez
Luc la promesse de Pierre de suivre Jésus jusque dans la mort, et
surtout la scène doit s'être passée, selon la tradition utilisée par le
quatrième évangile, également au moment du dernier repas; car
le discours dans lequel l'auteur de l'évangile johannique l'a placée
suit la multiplication des pains considérée par lui comme type de
l'Eucharistie; d'autre part il rapporte en même temps l'annonce
de la trahison de Judas qui primitivement appartient à ce même
cadre. Mais d'un autre côté, Jean 6:69 a de commun avec Matt.
16:17 le fait que Pierre confesse: Tu es le Saint de Dieu. Le rapport
avec Matt. 16:17 apparaît plus clairement encore lorsque nous
tenons compte du fait généralement reconnu que le titre « le saint
de Dieu » n'est qu'une variante du titre « fils de Dieu ».[22] A la

rigueur, on pourrait mentionner encore un rapport plus indirect entre Jean 6:70 et Matt. 16:17 ss. En réponse à la confession de Pierre, Jésus souligne la place exceptionnelle des douze tout en prédisant la trahison de Judas qui est opposée ici à l'attitude de Pierre: « ne vous ai-je pas choisis les douze, et l'un d'entre vous est un diable.»

Nous avons donc affaire en quelque sorte à un rapport triangulaire: Matt. 16 et Luc 22 s'accordent en ce qui concerne la prédiction du rôle prédominant de Pierre; Matt. 16 et Jean 6 s'accordent en ce qui concerne la confession de Pierre: Tu es le Fils (le Saint) de Dieu; Jean 6 et Luc 22 s'accordent en ce qui concerne la promesse de Pierre de suivre Jésus et en ce qui concerne le cadre de la scène, le dernier repas. La conclusion s'impose: à la base des trois récits, il y a comme *source commune* un récit appartenant à une tradition plus ancienne et dont nous pouvons indiquer les éléments suivants: lors du dernier repas (ou immédiatement après lui), Pierre dit à Jésus: Tu es le fils de Dieu, et lui promet de le suivre jusque dans la mort. Jesus lui répond que c'est Dieu qui lui a révélé le secret concernant sa personne, et il lui annonce son reniement, mais lui prédit en même temps qu'il aura une tâche particulière à remplir parmi ses frères qui tomberont dans la même tentation que lui.

Chacun des trois évangélistes, Matthieu, Luc et Jean, a fait un autre usage de cette vieille tradition, et c'est ainsi que s'expliquent les divergences. Nous reviendrons tout à l'heure sur le but particulier qu'a poursuivi Matthieu en cet endroit qui est le point de départ de la présente étude. Essayons d'abord d'expliquer les tendances de Luc et de l'évangile johannique. Luc a omis au chap. 22 la confession christologique de Pierre. C'est qu'à l'endroit où il a rapporté le récit de Marc 8:28–33, c'est -à-dire dans Luc 9:18 ss., il a supprimé la pointe du récit, la protestation de Pierre et l'ordre que lui adresse Jésus: Arrière de moi, Satan! Cette conclusion l'a manifestement choqué. Dans le récit ainsi tronqué, la déclaration de Pierre: tu es le Messie de Dieu, prend alors, contrairement à son sens primitif dans Marc. 8:27–33, le caractère d'une confession *légitime*. Ainsi Luc a pu se passer de la vraie confession à l'endroit (chap. 22) où il a rapporté le dernier entretien avec Pierre.

Pourquoi le quatrième évangéliste a-t-il omis la prédiction du rôle particulier que jouera Pierre parmi ses frères selon Matt. 16:18 s. et Luc 22:31 s.? Peut-être est-ce en rapport avec le fait que dans cet évangile il y a une certaine concurrence entre Pierre et le disciple bien aimé.

C'est seulement au chap. 21, ajouté à l'évangile johannique plus tard, qu'il est question dans le dialogue déjà mentionné, chap. 21:15 ss., de la mission de Pierre « pais mes brebis », dans un contexte tout analogue à celui que nous étudions en ce moment. Ici il n'y a pas vraiment concurrence, puisque les privilèges des deux disciples sont nettement délimités. Quoiqu'il en soit, nous pouvons ajouter ce passage Jean 21:15 ss. comme un quatrième témoin de l'ancienne tradition telle que nous l'avons reconstruite. En effet, l'auteur de Jean 21 doit l'avoir connue également. Car le dialogue entre Jésus et Pierre v. 15 ss. tout en se plaçant après la résurrection, est orienté dans le même sens et construit de façon à suggérer au lecteur le souvenir de cet autre récit qui joue du vivant de Jésus.

Quant à l'auteur du corps du quatrième évangile, le fait qu'au chap. 6:66 ss. il a utilisé cette vieille tradition se trouve encore confirmé par l'entrée en scène des douze qui en tant que groupe interviennent seulement à cet endroit de l'évangile johannique. Dans le reste de son livre, l'auteur ignore le schème des douze. Il y a des disciples très intimes, tels Natanael et Lazare, qui ne font pas partie des douze.[23] L'évangéliste les a introduits ici sous l'influence du récit qui lui a servi de base.

3

Il nous reste à voir pour quelle raison Matthieu a inséré cette vieille tradition dans le cadre du récit de Césarée de Philippe. Le contraste entre ces deux péricopes est tel qu'il est difficile d'admettre que l'évangéliste ne l'ait pas remarqué. Nous avions pensé autrefois que c'était un rapprochement plus ou moins superficiel qui l'aurait amené à combiner les deux récits, Pierre disant, dans l'un (à Césarée de Philippe), à Jésus qui il était; Jésus disant, dans l'autre, à Pierre qui il était.

Après avoir constaté cependant l'opposition christologique entre la proclamation diabolique du Messie par Pierre dans Marc. 8, et la confession du fils de Dieu, inspiré à Pierre par Dieu, nous ne pouvons plus croire que Matthieu ait vraiment méconnu le sens du récit de Marc. Il faut admettre plutôt qu'il y a eu *intention* de sa part: il veut corriger l'impression pénible que devait laisser le récit

de la scène de Marc 8 qu'il reproduit fidèlement et dans lequel
Pierre en proclamant Jésus Messie est le porte-parole du diable
pour imposer à Jésus le rôle politique du Messie juif et pour le
détourner de la voie de l'ebed Yahveh. Nous avons vu que Luc
a été choqué également par ce récit. Voilà pourquoi il l'a tronqué
en supprimant précisément l'essai de Pierre de tenter Jésus et la
parole si sévère de Jésus: « Arrière de moi, Satan! ». Matthieu a
reproduit le récit de Marc intégralement, mais en ce faisant, il a
tenu à lui juxtaposer immédiatement cet autre récit qu'il a trouvé
à un autre endroit de la tradition: la vraie confession de Pierre
proclamant Jésus fils de Dieu.

Ce rapprochement répondait d'autant plus à l'intention de
Matthieu que ce deuxième récit qui a pour cadre le dernier repas,
semble avoir mentionné lui aussi le *diable*, mais de manière à
montrer au contraire, Pierre se défendant et défendant ses frères
contre ses attaques. Ainsi dans Luc 22:31, Jésus dit: « Satan vous a
réclamés… ». Le quatrième évangile oppose Pierre qui confesse le
Saint de Dieu à Judas Iskariot qui est « un diable » (Jean 6:70).
D'après la variante que donne Matthieu du même récit, les
« portes de l'enfer ne prévaudront pas » contre le qehal que Jésus
bâtira sur Pierre le Roc. Alors que dans le récit de Césarée de
Philippe Pierre est l'instrument du diable, il est dans le récit de sa
confession lors du dernier repas, au contraire, celui qui malgré sa
défaillance au moment du reniement finira par triompher sur lui.
Ainsi Matthieu a pu rapporter sans hésitation la fin du récit de
Césarée de Philippe avec la parole si sévère de Jésus. En combinant
les deux récits, il rappelle implicitement que le dialogue de Césarée
de Philippe n'est pas le dernier mot. Il lui enlève par avance ce
qu'il peut avoir de choquant.

Les différences, en ce qui concerne la future mission de Pierre,
entre les deux variantes, celle de Luc 22 et celle de Matthieu 16 qui
est beaucoup plus développée, s'expliquent probablement par la
même préoccupation de Matthieu.[24] En vertu de la place représen-
tative qu'occupe Pierre parmi les disciples dans l'ensemble de
la tradition synoptique,[25] Matthieu a ainsi placé à cet endroit aussi
le logion de Jésus sur la signification du nom Kephas qui, selon
d'autres récits évangéliques,[26] a été conféré à Pierre à un autre
moment. Au point de vue de sa signification, cet épisode s'accorde
parfaitement avec la parole de Luc 22:31 ss. Il est d'ailleurs invrai-
semblable que le surnom « Roc » (Kephas) ait été donné à Pierre

seulement plus tard par la communauté primitive. Mais si c'est
Jésus qui l'a appelé ainsi, il doit en avoir donné l'explication.

En outre, Matthieu pouvait considérer comme légitime de
reproduire au même endroit les logia relatifs au fait de « lier » et
de « délier » qui appliqués à tous les disciples se trouvent dans
Matt. 18:18 et sous une forme différente dans Jean 20:23. Il est
conforme à la tradition synoptique que Pierre est, en toutes choses,
le porte-parole et le représentant des autres disciples, en bien et en
mal. Ici comme ailleurs, Matthieu a donc réuni des logia qui dans
la tradition antérieure étaient isolés ou répartis sur plusieurs récits
différents.

NOTES

[1] F. M. Braun, *Aspects nouveaux du problème de l'Eglise* (1942). Trad. alle-
mande: *Neues Licht auf die Kirche* (1946).

[2] *Der Quellort der Kirchenidee* (Festgabe für A. Harnack, 1921), 142 ss.

[3] *Die Kirche des Urchristentums* (Festgabe für Ad. Deissmann, 1927), 259 ss.;
id. TWNT 3 (1936), Art. ἐκκλησία. Trad. anglaise: *The Church* (*Bible Key
Words* from TWNT, 1950).

[4] *Pierre, disciple, apôtre, martyr* (1952).

[5] *S. Pierre*, 188; A. Oepke « Der Herrenspruch über die Kirche, Matt 16,
17–19, in der neuesten Forschung », *Studia Theologica* (1948/50), 111, note 1.

[6] Une thèse semblable, mais sur une base un peu différente, a été défendue
déjà par R. Liechtenhan, *Die urchristliche Mission* (1946), 9 ss. Il considère Luc
22:31 ss. comme la forme originale de Matt. 16:17 ss.

[7] *Der Rahmen der Geschichte Jesu* (1919).

[8] *Die Kirche des Urchristentums*, 283.

[9] *Ibid.*

[10] Défendue entre autres par H. J. Holtzmann, HKNT, 1, *ad loc.*

[11] K. L. Schmidt, *Die Kirche des Urchristentums*, 281, appelle cette thèse « zu
grobschlächtig, um ernst genommen zu werden ».

[12] P. 154 ss.

[13] Contrairement à ce que pense R. Bultmann, « Die Frage nach dem mes-
sianischen Bewusstsein Jesu und das Petrus-Bekenntnis » ZNTW (1919/20),
165 ss.

[14] O. Cullmann, *Der Staat im Neuen Testament* (1956); id., *Die Christologie des
Neuen Testaments* (1957; 2ᵉ éd. 1958), 111 ss.

[15] Cette thèse a été défendue surtout par E. Stauffer, « Zur Vor- und Frühgeschichte des *Primatus Petri* » *Zeitschrift für Kirchengeschichte* (1943–44), 1 ss.;
R. Bultmann, *Theologie des Neuen Testaments* (1953), 46; O. J. F. Seitz, « Upon
this Rock: A critical re-examination of Matt. 16:17–19 », JBL (1950), 329 ss.

[16] O. J. F. Seitz, *op. cit.*, 330, insiste sur cette différence de forme pour nier le
rapport entre les deux textes. Mais nous allons voir que cette différence qui

s'explique par la tendance particulière de Matthieu ne saurait infirmer notre thèse.

[17] Marc 14:26–31 rapporte seulement la prédiction du reniement. N'a-t-il pas connu la tradition qui réunit avec elle la prédiction du futur rôle de Pierre ? Dans ce cas, celle-ci tout en étant antérieure à Matthieu serait probablement plus récente que Marc.

[18] O. Cullmann, *Die Christologie des Neuen Testaments* (2ᵉ éd. 1958), 276 ss.

[19] *Die Christologie des Neuen Testaments*, 281 ss.

[20] À la deuxième partie: «personne ne connaît le Père si ce n'est le Fils, et celui à qui il (le Fils) veut le révéler», pourrait avoir correspondue primitivement la première partie sous une forme plus complète: « personne ne connaît le Fils si ce n'est le Père et celui à qui il (le Père) veut le révéler ». Les variantes attestées par l'histoire du texte pourraient expliquer le fait que dans la première partie le second membre de phrase soit tombé.

[21] Meyer, 10. éd. (1910), *ad loc.*

[22] Jean 10:36; Luc 1:32, 35. Voir O. Cullmann, *Die Christologie des Neuen Testaments*, 292.

[23] Ce fait est en rapport avec la question de l'auteur qui semble avoir appartenu lui-même à un milieu différent de celui des douze.

[24] Ainsi les objections formulées par O. J. F. Seitz, *op. cit.*, contre le rapprochement entre Luc 22:31 ss. et Matt. 16:17 ss. tombent.

[25] *S. Pierre*, 19 ss.

[26] *S. Pierre*, 14 ss.

THE PRIMITIVE CATECHISM AND THE SAYINGS OF JESUS

by

C. H. DODD

THE critic of the Gospels, however 'objective' he seeks to be, can hardly get on without some presuppositions, however hypothetical and tentative. I may as well say at once, therefore, that I start with the presupposition that the community which claimed Jesus as its founder is likely to have preserved some memory of what he taught. That they may sometimes have misremembered, or misunderstood, what he said, or deliberately paraphrased[1] or expanded it to make it more intelligible or more 'contemporary', that they may even in honest error have fathered upon him things he had not said, is likely enough. But the presupposition to which I have confessed seems on general grounds more probable than the assumption (which appears often to be made tacitly) that the early Christians had forgotten, within a generation, almost everything that Jesus had said, and found themselves obliged to think up maxims to meet the needs of their changing circumstances, maxims which they then attributed (in all reverence, no doubt) to 'the Lord'. If however the early Church did treasure the memory of sayings of Jesus, the attempt to recover them is a legitimate enterprise, and the criticism of the Gospels, with the examination of the tradition that lies behind them and the *Sitz im Leben* of various elements in it, has the ultimate purpose (over and above any light it may throw on the early history of the Church) of working back to a point as near as we can hope to get to what Jesus actually said. This purpose may be served by the attempt to identify, as far as possible, the channels through which the sayings may have been transmitted, in order to estimate the extent to which the accuracy of the report may be trusted, or, on the other hand, its content may have been subject to modifying influences.

There has in recent years been much inquisition after such channels of transmission, especially with the aid of the methods of form-criticism, and not without valuable results; but it may be worth while going over some of the ground once more.

It is natural to assume that the sayings of Jesus were recalled to serve the purpose of instruction in the principles of Christian belief and practice. Indeed, that is perhaps a glimpse of the obvious. In itself it does not get us very far, for our direct knowledge of methods of instruction in the early Church is limited, and the argument does not always avoid the danger of slipping into a circle. In one department, however, I think we may now say that we have at any rate a little solid knowledge: I mean the elementary instruction given to candidates for admission to the Church as preparation for their baptism, commonly described as *catechesis*. I would refer in particular to the work of the Archbishop of Quebec[2] and Dr. E. G. Selwyn[3] on catechetical material in the Epistles. They have, I believe, laid down lines on which it is possible to envisage what the former calls the Primitive Catechism—fragmentarily, no doubt, but as something that one can work with. In order to do so it is not necessary to accept all the details of their ingenious reconstructions. But I believe we are entitled to assume that forms of teaching of the kind envisaged were traditional during the New Testament period. Assuming that, I raise the question, Is this the kind of thing which served as channel for the transmission of the sayings of Jesus? And I shall try by 'sampling' to suggest an answer.

In the first place we may recall that we have evidence for the beginnings, at any rate, of some traditional scheme of teaching at a very early date. Already in what is probably the earliest extant Christian document, Paul's First Epistle to the Thessalonians, we find references to a 'tradition' (2:13, 4:1–8; 2 Thess. 2:15, 3:6) which the recipients of the letter had received from the apostles. As they were Christians of no more than a few weeks' standing, we may take it that the writer is recalling teaching which he had given either as *catechesis* in the strict sense, or at any rate as elementary instruction for new converts. The following topics are either expressly stated or necessarily implied to have formed part of this fundamental instruction: (i) theological dogmas: monotheism and the repudiation of idolatry; Jesus the Son of God; His resurrection and second advent; salvation from the Wrath (1:9–10); the calling of the Church into the kingdom and glory of God (2:12); (ii) ethical precepts (παραγγελίαι, i.e. 'marching orders', 4:2, 11, cf. 2 Thess. 3:6, 10, 12): the holiness of the Christian calling; repudiation of pagan vices; the law of charity (4:3-9); eschatological motives (5:2: note αὐτοὶ ἀκριβῶς οἴδατε—this is among the things they have already learnt).

So much is clearly the minimum content of the παράδοσις. That it actually contained more than this there can be little doubt. In particular, the injunctions regarding Church order and discipline in 5:12-22 are given with an allusive brevity which would be more in place in recalling maxims already familiar than in breaking fresh ground. In 2 Thess. 3:7-10 similar injunctions are expressly said to have been given previously (τὴν παράδοσιν ἣν παρελάβετε ... ὅτε ἦμεν πρὸς ὑμᾶς τοῦτο παρηγγέλλομεν ὑμῖν — note the imperfect tense of continuous or habitual action).[4] And it is noteworthy that under this head the mutual duties of members of the Church expand into universal social duties (πάντοτε τὸ ἀγαθὸν διώκετε εἰς ἀλλήλους καὶ εἰς πάντας, 1 Thess. 5:15), which may have been specified in the actual teaching. Similarly, we must suppose that a good deal of the eschatological *paraenesis* in 5:3-10 comes under the rubric, ἀκριβῶς οἴδατε, although these words apply directly only to the content of 5:2.

We see already emerging a 'pattern of teaching' (τύπος διδαχῆς, Rom. 6:17), the general lines of which appear in other epistles. Omitting for our present purpose the properly theological portions, we may set out the table of contents somewhat as follows:

A. The holiness of the Christian calling.

B. The repudiation of pagan vices, leading up to—

C. The assertion of the Christian law of charity (ἀγάπη, including φιλαδελφία).

D. Eschatological motives.

E. The order and discipline of the Church: duties of its members to one another; [social duties at large].

These topics tend to reappear in combination in the 'ethical section' of various epistles. Even the long and comprehensive outline of Christian ethics in Rom. 12-13 follows with little divergence the plan of the παραγγελίαι of 1 Thessalonians. Starting with the holiness of the Christian calling (A), here under the figure of sacrifice (12:1-2), the writer moves on to the theme of the unity of the Church and the functions of its members (E) (12:3-8); then comes a long section applying the law of charity (C) to Christian conduct within the community (φιλαδελφία, 12:10-16) and to social duties in general (12:17-13:7), and subsuming it all once again under the law of charity (13:8-10); he then finishes with a section of eschatological *paraenesis* (D),[5] in terms closely similar in part to those of 1 Thess. 5:2-10. Only the section on the repudiation of pagan vices is missing, and this theme has been dismissed in ch. I.

It is not necessary here to trace the pattern in other epistles, where it has been amply studied. But it is noteworthy that it still underlies the detailed manual of instruction known as 'The Teaching of the Lord through the Twelve Apostles' (commonly referred to as *Didache*). There is nothing indeed expressly corresponding with section A, on the holiness of the Christian calling, but the contrast between pagan vices and the Christian law of charity (B, C) is here, only in reverse order, in the passage on the Two Ways (1-6). The familiar list of vices in 5 leaves no doubt where it belongs. There follows an elaborate section on Church order and discipline (D), (7-15). It contains a great deal for which earlier examples of the τύπος διδαχῆς found no place, including liturgical matter, but in the less specialized sections familiar turns of phrase are frequent enough to arrest the attention of the reader who has earlier writings in mind. Finally we have a passage which combines apocalyptic prediction with *paraenesis* (D) in the traditional manner (16). The *Didache* is of course not a 'catechism' in the proper sense, but it comprises a large amount of catechetical material, some of it closely akin to passages in the epistles, and it gives evidence of the long persistence of a pattern once established.

It is indeed the pattern itself which is the constant element. There is not sufficient evidence of a complete documentary catechism from which various writers might be supposed to quote. All that we are entitled to infer is a kind of programme or schedule of instruction, which could be filled in and expanded orally, no doubt, in various ways. Nevertheless, in passages which we may suppose to be following the established pattern we frequently discern a common style, and this style is often in contrast with the habitual style of the author concerned.[6] We may take it to be the style of early Christian *catechesis*. It has analogues in the style of the Jewish Wisdom literature, and of documents like the *Testaments of the Twelve Patriarchs* and the *Manual of Discipline* from

Qumran, and also in Jewish-Hellenistic propaganda-literature such as that of the pseudo-Phocylides. On the other side it has some resemblance to the style of Greek gnomic writers.[7] Agreeably with these indications from style we note that in form and often in content the early Christian *catechesis* has clear points of contact both with forms used in the admission of proselytes to Judaism,[8] on the one hand, and, on the other hand, with popular Stoic teaching. That is to say, it bears traces of precisely those influences which we should expect to have helped to mould the practice of the new community as it first grew up in a Jewish environment and then moved out into the Graeco-Roman world, following largely in the tracks of Jewish-Hellenistic missionaries. If we are to conjecture a date for the more or less definite fixing of the pattern, we should be led, it seems, to the earliest period in which Greek-speaking converts from paganism began to enter the Church in such numbers that the need for a standardized *catechesis* became pressing. This period might perhaps begin with the rise of a Gentile Christianity at Antioch, and, as we have seen, the ethical παράδοσις was already in existence at any rate by the time of Paul's visit to Thessalonica, A.D. 49.

The way in which the content of these largely inherited forms was transformed by distinctively Christian motives I have tried to illustrate elsewhere.[9] The question before us here is a different one. Granted that we have a not inadequate general picture of the forms of catechetical instruction employed in the early Church during its formative period, can these be related to the teaching of Jesus as presented in the Gospels in such a way that they may reasonably be regarded as a channel through which His sayings were transmitted during the period of oral tradition before the Gospels were written?

The first general observation that occurs is that the pattern of teaching almost always includes a passage, which tends to be placed at the end, appealing to eschatological motives for Christian conduct, and that in the Gospels eschatological *paraenesis* holds a similar place. In all three Synoptics the report of the teaching of Jesus closes with the Eschatological Discourse, which has its equivalent in portions of the Farewell Discourses in the Fourth Gospel.[10] It is a probable inference that the traditional order of *catechesis* determined, to this extent at least, the arrangement of material in the Gospels.

Moreover, traces of its influence are perhaps not confined to the composition of the Gospels as a final product, but are to be found also in some of their constituent parts, which may point to earlier sources constructed on a similar plan.

The Great Sermon, in its Matthaean form, ends on an eschatological note. The reference in Matt. 7:22 to ἐκείνη ἡ ἡμέρα makes it clear that this evangelist at least understood these sayings in an eschatological sense, and that he took the storm and floods of the parable of the Two Builders as symbols of the coming Judgment. With this clue, it is possible to suspect a wider influence of the general pattern in the structure of the Sermon as a whole. The Beatitudes, with the sayings immediately following (5:3-16), may be regarded as an equivalent for the section on the holiness of the Christian calling (A). Then comes a long section in which, as in sections B and C, the new Christian way is contrasted with the old ways which the convert is leaving (5:17-48). Like the *catechesis*, it culminates in the statement of the Christian law of charity, but where the *catechesis* contrasts the Christian way with the vices of paganism, the Sermon points the contrast with the casuistry of scribal Judaism. The next section of the Sermon (6:1-18) deals with almsgiving, fasting and prayer (corporate prayer, since the model provided is in the first person plural), and this would readily fall into the section (E) about Church order and discipline, to which also the sayings about pearls before swine (7:6) and about false prophets (7:15-20) might reasonably be assigned. Both of these themes, as well as those of prayer and fasting, are integral parts of the corresponding section in the *Didache* (8, 9:5, 11:3-5). The intervening sections of the Sermon fall outside the common pattern.

In the Lucan form of the Sermon it is much more difficult to discern traces of the catechetical scheme. Here the Beatitudes (with their balancing Woes) no longer have the character which they show in Matthew.[11] The Christian law of charity is stated, but without the contrast with the old ways. The saying about the tree and its fruit (6:43-4) is given without the application to false prophets which it has in Matthew, and so loses its relevance to Church discipline. The saying about those who say 'Lord, Lord' is given without its eschatological setting.[12] The parable of the Two Builders similarly has no expressly eschatological reference.

When source analysis has done all it can do, the relation between the Matthaean and the Lucan forms of the Sermon remains enigmatic. It seems, however, not too rash to infer that the Matthaean form has been influenced at some stage by a form of catechetical instruction, if it is not based upon it. If so, it must have been a Jewish-Christian form, for the Hellenistic element which we have noted in the *catechesis* of the epistles is entirely absent from the Sermon, and paganism is not in view. Whether the First Evangelist made use of a pre-existing document based upon a form of Jewish-Christian catechism, or being himself familiar with some such form, organized his material on its pattern, the *catechesis* in some form seems to have served as a vehicle for the transmission of part at least of the material comprised in the Sermon.

Although the Lucan version of the Sermon thus appears to retain little of the traditional form of *catechesis*, some of the material embodied in the Matthaean Sermon occurs in a different context in Luke (12:22–34), where it leads up at once to a passage which has much in common with the Eschatological Discourse (12:35–46), as well as with the eschatological section (D) of the common form of *catechesis*. That we may have traces here of an earlier source (whether documentary or oral) which followed the traditional order of the *catechesis*, and ended with a piece of eschatological *paraenesis*, is a not unreasonable conjecture. If so, it has become disintegrated through combination with extraneous material.

So far we have been concerned only with the form and sequence of the *catechesis* as they reappear in the Gospels. We may now inquire how far the contents show significant points of similarity in language or substance. Here again we turn to the eschatological section. The main burden of this section in the *catechesis* is the attitude and conduct demanded of the Christian in view of the fact that the End is near but its date uncertain: τὸ τέλος ἤγγικεν (1 Pet. 4:7), ἡ παρουσία τοῦ κυρίου ἤγγικεν (Jas. 5:8), ἡ ἡμέρα ἤγγικεν (Rom. 13:12), ἡμέρα κυρίου ὡς κλέπτης ἔρχεται (1 Thess. 5:2), and the like. The 'Day of the Lord' tends to be thought of as the dawn coming to end the night, and this brings in the antitheses of light and darkness, sleep and wakefulness, drunkenness and sobriety, which are found in Jewish contexts but are also especially beloved of Hellenistic moralists.[13] The recurrent key-words are ἐξ ὕπνου ἐγερθῆναι, γρηγορεῖν, ἀγρυπνεῖν,[14] νήφειν, σωφρονεῖν, in James μακροθυμεῖν. A note of mili-

tancy is not far below the surface: in 1 Thess. 5:8 the call for
wakefulness and sobriety suggests the armed Christian warrior;
in Rom. 13:12, similarly, since dawn is at hand the Christian must
put on τὰ ὅπλα τοῦ φωτός; in 1 Pet. 5:8–9 νήψατε γρηγορήσατε is
followed by the call to resist (ἀντιστῆναι) the devil, 'armed',
perhaps, with the mind of Christ (τὴν αὐτὴν ἔννοιαν ὁπλίσασθε,
4:1). In 1 Pet. 4:7 the idea of wakefulness or sobriety in view of
the nearness of the End is specifically associated with prayer:
πάντων δὲ τὸ τέλος ἤγγικεν · σωφρονήσατε οὖν καὶ νήψατε εἰς
προσευχάς. In Ephesians, where explicit eschatology is only faintly
present, the whole of the eschatological *paraenesis* is reduced to an
eloquent passage upon the Christian warfare against the powers of
darkness (6:10–17). The picture of the Christian warrior equipped
with the πανοπλία τοῦ θεοῦ is reminiscent of the strongly eschatological passage in 1 Thess. 5:7–9, but more elaborate. The exhortation to sleepless vigilance, which is in itself entirely germane to
the military imagery, is here, as in 1 Pet. 4:7, associated with
prayer: προσευχόμενοι ἐν παντὶ καιρῷ ἐν πνεύματι καὶ εἰς αὐτὸ
ἀγρυπνοῦντες ἐν πάσῃ προσκαρτερήσει (6:18). In the corresponding
passage of Colossians (4:2–3) the exhortation to perseverance and
wakefulness is again associated with prayer, but it has lost even its
vestigial connection with eschatology, occurring in a context
which has more affinity with the section on Church order in
1 Thess. 5:12–22 (note ἀδιαλείπτως προσεύχεσθε, 5:17).[15] It is
perhaps significant that when all the rest of the eschatological
paraenesis has faded out, γρηγορεῖτε, ἀγρυπνεῖτε remains as its permanent legacy to the Christian moral ideal.

We now turn to the Gospels, and primarily to the Eschatological Discourse which concludes the report of the teaching of
Jesus. The burden of the *paraenesis* here is closely similar to that
of the eschatological section of the *catechesis*, and its style, though
not identical, is sufficiently similar, and sufficiently unlike the prevailing style of some other parts of the Gospels, to warrant the
belief that some relation existed between them at an early stage
in the formation of the tradition.

Here again the motive for conduct is found in the nearness of
the End and the uncertainty of its date, which should lead the
Christian to be wakeful and alert: ἐγγύς ἐστιν ἐπὶ θύραις . . .
ἀγρυπνεῖτε, οὐκ οἴδατε γὰρ πότε ὁ καιρός ἐστιν . . . γρηγορεῖτε οὖν
. . . πᾶσιν λέγω, γρηγορεῖτε (Mark 13:29, 33, 37,); γρηγορεῖτε οὖν

I

ὅτι οὐκ οἴδατε τὴν ἡμέραν οὐδὲ τὴν ὥραν (Matt. 25:13); and the like. As the various forms of *catechesis* call for μακροθυμία under trial, and for 'armed' resistance in the spiritual conflict, so the Eschatological Discourse calls for ὑπομονή to the end (Mark 13:13, Luke 21:19).

In the Lucan form of the Discourse a passage (21:34–6) is introduced which has a striking likeness to the language of eschatological *paraenesis* in the catechetical sections of the epistles, chiefly of 1 Thessalonians:

Προσέχετε δὲ ἑαυτοῖς	
μήποτε βαρηθῶσιν ὑμων αἱ καρδίαι	
ἐν κραιπάλῃ¹⁶ καὶ μέθῃ καὶ μερίμναις βιωτικαῖς,	Cf. 1 Thess. 5:7
καὶ ἐπιστῇ ἐφ᾽ ὑμᾶς αἰφνίδιος ἡ ἡμέρα ἐκείνη . . .	Cf. 1 Thess. 5:3
ἀγρυπνεῖτε δὲ ἐν παντὶ καιρῷ δεόμενοι . . .	Cf. Eph. 6:18,
	1 Pet. 4:7
ἵνα κατίσχυσητε ἐκφυγεῖν ταῦτα πάντα . . .	Cf. 1 Thess. 5:3
καὶ σταθῆναι ἔμπροσθεν τοῦ υἱοῦ τοῦ ἀνθρώπου	Cf. Eph. 6:13

It is improbable that the evangelist was drawing upon the epistles for his material; but if he was (as I have suggested) following the general arrangement of a common form of *catechesis*, its language too may well have been in his mind.¹⁷ It is noteworthy that the language here belongs more particularly to the Hellenistic strain in the early *catechesis*. Here, then, there is good reason to suppose that the primitive catechism, in serving as a vehicle for transmitting the teaching of Jesus, has influenced the language of the sayings.

In the same passage of 1 Thessalonians which contains these striking parallels with Luke, the unexpectedness of the End is expressed in the terms: ἡμέρα κυρίου ὡς κλέπτης ἐν νυκτὶ οὕτως ἔρχεται. The image fits in well with the sustained imagery of day and night, sleeping and waking, which pervades the passage. Yet it directly recalls a parable which occurs as part of the Eschatological Discourse in Matthew (24:43–4), and in a passage of Luke which I have conjectured to represent the eschatological conclusion of a sequence which he derived from some earlier source (12:39). Are we to say that this also passed out of the *catechesis* into the tradition of the sayings of Jesus? No one, surely, would seriously contend that the parable, with its characteristically swift and vivid evocation of a situation in real life, is secondary, and the passing simile in 1 Thess. 5:2—one of a series of rhetorical figures running through the passage—primary. It is a curious fact that in the Lucan form of the parable there is nothing about night or about wakefulness: εἰ ᾔδει ὁ οἰκοεπότης ποίᾳ ὥρᾳ ὁ κλέπτης ἔρχεται, οὐκ ἂν ἀφῆκεν διορυχθῆναι τὸν οἶκον αὐτοῦ. So far as we are told, the raid might have taken place either by night or by day; ὥρα would serve for either. The householder may have been at fault, not in falling asleep, but in going from home without providing protection for his property. The moral is not, 'Keep awake', but simply, 'Be prepared': γίνεσθε ἕτοιμοι, ὅτι ᾗ ὥρᾳ οὐ δοκεῖτε ὁ υἱὸς τοῦ ἀνθρώπου ἔρχεται. It is Matthew here who has introduced the terms φυλακή (implying night) for ὥρα, and ἐγρηγόρησεν ἄν, and so associated the parable with the *paraenesis* about night and day, sleeping and waking. It appears that these traits may have crept in from the *catechesis*. Yet as regards the substance of the matter we cannot doubt that the Gospel parable has priority.

If so, it would follow that even where the evangelists seem to be following the catechetical pattern as a general guide, they were acquainted also with a tradition of the sayings of Jesus which had been transmitted (by whatever channel) independently of the τύπος διδαχῆς. Little, in fact, of the rich and varied material embodied in the Eschatological Discourse by the several evangelists could plausibly be derived directly from the catechetical instruction as we know it from the epistles. Its style for the most part is widely different. But it may well be that material transmitted by other channels was used to illustrate and enforce articles of the *catechesis*. Thus when the teacher reached the point at which he must deal with themes falling under the catch-heading, τὸ τέλος ἤγγικεν · γρηγορεῖτε, he might introduce prophetic words or parables of Jesus for which he must have been indebted to a richer strain of tradition. Sometimes the saying or parable might be absorbed into the form of *catechesis*, losing in the process something of its characteristic stamp, like the parable of the Thief in 1 Thess. 5:2. At other times the parable itself might get a twist to make it fit a 'moral' derived from the *catechesis*; and that would explain how certain parables—the 'eschatological' parables in particular—have (as I believe) suffered a certain shift of meaning in transmission.[18]

No general conclusion could legitimately be drawn without a

much fuller examination of the material, but the 'samples' we have
taken seem, so far as they go, to point to some such conclusion as
this: the catechetical instruction of the early Church was largely
based upon earlier models, partly Jewish, partly Hellenistic. It was
moulded by distinctively Christian motives partly drawn from the
teaching of Jesus as it was remembered at an early date.[19] It was
a convenient framework within which remembered sayings of
Jesus could be organized for teaching purposes, and so provided
an occasion for preserving the sayings rather than the means by
which they were preserved. In any case it does not appear to be
the main channel through which the tradition came down, but
presupposes an independent tradition upon which it could draw,
and by which it was influenced, while it also exerted a reciprocal
influence. The extent to which the catechetical scheme could ab-
sorb sayings of Jesus is illustrated by those sections of the *Didache*
in which the formula of the 'Two Ways' is filled out with adapta-
tions of sayings of Jesus which are otherwise known to us from the
Gospels, though there is no need to suppose that our written
Gospels were a source for the *Didache*. The other side, the influence of the *catechesis* on the Gospels, would evidently repay further
examination, but it was limited.

NOTES

[1] The sayings were in any case translated; and intelligent translation without
any element of paraphrase is, as experience shows, a difficult thing.

[2] P. Carrington, *The Primitive Christian Catechism*.

[3] E. G. Selwyn, *The First Epistle of St. Peter*, Essay II, 363–466.

[4] I see no sufficient reason for rejecting the evidence of 2 Thessalonians. The
objections to Pauline authorship have no great weight, if we allow for the
probability that in 2:6–10 we have material drawn from some Christian prophecy or apocalypse. If however the non-Pauline turns of phrase suggest a different authorship, Silvanus, after all, is named in the superscription, even though
it is Paul who signs at the end.

[5] In Romans the eschatological section concludes the catechetical material
(for ch. 14 belongs to a different category). In 1 Thess., as we have seen, it
precedes the section on Church order. But in that epistle Paul had special
reasons for including fresh teaching (οὐ θέλομεν ὑμᾶς ἀγνοεῖν, 4:13) upon
eschatology, and he has appended to it a reminder of teaching already known,
before going on to Church order. In James, as in 1 Thess. a section of eschatological *paraenesis* (5:7–9) precedes a passage relating to discipline and practice
in the Church (5:13–16). In 1 Peter there are two sequences of catechetical
material; in the first, a brief piece of eschatological *paraenesis* (4:7) is sandwiched

between the repudiation of pagan vices (4:3–6) and the affirmation of the law of ἀγάπη (4:8–9), which in turn is followed by a section on Church order; in the second, the characteristic injunctions associated with eschatological *paraenesis* follow the section on Church order, and virtually close the epistle (5:6–9). In Ephesians the passage corresponding with the eschatological *paraenesis* forms the virtual close of the epistle (6:10–18). In the *Didache* there is a full-scale eschatological section at the end. It is evident that the sequence of sections varies, but the eschatological section tends to gravitate to the close of the *catechesis*.

⁶ I have illustrated this in *Gospel and Law*, 17–20.

⁷ See H. Chadwick, *The Sententiae of Sextus* (TS., new series, no. 5), introduction.

⁸ See D. Daube, 'A Baptismal Catechism', in *The New Testament and Rabbinic Judaism*, 106–40.

⁹ In *Gospel and Law*, 25–45.

¹⁰ See my *Interpretation of the Fourth Gospel*, 390–6.

¹¹ See my essay on the Beatitudes in *Mélanges Bibliques rédigés en l'honneur de André Robert* (1957).

¹² Though the eschatological sayings accompanying it were known to Luke in another version, see p. 112.

¹³ See my book *The Bible and the Greeks*, 187–91.

¹⁴ The meaning of these two verbs is substantially the same. The shade of meaning is perhaps something like that between 'to keep awake' and 'to be sleepless': 'αγουπνία is insomnia. Neither means 'to watch' in the modern sense of that term, which is either θεωρεῖν, or παρατηρεῖν, φυλάττειν, or the like.

¹⁵ Prayer, along with fasting, comes in the section on Church order and discipline in the *Didache* (viii), and so also, as I have suggested (p. 111) in the *catechesis* behind the Sermon on the Mount. There is in Colossians no section properly devoted to Church order; in Ephesians it is represented, but of normal sequence, by 4:1–16.

¹⁶ Cf. *Corp. Herm.* vii. 27: νήψατε, παύσασθε κραιπαλῶντες, and see my *Parables of the Kingdom*, p. 157.

¹⁷ Note that Luke has here introduced the association of prayer with the wakefulness, endurance and steadfastness required of the Christian in view of the critical situation. In the epistles, as we have seen, this association is peculiar to Ephesians, Colossians and 1 Peter. But it is far more impressively and memorably affirmed in a passage of the Gospels which ostensibly does not belong to the record of the teaching of Jesus, Mark 14:38: γρηγορεῖτε καὶ προσεύχεσθε. The passage is an organic part of the Passion narrative. Yet Mark was probably not unaware of its didactic value, or of its aptness to the theme of sleeping and waking in the *catechesis*. I would suggest that we have here an instance of the reciprocal influence between the *catechesis* and other branches of the tradition, to which I point in the conclusion of this essay, p. 115. The constant emphasis on the duty of wakefulness helped to keep in memory this element in the story of the Passion of the Lord: that at the crisis of His fate his disciples were in fact asleep. The words which Jesus was remembered to have addressed to them, with reference to the immediate crisis which was upon them, were adapted by Luke (or his source) to the expected crisis of the second advent, and they also passed into the *catechesis* in some of its forms, where the association of wakefulness with

prayer proved, it seems, more durable than its association with the expectation of the approaching End.

[18] See *Parables of the Kingdom*, 154–74.

[19] Partly also, and perhaps more importantly, by motives drawn directly from the central truths of the Gospel as embodied in the *kerygma*. See *Gospel and Law*, 25–45.

SON OF MAN—*FORSCHUNG* SINCE
'THE TEACHING OF JESUS'[1]

by

A. J. B. HIGGINS

A COMPLETE survey of the bewildering mass of material on the Son of Man problem which has been produced during the quarter of a century since the publication of Professor Manson's book is impossible here. In the far from easy task of selection some names and even some not insignificant contributions to the subject have perforce been omitted. What is attempted is a sketch of the main lines of discussion of a topic which has been uppermost in my mind since my interest in it was first aroused by Dr. Manson's book and by his lectures in the Faculty of Theology in Manchester University—a topic to which I hope to return on a later occasion. Much less is it within the scope of this paper to review the progress of the debate on the whole problem of the eschatological teaching of Jesus, of which the Son of Man question, however important in itself, is but an integral part.[2] A few remarks will suffice. Schweitzer's 'thorough-going' (*konsequent*) eschatology, which he still retains (see his introduction to the third edition (1954) of *The Quest of the Historical Jesus*) has been revived by M. Werner in *Die Entstehung des christlichen Dogmas* (1941, 2nd edn., 1954; Eng. trans. (in a shortened form), *The Formation of Christian Dogma* (1957)), who is opposed by W. Michaelis in *Der Herr verzieht nicht die Verheissung* (1942), especially pp. 58 ff. To the latter should now be added H. Schuster's important article, 'Die konsequente Eschatologie in der Interpretation des neuen Testaments, kritisch betrachtet', ZNTW 47 (1956), 1–25. The whole question is fully discussed by W. G. Kümmel in *Promise and Fulfilment* (1957). Even C. H. Dodd (in *The Coming of Christ* (1951)) has modified his earlier thesis of 'realized eschatology' by allowing for the parousia of the Son of

Man (beyond history) and by distinguishing this from the resurrection as an event within history.[3]

Dr. Manson followed up his now well-known examination of
the Son of Man sayings in the Synoptic Gospels in *The Teaching
of Jesus* (211 ff., 263 ff.) with *Son of Man* (1950) and with a summary of his conclusions in *The Servant-Messiah* (1953), 72–4, on
which the following outline, with some use of his own language,
is based.

(1) ' "Son of man" is a symbol, an apocalyptic counter.'

(2) 'Jesus took it from the book of Daniel. We have good
evidence that he knew of the Danielic Son of man, and no reason
to think that he knew of any other.'

(3) In Daniel 'Son of Man' is not a Messiah but a symbol for
' "the people of the saints of the Most High", who are to receive
the coming kingdom.'

(4) 'The "receiving of the kingdom" is a comprehensive term
for the vindication of Israel and the fulfilment of the promises
made to the dynasty of David. The "people of the saints of the
Most High" is the actualization in history of the Israelite ideal.
So the Son of man idea in Daniel links the Davidic hope to the
Israelite ideal.'

(5) The answer of Jesus to the questions: 'How does the kingdom come to the Son of man? and, What is the Israelite ideal?'
is to define Son of man in terms of the Deutero-Isaianic Servant
of the Lord.

(6) This definition is worked out especially in the Son of man
sayings, in 'the closely parallel sayings on the task of the disciples',
and in the ministry of Jesus.

(7) Not only the Messiah but Israel, or a believing remnant
within Israel, must be the Servant.

(8) The Messiah is the embodiment not only of the Israelite
ideal, but of the true Israel. Here the Hebrew conception of corporate personality and of oscillation[4] between the pluralistic and
individualistic understandings of the social group makes possible
'the transition from Son of man as a name for the people of the
saints of the Most High to Son of man as a messianic title'.

(9) 'The kingdom of God is *God's* kingdom', and it has come
to Israel in Jesus as the realization of the Israelite ideal.

The salient points then are: (*a*) The Son of Man in the Gospels
is of apocalyptic origin; (*b*) Jesus derived the term and its meaning

from the book of Daniel; (*c*) the Danielic figure is a corporate one; (*d*) Jesus understood Son of Man in terms of the suffering Servant; (*e*) the Son of Man in the Gospels is a corporate as well as an individual conception.

A preliminary question, however, is that of the origin of the Son of Man conception in Judaism. In a sense this may be regarded as lying outside the problem of the significance of the figure in the Synoptic Gospels, especially if the non-apocalyptic view of its provenance is adopted. But the question of ultimate origins is also strictly irrelevant if Dr. Manson's opinion is followed that there is 'no reason to think that he [Jesus] knew of any other' Son of Man than the Danielic.[5] If, however, a wider view is adopted, the two questions are intimately connected: it is possible that Jesus was influenced by current Jewish ideas of the Son of Man which retained, though in a considerably modified form, the marks of their foreign origin.

Bousset, von Gall, Gressmann, Reitzenstein and others have found the ultimate source of the Son of Man in oriental and Hellenistic conceptions of the *Urmensch, Anthropos,* or primordial man, particularly in its Gnostic form of the Redeemer. Among recent surveys may be mentioned those of H. L. Jansen,[6] W. Manson,[7] and especially S. Mowinckel who provides copious references to the vast literature.[8] The last named holds that the fact that the *Anthropos* in most Gnostic systems has 'acquired a certain element of the eschatological redeemer' is due to his having already assumed this role in certain circles of Persian religion, and with earlier scholars points especially to the Gayomartian sect (p. 429). R. Bultmann, the indefatigable champion of the theory of pervasive Gnostic influence in Christianity, attributes the Christian Redeemer-conception to Gnosticism.[9] But the Gnostic texts found at Nag Hammadi in 1945 suggest that such ideas may need at least some revision: there is no 'pre-Christian Gnostic redeemer' in the mid-second-century *Gospel of Truth* (edited by M. Malinine, H. C. Puech and G. Quispel as *Evangelium Veritatis* (1956)). G. Quispel writes: 'There would appear to be good grounds for supposing that it was from Christianity that the conception of redemption and the figure of the Redeemer were taken over into Gnosticism. A pre-Christian redeemer and an Iranian mystery of redemption perhaps never existed.'[10] Further, he believes the texts show that Gnostic speculations about the

Heavenly Man are traceable to heterodox Jewish traditions about Adam. Certainly the idea of the Man was not strange to Judaism with its belief in the creation of man in the divine image.[11] But it would be as unwise to over-emphasize the importance of Judaism as it would that of Christianity.[12]

Another aspect of the problem is the relationship between the Son of Man and the Messiah. Mowinckel sharply distinguishes the derivation of the Son of Man from the oriental *Urmensch* and that of the Messiah from the Israelite adaptation of oriental kingship: the Son of Man is not connected with the king. A. Bentzen[13] represented a different school of thought and found a closer connection in the Old Testament between the two figures than Mowinckel does. He pointed to Gen. 1 and Ps. 8 as parallels, and in Ps. 8 (also Ps. 80:18) the king is called Son of Man. H. Riesenfeld,[14] with Bonsirven and Küppers, conflates the Son of Man and the Messiah, asserting that the differences between them are often exaggerated at the expense of the similarities. Mowinckel answers Riesenfeld's view that the transcendent and divine features of the Son of Man are derived, like those of the Messiah, from oriental royal ideology, in *He That Cometh*, 467.

A. Feuillet[15] has taken a completely different line by attempting to account for the Jewish Son of Man figure (as it appears in Daniel) without recourse to foreign influence. He describes the figure as a kind of visible manifestation of the invisible divine glory in human form like that in Ezek. 1:26, by which it is influenced (p. 187), and as the result of the influence of sapiential literature on the prophetic conception of the Messiah through the divine hypostasis Wisdom. This hypothesis of 'sapiential Messianism' is examined by J. Coppens and rejected:[16] the figure of Wisdom is too closely bound up with the being of God to be a prototype of the Son of Man, who is distinct from God.

T. F. Glasson, who deprecates the *Urmensch* and similar theories, finds the origin of the Son of Man figure in Dan. 7 in the very similar vision of Enoch in 1 En. 14.[17] He does not mean to suggest that the writer of Dan. 7 made the identification with Enoch, but he points to the identification of the Son of Man and Enoch in 1 En. 71.

The *Similitudes of Enoch* (1 En. 37–71) show, in the opinion of many scholars, that in the time of Jesus certain Jewish apocalyptic circles cherished hopes in the coming of a Son of Man, a celestial figure, to deliver the righteous (Israelites) and to execute judgment on the wicked. Whatever view is adopted about the origin of this conception and the body of ideas bound up with it, various opinions have been held as to the indebtedness of Jesus to them.

There are still occasional attempts to support the hypothesis that Jesus owed little or nothing to apocalyptic and that his use of the title Son of Man is based primarily on Ezekiel.[18] Pierson Parker[19] holds that the title as used by Jesus (and his predecessors) 'carried no messianic implication at all', was drawn from Old Testament passages other than Dan. 7:13, such as Dan. 8:17 and numerous occurrences in Ezekiel where Son of Man simply means 'man', and denotes prophetic leadership. According to W. A. Curtis (*Jesus Christ the Teacher* (1943)), Son of Man was not a current Messianic apocalyptic title, otherwise Jesus would have discouraged its use as he did that of the term Messiah. The expression has no Messianic meaning in the Old Testament, not even in Dan. 7:13, where what we have is 'one like a son of man'. Jesus' use of the term therefore cannot be Messianic, but denotes himself as representative, typical, or true man. *Ben 'ādhām* in Ezekiel (nearly a hundred times) is regarded as the main source of the self-designation of Jesus, and this was fundamentally prophetic in intention. G. S. Duncan's book *Jesus, Son of Man* (1947) is perhaps the most notable recent work on these lines. Its subtitle, 'Studies Contributory to a Modern Portrait', is reminiscent of Harnack and the writers of the 'liberal' lives of Jesus, and although Duncan allows more content to the concept of Messiahship than did Harnack, he portrays Jesus as primarily a prophetic Son of Man and as having derived the title and his understanding of it from Ezekiel. The apocalyptic associations of the Son of Man are therefore discarded; the apocalyptic hope of the final consummation of the kingdom of God is said to be quite alien to the thought of Jesus; and the parousia is interpreted in the sense of the future aspect of his one coming which has taken place because the kingdom of God has come in him. Of the use of Dan. 7:13 by Jesus before the high priest Duncan writes that

we need not be surprised if Jesus, recognising Himself to be, in a most truly spiritual sense, the Man in whom God's ideals and purposes for men were to be fulfilled, should have dared to believe that this and all such Scripture references to exaltation and authority, whether on the part of the Son of Man or some other such figure, were to be fulfilled in Himself (p. 191).

It is questionable whether the apocalyptic Son of Man can be relegated to the periphery in this way, and if Jesus borrowed from Ezekiel, his scant references to the Spirit are in surprising contrast to the frequent association in Ezekiel of the 'son of man' and the Spirit. Nor is there much force in Duncan's argument from the frequency of the term in Ezekiel as compared with the 'one phrase in Daniel vii:13' (p. 145, n. 3). A similar position is adopted by J. Y. Campbell.[20]

There is no purely *philological* obstacle to the belief that *bar nāšā'*, represented in the Gospels by Son of Man, could be a title, although in early Palestinian Aramaic, but not very commonly, it means 'a man', much as ἄνθρωπος became a title in Gnosticism.[21] J. Y. Campbell ('The Origin and Meaning of the Term Son of Man', JTS 48 (1947), 145–55) suggested that Jesus used it of himself but not as a title, and in the form *hahû' bar nāšā'* as a more distinctive equivalent of *hahû' gabhrâ'*, 'this man' or 'I', which would account for the Greek ὁ υἱὸς τοῦ ἀνθρώπου.[22]

There is still to be found the opinion that Jesus did not allude to himself as Son of Man at all. According to F. C. Grant in *The Gospel of the Kingdom* (1940) the Son of Man Christology is a creation of the early church, and the coexistence of different Christologies—Messiah, Son of David, Son of Man—militates against any one of them having originated with Jesus.[23]

R. Bultmann opens his *Theology of the New Testament* (i (1952)) with often quoted words: '*The message of Jesus* is a presupposition for the theology of the New Testament rather than a part of that theology itself'. His message was of the imminence of the reign of God, whose dawning was manifest already in his own words and works. Now is the time for *decision*, for soon will come the judgment exercised by God or by his representative the Son of Man who will arrive on the clouds of heaven. Jesus, although in his own person the sign of the times, did not demand belief in himself or declare himself Messiah. He came as a prophet or rabbi without any Messianic consciousness whatever, either of the political Davidic or the apocalyptic Son of Man variety, and points ahead to the Son of Man as another than himself (p. 9). Bultmann sharply distinguishes between sayings which allude to the Son of Man's passion, death, and resurrection and those which refer

to his parousia. The two groups had originally no connection
with one another, for the passion sayings say nothing of the
parousia and the parousia sayings nothing of the death and
resurrection of the Son of Man. The latter are judged to be
the older, and probably authentic utterances of Jesus; the former,
unrepresented in Q, are probably creations of the Hellenistic
church which had lost the meaning of the expression Son of Man
and identified the figure with Jesus. We have here an illuminating and crucial example of the significance of the opening
sentence in Bultmann's book.[24] T. F. Glasson in *The Second Advent* (1945), on the assumption that Jesus did not think in apocalyptic terms at all, though he regarded himself as Son of Man,
reinterpreting Dan. 7 in terms of the Suffering Servant, reaches a
result diametrically opposed to Bultmann's, for it is those very
parousia sayings, accepted by Bultmann as genuine, which he pronounces unauthentic. A different explanation of the apparent
reference of Son of Man sayings to another person than Jesus himself is that of J. Schniewind,[25] to whom they are part and parcel
of Jesus' own Messianic secret—he is the hidden Messiah on earth.

The only direct available evidence for the existence of Son of
Man as a Messianic title in pre-Christian Judaism is Dan. 7 and
1 En. 37–71. According to Mowinckel Dan. 7 itself is directly
important evidence for belief in an individual Son of Man about
200 B.C., which it reinterprets in a corporate sense.[26] The *Similitudes of Enoch* show that, though of a different origin from the
Messiah, this Son of Man in certain apocalyptic circles had come
o be regarded as the Messiah,[27] The more usual view is that the
figure in the *Similitudes* is an individualization of the corporate
figure symbolic of 'the saints of the Most High' in Dan. 7. Thus,
for example, J. W. Bowman, while admitting the possibility of
influence from other sources, is content with Dan. 7 as the origin
of the Son of Man in 1 En.[28] Among recent writers who assume
Son of Man to have become a Messianic title before the time of
Jesus, at least in certain circles, may be mentioned N. Johansson,[29]
W. Manson,[30] J. W. Bowman,[31] E. Sjöberg,[32] W. F. Albright,[33]
R. Bultmann,[34] R. Leivestad[35] and O. Cullmann.[36] That the
term was not a Messianic title in pre-Christian Judaism is held,
among others, by Pierson Parker,[37] H. H. Rowley,[38] M. S. Ens-
lin[39] and R. H. Fuller.[40] This attitude is largely determined by
doubts concerning the common assumption of a pre-Christian

date for the *Similitudes of Enoch*. The most severe depreciation of
them in recent years is that of J. Y. Campbell,[41] who points to
the late date of the manuscripts, none of which is earlier than the
sixteenth century, and regards the work as quite valueless as
evidence for Jewish ideas about the Son of Man; the title may be
the work of Christian interpolators. More recently doubts about
the pre-Christian date of the *Similitudes* have been expressed by
C. H. Dodd[42] and R. H. Fuller.[43]

The majority of critics continue to regard the Son of Man in
the Gospels as of apocalyptic origin and to attribute the usage to
Jesus himself. But there remains a sharp cleavage of opinion as to
whether Dan. 7 or 1 En. is the source from which he drew.

Those who agree with Dr. Manson that Dan. and not 1 En. is
the source of the self-designation of Jesus, and that the Danielic
figure is a corporate symbol are, of course, numerous. But there
is very little unqualified acceptance of his suggestion that Jesus'
own use of the term Son of Man is also corporate. C. J. Cadoux
in *The Historic Mission of Jesus* (1941), especially 90–103, whole-
heartedly adopted the thesis.[44] M. Black thinks that 'the communal meaning is not only possible, but highly probable, and may
be the true one, but it is doubtful if, in any case, it is the only
one. . . .' [45] The disagreement on this point is in some cases complete. C. C. McCown[46] brings forward four objections. (1) No
Gospel passage suggests that Jesus and his followers, forming a
corporate entity, are described as Son of Man; (2) the Son of Man
in 1 En. was probably known to them; (3) 'the increasing popu-
larity of angelology and hypostatization looks toward an indi-
vidualizing of such figures rather than the more abstract corporate use of the terms'; (4) there is no need to look beyond the
ideas of the guardian angel or the *fravashi* to explain the conception. E. Percy[47] rejects Dr. Manson's theory without discussion.
E. Sjöberg[48] sees in Dr. Manson's hypothesis an unjustifiable conclusion drawn from the (mistaken) corporate interpretation of
Dan. 7 and from his opinion that Jesus drew from the passage
directly without reference to contemporary Jewish exegesis of it.[49]

On the other hand, it is recognized by some of those who cannot accept the theory as Dr. Manson states it that it contains
valuable elements of truth. R. N. Flew emphasizes the value of
the connection of the remnant idea with that of the Messiah in
Dr. Manson's treatment.[50] V. Taylor in *Jesus and His Sacrifice*

(1943), 29, did not think it necessary to discuss the societary view because Dr. Manson himself holds that Jesus came to restrict the title to himself. Later, however, in a valuable treatment of the question, he made two important points. (1) 'Apart, therefore, from discussions concerning "the Son of Man" a communal element in his teaching is a vital clue to his mission. If this is so, the significance of the title, important and revealing as it is, is not a decisive issue. The thing signified, and not the name, is the primary consideration. The value of the collective interpretation is that it names the community otherwise implied.' [51] (2) He suggested that, even if the communal interpretation is not conclusive, it is possible that the early church applied to the second coming of Christ parousia sayings which, belonging to the earlier period of the ministry, originally referred to the elect community as the Son of Man.[52] This should be taken in conjunction with Taylor's earlier article 'The "Son of Man" Sayings Relating to the Parousia' in ET 58 (1946), 12–15, the thesis of which is summarized in general terms in *The Interpreter's Bible* vii (1951), 118 f.; cf. also his *The Gospel according to St. Mark* (1952), 383 f.; *The Names of Jesus* (1953), 33 f. H. H. Rowley seems to be thinking on somewhat similar lines when he remarks that it is in passages concerning the future coming of the Son of Man that 'the collective understanding of the phrase is attended with the least difficulty'.[53] J. W. Bowman is impressed by the corporate understanding of the term Son of Man but, denying the presence of apocalyptic eschatology in the thought of Jesus, he regards it as referring to Jesus and the church which it was his 'intention' to establish.[54] Cullmann sees both in Dan. 7:13 and in Jesus' use of the phrase Son of Man a collective sense, but with the individual aspect more prominent.[55] Finally, the view supported by Mowinckel (mentioned earlier) that in Dan. 7 we have a corporate interpretation of an individual Son of Man who was an object of belief before the time of Jesus, invites the question whether (if it is accepted) Jesus would have been more likely to appeal directly to the scriptural passage to the neglect of the supposed current belief than to the latter itself. Perhaps both motives should be allowed for, and if so we should have a reasonable explanation of the variation between the personal and collective uses of the term Son of Man. In any case it is probably a mistake to regard Dan. 7 as the sole source of the title in the Gospels.

R. Otto's once widely influential book[56] offered suggestions concerning the Son of Man problem which, while ingenious, have not commended themselves to most scholars. Otto is to be classed with the supporters of 1 En. as the direct source of Jesus' self-designation. According to him Jesus was a charismatic preacher of the imminence of the Kingdom of God who was so influenced by Persian ideas mediated in Galilee through the Enochic literature that he came to think of his mission in terms derived from its teaching. Enoch was 'a prophet of the eschatological Son of Man', who 'would be exalted to become the one whom he had proclaimed' (p. 213).

But although he himself was the future Son of Man, he did not proclaim himself as the Son of Man . . . Similarly Jesus knew himself to be the 'filius hominis praedestinatus'; therefore he summoned, worked, and acted as the one upon whom the choice had fallen; he worked proleptically with the powers of the Son of Man, with divine commission and divine anointing; but he did not deliver teachings in regard to his being the Son of Man, any more than did Enoch (p. 219).

The basis of this theory is 1 En. 71:14, where alone in the *Similitudes* is Enoch identified with the Son of Man who, Otto tentatively conjectured, is the *fravashi* or heavenly counterpart of Enoch. Rowley's comment is worth quoting. 'My difficulty with Otto's view is that if 1 Enoch identifies Enoch with the Son of Man, and if 1 Enoch influenced our Lord's assumption of the title Son of Man, the implied identification of Himself with Enoch might have been expected to leave some trace in the Gospels.' [57] More serious for Otto's whole hypothesis is the problem of the relation of chapter 71 to the rest of the *Similitudes*.[58] Other writers who find in 1 En. the source of the Son of Man in the Gospels are N. Johansson (*op. cit.*, 183 f., 301), C. C. McCown (*op. cit.*, 9) and E. Stauffer (*New Testament Theology* (1955), 108–11 (in addition to Dan. 7)). But opponents of this derivation are many, and include C. J. Cadoux (*op. cit.*, 98 f.), V. Taylor (see last footnote), T. F. Glasson (*op. cit.*, 45 ff.), J. W. Bowman (*The Religion of Maturity* (1948), 255–7), and J. W. Doeve (*Jewish Hermeneutics in the Synoptic Gospels and Acts* (1954), 136).

Others allow the possibility of knowledge among Jesus and his followers of current ideas about a future superhuman judge and ruler, without necessarily direct dependence on 1 En. J. Lowe[59] thinks '*Enoch* or something like it' in addition to Daniel is presupposed by Gospel usage. M. Goguel[60] thought the expression '*this* Son of Man' in 1 En. points to an already known but not common conception. Similar views are held, among others, by E. Percy[61] and E. Sjöberg.[62]

E. Lohmeyer[63] dealt with the Son of Man question as part of his theory of two centres of primitive Christianity: the Son of Man (and Kyrios) Christology was characteristic of Galilaean belief, that of the Messiah belonged to Jerusalem. Of this Bultmann provides a brief critique (approved by Percy, *op. cit.*, 244, n.) in his *Theology of the New Testament* i (1952), 52 f.: the two titles do not imply two different types of Christology. Cullmann (*op. cit.*, 168) judges that Christologies cannot be differentiated in this way on a geographical basis.

Those who, with Dr. Manson, believe that Jesus invested the Son of Man title (derived from Dan. 7) with traits of the Suffering Servant are too numerous to mention. But there is a lack of agreement as to whether Jesus was original in this or whether Judaism was already familiar with the idea of a suffering Son of Man. While the great majority of supporters of originality think of Dan., R. H. Charles[64] and, in our period, Otto[65] have traced the thought of Jesus to a synthesis of the Servant conception and the *Enochic* Son of Man. Protagonists of the other view include some who find a suffering Son of Man already in the Old Testament. Thus W. D. Davies[66] thinks that Dan. 7:21, 25 points in this direction because the Son of Man represents the persecuted saints of the Most High. A similar view is adopted by C. H. Dodd[67] and C. F. D. Moule.[68] This kind of exegesis is rejected by H. H. Rowley who writes that there is no thought of a suffering Son of Man because the 'saints suffered before the appearance of the Son of Man, for this is a figure for the saints only after they are invested with power'.[69] More commonly, however, it is 1 En. 37–71 to which appeal is made: a suffering and dying Son of Man is conceived after the pattern of the Servant. The most notable recent attempt to support this thesis is that of J. Jeremias.[70] J. Héring[71] signified his rejection of such ideas, but the most thorough refutation is that of Sjöberg.[72] Mowinckel, following Sjöberg, adduces impressive and cogent arguments against the supposition that pre-Christian Judaism cherished any belief in a suffering and dying Son of Man.[73] In Mowinckel's opinion such

K

a supposition is due to misuse of verbal similarities.[74] To illustrate
the almost confusing variety of opinions on this question it is sufficient to refer to the fact that while C. R. North finds no evidence
that the Son of Man in the *Similitudes* is to suffer, he yet sees there
a real identification of the Son of Man and the Servant.[75] W.
Manson, in his valuable study *Jesus the Messiah* (1943), appears at
times almost to equate Son of Man and Servant in pre-Christian
Judaism, but does not intend actually to do so. He writes:

> In Biblical and Jewish belief the ideas Son of God, Servant of the
> Lord, and Son of Man, however separate they may have been in origin,
> had come to signify only variant phases of the one Messianic idea, and
> approaches to an actual synthesis of the features of all three had already
> taken place in I Enoch. . . . The sufferings of Jesus are predicted in the
> form of a dogma relating to the Son of Man. But this dogma is not only
> not derivable from Jewish apocalyptic tradition but stands in extreme
> paradoxical relation to it. That the Son of Man enters on his heavenly
> glory through humiliation and self-sacrifice was an idea which despite
> Isa. liii had not entered into the Messianic calculations of Judaism.[76]

Some scholars have denied to the thought of Jesus any association of the ideas of the Kingdom of God and the Son of Man. Of
these two concepts in his teaching H. B. Sharman writes that
'they create the impression of two foci that do not belong to the
same ellipse', and that 'the Son of Man has no kingdom and the
Kingdom of God has no Son of Man'.[77] Although the question
cannot be pursued here, a strong case can be made out for the
opposite view that the association of the two ideas belongs to the
earliest stratum of the tradition, and to the thought of Jesus himself.[78] In fact, it is difficult to imagine anything else if he was
dependent on Dan. 7.

This survey may conclude with another topic in some ways
germane to the connection between the Kingdom of God and the
Son of Man. Was Jesus, in thinking of himself as the Son of Man,
concerned primarily with the future, in view of the fact that in
Judaism the Son of Man is an entirely eschatological figure? R. H.
Fuller regards Jesus as exercising proleptically the functions of the
eschatological Son of Man in his earthly ministry viewed as the
Kingdom in action in advance of its full coming. Jesus is the Son
of Man designate: he 'is not yet the Son of Man (which is essentially a triumphant figure). But he acts as the one destined to be
the triumphant Son of Man already during his ministry and

humiliation. The Kingdom and the Son of Man "spill over" or "jut out", as it were, on to this side of the cross, yet the cross itself remains the decisive event which sets both in motion'.[79] J. Héring denies to Jesus any Messianic claim, while yet holding him to have looked to the coming of the Son of Man of Dan. and 1 En. and to his future identity with him.[80] Théo Preiss appeals to the idea of the Messianic secret: the use by Jesus of the term *bar nāšā'* forms part of this, serving both to indicate and to conceal the mystery of his person as the Son of Man who will be revealed in glory only at the parousia.[81] Sjöberg does the same. If Jesus claimed to be the Messiah-Son of Man, it was as *hidden*, since he appeared on earth before the *Endzeit*, when alone the Son of Man is fully revealed.[82] That Jesus appeared as Son of Man before the *Endzeit*, to which that figure properly belongs, is stressed by Cullmann in his important chapter on the title in *Die Christologie des Neuen Testaments*. He emphasizes the originality of the thought of Jesus about himself as the eschatological Son of Man already present on earth, a thought which finds its explanation in his transference of Jewish eschatological conceptions into the present, for in his teaching the *Endzeit* has already arrived.

NOTES

[1] 1931, 2nd edn., 1935; cf. also 'Mark ii. 27 f.', *Coniectanea Neotestamentica* 11 (*in honorem* A. Fridrichsen, 1947), 138–46; *The Church's Ministry* (1948), 18 ff.; *The Beginning of the Gospel* (1950), 23; 'The Son of Man in Daniel, Enoch and the Gospels', BJRL 32 (1950), 171–93 (cited as *Son of Man*); 'Realized Eschatology and the Messianic Secret', *Studies in the Gospels* (essays in memory of R. H. Lightfoot, ed. D. E. Nineham, 1955), 209–22. Recent surveys of the Son of Man problem include: N. Schmidt, 'Recent Study of the Term "Son of Man"', JBL 45 (1926), 326–49; A. S. Peake, *The Servant of Yahweh* (1931), 220–37; H. Riesenfeld, *Jésus Transfiguré* (1947), 307–13; C. C. McCown, 'Jesus, Son of Man: a survey of recent discussion', JR 28 (1948), 1–12; Bauer-Arndt-Gingrich, *A Greek-English Lexicon of the New Testament*, etc. (1957), 842 f.

[2] See e.g. A. N. Wilder, *Eschatology and Ethics in the Teaching of Jesus* (2nd edn., 1950); G. R. Beasley-Murray, *Jesus and the Future* (1954) and *A Commentary on Mark Thirteen* (1957); J. Jeremias, *The Parables of Jesus* (1954); J. A. T. Robinson, *Jesus and His Coming* (1957). See the useful articles on New Testament eschatology by C. K. Barrett in SJT 6 (1953), 136–55, 225–43, and G. R. Beasley-Murray in ET 64 (1953), 312–16; also E. Grässer, *Das Problem der Parusieverzögerung in den synoptischen Evangelien und in der Apostelgeschichte* (BZNW 22 (1957)), with which cf. O. Cullmann, 'Parusieverzögerung und Urchristentum', TLZ 83 (1958), 2–12.

[3] Aspects of the Son of Man question not treated here include the use of the term in the Fourth Gospel (cf. C. H. Dodd, *The Interpretation of the Fourth Gospel* (1953), 241 ff.; C. K. Barrett, *The Gospel according to St. John* (1955); R. H. Lightfoot, *St. John's Gospel* (1956); S. Schulz, *Untersuchungen zur Menschensohn-Christologie im Johannesevangelium* (1957); also E. M. Sidebottom, 'The Son of Man as Man in the Fourth Gospel', ET 68 (1957), 231-5, 280-3); 'Man' in St. Paul (cf. E. Stauffer, *New Testament Theology* (1955), 111, O. Cullmann, *Die Christologie des Neuen Testaments* (1957), 169-86, who continues with a discussion of Son of Man in the rest of the New Testament, including the Fourth Gospel (186-93). I am indebted to Dr. Cullmann for kindly allowing me to see the proofs of part of his book before publication); the survival of the title in early Judaistic Christianity (H. J. Schoeps, *Theologie und Geschichte des Judenchristentums* (1949), 78-82; E. Stauffer, *op. cit.*, 328; O. Cullmann, *op. cit.*, 194 f.). The connection between the Son of Man and Enoch has been much discussed. In addition to the literature referred to in the course of this paper may be mentioned C. P. van Andel, *De Structuur van de Henoch-Traditie en het Nieuwe Testament* (1955). No reference is made to the Qumran documents in which the title Son of Man has not been found. Cullmann, *op. cit.*, 143, calls attention to the possible presence of the idea of the Second Adam in 1 QS 4, 23. The suggestion of some scholars (e.g. M. Black in SJT 6 (1953), 8; F. F. Bruce, *Second Thoughts on the Dead Sea Scrolls* (1956), 103) that the Qumran community's self-identification with the Servant of the Lord in 2 Isa. (1 QS 8, 1 ff.) may be extended to include also the symbolic Son of Man figure in Dan. 7 (cf. CD xx, 8 (IX, 33B)) is doubtful because it rests on inferences only, and these in turn depend on a view of the relation between the two passages which is not demonstrable.

[4] Dr. Manson admits in *Son of Man*, 190, that he allowed insufficient weight to this in *The Teaching of Jesus*.

[5] *The Servant-Messiah*, 72.

[6] *Die Henochgestalt. Eine vergleichende religionsgeschichtliche Untersuchung* (1939), 86 ff. His suggestion that the Son of Man is a kind of Jewish counterpart to the Babylonian-Chaldaean god of wisdom Ea-Oannes is rejected by N. A. Dahl, *Das Volk Gottes* (1941), 297.

[7] *Jesus the Messiah* (1943), 174 ff.

[8] *He That Cometh* (1956), 420 ff.; but his whole long treatment of the Son of Man (346-450) deserves the closest attention.

[9] E.g. *Das Evangelium des Johannes* (1950), 10 f.

[10] *The Jung Codex:* three studies by H. C. Puech, G. Quispel and W. C. van Unnik translated and edited by F. L. Cross (1955), 78.

[11] Cf. O. Cullmann, *Die Christologie des Neuen Testaments* (1957), 144.

[12] Cf. M. Black in SJT 7 (1954), 177: 'The ubiquity of the conception [of the Heavenly Man-Redeemer] in the middle and further East from the second century A.D. onwards in so many forms is difficult to explain as due entirely to Christian influence.'

[13] *King and Messiah* (1955), 43.

[14] *Jésus Transfiguré* (1947), 62-4; 'Behind the Son of Man as well as behind the Messiah there is the idea of the king', in his essay 'The Mythological Background of New Testament Christology', *The Background of the New Testament*

and its Eschatology, ed. W. D. Davies and D. Daube (in honour of C. H. Dodd, 1956), 86.

15 'Le fils de l'homme de Daniel et la tradition biblique', RB 60 (1953), 170–202, 321–46.

16 'Le messianisme sapiential et les origines littéraires du Fils de l'homme daniélique', *Wisdom in Israel and in the Ancient Near East* [H. H. Rowley Festschrift], ed. M. Noth and D. Winton Thomas (*Supplements to* VT 3 (1955)), 33–41.

17 *The Second Advent* (1945), 14 ff. This suggestion is accepted by J. W. Bowman, *The Religion of Maturity* (1948), 225.

18 Cf. earlier E. A. Abbott, *The Son of Man* (1910) and D. Völter, *Die Menschensohn-Frage neu untersucht* (1916). J. Christensen in an article on Mark 14:21 (ὑπάγει) in *Studia Theologica* 10 (1957), 28–39, calls attention to the neglect of Ezek. 12 and its theme of 'departure', and thinks that both Ezekiel and apocalyptic must be taken into account.

19 'The Meaning of "Son of Man" ', JBL 60 (1941), 151–7.

20 'Son of Man', *A Theological Word Book of the Bible*, ed. A. Richardson (1950), 231 f. For a critique of the Ezekielic view see R. H. Fuller, *The Mission and Achievement of Jesus* (1954), 99–102; cf. T. W. Manson, *Son of Man*, 172 f., and E. Percy, *Die Botschaft Jesu* (1953), 256 f.

21 Cf. E. Sjöberg, *Der Menschensohn im äthiopischen Henochbuch* (1946), 40 ff.; M. Goguel, *Jésus* (1950), 246 f.; S. Mowinckel, *op. cit.*, 346 f.; O. Cullmann, *op. cit.*, 139 f.

22 But unfortunately for this theory *hahû' bar nāšā'* is nowhere found; cf. M. Black in ET 60 (1948), 34.

23 See especially 64–6, 153–60, and for other names C. C. McCown in JR 28 (1948), 6; also now J. Knox, *The Death of Christ* (1958).

24 In a third category of sayings which concern the Son of Man's earthly activities it is a matter of mistranslation of the Aramaic where it means 'man' or 'I'. For criticism of Bultmann's differentiation of two main groups of Son of Man sayings see E. Percy's remarks in *Die Botschaft Jesu* (1953), 245–9, especially the statement (p. 247): 'ihr [the primitive church] war aber der Tod und die Erhöhung Jesu als Voraussetzung seiner Wiederkunft als der "Menschensohn" bekannt. Für sie gab es deshalb kein Bedürfnis, die Parusie Jesu mit seinem Hingang durch den Tod und die Himmelfahrt zu verbinden, und die Überlieferung der Parusieworte ist selbstverständlich von dem Bedürfnis der christlichen Gemeinde nach Belehrung und Ermahnung bestimmt.' Cullmann, *op. cit.*, 159, thinks Bultmann's hypothesis creates more difficulties than it solves. G. Bornkamm, *Jesus von Nazareth* (2nd edn., 1957), 160 ff., 206 ff., agreeing with Bultmann's view of the parousia sayings, attributes the use of Son of Man as a self-designation of Jesus to the creativity of Christian prophets in the early Palestinian church.

25 *Das Evangelium nach Markus* (1956), 55, 120, 174.

26 *Op. cit.*, 352.

27 *Op. cit.*, 360–2.

28 *The Religion of Maturity* (1948), 225.

29 *Parakletoi* (1940), 101.

30 *Op. cit.*, 102, who also refers to a certain synthesis of features in the Son of

Man derived from the Davidic Messiah and the Servant (99, 101, 173 f.).

[31] *The Intention of Jesus* (1945), 109, 127 f.

[32] *Der Menschensohn im äthiopischen Henochbuch* (1946), 140 ff.

[33] *From the Stone Age to Christianity* (2nd edn., 1946), 292.

[34] *Theology of the New Testament* i (1952), 52 f.

[35] *Christ the Conqueror* (1954), 9.

[36] *Op. cit.*, 140 ff.

[37] *Op. cit.*, 151-3.

[38] *The Relevance of Apocalyptic* (1944), 29 f., 56 f.; *The Servant of the Lord* (1952), 80-2.

[39] *The Interpreter's Bible* vii (1951), 113.

[40] *Op. cit.*, 98, 106, 108.

[41] JTS 48 (1947), 145 ff.

[42] *According to the Scriptures* (1952), 116; *The Interpretation of the Fourth Gospel* (1953), 242 f.

[43] *Op. cit.*, 98; cf. also T. F. Glasson, *op. cit.*, 57 ff., and A. J. B. Higgins, *The Christian Significance of the Old Testament* (1949), 150-3, though I now feel the view there expressed requires reconsideration.

[44] For earlier advocates of the corporate interpretation in various forms see Cadoux's book, 100, n. 2.

[45] 'The "Son of Man" in the Teaching of Jesus', ET 60 (1948), 32-6 (33). F. V. Filson in *Jesus Christ the Risen Lord* (1956), 142, goes no further than to allow the possibility of the collective meaning alongside the predominant personal reference.

[46] JR 28 (1948), 9.

[47] *Op. cit.*, 239, n. 1; cf. A. Feuillet, *op. cit.*, 344: 'relève de la haute fantaisie'.

[48] *Der verborgene Menschensohn in den Evangelien* (1955), 241, n.

[49] Cf. also H. Roberts, *Jesus and the Kingdom of God* (1955), 32; W. G. Kümmel, *Promise and Fulfilment* (1957), 46.

[50] *Jesus and His Church* (2nd edn., 1943), 54 f.; cf. T. F. Glasson, *op. cit.*, 54 f.

[51] *The Life and Ministry of Jesus* (1954), 75.

[52] *Ibid.*, 73.

[53] *The Relevance of Apocalyptic* (1944), 115; cf. *The Servant of the Lord* (1952), 81, n. 4; *The Unity of the Bible* (1953), 125, n. 1.

[54] *The Intention of Jesus* (1945), 165 ff.; *The Religion of Maturity* (1948), 235 ff.

[55] *Op. cit.*, 159; cf. *The Early Church*, ed. A. J. B. Higgins (1956), 130.

[56] *Reichgottes und Menschensohn* (1934), Eng. trans. *The Kingdom of God and the Son of Man* (1938, 2nd edn., 1943); there is a valuable critique by C. F. Evans in ET 65 (1954), 303-6.

[57] *The Relevance of Apocalyptic* (1944), 56, n.

[58] Among recent discussions of chapters 70 and 71 in relation to the *Similitudes* and the consequent connection between Enoch and the Son of Man see P. Volz, *Die Eschatologie der jüdischen Gemeinde im neutestamentlichen Zeitalter* (1934), 21, 25; J. Bowman, ET 59 (1948), 287; M. Black, ET 60 (1948), 12-14, also JTS, new series 3 (1952), 4-10 (the chapters represent an older Son of Man-Enoch tradition, integral to 1 En., 'out of which the *Similitudes* have grown, by a re-writing of the Enoch legend in support of a doctrine of a supernatural Messiah,

foreign to the original conception of 1 Enoch' (8)); H. Bietenhard, *Die himmische Welt im Urchristentum und Spätjudentum* (1951), 146 ff.; Mowinckel, *op. cit.*, 437 ff. (it is 'inconceivable' that chapter 71 depicts Enoch as becoming one with the Son of Man (444), as Sjöberg, who thinks it does, himself admits (*Der Menschensohn im äthiopischen Henochbuch* (1946), 187)); E. Percy, *op. cit.*, 256–9; T. W. Manson, *The Teaching of Jesus*, 228 f., and *Son of Man*, 176 ff. Dr. Manson's opinion (reached independently of Messel's earlier collective view) is that the Son of Man in 1 En. is collective as in Dan. 7 except for chapters 70 f., in which Enoch becomes the nucleus of the elect community and the first historical actualization of the Son of Man who is not so much 'pre-existent' as 'an idea in the mind of God' (*Son of Man*, 188 f., to which Sjöberg replies in *Der verborgene Menschensohn in den Evangelien* (1955), 45, n. 2). For criticism of Otto's theory in general see, e.g. V. Taylor, *Jesus and His Sacrifice* (1943), 26 f.; W. Manson, *op. cit.*, 119 f.; T. F. Glasson, *op. cit.*, 48 ff.

[59] JTS 47 (1946), 81 f.

[60] *Op. cit.*, 248.

[61] *Op. cit.*, 257.

[62] *Der verborgene Menschensohn in den Evangelien* (1955), 242.

[63] *Galiläa und Jerusalem* (1936), followed by F. C. Grant, *op. cit.*, 54, and in *The Interpreter's Bible* vii (1951), 641, 849.

[64] *The Book of Enoch translated* (2nd edn., 1912), 306.

[65] *Op. cit.*, 244 ff.

[66] *Paul and Rabbinic Judaism* (1948), 280, n. 1.

[67] *According to the Scriptures* (1952), 117, n. 2.

[68] *Bulletin* 3 (1952) of the *Studiorum Novi Testamenti Societas*, 40 ff.

[69] *The Servant of the Lord* (1952), 62, n. 2.

[70] *The Servant of God* (1957), 58 ff., translated from art. παῖς θεοῦ in TWNT; cf. *Aux Sources de la Tradition chrétienne* [M. Goguel Festschrift] (1950), 113 ff.; also W. D. Davies, *op. cit.*, 279 f.

[71] *Le Royaume de Dieu et sa Venue* (1937), 80, n.

[72] *Der Menschensohn im äthiopischen Henochbuch* (1946), 116 ff., cf. also his *Der verborgene Menschensohn in den Evangelien* (1955), 70 f., 257.

[73] *Op. cit.*, 410 ff.; neither was there any conception of a suffering and dying national Messiah, 325 ff.

[74] *Ibid.*, 366, n. 3.

[75] *The Suffering Servant in Deutero-Isaiah* (2nd edn., 1956), 7 f.

[76] *Jesus the Messiah*, 110, 116.

[77] *Son of Man and Kingdom of God* (1944), 89; cf. H. A. Guy, *The New Testament Doctrine of the 'Last Things'* (1948), 81.

[78] Cf. W. Manson, *op. cit.*, 66, 113; J. W. Doeve, *op. cit.*, 119 ff.

[79] *Op. cit.*, 107 f.

[80] *Op. cit.*, 96 ff.

[81] *Le fils de l'homme* (1951), 44 f.

[82] *Der verborgene Menschensohn in den Evangelien* (1955), 218 f.

PAARWEISE SENDUNG IM NEUEN TESTAMENT

von

J. JEREMIAS

---

1. DAS SPÄTJUDENTUM

WÄHREND dem Alten Testament die paarweise Sendung von Boten als Brauch nicht bekannt zu sein scheint, ist in der rabbinischen Literatur wiederholt davon die Rede, daß zwei Gelehrtenschüler oder zwei Schriftgelehrte zusammen mit einem Auftrag entsandt werden. Sie werden dann gewöhnlich unter der Bezeichnung *zugh* = ζεῦγος (ein Paar, zwei Jochgenossen) zusammengefaßt.[1]

Bei den Aufträgen, die die Jochgenossen gemeinsam auszuführen haben, kann es sich um *private Botengänge für den Lehrer* handeln. So schickt Rabban Gamaliel II. (um 90), als ihm ein Sohn erkrankte, zwei seiner Schüler (*šᵉne thalmidhe ḥᵃkhamim*) zu R. Ḥanina bhen Dosa mit der Bitte, daß dieser als großer Beter bekannte Mann für ihn um Heilung beten möge.[2]

R. Šimʿon ben Joḥai (um 150) schickt ein Schülerpaar (*zugh eḥadh šel talmidhe ḥᵃkhamim*) aus, um in Erfahrung zu bringen, worüber sich drei seiner Kollegen unterhalten.[3] Und Abbaje (280–338/9) gibt einem Schriftgelehrtenpaar (*zugha dhᵉrabbanan*) den Auftrag, einen frommen Bader auf die Probe zu stellen.[4]

Doch handelt es sich bei den Funktionen, zu deren Ausübung ein Paar von Gelehrten entsandt wurde, zumeist um solche *offizieller Art*. So lesen wir b Sanh 26a: „R. Ḥijja bhar Zarnoḳi und R. Šimʿon ben Jehoṣadhaḳ (um 250) reisten nach Asia, um das Jahr zu interkalieren", d. h., da die Schaltung nur in Palästina verfügt werden durfte:[5] sie überbrachten der kleinasiatischen Judenschaft als Sendboten die offizielle Mitteilung, daß die Einschaltung eines Monats von der palästinischen Behörde beschlossen worden sei.[6]

Nach Sanh 6. 1 hat ein zur Steinigung Verurteilter das Recht, sich vom Weg zur Richtstätte nochmals zum Gerichtssaal zurückführen zu lassen, selbst vier, ja fünf Mal, wenn er etwas Erhebliches zu seiner Entlastung vorzubringen hat. „Aber woher weiß man das (daß seine Vorbringungen erheblich sind)?" Der eben erwähnte Abbaje schlägt vor: „Man gebe ihm (dem Delinquenten) ein Schriftgelehrtenpaar (*zugha dhᵉrabbanan*) mit (auf den Weg zur Richtstätte)." [7]

Ein Auftrag wird zwar nicht ausdrücklich erwähnt in einem lauter Decknamen verwendenden Geheimbrief, der berichtet, daß ein aus Tiberias kommendes Gelehrtenpaar (*zugh*) von den Römern gefangen genommen worden, ihnen jedoch wieder entkommen sei;[8] angesichts der Wichtigkeit, die der Angelegenheit beigemessen wird, und angesichts der Verwendung des Terminus *zugh* wird man aber mit Sicherheit annehmen dürfen, daß auch dieses ζεῦγος von Gelehrten in offizieller Mission unterwegs war.

Eine jüdische Inschrift aus *Venosa* in Apulien (5./6. Jhdt.), Grabinschrift einer vierzehnjährigen *Faustina*, erwähnt, daß dieser ‚zwei Apostel und zwei Schriftgelehrte' die Grabrede hielten (*QVEI DIXERVNT TRHNVS DVO APOSTVLI ET DVO REBBITES*).[9] Die Inschrift ist berühmt, weil sie der einzige jüdische Beleg dafür ist, daß die offiziellen Sendboten des palästinischen Mutterlandes in der Diaspora den Titel ἀπόστολος, latinisiert *apostuli*, trugen. Sie bestätigt zugleich, daß es üblich war, diese bevollmächtigten Sendboten paarweise auszusenden.[10] Dafür spricht auch das reiche neutestamentliche Belegmaterial für die paarweise Sendung von Boten und eine Midhrasch-Stelle, die den Brauch der paarweisen Sendung schon in der Mosesgeschichte wiederfindet: Moses und Aaron bezeichnen sich hier als „Sendboten Gottes" (*šᵉluḥaw šel hḳb"h*).[11] Ob daneben bei offiziellen Aufträgen auch die Sendung von drei Boten vorkam, ist nicht sicher. Zwar berichtet der palästinische Talmud, der Patriarch Jehudha III. (um 300) habe drei Bevollmächtigte, R. Ḥijja II., R. ʼAsi und R. ʼAmmi, in die Ortschaften Palästinas gesandt, umd ort Bibel- und Mischnalehrer einzusetzen;[12] doch beschränken die beiden Parallelüberlieferungen zu dieser Stelle übereinstimmend die Zahl der Boten auf zwei,[13] vermutlich mit Recht.[14] Besser bezeugt zu sein scheint die Sendung eines einzelnen Bevollmächtigten, weil für sie das Beispiel des Saulus angeführt werden könnte (Apg. 9:1–2; 22:5; 26:12); doch hat Saulus

Begleiter neben sich, und es wäre durchaus denkbar, daß sich unter diesen der Jochgenosse befand, an dem aber die christliche Überlieferung kein Interesse gehabte hätte. Obwohl die Entsendung einzelner Boten vorkam, dürfte doch die paarweise Sendung die Regel gewesen sein.

Fragen wir, warum man die Boten paarweise aussandte, so wird man zunächst an die Unsicherheit der Reiseverhältnisse zu denken haben: die Botschaft war durch zwei Boten besser geschützt. Hinzu kam aber sicherlich ein zweites Motiv, das aus der alttestamentlichen Vorschrift zu erschließen ist, daß, vor allem bei Kapitalverfahren, die übereinstimmende Aussage von zwei oder drei Belastungszeugen Voraussetzung für die gerichtliche Verurteilung sein solle:[15] Erst die Übereinstimmung der Aussage von mindestens zwei Zeugen macht diese glaubwürdig. *Entsprechend hat der Wortführende der beiden Sendboten* (vgl. Apg. 14:12: ὁ ἡγούμενος τοῦ λόγου) *den Jochgenossen zur Bestätigung der Botschaft neben sich.*

2. DAS NEUE TESTAMENT

Im Neuen Testament spielt die paarweise Sendung eine große Rolle. Wir stellen die wenigen Stellen voran, an denen es sich um einen reinen Botendienst handelt: Johannes der Täufer sandte nach Lk. 7:18 (anders Mt. 11:2) zwei seiner Jünger vom Gefängnis aus zu Jesus, dieser je zwei Jünger zur Abholung des Esels für den Einzug (Mk. 11:1; Mt. 21:1; Lk. 19:29) und zur Vorbereitung der Passafeier (Mk. 14:13; nach Lk. 22:8: Petrus und Johannes),[16] die Brüder von Lydda zwei Boten zu Petrus (Apg. 9:38), Cornelius zwei Sklaven unter dem Schutz eines Soldaten ebenfalls zu Petrus (10:7, 20). Uns kommt es auf die übrigen Fälle an, in denen es sich durchweg bei den Jochgenossen um mit besonderer Vollmacht ausgestattete Sendboten handelt.

(a)

Nach Mk. 6:7 hat *Jesus* die Zwölf δύο δύο ausgesandt, um den Anbruch der Gottesherrschaft durch Austreibung der unreinen Geister zu proklamieren. Diese klassische Belegstelle wird von den beiden synoptischen Seitenreferenten insofern gestützt, als einerseits Matthäus (10:2–4) und die Apostelgeschichte (1:13) die Namenliste der Jünger Jesu paarweise aufgliedern,[17] andererseits

Lukas die paarweise Sendung von den Siebzig berichtet: nach Lk. 10:1 hätte Jesus 35 Botenpaare vor sich hergesandt.[18] Die historische Glaubwürdigkeit der Nachricht, daß Jesus die Sendboten paarweise aussandte, wird durch die Beobachtung gestützt, daß die Aufteilung der Zwölf auf sechs Botenpaare zu der eschatologischen Funktion der Zwölfzahl, wie sie Mt. 19:28 zum Ausdruck gebracht wird, in einer gewissen Spannung steht. In der Aussendung bevollmächtigter Botenpaare kommt das von sämtlichen Evangelien bezeugte Hoheitsbewußtsein Jesu, *der* Gottgesandte zu sein (Mt. 15:24; Mk. 9:37; Lk. 4:18; Joh. 5:36 ff. u. ö.), zum sichtbaren Ausdruck. Dasselbe gibt von der Zwölfzahl.

(b)

Nach Jesu Vorbild hat die *Jerusalemer Urgemeinde* wiederholt bevollmächtigte Sendboten paarweise ausgesandt. Petrus und Johannes, die in der Jüngerliste Apg. 1:13 als erstes Paar genannt werden, werden als Jochgenossen nach Samaria geschickt (Apg. 8:14); schon vorher treten sie zusammen auf[19] und bezeugen Christus, wobei Petrus der Wortführer ist (3:1, 4, 6, 12; 4:8). Ein weiteres Botenpaar der Jerusalemer Urgemeinde sind die Propheten Judas Barsabbas und Silas, die zusammen mit dem antiochenischen Botenpaar Paulus und Barnabas nach Antiochia geschickt werden (15:22, 27, 32). Gewiß kommt daneben auch die Sendung eines einzelnen vor; so wird z. B. Barnabas von der Urgemeinde allein nach Antiochia geschickt (11:22); aber es ist doch bezeichnend, daß er sich in der Person des Saulus einen Mitarbeiter holt (11:25 f.). Wir werden nach alledem schwerlich fehl gehen, wenn wir auch Andronikus und Junias, von denen Paulus sagt: οἵτινές εἰσιν ἐπίσημοι ἐν τοῖς ἀποστόλοις, οἳ καὶ πρὸ ἐμοῦ γέγοναν ἐν Χριστῷ (Röm. 16:7), als Sendbotenpaar der Urgemeinde ansprechen und wenn wir annehmen, daß es sich bei den mit Empfehlungsbriefen von Jerusalem ausgesandten Christusaposteln, mit denen sich Paulus 2 Kor. 10–13 auseinandersetzen muß,[20] und dann wohl auch bei den τινὲς ἀπὸ Ἰακώβου (Gal. 2:12) je um ein Botenpaar gehandelt hat. Aber selbst wenn man von den beiden zuletzt genannten Fällen, in denen die Zweizahl nicht ausdrücklich genannt ist, absieht: die Tatsache, daß die Urgemeinde bevollmächtigte Botenpaare ausgesandt hat, steht fest – und ist nicht selbstverständlich. In ihr spiegeln sich Gewißheit und Anspruch, das eschatologische Gottesvolk zu sein.

(c)

Dieses Bewußtsein blieb nicht der Jerusalemer Urgemeinde
vorbehalten, sondern wurde - was wiederum nicht selbstverständlich ist - in gleicher Weise von der *Gemeinde in Antiochia*
zum Ausdruck gebracht. Sie sendet zunächst Paulus und Barnabas wiederholt als Jochgenossen aus: nach Jerusalem (Apg.
11:30; Gal. 2:1; Apg. 15:1-2, 12) und zur Heidenmission (Apg.
13:2 f.);[21] im ersten Falle zog Titus als dritter mit (Gal. 2:1), im
zweiten Falle Johannes Markus (Apg. 13:5). Da Markus ausdrücklich als ὑπηρέτης bezeichnet wird (Apg. 13:5), wird wohl
Titus dieselbe Funktion gehabt haben. Paulus hatte die Funktion
des Wortführers (Apg. 14:12).

Bei einer späteren Aussendung schickt die antiochenische
Gemeinde zwei Botenpaare aus: Barnabas und Markus (Apg.
15:39) sowie Paulus und Silas (15:40). Die Präskripte 1 Thess. 1:1;
2 Thess. 1:1 bestätigen die Nachricht der gemeinsamen Entsendung des Paulus und Silas; der in diesen beiden Präskripten an
dritter Stelle genannte Timotheus dürfte wiederum die Funktion
des Dieners ausgeübt haben. Wenn endlich seit der 3. Missionsreise in den Präskripten der Paulusbriefe wiederholt Timotheus
allein neben Paulus als Mitabsender erscheint (2 Kor. 1:1; Phil.
1:1; Kol. 1:1; Philem. 1), so wird man vermuten dürfen, daß
Timotheus zu Beginn der 3. Missionsreise seitens der antiochenischen Gemeinde zum Jochgenossen des Paulus an Stelle des Silas
bestimmt worden war.

Phil. 4:3 redet Paulus einen uns Unbekannten mit γνήσιε
σύζυγε an. Man hat viel darüber gerätselt, wen Paulus gemeint
haben könne.[22] Die Fassung von σύζυγος als Eigenname muß
ausscheiden, weil es dafür keinen Beleg gibt. In der alten Kirche
dachte man gelegentlich seit Klemens von Alexandria[23] und Ori-
genes[24] - sehr phantastisch - an die Frau des Apostels. Die
beliebte Deutung auf Epaphroditus stößt sich mit dem Umstand,
daß er der Briefüberbringer zu sein scheint (Phil. 2:29). Geht man,
wie es methodisch das Gewiesene ist, von dem spätjüdischen
Sprachgebrauch aus, so kommt, da Timotheus wegen Phil. 1:1
ausscheidet, nur Silas, der Jochgenosse der 2. Missionsreise, in
Frage. Er war Mitbegründer der Gemeinde von Philippi (Apg.
16:19), und nichts hindert, ihn zur Zeit der Abfassung des Philip-
perbriefes, wie immer man diesen datiert, in Philippi zu vermuten.

Daß auch die *paulinischen* Gemeinden, ebenso wie Antiochia, Botenpaare ausgesandt haben, zeigt mit Sicherheit 2 Kor. 8:23: ἀπόστολοι ἐκκλησιῶν. Es handelt sich bei diesen „Sendboten der Gemeinden" um die beiden v. 18–22 erwähnten Brüder, die auf Beschluß der (mazedonischen?) Gemeinden Paulus bei der Durchführung der Kollekte unterstützen sollten. Es liegt nahe, mit fast allen Kommentatoren von hier aus Apg. 20:4 zu deuten und dort Botenpaare erwähnt zu finden, die von den Gemeinden mit der Überbringung der Kollekte nach Jerusalem beauftragt waren. Auf jeden Fall ist es auffällig, daß von den acht (nicht, wie man gewöhnlich liest, sieben, denn Lukas ist der achte) Reisebegleitern des Apostels sechs ausdrücklich paarweise zusammengefaßt werden: Θεσσαλονικέων δὲ Ἀρίσταρχος καὶ Σέκουνδος, καὶ Γάϊος Δερβαῖος καὶ Τιμόθεος, Ἀσιανοὶ δὲ Τύχικος καὶ Τρόφιμος. Aristarch und Sekundus vertreten also die Gemeinde von Saloniki, Gaius und Timotheus die südgalatischen Gemeinden, Tychikus und Trophimus die Gemeinden der Provinz Asia. Möglicherweise haben auch die restlichen beiden Männer, Σώπατρος Πύρρου Βεροιαῖος und Lukas, ein Sendbotenpaar gebildet.

Sonst wäre nur noch Heb. 13:23 zu nennen. Haben der Briefschreiber und Timotheus ein Sendbotenpaar der Empfängergemeinde des Briefes (vermutlich Rom) gebildet?

(d)

Auch *Paulus* selbst hat wiederholt bevollmächtigte Botenpaare zu besonderen Aufträgen entsandt: Apg. 19:22 Timotheus und Erastus, 2 Kor. 12:18 Titus und einen Bruder,[25] Kol. 4:7–9 Tychikus und Onesimus, Titus 3:13 Zenas und Apollos.[26]

(e)

Selbst *Gott* sendet wiederholt seine Boten paarweise. In gewissem Sinn bilden schon Gesetz und Propheten ein Botenpaar, durch das er redet. Nicht nur die Essener, sondern – wie die Barkochba-Münzen zeigen – auch die Synagoge erwarteten in der Endzeit zwei gesalbte Gottesboten, den gesalbten König und den gesalbten Hohenpriester. Eine andere verbreitete volkstümliche Erwartung erhoffte (Deut. 18:15, 18 [Prophet wie Moses] und Mal. 3:23 [wiederkehrender Elias] kombinierend) das Kommen von zwei Vorläufern des Messias;[27] von hier aus wird sich die Erscheinung

des Elias mit Moses (Mk. 9:4)[28] auf dem Verklärungsberge er-
klären.[29] Ein himmlisches Botenpaar erscheint wiederholt in den
Ostergeschichten: Lk. 24:4; Joh. 20:11 f.; Apg. 1:10. Zwei
Bußprediger wird Gott in der Endzeit senden: Apk. 11:3 ff., in
Erfüllung des Sacharjawortes (Sach. 4:3, 11–14) von den zwei
Ölbäumen und zwei Leuchtern (Apk. 11:4).[30] Auch die gott-
feindliche Macht hat sich in der Mosezeit des Botenpaares bedient
(2 Tim. 3:8: Jannes und Jambres).

(f)

Immer geht es bei der Entsendung von Botenpaaren um die
Bekräftigung der Botschaft durch den Jochgenossen. *Einer* steht
außerhalb der Regel und bedarf der menschlichen Bekräftigung
nicht: der Sendbote Gottes schlechthin, ὁ ἀπόστολος καὶ ἀρχιερεὺς
τῆς ὁμολογίας ἡμῶν Ἰησοῦς (Heb. 3:1). Zwar hat er selbst in einem
seiner Gleichnisse den Täufer als Gottesboten neben sich gestellt
(Mt. 11:16–19 par. Lk. 7:31–35), aber er sprach hier aus der Sicht
des Volkes. Das Johannesevangelium hat die Problematik stark
empfunden, die in der Beschränkung des Zeugnisses des Gott-
gesandten auf das Selbstzeugnis beschlossen liegt, und sie immer
wieder aufgeworfen. Seine Antwort lautet: Der Gottgesandte
läßt kein menschliches, seine Sendung bestätigendes Zeugnis gelten, auch nicht da, wo es sich ihm anbietet, seitens des Täufers
(Joh. 5:33 f.). Die Bestätigung seiner Sendung liegt vielmehr in
den Werken, die er tut, und im Zeugnis des Vaters (5:36 f.).

ANMERKUNGEN

[1] Mit diesem *terminus technicus* bezeichnete man auch die fünf P Abh I. 4–15
genannten Gelehrtenpaare (*hazzughoth*), die angeblich seit dem 2. Jhdt. v. Chr.
bis auf Hillel (20 v. Chr.) die Tradition verbürgten; nach jSoṭ IX. 24a.25, ed.
Venedig 1523, hätte die Zeit der *zughoth* sogar schon mit Moses' Tod begonnen.
[2] bB^er 34b (Bar.); jB^er V.9d.20.
[3] Gen r 35.4 zu 9:16.
[4] bTaʿan 21b gegen Ende. Diese drei Beispiele stellte A. Schlatter, *Der Evangelist Matthäus* (1929), 326 zusammen.
[5] Tos Sanh 2.13; jSanh I.19a.1; jNedh VI.40a.27; bSanh 11b.
[6] H. Graetz, *Geschichte der Juden vom Untergang des jüdischen Staates bis zum
Abschluß des Talmud*, 2. Aufl. (1865), 478.
[7] bJoma 85b; bSanh 43a.
[8] bSanh 12a.
[9] J.-B. Frey, *Corpus Inscriptionum Iudaicarum* i (1936), 438 (No. 611).
[10] So auch K. H. Rengstorf, Ἀποστέλλω κτλ., TWNT, i (1933), 417.

[11] Ex r 5.14 zu 5:1.

[12] jHᵃgh I.76c.26.

[13] Pᵉsikṭa dhᵉRabh Kahᵃna, ed. S. Buber (1868), 120b.18 nennt R. Dosa und R. 'Ammi (MS. Oxford: R. Jose und R. 'Amma; MS. Parma: R. 'Amma und R. 'Asi); Midhr Klagelieder, Einleitung 2: R. 'Asi und R. 'Ammi.

[14] So auch H. L. Strack, *Einleitung in Talmud und Midraš*, 5. Aufl. (1921), 141.

[15] Deut. 17:6; 19:15; Num. 35:30. Die Vorschrift wird im Neuen Testament oft erwähnt: Mt. 18:16; Joh. 8:17; 2 Kor. 13:1; 1 Tim. 5:19; Heb. 10:28; vgl. Mt. 26:60. Siehe unten Korrekturzusatz.

[16] Auch Lk. 9:52 wäre hier zu nennen, falls — wie doch recht wahrscheinlich — Jakobus und Johannes (v. 54) die abgewiesenen Quartiermacher sind.

[17] Bei Mt. mit Ausnahme der ersten vier Namen; dagegen gibt Apg. 1:13 durch das τε am Anfang zu erkennen, daß auch die ersten vier Namen als zwei Paare gelesen werden sollen.

[18] Auch an die Geschichte der Berufung der beiden Brüderpaare Petrus-Andreas und Jakobus-Johannes (Mk. 1:16-20; Mt. 4:18-22; vgl. Lk. 5:1-11) sowie an die beiden Johannesjünger (Joh. 1:35, 37, 40), von denen einer Andreas war (1:40), wird man sich in diesem Zusammenhang zu erinnern haben. Doch werden in den Apostelkatalogen die beiden Brüderpaare nur von Matthäus (10:2) und Lukas (6:14) zusammen genannt, anders Markus (3:16-18: Petrus-Jakobus-Johannes-Andreas) und die Apostelgeschichte (1:13: Petrus-Johannes-Jakobus-Andreas).

[19] Vgl. auch Joh. 21:7, 20 ff.; Lk. 22:8.

[20] Über diese Jerusalemer Visitatoren vgl. E. Käsemann, 'Die Legitimität des Apostels', ZNTW 41 (1942), 33-71.

[21] Vgl. die Nennung dieser beiden Sendboten 1 Kor. 9:6.

[22] BGDW, 5. Aufl. (1958), 1536.

[23] *Strom.* III.53.1.

[24] *Comm. in ep. ad Rom.* 1.1.

[25] Hier handelt es sich um die 1. Reise des Titus nach Korinth. Bei der 2. Reise war er, wie wir sahen, von einem von den Gemeinden bevollmächtigten Botenpaar begleitet.

[26] Vgl. noch 2 Tim. 4:11: Timotheus soll mit Markus nach Rom kommen.

[27] Äth. Hen. 90:31; 4 Esr. 6:26; Apk. 11:3 ff.; Apk. Petr. 2; *Koptische Elias-Apk.*, ed. G. Steindorff, TU II 3a (1899), 163 f., 169 u. ö.

[28] Die Seitenreferenten Mt. 17:3; Lk. 9:30 stellen die historische Reihenfolge durch Umstellung her.

[29] J. Jeremias, ʽΗλ(ε)ίας, TWNT, ii (1935), 940 f.

[30] *Ebd.*, 941-3.

Korrekturzusatz: Während des Druckes erschien die Utrechter Dissertation von H. van Vliet, *No Single Testimony. A study on the adoption of the law of Deut.* 19:15 par. *into the New Testament*, Utrecht, 1958. Die Arbeit bringt reichhaltiges Material über den großen Einfluß von Deut. 19:15 auf das spätjüdische Prozeßrecht und das neutestamentliche Verständnis von Zeuge und Zeugnis, geht aber auf die paarweise Sendung von Boten nicht ein.

GALATIANS 1:18 *ΙΣΤΟΡΗΣΑΙ ΚΗΦΑΝ*

by

G. D. KILPATRICK

FOR *ἱστορῆσαι Κηφᾶν* (v.l. *Πέτρον*), Gal. 1:18, the Authorized Version has 'to see Peter' and the Revised Version 'to visit Cephas'. These renderings of the verb come as a surprise when we recall its use in older Greek as shown for example in the article on *ἱστορέω* in Liddell and Scott with its explicit reference to this passage: '*visit* a person for the purpose of inquiry, *Κηφᾶν, Ep. Gal.* 1:18'. None the less versions and ancient commentators seem content with the range of meanings indicated by the Authorized Version and the Revised Version.

The Authorized Version is supported by the three versions whose evidence is most important, the Latin, the Coptic and the Syriac. The Latin according to Wordsworth and White has uniformly *uidere*. The Coptic, both Sahidic and Bohairic, treats the word as the equivalent of 'see'. The Peshitta and Harclean Syriac use forms of *ḥz'*, the primary meaning of which in both Hebrew and Aramaic is 'to see'. Photius refers to this interpretation: *ἢ οὕτωσ. παρὰ Πέτρου οὐκ ἔμαθον, μόνον εἶδον αὐτόν. παρὰ Ἰακώβου οὐκ ἔμαθον, κἀκεῖνον γὰρ μόνον εἶδον.*[1]

The later commentators were not content with this interpretation which they seemed to know. Chrysostom,[2] to whom Cramer's *Catenae* makes no substantial addition, has three points: (1) he perceives that *ἱστορῆσαι* must here mean more than 'see', *οὐκ εἶπεν, ἰδεῖν Πέτρον, ἀλλ᾽ ἱστορῆσαι Πέτρον, ὅπερ οἱ τὰς μεγάλασ πόλεισ καὶ λαμπρὰσ καταμανθάνοντεσ λέγουσιν,* (2) he will not allow the meaning 'to get information, knowledge from Peter', *οὐκ ὡσ μαθησόμενόσ τι παρ᾽ αὐτοῦ οὐδὲ ὡσ διόρθωσίν τινα δεξόμενοσ,* (3) he decides for the sense *ἰδεῖν αὐτὸν καὶ τιμῆσαι τῇ παρουσίᾳ.* Theodoret[3] concisely supports points (2) and (3), *Καὶ τοῦτο πάλιν δείκνυσιν αὐτοῦ τὴν ἀρετὴν τῆσ ψυχῆσ. Καὶ γὰρ μὴ δεόμενοσ ἀνθρω-πίνησ διδασκαλίασ, ἄτε δὴ ταύτην παρὰ τοῦ Θεοῦ τῶν ὅλων δεξάμενοσ,*

τὴν πρέπουσαν ἀπονέμει τῷ κορυφαίῳ τιμήν. Τούτου γὰρ χάριν πρὸσ
αὐτὸν ἀπελήλυθει, οὐχ ἵνα τι παρ᾽ αὐτοῦ μάθῃ, ἀλλ᾽ ἵνα μόνον θεάση-
ται. Δείκνυσι δὲ καὶ τὸ φίλτρον. The Latin version of Theodore
of Mopsuestia[4] certainly agrees with (2): euidens est ergo quo-
niam neque tunc ut aliquid disceret ascendit. He may have (3)
in mind also: 'et ut ne uideatur per omnia contempsisse apostolos:
"deinde post annos tres ascendi Hierosolimis uidere Petrum." et
ita affectum quem erga Petrum uidendum habebat explicans, et
quod sollicitudinem expenderet, ut redderet ei quod debebat.'

As the Latin has *uidere* for ἱστορῆσαι, the Latin commentators
cannot easily make Chrysostom's distinction between ἰδεῖν and
ἱστορῆσαι. Victorinus[5] has Chrysostom's point (2) in mind and
develops (3): 'deinde subiungit causam, uidere Petrum. Etenim
si in Petro fundamentum ecclesiae positum est, ut in euangelio
dictum; cui reuelata erant omnia Paulus sciuit uidere se debere
Petrum; quasi eum, cui tanta auctoritas a Christo data esset, non
ut ab eo aliquid disceret.' Ambrosiaster[6] has the same interpretation. Jerome[7] takes it up: 'nam et quod uisus (Al. jussus) sit
ire Hierosolymam, ad hoc isse ut uideret apostolum, non discendi studio, quia et ipse eumdem praedicationis haberet aucto-
rem; sed honoris priori apostolo deferendi.' Pelagius[8] could
hardly be briefer: 'uidendi gratia, non discendi.' Augustine's[9]
comment is: 'Si cum euangelizasset Paulus in Arabia, postea uidit
Petrum, non ideo ut per ipsum Petrum disceret Euangelium; nam
ante eum utique uidisset: sed ut fraternam caritatem etiam cor-
porali notitia cumularet.'

These quotations have much in common, enough perhaps for
us to be able to outline the history of the ancient exposition of
this passage. The oldest interpretation is that of the versions which
treat ἱστορῆσαι as the equivalent of ἰδεῖν. As Photius notes this
interpretation and Chrysostom rejects it, it existed in Greek and
the Latin and Syriac renderings suggest that it is as old as the
second century. The fact that much of Chrysostom's comment is
shared by Latin commentators who were either a little earlier
than he or his contemporaries shows that his interpretation is older
than the middle of the fourth century. Perhaps it belonged to the
Antiochene tradition of exegesis.

The point of departure for this later interpretation is Chrysostom's distinction between ἱστορῆσαι and ἰδεῖν. The renderings
of the versions are inadequate and even the Latin commentators,

L

though they have to expound *uidere* frequently, read more into the word than it can be expected to mean of itself. The commentators are equally clear that the meaning of ἱστορεῖν 'to get knowledge or information' is inapplicable. They argue that St. Paul had already received the requisite knowledge by revelation and so had no need to visit St. Peter for that purpose. In agreement with Chrysostom most commentators make St. Paul visit St. Peter to pay his respects. For St. Augustine it is merely a token of friendship. For Victorinus and Ambrosiaster it is an acknowledgment of the primacy of Peter.

In support of Chrysostom's contention that ἱστορῆσαι is not merely an equivalent of ἰδεῖν is the following evidence on the use of the word. It appears first in Aeschylus and continues in use throughout Hellenistic, Roman and Byzantine times, but it occurs only here in St. Paul, and, except for three passages in I Esdras where it means 'narrate', it does not appear elsewhere in the LXX, the Pseudepigrapha, the New Testament, or the Apostolic Fathers.

It is said that the more we use a word the less it means. If we may reverse this, the more rarely we use a word, the more of its full meaning it is likely to retain when it is used. While this maxim does not hold good universally, it seems applicable to the present instance. St. Paul we may assume would not have chosen a word unparalleled in his own vocabulary and so rare in Biblical Greek, had he not wanted it to bear a meaning which could not have been expressed as well by a commoner term. To this extent to treat ἱστορῆσαι as a mere equivalent of ἰδεῖν is unsatisfactory and unconvincing.

This point being granted, we may examine the other possible meanings of the word. St. Augustine thought that it described a fraternal visit, other commentators that it was used of the visit paid by an apostle to his superior colleague and even read into the occasion a reference to the primacy of Peter. Modern suggestions are that it means 'to get to know, to become acquainted with'. Finally, there is the meaning suggested by Liddell and Scott mentioned above.

Liddell and Scott's article on ἱστορέω is probably the best guide to the meaning of the word. It can be supplemented by the quotations in Schlier's commentary, in Bauer's *Wörterbuch* and in Sophocles' *Lexicon*. These together with the references in the indices to the principal authors of the time give us enough material to discern how the word is used in the New Testament period. In view of this sufficiency of early evidence and of the possibility of the word gradually changing its meaning there seems no reason to enquire how writers later than the beginning of the second century used it.

Liddell and Scott give as the first meaning of ἱστορέω 'inquire into or about a thing', 'inquire about a person'. With this meaning the verb takes an accusative of the thing or person in question. As it can also take an accusative of the person of whom inquiry is made it sometimes takes a double accusative. From this double use of the accusative our alternatives arise.

Let us begin our ἱστορία or inquiry by examining the first meaning that Liddell and Scott give, that of inquiry into or about a person or thing. Plutarch[10] has an interesting example of the use of ἱστορεῖν for 'getting information' about both persons and things. Aristippus is so excited by what he hears of Socrates that he is beside himself, ἄχρισ οὗ πλεύσασ ᾿Αθήναζε διψῶν καὶ διακεκαυμένοσ ἠρύσατο τῆσ πηγῆσ καὶ τὸν ἄνδρα καὶ τοὺσ λόγουσ αὐτοῦ καὶ τὴν φιλοσοφίαν ἱστόρησεν. He found out about the man, his utterances and his philosophy, But we may exclude at once the explanation that ἱστορῆσαι Κηφᾶν meant 'to inquire into, investigate, Cephas'.

ἱστορεῖν with the accusative of the thing means 'to inquire into it, to examine it for the sake of knowledge'. It can then come to mean 'to go and examine it' first for the sake of knowledge and then out of curiosity. From this comes the sense of visiting famous monuments or cities to which Chrysostom referred. It is amply illustrated from the papyri in Moulton and Milligan, *The Vocabulary of the Greek Testament*. It is noteworthy however that this use of the term is confined to things. There seems to be no examples where it is necessarily used of persons. We can see something of this distinction in English. We can talk of visiting the Tower of London, but when we speak of visiting Gladstone or Churchill our meaning is quite different. It is at this point then that Chrysostom's suggestion comes to grief. He refers solely to great cities. An example of the word used of persons in New Testament times which demonstrably and necessarily has this sense has still to be produced. We must not be misled by a clause in Josephus.[11] He describes how Lot's wife was turned into a pillar (στήλην) of salt and goes on: ἱστόρησα δ᾿ αὐτήν, ἔτι γὰρ νῦν διαμένει. Josephus does not mean that he has paid a tourist's visit or a social call on Lot's wife but that he has investigated the pillar.

There remains however one other proposed development of this meaning of ἱστορεῖν to examine. It is sometimes suggested that it means 'visit' in the sense of 'pay a call' on someone, a social activity. For this there is no convincing Greek example and we can suspect that the ambiguity of such English words as 'visit' has been responsible for the suggestion. Nor is it clear why St. Paul should visit St. Peter, but should see St. James without visiting him.

Our examination of the construction of ἱστορεῖν with the accusative of the person as the object of the inquiry has shown that none of the proposed meanings of the word derived from this construction are satisfactory. Convincing examples of such meanings are lacking and the interpretations fail to suggest a reason why St. Peter alone as distinct from St. James should be the object of such an activity.

There remains the interpretation suggested by Liddell and Scott. It requires no linguistic defence. It retains its full meaning, thus satisfying a condition suggested by the rarity of its occurrence in Biblical Greek and Early Christian texts. The only question is: does it satisfy the conditions of the context? St. Paul seeks information from St. Peter and not from St. James. Is there any information that the one had to give him that the other could not provide? St. Peter had been an eyewitness and disciple of Jesus. St. James could not claim to be a comparable informant about the teaching and the ministry. We know then of one kind of information for which St. Paul would go to St. Peter rather than St. James, information about Jesus' teaching and ministry.

There may seem to be one difficulty in the suggestion that St. Paul would have sought information about Jesus from St. Peter. According to Gal. 1:12 St. Paul did not receive his gospel from men nor was he taught it but it came to him through a revelation of Jesus Christ. If St. Paul received his gospel by revelation, what need had he to get information about Jesus from St. Peter? That would put him in the position of being taught, which he denies. This difficulty turns on the meaning of εὐαγγέλιον in Galatians. If the word there means information about Jesus the difficulty is insuperable: if however it means something different then the difficulty disappears.

In a study of the meaning of ὀρθοποδεῖν[12] it was argued that the phrase described some kind of progress toward the truth of the gospel. This exposition has implications for the meaning of εὐαγγέλιον. Thus the two inquiries into the interpretation of ἱστορῆσαι Κηφᾶν and of ὀρθοποδεῖν find this point of contact in the significance of εὐαγγέλιον.[13] For the present we may conclude that provided that the meaning of εὐαγγέλιον raises no difficulty, ἱστορῆσαι Κηφᾶν at Gal. 1:18 is to be taken as meaning 'to get information from Cephas'.

NOTES

[1] Staab, *Pauluskommentare aus der Griechischen Kirche* (1933), 605.

[2] Field, *Chrysostomi Homiliae in Epistolas Paulinas*, iv, 29, or Migne, *P.G.*, lxi, 651.

[3] Migne, *P.G.*, lxxxii, 468.

[4] Swete, *Theodore of Mopsuestia on the Minor Epistles o St. Paul*, i, 14.

[5] Migne, *P.L.*, viii, 1155.

[6] Migne, *P.L.*, xvii, 364.

[7] Migne, *P.L.*, xxvi, 354.

[8] Souter, Pelagius's *Expositions of Thirteen Epistles of St. Paul*, ii, 311.

[9] Migne, *P.L.*, xxxv, 2110.

[10] Plutarch, *Moralia* 516C, *De Curiositate* 2; iii, 314 in the last Teubner edition.

[11] *Ant.* i, 203.

[12] *Neutestamentliche Studien für Bultmann*, 269–74.

[13] I propose on another occasion to examine the meaning of εὐαγγέλιον in Galatians.

NOTES ON THE ARGUMENT OF ROMANS
(CHAPTERS 1–8)

by

W. MANSON

QUESTIONS numerous as bees about a hive beset the critical approach to the Epistle to the Romans, but in the main the interest settles down around two primary concerns. One relates to the character of the Roman Christian community: Was it Jewish-Christian or Gentile-Christian in its composition, and is any evidence on the point to be extracted from the Epistle? The problem here lies in the circumstance that while the writer names his readers as Gentiles or assumes their Gentilic character, he everywhere argues with them as if their religious background was Jewish. The other question starts from the Epistle itself: Does its matter stand in substantive and apposite relation to the character of the Roman community, or is it possible that a general statement of Pauline evangelistic teaching was incorporated with covering matter in the Apostle's letter to the as yet unvisited Church at Rome? The latter view has been advanced to account for the existence of variant recensions of the Epistle in the early centuries. Less doubtfully it may help to explain the dislocation between the Gentile-Christian address of the latter and the predominantly Jewish-Christian orientation of the subject-matter.

1. The question regarding the origin and religious history of the Roman Christian community has an interest going beyond any precise conclusions to be drawn from the Epistle. We have to distinguish the Church-history issue from the literary problem posed by the letter. A tradition handed down by the patristic commentator 'Ambrosiaster' (*c.* 370) states that the Roman Christians were originally Gentiles, but received the gospel from believing Jews who *tradiderunt Romanis ut Christum profitentes legem servarent.* Without having seen any miracles or been visited by any apostle

they had taken up the Christian faith *ritu licet Judaico*.[1] This interesting tradition was taken by F. C. Baur, together with what
appeared to be the supporting evidence of St. Paul's Epistle, to
establish the Judaic character of Roman Christianity. With the
waning of the influence of Baur's theoretical construction of
Church history, there came a reaction away from this position.
The Gentile character of the Church has been affirmed by a
majority of modern scholars, a notable exception being the historian Eduard Meyer,[2] who has re-asserted its Judaic complexion,
and certainly if St. Paul's letter was composed with an eye on the
Roman community, it is difficult to see that any other conclusion
than Meyer's is satisfactory. The present writer has elsewhere set
down what seems to him irresistible material arguments in favour
of the Judaic view.[3] Two considerations are of quite paramount
importance. (*a*) There is the circumstance already noted that,
while the Apostle names or classifies his readers as among the
'Gentiles' (1:5, 6, 1:13, 11:13, 15:16, etc.), he argues with them
everywhere as if their religious training was Jewish (e.g. 4:1, 7:1,
7:6, 9, 10, etc. (*b*) There is the striking absence in the Epistle of
allusion to those characteristic aberrations of a speculative-gnostic
type which in other letters, such as Galatians, 1 Corinthians, and
Colossians, are associated with Gentile Churches. All these considerations would, however, lose their force if there was a reason
to think that the didactic substance of the Epistle was not originally framed with specific reference to Rome.

2. The textual phenomena presented by the Epistle constitute,
in Lietzmann's words, 'ein eigenes und höchst kompliziertes
Problem'.[4] There is, first, the well-known textual disturbance
manifest in the variant positions of the doxology which our best
uncial authorities exhibit at 16:25–7. There is, secondly, the omission in G of ἐν Ῥώμῃ at 1:7 and of τοῖς ἐν Ῥώμῃ at 1:15. Dr. Kirsopp
Lake has submitted these phenomena to patient examination,[5] and
decides on the strength of evidence drawn from the chapter-
divisions of Codex Amiatinus of the Vulgate, from Cyprian's
Testimonia, and from Tertullian, that in the second and succeed-
ing centuries a recension of Romans was current which omitted
chapters 15 and 16 and ended with the doxology at 14:23. This
recension also lacked the references to Rome in 1:7 and 1:15, and
was only gradually abandoned, Lake thinks, in favour of the long
recension. Nevertheless Lake has to admit the genuinely Pauline

authorship of chapter 15. It is organically connected with chapter 14, and cannot be considered a later addition to the short recension by another hand. 'We have to face the existence of the long recension as genuinely Pauline.' Lake offers in explanation of the two recensions the alternative hypotheses: either (1) St. Paul's letter was the long recension, and the short recension was made by someone else (Marcion), or (2) St. Paul wrote both recensions, 'issuing the letter in two forms, either simultaneously or successively'.[6] Lake personally inclines to the latter view.

The case for this hypothesis, however, according to which the Apostle emitted, simultaneously or successively, two different versions of his letter, creates difficulties. It leaves unsolved the question, what then did Marcion do? According to the statement in Rufinus' translation of Origen's Commentary on Romans 16:25–7), Marcion removed the Doxology from the Epistle (*penitus abstulit*) and also cut away everything from 14:23 to the end (*usque ad finem cuncta dissecuit*). If this means anything, it means that Marcion's basis of operations was the longer recension which extended beyond 14:23. Marcion had this longer text, and if what he did was not to *produce* the short recension, what was it? To assume the currency of a short recension in the West in order to avoid the conclusion that Cyprian, Tertullian, and the chapter-divisions of Codex Amiatinus were somehow all indebted to Marcion for their text of Romans is to save the face of these authorities at the expense of putting Marcion out of business. The case, then, is against a short text of Romans having existed in the West before, and independently of Marcion. What was first there was a longer text including at least chapter 15.

A more helpful approach to a solution of the problem has been offered by Dr. T. W. Manson.[7], and is discussed by Dr. Johannes Munck.[8] Basing his position on Chester-Beatty Papyrus Codex 46 which was not available when Lake wrote his *Earlier Epistles*, but which contains the doxology at the end of Romans 15, Manson contends that this third-century codex incorporates the original form of the letter which St. Paul sent to Rome, and which was the basis on which Marcion got to work. As St. Paul wrote the letter, it was without the doxology and chapter 16, but the argument is that a copy was simultaneously sent to Ephesus, occasion being taken by the Apostle to add chapter 16 with its personal greetings to Ephesian friends. This composite copy came later *via* Ephesus to Egypt, and there the Roman and Ephesian texts were worked together into the final form now represented by Papyrus Codex 46.

The reason why St. Paul sent a copy to Ephesus as well as to Rome was that the letter epitomized the main theological positions reached by himself in the course of his long controversy over the relations of Law and Gospel in the Churches. The didactic substance of the letter was not originally framed with a view to the Roman Church. Perhaps in this way we account for the dislocation between the Gentile address of Romans and the intimate Jewish colour and background of its theology.

ANALYSIS OF THE EPISTLE

I. Apostolic Salutation and Address to the Roman Church (1:1-17)

This touches on three main topics.

(1) The subject of the Apostle's gospel is the Son of God, Jesus Christ, whose revelational significance the Apostle defines by reference to the two successive stages of His manifestation: (*a*) the earthly life (κατὰ σάρκα) in which Jesus appeared as Davidic Messiah, (*b*) the post-resurrection existence (κατὰ πνεῦμα ἁγιωσύνης) in which He is 'definitively presented' through the Holy Spirit as Son of God 'in power' (1:3-4). It is the same Son of God who is demonstrated in both stadia. The antithetic terms 'flesh', 'spirit' do not divide His substance but unfold the economy of His manifestation. The sublimation of the first phase in the second, by which the second becomes definitive for the understanding of the whole presentation, makes this passage the key to the enigmatic word (2 Cor. 5:16) about our no longer knowing Christ after the flesh. The Jesus of Jewish history is also supra-historical.

(2) The Apostle's interest in the Roman Christians (1:10, cf. 15:23) rests on his commission to preach the gospel 'among all the Gentiles' (1:5, 1:14): compare 15:16, 'that I should be a priest (λειτουργός) of Christ Jesus to the Gentiles, exercising the sacral office in the sphere of the gospel of God.' The Gentile-Christian character of the Church addressed seems clearly indicated unless the term 'Gentiles' is given a merely geographical connotation. The special purpose of St. Paul's projected visit to Rome is the

communication of a 'spiritual gift' (χάρισμα), but the Apostle
with the delicacy natural to one approaching a Church not
founded by, or known to himself, amends this into: 'that I may
share with you the encouragement which our common faith
inspires, yours and mine' (1:11–12). So explained the 'spiritual
gift' is not necessarily an imparting of apostolic order or foundation to an *ex hypothesi* as yet inchoate religious community, but
rather a contribution to the common faith.

(3) Faced by daunting circumstances, the multiplicity of salva-
tion-cults offered to mankind in the contemporary world, the
antipathy of Jews and Judaizing Christians to his teaching, and the
aversion of those who dislike him and fancy he will not show
his face among them (cf. 1 Cor. 4:18 f.), the Apostle comes to
Rome and relies on the gospel as God's instrument for effecting
men's 'salvation'. In a world that yearns for redemption, he has
found it to be God's δύναμις, God's way of getting that redemption accomplished (1:16. Cf. 1 Cor. 1:21–4), and this because it
opens up a 'righteousness of God' for men, a way of salvation
which does justice to the moral reality of God's relations with
men, while at the same time enabling men's restoration to right
relations with God. At the supreme crisis in history marked by
the coming of Jesus Christ, God's righteousness, while declaring
His condemnation of the world's sin (ὀργή, κρίμα, δικαιοκρισία),
offers absolution (δικαιοσύνη θεοῦ) through the work of Christ.

II. THE RIGHTEOUSNESS OF GOD

A. *This Righteousness of God is on its negative side His Judgement
upon a world that is apostate from Himself* (1:18–3:20). The indictment is directed against (*a*) the ethnic world (1:18–32), (*b*) the
Jewish people (2:1–29), (*c*) the guilt of all humanity before God
(3:1–20).

The verb ἀποκαλύπτεται (1:18) indicates, when taken with the
same term in 1:17, that the 'Wrath' of God here introduced belongs to the same disclosure as His 'Righteousness'. It is organic
to the gospel as a sign of the eschatological crisis, the κρίσις τοῦ
κόσμου τούτου (John 12:21), which has come with Christ. While
the indictment of the ethnic and the Jewish worlds in these chapters is grounded formally on the moral facts of the human situation, the real starting-point is Christ and His cross. This has given
the Apostle the luminous centre from which he looks at the sin

of the world, the holiness of God, and the grace and wonder of forgiveness. The latency of the gospel under the indictment appears clearly when the edge of the argument happens to be turned up as it is in 2:16.

(*a*) The gravamen of the charge against the pagan world is that it has rejected the divine revelation given to it in creation. God has made His eternal power and divinity known, not indeed to the eye, but to the mind or νοῦς of man (1:19–20). The indictment follows the lines of the traditional Jewish-Hellenistic theology developed at Alexandria (cf. Wisdom 13), but has a vigour and force which are Paul's own. The nations have turned from revelation to embrace the 'lie' of idolatry, and God has handed them over to the moral consequences of their apostasy. 'Because (despite the evidence offered) they refused to acknowledge God as real, God has given them over to a mind now void of all sense of the real' (1:28). Nothing is said about eschatological promises being given to the world at large.

(*b*) In 2:1–29 the argument graduates from the Gentiles to the Jews, whose guilt lies in the pride which has led them, as the privileged recipients of an eschatological revelation, to overlook the moral realities of their existing situation. If in the preceding section the Apostle had Wisdom 13 in mind, here he is thinking of Wisdom 15 where the Jewish writer turns from the heathen with the comforting reflection: 'But Thou, our God, art gracious, true, long-suffering. . . . Even if we sin, we are Thine, etc.' This delusion of the Jew lies behind the Apostle's taunt in 2:3–4. While acknowledging the magnificent privilege of the Diaspora Jew (2:17–20), he presses the rigour of God's ethical demand. The Jew has in the Law 'the very embodiment of religious knowledge and divine truth', but the Gentile also has an inward law, the sanctions of which he recognizes in conscience, philosophy, and life. Thus Jew and Gentile stand alike before the one tribunal of God's inexorable holiness, and this, according to the Apostle's gospel, is the judgment-seat of Christ (2:16).

(*c*) In 3:1–21 the Apostle sums up. The tests of law and truth have as applied to men revealed their total bankruptcy in a moral point of view. No righteousness but that of God remains. If man's relation to God is to be rectified, it must be by the operation of that divine righteousness, not man's own. Διὰ γὰρ νόμου comes only ἐπίγνωσις ἁμαρτίας (3:20).

B. *The Righteousness of God is in its positive aspect the Atonement effected for us by God in Jesus Christ, who is the* ʿΙλαστήριον, *the Agent or Ground set forward by God for the Expiation of sin* (3:21–5:21).

The Apostle here presents the Righteousness of God as (*a*) manifested (πεφανέρωται) in Jesus Christ (3:21–30), (*b*) underlying the Old Testament and establishing the Law (3:31–4:25), (*c*) verified by its results in Christian experience (5:1–11), and (*d*) marking the Great Divide between the past world-age of Sin and Death and a new world-age of Righteousness and Life (5:12–21).

(*a*) This righteousness is χωρὶς νόμου, but being prefigured in the law and the prophets it signifies no dismissal of law as an eternal factor in the determination of divine-human relations. Rather it means the transcending of law by the gracious act of God in Christ. If law is marked off from this transaction, it is, as Denney says, in the sense in which a Jew laid stress on his fulfilment of the Mosaic commandments or a Gentile on his life according to natural law as constituting a claim upon God. All such claim is excluded by the moral failure of the recipients (3:23) and by the nature of the 'redemption' (ἀπολύτρωσις) effected for men in the 'forth-setting' of the Christ as our ἱλαστήριον. He is the manifestation (ἔνδειξις) of God's will so to present His righteousness as effectually to cover us with regard both to past guilt and to the institution of a totally new relation between God and our souls (3:25–6). Faith, the condition of acceptance, is essentially the abandonment of all self-righteousness, it is the casting of ourselves on God (3:27–8). The language employed—the 'forth-setting' of Christ and the 'exhibition' of divine righteousness—is to be understood in a dynamic and activist, not in a merely demonstrative sense, God has acted not merely to vindicate His integrity (3:25) but to make His righteousness *operative* henceforth in us (3:26). The result is the supersession of legal religion (3:27).

In this exposition the expiatory sacrifice of Christ is the pivotal conception on which the relations of God and man are finally seen to turn. While elsewhere (Gal. 3:13; 2 Cor. 5:21; Rom. 8:3–4) other metaphors are employed to describe the redemptive work of Christ, the expressions all converge on His being an *ʾasham* for the guilt of men. The righteousness of God is thus no mere overflowing of His goodness and mercy, but is conditioned by the atoning act of Jesus, in whom alone the reality of sin is grappled with and disposed of, and the righteousness of God made *transitive* to us as the only righteousness we can ever have. In this representation—

(i) 'Righteousness' retains its biblical sense, in which it has been defined as 'the triumphant assertion or action of God's sovereign will, whether in requiring obedience, or in achieving victory over man's rebellion, or in victoriously accomplishing man's salvation'. It is used here in this third or eschatological sense.

(ii) The righteousness of God is a concept primordial to Christianity, for it is implied in our Lord's requirement 'Repent', for 'the Kingdom of God is at hand' (Mark 1:15), also in His word, 'seek first the Kingdom and the righteousness of God' (Matt. 6:33). In response to this demand men may turn, and their lives take a new direction towards God, but can they give themselves a new mentality, a new nature, a new heart? And faced by the Sermon on the Mount, man may acknowledge the perfection of God's commandment, but can he achieve full obedience to it by his own power or righteousness? Inevitably what God here requires He must Himself put our way. Christianity sees this truth flashing in the vicarious obedience and sacrifice of Jesus Christ.

(*b*) St. Paul's particular description of this communicated 'righteousness' as justification by 'faith' is due to his doctrine being hammered out on the anvil of his anti-Jewish conflict in which his gospel of grace was opposed by determined insistence on 'works'. Over against the latter position the Apostle contends that the gospel is the true vindication of the law (νόμον ἱστάνομεν, 3:31), since the law itself preaches faith. In proof he cites God's acceptance of Abraham (Gen. 15:6) and the blessedness of the forgiven whose sins are 'covered' (Ps. 31:1–2). Law, prophecy, and the hagiographa attest a righteousness conferred upon and covering man which is not man's own but God's. While the appeal to Abraham leaves much in the Abraham story out of account, at one point it brings the patriarch's faith very close to the substance of the Christian religion, and that is where Abraham's faith in God's promise is interpreted as essentially 'faith in the God who gives life to the dead' (4:17), thus being an anticipation of Christian trust in the resurrection of Jesus (4:24–5).

(*c*) In Romans 5:1–11 the doctrine of divine Righteousness is taken to the test of Christian experience. As 'justified' by faith, that is, as covered by the saving action of God in Christ, we are taken out of the condemnation of the sinful consciousness into a

status of grace and peace, and are given a new hope through God
(5:1–2). St. Paul analyses the nature of the Christian's assurance
that the tide in divine–human relations has turned (5:3–4), finding
its ground in the palpable fact that 'the love of God has been
poured into our hearts through the Holy Spirit imparted to us'
(5:5). When the persecutor of the Church capitulated to Christ,
he had identified the upsurge of love in his own soul with the
experience which the Nazarenes described as the descent of the
Holy Spirit. Now, in stammering words that necessitate more
than one effort at successful expression, he sets over against all
limited human ideas of justice the ineffable proof of divine love
given in the fact—he is thinking of himself—that 'while we were
still sinners, Christ died for us' (5:6–8). This release of love in
Christian hearts is for the Apostle the sign that the eschatological
order of grace has broken into time. The 'much more' argument
significantly makes its entrance at this point (5:9–10). 'If, being
enemies, we were reconciled to God by the death of His Son,
much more, being now reconciled, we shall attain salvation by
His life.' This statement is important as asserting the Christological basis of the whole Christian life: cf. chapters 6–8.

(d) The note of 'triumph' (5:11) suitably introduces a section
in which the Apostle, conscious of having attained a climax in his
argument, is conscious also of having reached the high watershed
of Heilsgeschichte (5:12–21). From the altitude at which he can say
'We have received the Reconciliation (τὴν καταλλαγήν)', the
entire past history of the race appears as a domination of life by
death through the separation of man from God by sin. 'As
through one man sin entered the cosmos, and death through sin,
and thus death passed to all men because all men sinned' (5:12)—
the sentence which has started off with words derived from
Wisd. 2:24 here breaks off, because the writer is diverted at this
moment by the necessity (5:13–14) of explaining some of his
terms, leaving his further meaning to be supplied from the sequel.
But certain things are clear. Heilsgeschichte divides into two aeons.
At the head of the first stands Adam in corporate relation with
the race. At the head of the other stands Jesus Christ, head of the
new humanity through His representative action on our behalf.
Over against the 'fall' or 'trespass' of Adam (παράπτωμα, παρακοή)
stands Christ's 'act of righteousness' or 'obedience' (δικαίωμα,
ὑπακοή), over against 'condemnation' (κατάκριμα) stands 'acquit-

tal' or 'justification' (δικαίωσις ζωῆς, δικαιοσύνη), over against the reign of death through sin stands the reign of life through 'righteousness'. But, as St. Paul insists, this is no mere balancing of accounts. 'It is not a case of the gift of grace (χάρισμα) merely corresponding to the transgression' (παράπτωμα, 5:15). The old order is overwhelmingly reversed: 'Where sin (multiplied by law) has come to its full measure, grace has flowed beyond all measure' (5:20).

One or two comments may here be made,

(i) Grace has come when, through the operation of law, sin had attained its full quantum (5:20).

(ii) The two orders, the new and the old, now exist in the world together.

(iii) The order of sin dates from Adam, whose express act of disobedience introduced it, but the organic connection between Adam's sin and ours is not made clear. If indeed the statement ἐφ' ᾧ πάντες ἥμαρτον should refer to men's individual sins, we have here an overlag from the Jewish position that every man is the Adam of his own soul, but this would have no counterpart on the Christian side of the account. It is therefore better to take the ἐφ' ᾧ (Old Latin *in quo*) as bringing out the corporate solidarity of human guilt—'all men sinned in Adam'.

(iv) Death is conceived not merely biologically but theologically or, if the expression may be allowed, *sacramentally*: that is, biological death is the sign or symbol of the extinction of man's spiritual life in God. That loss is now made good in the 'eternal life', also sacramental, which the righteous act of Christ has procured (5:21).

C. *The Righteousness of God in its concrete effects is the Incorporation of our lives into Christ through the Spirit. Here is the radical meaning of Justification by Grace and the finality of Christian Faith* (6:1–8: 39).

The argument takes account (*a*) of what is effected in Christian baptism (6:3–14), (*b*) of the new service into which Christians have entered (6:15–7:6), (*d*) of the dethronement of sin and the victory of life in the new Christian order (8:1–39). Into this scheme is intercalated (*c*) a dialectical analysis of the nature of life under law (7:7–25).

(*a*) The Apostle, concerned to establish that Christians reconciled to God by the death of His Son will be saved by His Life (5:10), dismisses first the captious charge that to emphasize abounding grace is to put a premium on sin: 'Are we to continue in sin that grace may abound?' (cf. 3:7-8). His answer is that this charge forgets the nature of what takes place in Christian baptism. Lietzmann suggests that St. Paul here is merely trying to give an ethical direction to the sacramentalist tendencies of Hellenistic Christians. The truth rather is—cf. 6:3 'Do you not know, etc.?' —that he is *injecting* a profounder and more radical sacramentalism into their ordinary thinking. He is not so much qualifying the sacramental as raising it to its full significance for faith. The ordinary Christian interpreted baptism as a cleansing from sin, or as an initiation into the eschatological community of salvation. St. Paul insists that it means the incorporation of the Christian into Christ, so that sacramentally he is dead in Christ to sin, and alive in Him to righteousness. 'Do you not know that all of us who were baptized into Christ (i.e. to belong to Him) were baptized into His death (i.e. to share His death and resurrection)?' The Apostle illustrates this truth by reference to the symbolism of the rite (6:4). Baptism is the ὁμοίωμα, the concrete representation, or effectual sign, of Christ's death and life in its application to the Christian. 'Our former personality has been crucified with Him that the sinful body might be rendered inactive . . . He who is dead has been pronounced free from sin' (6:6-7). But though this status in Christ is sacramentally complete, it has to be ethically actualized by faith (6:8), knowledge (6:9), and obedience (6:12-14). Clearly St. Paul is here not abandoning justification by faith for a new ground of life in 'Christ-mysticism', but showing Christ-mysticism to be the conclusion to which by inner logic justification leads.

(*b*) Against antinomian dangers St. Paul also places the fact that the transition from law to grace leaves no middle ground of autonomous Christian freedom (6:14-23). He hesitates to apply the word δουλεία to the life of grace, but does not reject it altogether. The biblical term *'ebed* primarily connotes personal obligation to a master and, as such, St. Paul retains it. Changing the metaphor, he compares the transition from law to Christ to the release of a woman from marriage by the death of her husband (7:1-6). The illustration is not happy, for the law does not die. The Apostle's point, however, is that the Christian is freed from law through the death of Christ (διὰ τοῦ σώματος τοῦ Χριστοῦ) in order to transfer to the risen Lord his total devotion.

(c) The sinister part ascribed to law as inciting sinful παθήματα in the soul wedded to it (7:5–6) and generally the intimate conjunction in which it stands with the sin-flesh-death complex of ideas leads the Apostle at this point to clear up certain ambiguities in his teaching. Apart altogether from his indicting of Jewish legalism in its opposition to the gospel as enmity towards God, certain expressions of his seemed to suggest that he made the law responsible for sin (7:7). This idea Paul repels. As that which exposes sin, the law stands off from sin, flesh, and death as 'spiritual', as 'holy and just and good' (7:12–14) On the other hand, and bearing in mind the question (6:15): 'Are we ever to sin because we are not ὑπὸ νόμον but ὑπὸ χάριν', St. Paul has to dispel the opposite assumption that the practice of law *per se* has saving value. There were in his Churches those who, like the persons indicted in Gal. 3:2–5, had started the Christian life in dependence on the Spirit but later proposed to supplement faith by legal observances. St. Paul's answer in Galatians is well-known, but possibly the existence elsewhere of the same tendencies explains why at this point, when defending the principle that the Christian is not under law but under grace, he throws the weight of his argument into what is really a psycho-analytic exposure of the state of the soul ὑπὸ νόμον. In the whole delineation accordingly (7:7–25) no account is taken for the moment of the element of grace either in Judaism or in Christianity. The Apostle affirms:

(i) That while law exposes sin, it has also the psychological effect of exciting it (7:7–8). Rebellious instincts, latent or moribund in the soul, are aroused by the No of the commandment, and St. Paul says he has not been a stranger to the experience (7:9–11). But was there ever an actual time when Paul lived χωρὶς νόμου? The difficulty of locating such a time in his historical experience, coupled with the hyperbolical nature of his expressions—'I died' (ἀπέθανον) and 'Sin deceived me' (ἐξηπάτησεν, recalling the language used of the serpent by Eve in Gen. 3:13, LXX)—suggests that here the Apostle is not speaking historically of himself, but theologically. He is seeing all human life, his own included, against the background of Gen. 3.

(ii) Man's weakness ὑπὸ νόμον is grounded in the circumstance that, though the commandment is beneficent, sin has invaded and

M

usurped control over his σάρξ. It is the essence of demonic evil that it takes the holy law of God and makes it an instrument of ruin to our corrupted nature (7:13-15). Paul, like every son of Adam, recognizes himself as in this matter 'sold' (πεπραμένος) under sin. The law, though exposing sin, cannot extricate us from its demonic sway.

(iii) What follows in 7:15-25 is a dialectical analysis of the slave-relation so described. The Greek Fathers, founding on the hopelessness of the condition depicted, have seen in the chapter a transparent account of the Apostle's pre-baptismal experience, the Western Fathers, notably St. Augustine, and the Reformers, especially Calvin, founding on the goodness of the will or νοῦς engaged in the conflict, having given the analysis a post-baptismal reference. But if the Apostle was writing of his unregenerate experience in Judaism, why have the glory and grace of God vanished from the Torah? And if he was writing of his Christian experience, why is no mention of grace made until the end (7:24)? If we take the representation as autobiographical in any strict or real sense, we are in the curious position of having to say that *either it reflects a Judaism in which the glory has passed from the law, or a Christianity in which the glory has not yet arisen on the gospel!* For this reason the chapter should be taken rather as a dialectical analysis of the state of the naturally sin-enslaved soul ὑπὸ νόμον. This is made definitely certain by the conclusion of the argument in 7:25, where the subject of the representation is described as αὐτὸς ἐγώ.

(*d*) With chapter 8 we pass out again into the sunshine of the life of grace. The κατακρίμα inseparable from life under the law (cf. 3:20) has been lifted not only by the acts of divine grace asserted in 3:21-26 and 5:12-21 but by the supplementary proofs established in 6:1-7:6 that the Christian life is no more a life in sin. A new principle, 'the law of the Spirit of life in Christ Jesus', has become operative in it, ending the bondage under sin and death to which the former life was subject (8:2). For—and here St. Paul's conception expands to take in the full cosmic and apocalyptic dimensions of the Christian redemption—God's act in sending His Son to be incorporated in humanity and to become a sin-offering for us has dethroned sin from its absolute empire in our nature, and has introduced the Age of the Spirit (8:3-4). Christian life is life on this renewed level, i.e. the eschatological order of God has intersected our life in time, and we, though still in the flesh, are sustained by the Spirit, or, as St. Paul alternatively puts it, by the indwelling of Christ. St. Paul analyses the nature of this life in grace.

(i) It is a life in which tension still exists between flesh and spirit, between the old nature and the new (8:4–11). Though dethroned by Christ's victory, sin has not been finally disarmed, because the existing world-order has not yet come to its end: 'the body indeed is dead on account of the sin (for which Christ suffered), and the spirit is alive on account of the righteousness (which He has achieved') (8:10). But what has thus been sacramentally certified in baptism (6:3–14) has to be completed by the hallowing of personal life.

(ii) It is a life in which, through the new orientation of our spirits to the Spirit of God, man's sonship to God is recovered (8:12–17). St. Paul may well be thinking here of the position of simple Christians who, unable to rise to the height of his great argument—'no condemnation', 'peace with God', life with risen Christ—plead that all they can do is to fall on their knees and cry 'Our Father!' The Apostle accepts this protestation as itself the veriest proof of the Spirit's presence with believers (8:15–16. Cf. Gal. 4:6–7), but points out that God, having restored us to sonship, is not yet done with us. He has a future for His children: which is to make them 'inheritors of God and co-inheritors with Christ', if they accept present suffering with Christ as the condition of sharing His glory (8:17).

(iii) The suffering and frustration of present existence must be seen against the bright counterfoil of the glory towards which both in the cosmos and in the individual life, God's purpose of redemption is working (8:18–30). A *cosmic* redemption is proposed, of which man's spiritual redemption is a present first instalment. While man possesses the first-fruit of the Spirit, nature has to wait for its deliverance until man's re-instatement in the image of God is completed by the redemption of his 'body', which awaits the Resurrection (8:22–23). It is plain here that St. Paul thinks of man's present redemption as limited to his spirit. Meantime the Holy Spirit assists our weakness; a striking instance is the spiritual power of prayer (8:26–8).

(iv) In the end the Christian's assurance lies in the inalienable love of God, signified to us in His foreknowledge and predestination of us, in our calling, in our justification, and in God's final purpose to glorify us (8:29–30). The Christian argument is un-answerable when we think of what is involved in the Incarnation and in the Death of the Redeemer (8:31–2), and on this note St. Paul ends. The Christian in his good fight of faith has over-whelming powers working on his side; for over against the physical forces of life and death, the arbitrary tyranny of demonic spirits, the unknown contingencies of present and future history, and the malign influence of the stellar powers, the Christian trusts that the Love of God in Christ will never forsake him (8:33–9).

It has not been possible within the limits of this survey to in-clude chapters 9–11, dealing with 'The Righteousness of God in History', nor to bring to a fuller conclusion the question raised at the beginning concerning the relation of the matter of the Epistle to the specific community addressed. On this question, however, it seems probable that, even if the subject-matter was not originally thought out with an eye on the Roman Church, which is not certain, but represents the mature product of years of earlier debate with Jews and Gentiles throughout the world, the first occasion of its commitment to writing may well have been the Apostle's desire to open communications with the un-visited Church at Rome. Personal touches pervade the writing, and the design to give literary embodiment to the matter may have shaped itself in the writer's mind as the conveying of a truly apostolic charisma. In this matter the critical hypothesis of Dr. T. W. Manson is distinctly helpful.

NOTES

[1] On the 'Ambrosiaster' passage see Sanday and Headlam's Commentary, p. xxv, and Zahn's *Introduction*, i, 431 f.

[2] *Ursprung und Anfänge des Christentums* (1923), iii, 465–7.

[3] W. Manson, *Epistle to the Hebrews* (1951), 172–84.

[4] HNT, *An die Römer*, 130.

[5] *Earlier Epistles of St. Paul* (1914), 335–70.

[6] Kirsopp Lake, *op. cit.*, 349–50.

[7] Article on 'St. Paul's Letter to the Romans—and Others', BJRL, 31 (1948), 224–40.

[8] *Paulus und die Heilsgeschichte* (1954), 191–4.

THE INTENTION OF THE EVANGELISTS

by

C. F. D. MOULE

THE great scholar in whose honour this essay was offered might well have found in it much with which to disagree. But there are at least aspects of it which he would probably have supported; and at any rate nothing can alter the fact—whether or not the essay provides evidence of it—that the writer, in common with all present-day students of the New Testament, owes him an incalculable debt.

The view here presented[1] is that, at the time when the Gospels were being written and first used, the Church was well aware of a distinction between 'the Jesus of history' and 'the Christ of faith', to use the modern clichés; and that, in so far as the Gospels were used in Christian worship at all (and we shall have to ask how far, after all, that was the case), they filled a place broadly comparable to the narrative parts of the Hebrew Scriptures in the Synagogue, as the historical background against which the interpretative writings might be read. The interpretative writings for the Synagogue, one may presume, were, in the main, the Latter Prophets and many of the Writings; for the Christian Church, mostly the apostolic epistles or homilies. The Gospels, it will be here suggested, fall not so much into this latter category as into the former: they were in intention less interpretation, liturgy and theology than narrative statement. It is just possibly this distinction which lies at the back of Ignatius' words (however highly charged they may be with other associations besides) in Philad. 5: . . . προσφυγὼν τῷ εὐαγγελίῳ ὡς σαρκὶ Ἰησοῦ καὶ τοῖς ἀποστόλοις ὡς πρεσβυτερίῳ ἐκκλησίας. So, ibid. 9, he writes: ἐξαίρετον δέ τι ἔχει τὸ εὐαγγέλιον, τὴν παρουσίαν τοῦ σωτῆρος, Κυρίου ἡμῶν Ἰησοῦ Χριστοῦ, τὸ πάθος αὐτοῦ, τὴν ἀνάστασιν. Lightfoot's very instructive note on the former passage, however, comes down in favour of τὸ εὐαγγέλιον *not* meaning a document, while οἱ ἀπόστολοι means apostolic comment on the events, itself including the Gospels.

Be that as it may, the present trend of thought about the New Testament is, if I interpret it aright, inclined to deny, or at the very least, to overlook, the consciousness of any such distinction in the early Church. We are taught, instead, that even St. Mark, let alone the other Gospels, was written 'from faith to faith':[2] that is, that, so far from being a mere collection of annals, it reflects the religious convictions of the community which was its cradle; that it represents an interpretation of Jesus in terms of Christian conviction; and, in short, belongs rather to liturgy and even to high theology than to history in any of its colder and more annalistic senses. Thus, even one who, like Archbishop Carrington, strenuously denies that the primitive Church had no concern for biography, holds nevertheless that Mark was designed to present Jesus as Son of Man and Son of God and to be read at Christian worship;[3] and here he has a large number of other scholars with him, however little he has carried conviction in the matter of his own 'lectionary' theory of the Gospel.[4]

Now, that the Gospels, or comparable material, had some place in worship who could wish to deny? The analogy with synagogue worship already implies thus much. Indeed, it is virtually demonstrable by the time of Justin, for he speaks (*Apol.* 67) of the reading of the ἀπομνημονεύματα of the apostles at Christian worship, and these 'reminiscences' must have been in some sense evangelic and are indeed actually called Gospels in *Apol.* 66, 3 (though this may be a gloss[5]). Possibly something of the same sort is intended in the command in 1 Tim. 4:13, πρόσεχε τῇ ἀναγνώσει, though that may well mean the reading of the Old Testament scriptures. At any rate, nobody could deny the strong probability that from very early times traditions about Jesus were recited or read at Christian worship. We are all familiar with the suggestion that the passion narrative may have been recited at the Eucharist. These Gospel traditions, accordingly, were doubtless framed within the context of Christian faith, so that no Christian writings are mere dispassionate narratives but are documents of faith, springing from such an estimate of the person of Jesus as belongs not to a sceptic but to an already convinced believer.

All this is undeniable, and no one in his senses would attempt to deny it. What may be questioned, however, is any implication of failure, in the primitive Christian community, to realize that there was some distinction in some sense—however impossible it was to draw it in practice—between 'history' and 'interpretation'. Further, it may be suggested that it is a mistake to regard use at worship as the primary function of the Gospels. The Synoptic Gospels, at any rate, are better explained as apologetic material; and even in the context of Christian worship, or of the instruction and edification of Christians, they represent little more than the element of historical foundation—the explanation of 'how it all started'.[6] After all, as to their 'outline' or framework, they are κήρυγμα; and the 'heralding' of the deeds of God in Jesus Christ is, in the first place, for the outsider, not for the already convinced Christian: it is evangelistic material; it is propaedeutic; it is that by which a man is first brought within reach of appropriating salvation.

It is only after this, and in the second place, that he is instructed further, and with more particular reference to the Christian *interpretation* of the facts, and is shown how to appropriate what the interpretation implies. Only then is he baptized and brought inside, thus beginning to experience the joint participation in the Holy Spirit. Only then does he find theology real and significant and begin to be nourished by life and worship within the body of Christ. Of course he will go on listening to and reading the narratives of how it all began; if he does not constantly return to these foundations, he will never secure the superstructure. But he will not be content with what the Gospels tell him; he will need the sort of theological interpretative matter provided by eucharistic worship and by the writings and sermons of Christian thinkers, in their capacity as prophets and teachers.

Viewed thus, the Gospels (or equivalent material now no longer extant) are first and foremost addressed '*from* faith', indeed, but not '*to* faith' so much as to unbelief. And such St. Luke's Gospel, for one, seems explicitly to declare itself. Theophilus has already been instructed; but there is nothing to say that he has yet come inside the Church. The purpose of the Gospel is to possess him of the facts—τὴν ἀσφάλειαν (1:4, cf. τὸ ἀσφαλές, 'the rights of the matter', Acts 22:30, 25:26). Dibelius,[7] while holding that the contents of the Gospel are in a deeper sense εὐαγγέλιον, and were meant also for readers who were already Christians, noted the impartial tone of the exordium; it is as though Luke were announcing a history: Λουκᾶ (Ἀντιοχέως) πράξεις Ἰησοῦ. But if the

Gospel is the Acts of Jesus, Dibelius went on to draw a striking contrast between it and the Acts of the Apostles. Holding that the Acts speeches were Luke's own compositions, skilfully designed to point his moral and help to tell his story, he emphasized that in the Gospel, by contrast, Luke contents himself almost entirely with sayings—not speeches—and sayings drawn from the tradition. Thus, a *prima facie* case, at least, can be made for regarding Luke's Gospel as intended primarily to 'tell the story'—and that for the outsider.[8]

The other Gospel which declares its purpose is St. John's. It is (20:31) ἵνα πιστεύητε ὅτι Ἰησοῦς ἐστιν ὁ χριστὸς ὁ υἱὸς τοῦ θεοῦ, καὶ ἵνα πιστεύοντες ζωὴν ἔχητε ἐν τῷ ὀνόματι αὐτοῦ. It is, as is well known, possible to interpret this as applying to those who have already come to believe, in the sense that the aim is to deepen or make constant that belief. But perhaps the more natural interpretation (despite the present tense, *si vera lectio*) is that the aim is to evoke belief—to bring outsiders within the fold of the believers. No doubt the other exegesis can be sustained: indeed, the opening words of 1 John provide a parallel, and they are clearly addressed to believers. But on the whole, there is a strong case for the view that the Fourth Gospel is more intelligible as a skilful apology to the pagan 'Gnostic' who had heard about Jesus but was misunderstanding him, and perhaps still more to the non-Christian Jew, than as primarily intended for the full believer.[9]

If, then, we may assume for the time being that both Luke and the Fourth Evangelist wrote with more than half an eye on outsiders—or at any rate on those who formed only the fringe of the Church and were not fully inside—what of the other two Evangelists? St. Matthew's Gospel never declares its purpose in so many words; but it does not take much reading between the lines to recognize that a large amount of its material would be eminently suitable for pastoral instruction in a Christian community which had come out from Judaism but was still beset by antagonistic Jews at close quarters and therefore required both directly apologetic material and also the narrative of 'how it all began', which is indirectly of great apologetic importance. It looks like ethical and religious instruction designed to equip Christians not only with spiritual help but also with intellectual guidance in facing attack from Jews. All the time it is presenting Christianity as true Judaism in contrast to the spurious Judaism of the anti-Christian Synagogue; and in this regard it is comparable to the Epistle to the Hebrews. It is both conciliatory to the heart of Judaism ('Think not that I came to destroy . . .') and also rigid in its insistence on the *differentia* of Christianity.[10]

Then what of Mark? The most significant fact about it, for the present inquiry, is simply its contents, which are not only within the framework of the κήρυγμα[11] but are themselves in the nature of κήρυγμα; and κήρυγμα is primarily the 'propaedeutic' for the outsider. Bishop Rawlinson, in his well-known commentary (p. xxii) described Mark as written 'partly to edify converts, and to satisfy a natural curiosity as to how Christianity began, and partly to supply Christian preachers with materials for missionary preaching, and partly also to furnish a kind of armoury of apologetic arguments for use in controversy with opponents, whether Jewish or heathen.' This seems to be a far more plausible account of it than those which view it first and foremost as liturgically or theologically conditioned. Bishop Rawlinson, it is true, ends the same paragraph by saying that 'the Evangelist's motives were not primarily historical; they were primarily religious.' But 'religious' requires defining; and there are contexts in which religion is best served by the historical. If Professor Cullmann has urged that it is a mistake to postulate two types of Christian worship—a 'synagogue' type and a 'temple' type—at any rate he does allow that it is possible to distinguish a meeting for missionary preaching from a meeting for the edification of the community (despite the fact that an unbeliever may be found wandering into the latter, 1 Cor. 14:23–5);[12] and (so, at least, it will be argued directly) it is the *preaching* that is primarily the content of Mark: the κήρυγμα for unbelievers.

Now there were many different types of unbeliever and outsider. Some were Jews, some were devout God-fearers—pagans who had been attracted by the lofty monotheism of the Jews without actually becoming proselytes. Some, if we conjecture aright, were deeply religious inquirers with a background of Hellenistic Saviour cults: not only deeply religious, but capable of understanding such a profoundly spiritual idea as, for instance, the idea of being nourished upon the life of the Saviour and finding life through his death. Others had to be fought with and stood up to: detractors, against whom it was vital that Christians should be armed with polemically effective material. Others again might be described as neutral: they were neither profound, spiritually or mentally, nor yet specially antagonistic: people for whom the first approach to Christianity might be the plain story of what God had achieved in Christ; and if (for the sake of argument) we are classifying the Gospels as though they were addressed, directly or indirectly, to outsiders, it will clearly be this third, 'average' group, for which Mark in particular is the best suited. The cosmopolitan crowds of Rome might well require this type of 'ammunition'.

The words 'directly or indirectly' have been used, since it may now be suggested (cf. Rawlinson *ut sup.*) that Matthew and Mark were both intended chiefly as instruction for *Christians*, though in order to familiarize them with what they needed as equipment for their evangelistic witness to outsiders; while John and Luke were meant as tracts, to be placed directly in the hands of individual readers representing outside inquirers of different types.[13]

But it is time to return to current orthodoxy. Current orthodoxy regarding Mark is, as we know, that it was, in some sense, a composition made up from little narratives and sayings into a structure of great theological significance, for use within the Christian community—perhaps actually at worship; at any rate, largely within the Christian circle, partly for edification, partly to convey theological teaching. After all, the sacraments certainly acted as vehicles of the Christian proclamation: Baptism and the Lord's Supper both represented the shape and sequence of the Gospel; they were epitomes of the Gospel. Why, then, should not the worshipping communities have cast their creed and their theology into the framework of some such narrative as is found in Mark, as well as dramatizing it in the sacraments? That is, *a priori*, plausible enough. Yet, if that was the primary purpose of the Gospels, why did they not include an estimate of the position and status of Christ comparable to that implied by the sacraments and explicitly articulated in the letters of St. Paul? Why are they not more credal? And, still more, why is there not some indication as to how Christ might be received and appropriated, or, in other words, how incorporation into the Body of Christ took place?[14]

What we have to visualize, it must be remembered, is a community of Christians (say at Rome) who would find it perfectly

natural to endorse the little creed at the beginning of Romans
(1:3 f.); who would know what was meant by trusting Christ
(Rom. 3:22), by having access through Christ to God (Rom.
5:2, 11), by being baptized into his death and fused with him in
a death and resurrection like his (Rom. 6:1–11), by being a single
body in union with Christ (Rom. 12:5) and by being possessed
of and by the Holy Spirit (Rom. 8). Now, if a Gospel like Mark
was indeed primarily an expression of the faith of a worshipping
community with such an experience and such a creed, and was
addressed to its own members, or to those who were in the act of
becoming such, how comes it that it exercises such extraordinary
—and, on this assumption, misplaced—restraint? It probably (if
we accept a well-supported reading in 1:1) twice directly desig-
nates Jesus Son of God—1:1, 13:32; otherwise only indirectly—
3:11, 5:7 (demoniacs), 14:61 (the high priest—but perhaps the
phrase is only messianic), 15:39 (the centurion), and 1:11, 9:7 (the
divine voice at the baptism and the transfiguration). It once (but
only by implication) represents him as claiming the title Lord—
12:36; it never calls him Saviour; it only twice alludes to his death
as redemptive—10:45, 14:24. It does not get anywhere near suggesting the possibility of disciples becoming more than disciples
so as to be living members incorporated in his body.[15] It knows
about dying so as to live (8:35), but this is by *following* Christ,
that is, by discipleship, rather than by membership, in the post-
resurrection manner. Seldom (as is familiar to all students of the
Gospels) is there any allusion to the Holy Spirit, and then not in
any characteristically Christian sense, but only in ways in which a
devout Jew might use it.[16]

It is difficult to understand how such a presentation of Christ
could have seemed adequate, if Mark was really intended primarily as a vehicle of praise and meditation for the worshipping
Church. Indeed, Mark's εὐαγγέλιον provides a striking contrast
to what Professor Einar Molland showed to be the content of
εὐαγγέλιον in Paul: '... der Inhalt des Evangeliums ist Jesus
Christus selbst. Die christologische Lehre von dem Präexistenten,
der Mensch wurde um uns zu erlösen, und den Kreuzestod
erlitt, der auferstanden ist und zur Rechten Gottes weilt, bildet
den Kern des Evangeliums.'[17] In Mark the good news is the good
news of the kingdom of God, announced by Jesus; in Paul it is
Christ himself offered in the preaching and the worship of the

Church. To the same effect are the words of R. Leivestad: 'When we read Mark's story of the passion, we are struck by the remarkable lack of theological interpretation. It is indeed surprising that the Easter tidings could ever be related in this sober, reporting style by members of the Christian Church . . . there is no clear hint at the metaphysical background.' [18]

Why did Mark not go on to portray (as indeed the Fourth Gospel did) the Saviour who gives his life in such a way that we are nourished by it, and whose risen body is that of which we are limbs—the Saviour of Baptism and of the Eucharist? It is not a matter of *disciplina arcani*, for the institution narrative is included. But it is a lack of theology. The Pauline theology which is sometimes claimed for Mark,[19] and which indeed it ought to display if it were primarily for the instructed and for use in worship is uncommonly difficult to demonstrate. The same applies, to take an instance from the other Synoptists, to the Lord's Prayer in Matthew and Luke, containing no word or phrase that is explicitly Christian; and to the Sermon on the Mount, with never a word about the grace of God or about that quality of conduct which is described as ἐν Κυρίῳ. Relevant to this, although in a different context, are Dr. Manson's own words:[20] 'It seems a little odd that if the story of Jesus was the creation of the Christian community, no use should have been made of the excellent material offered by one of the most able, active, and influential members of the community.'

Must we not, then, retrace our steps at least part of the way, and examine the ground for a fresh start? Suppose the worshipping communities, as well as 'singing hymns to Christ as God', as well as offering petitions to God in Christ's name, and celebrating sacraments in which they found themselves limbs of Christ and linked with one another, also recognized that their faith stood or fell with the sober facts of a story, and that it was vital to maintain the unbroken tradition of those facts? Would they not, from time to time, rehearse the narratives *as such*, first of one incident, then of another, doing their best to keep within the historical limits and not embroider the tale anachronistically, however well they knew its sequel and its inner meaning? Sometimes, obviously, they did embroider and distort, failing to recapture the historical situation. Sometimes, no doubt, they might, in the process, turn aside to underline a hint of something latent in a saying or a deed, which contemporaries had at the time failed to notice, but which subsequent events had exposed and shown to be significant. But sometimes, conversely, may they not have said, 'We would never have dreamed, considering the original facts, that afterwards they would come to be understood so differently?' And in such cases, would they not be all the more careful to keep the story as it was, not spoiling the contrast with what had followed, but rather enhancing it?[21]

It must be reiterated that, of course, this exercise of reminiscent reconstruction (in obedience, perhaps, to a command to remember Jesus) is in no way alien to worship. On the contrary, it corresponds, as has already been observed, to the historical and quasi-historical traditions of the Jews, more particularly to the story of the Exodus which underlay so much of Jewish prophecy, preaching, and worship.[22] But—and this is one of the chief contentions of this essay—it remains in some sense distinguishable from theological deductions, from the preaching of the way of salvation, and from adoration. It is only one ingredient in worship; and its very nature demands that, so far as possible, it be kept in this distinguishable condition and not overlaid by interpretation. And—another point—its purpose accordingly was not only or even chiefly to be used for worship. Still more, it was to equip Christians with a knowledge of their origins, for use in evangelism and apologetic. The real core of worship was the experience of the risen Christ within the Christian Church through participation in the Spirit. But Christians knew well that if they lost sight of the story behind that experience their worship would be like a house built on sand; and that if they preached salvation without the story of how it came they would be powerless as evangelists; and that if they could not explain how they came to stand where they did, they would be failing to give a reason for their hope.

Therefore, they cherished the narrative as something precious. It would be ludicrous to deny that ecclesiastical interests and theological value-judgments ever overlaid the story. It has been as good as demonstrated that they do. But that is not the point. The point is that the Christians knew the difference between the two —between the pre-resurrection situation and the post-resurrection situation—and that their aim was to try to tell faithfully the story of how the former led to the latter. And in actual fact, they succeeded better than is often allowed.

Two instances may not unprofitably be recalled. First, the saying about fasting in Mark 2:18 ff. and parallels. There can be little doubt that the primitive Church practised fasting: the Acts and the *Didache* are sufficient witness to this. So much so that it has naturally been suggested that the words 'The days will come when the bridegroom is taken away from them, and then they will fast on that day' are an addition by the early Church to justify the difference between their current practice and the non-fasting vindicated by the words of the Lord in the first part of the section. But even if this is granted (and it is not necessarily so), that only underlines the probability of the first part, at any rate, being genuine history. It appears to serve no 'useful' purpose in the primitive Church as a pointer to correct behaviour or procedure; indeed (on the assumption that the second part is an effort to justify current practice), it seems to have been positively embarrassing and perplexing. It is only 'useful' if it is allowed that the Church recognized as 'useful'—indeed, as vital—the reconstruction and preservation of what Jesus said and did in his ministry, *as distinct from* what the Holy Spirit was saying and doing at the time of narration (cf., of course, 1 Cor. 7:10, 12).[23] Secondly, may one dare to interpret the much-debated saying about parables in Mark 4:10-12 (with or without Dr. Manson's Targumic explanation of v. 12)[24] as likewise free from the doctrinaire distortions of the Church? May it not merely mean that nobody can receive the mystery of the kingdom of God without exercising his own responsibility to respond to it? Those who are outside, οἱ ἔξω, are not a fixed, unalterable class: they are merely those who, for lack of response, are at the time remaining 'outside'. In Mark 8:18 the Twelve themselves are in that class. At any time when a man has ears without hearing, he is 'outside'; whenever he listens, responds, and begins to ask for more, he is beginning to be within reach of the mystery. If that is what is meant, it is entirely conceivable within the historical ministry of Jesus. As for the linguistic difficulties in vv. 13-20, there seems to be much truth in the contention that they are by no means fatal to the substantial genuineness of the section.[25] This is not, of course, to ignore the ecclesiastical origin of the variants in the Matthean and Lucan versions: it is only to claim that, in its essence, the saying is not difficult to fit into a place in the ministry of Jesus.

In all this, nothing is further from the intention of this essay than to attempt the impossible (and, in any case, undesirable) feat of drawing an *ultimate* distinction between 'history' and 'interpretation'. Of course it was inevitable—especially for the profounder and more mystical type of mind—that the two should be seen as ultimately one: and the Fourth Gospel portrays the earthly story *sub specie aeternitatis*, perhaps for 'Gnostics' who would be quick to appreciate certain aspects of such a presentation and who were in sore need of conversion, away from dualism, to certain other aspects less familiar to them. But all the time, it may still be urged, the Christian communities were vividly aware of the necessity of trying to avoid romancing, and of not confusing post-resurrection experiences of incorporation in the Body of Christ with the pre-resurrection process of discipleship—of following, learning, imitating.[26] This does not mean for a moment that they wholly escaped the temptation to heighten the miraculous and to modify the details.[27] But the amazing thing is not that they have sometimes modified, but that they have generally resisted so phenomenally well the temptation to read back into the narrative the contemporary interpretation of Christ; and was not this due to a conscious resistance to the non-'historical' in the sense just indicated?

It is sometimes observed that the high, theologically developed Christology of the Fourth Gospel represented, in a sense, the earliest impulse of Christian preaching, while the Synoptists represent rather a mature reflectiveness, bringing with it a realization that some historical reconstruction of the antecedents had its place in the preaching of the Gospel, as well as a theological presentation of the meaning and power of the contemporary Christ active spiritually in his Church. To say so is not, of course, to reverse the Gospels chronologically, or to imply that the Fourth Gospel was not the crown of mature reflexion: it is simply to stress that the presentation of the power of the Risen Lord is itself an early and immediate instinct of the Christian Church, whereas the reconstruction of the narrative leading up to it is something more deliberately and more consciously undertaken. In any case, it still remains at least possible that even the Fourth Gospel was not primarily 'worship' but apologetic.[28]

What is here argued for, therefore, is that all four Gospels alike are to be interpreted as more than anything else evangelistic and apologetic in purpose; and that the Synoptic Gospels represent primarily the recognition that a vital element in evangelism is the plain story of what happened in the ministry of Jesus. Thus, all four are to be regarded as having been written primarily with a view to the outsider (*from* faith but *to* unbelief or ignorance), although, as has already been suggested, Luke and John are more likely to have been intended to be *read* by the outsider, whereas Matthew and Mark may well represent instruction for *Christians*, with a view to equipping them in their turn for spoken evangelism. Only secondarily, it is here suggested, would a Gospel have been intended for purposes of Christian worship—and, if for such a purpose, then for its more *instructional* side as distinct from its more directly *devotional* side. I have argued elsewhere,[29] indeed, that a good deal of homiletic matter in the Epistles of the New Testament bears traces of the use of the Gospel narratives as illustrative material. And the Justin passage already alluded to (*Apol.* 67) speaks of the president urging upon his hearers the imitation of the good things which had been read about. But even so, this would not be incompatible with the contention that it is worth while asking whether the primary purpose was not simply the maintenance, for apologetic purposes, of the historical story.

The one point in the Synoptics where all attempt at historical narrative seems to be abandoned is in the reference to the *rending of the veil*. This is surely symbolical *in intention*. Is it not as much as to say, 'Here realized eschatology begins'? But until that point is reached, narrative rather than theology is the intention.[30]

It is a familiar fact that St. Mark is the first known book of an absolutely new type. May it not be said that it is the result of a conscious desire to preserve the sporadic traditions of incidents and to set them on permanent record for evangelistic purposes, and that, since the outline of the Good News (which we know as the κήρυγμα) was already necessarily in use in Christian preaching (as it had been from the beginning), it was natural to attach these floating units to this already existing framework? Once this was done, it becomes easier to imagine Matthew as compiled for the same purpose but with much more material and with particular apologetic requirements in view; and Luke–Acts and John as written to be *read* by individuals or groups outside the fully convinced Christian congregation—the earliest known written apologies.

When this has been said, it must still be asked exactly how we envisage the ἀπομνημονεύματα fitting into Christian worship when they were so used: was the passion narrative read at the Eucharist? Was the baptism story read at baptisms? Were there other occasions in the course of worship when other narratives were read? Can we fit any such reminiscing into the picture of 1 Cor. 14? Or is it, indeed, significant that it is precisely to such a community that the Apostle addresses remarks which suggest that his friends are forgetting the historical in favour of direct revelation? But for the moment, it need only be reiterated that sooner or later the distinction between narrative and interpretation has to be made both in worship and in evangelism: and we gain nothing by assuming that the early church was indifferent to the distinction, however true it is that, at a deeper level, the two belong inseparably together and are complementary.

NOTES

[1] For a most interesting view of the origin of the Gospel tradition—different from that here advanced, but at more than one point relevant to this investigation—see H. Riesenfeld, *The Gospel Tradition and its Beginnings* (an address at 'The Four Gospels' Congress, Oxford, Sept. 1957), delivered just as the present essay is going to the Editor. See also the communication read by Bishop R. R. Williams at the same Congress, whose proceedings are to appear in TU issued by the Berlin Academy.

[2] The phrase is wrenched indeed from its context in Rom. 1:17, and made to mean something quite different. But it is convenient and intelligible in its modern context.

[3] See P. Carrington, *The Primitive Christian Calendar* (1940), 7, 9 ff.

[4] See the detailed criticism by W. D. Davies in *The Background of the New Testament and its Eschatology*, ed. W. D. Davies and D. Daube (1956), 124–52.

[5] See the late R. G. Heard, in NTS 1 (1954), 122 ff.

[6] It must be freely admitted that Justin, *Apol.* 67, 3, just cited, makes the apostolic reminiscences alternatives to lections not from the Law but from the Prophets.

[7] *Die Reden der Apostelgeschichte* (*Sitzungsberichte der Heidelberger Akademie*, 1949), translated in *Studies in the Acts of the Apostles* (1956), 138 ff.

[8] Cf. H. Conzelmann, *Die Mitte der Zeit* (1954), 5.

[9] For discussions of this point, see C. H. Dodd, *The Interpretation of the Fourth Gospel* (1953), 7–9; C. K. Barrett, *The Gospel according to St. John* (1955), *in loc.* and 114 ff.; and, for arguments in favour of a primarily Jewish 'audience', the paper by W. C. van Unnik at 'The Four Gospels' Congress (as in note 1 above).

[10] I cannot help thinking that this apologetic purpose deserves even more prominence than, e.g., G. D. Kilpatrick's liturgical interpretation suggests (*The Origins of the Gospel according to St. Matthew*, 1946). K. Stendahl (*The School of*

N

St. Matthew, 1954) agrees that there is material in Matthew, e.g. the 'Church discipline' material, which is not compatible with a purely liturgical use (28). His conclusions (35) might well be extended to make room for the apologetic motive. Incidentally, however, it is perplexing to find, in a Gospel apparently directed to that end, such seeming ignorance of Jewish customs as is implied by Matt. 27:62 ff. (the Jews treat with Gentiles about the guarding of the tomb on the day after *paraskeue*).

[11] The sense in which this statement is true may be examined in C. H. Dodd's famous article 'The Framework of the Gospel Narrative' (ET June, 1932, and *New Testament Studies*, 1953) and D. E. Nineham's criticism of it in *Studies in the Gospels*, 1955). See also my comments on the latter in JTS n.s. 7 (1956).

[12] *Early Christian Worship* (1953), 29.

[13] This raises questions, which I am not capable of answering, about the extent to which books or tracts could be produced and multiplied in communities so poor as, for the most part, the Christian communities were.

[14] The Fourth Gospel admittedly, though addressed to outsiders (if the suggestion already made be accepted) goes far further to meet this need than the other Gospels. But why should not that be because the outsiders in question were already of a deeply religious cast of mind?

[15] Cf. W. F. Flemington, *The New Testament Doctrine of Baptism* (1948), 95: 'It was only *after* that Act [the death and resurrection of Jesus] that the rite of Christian baptism could possess its full meaning and potency. Thus we need not feel any surprise that in the Synoptic Gospels there are no passages linking the teaching of Jesus about men as "sons of God" with baptism. The Synoptic silence about baptism is a measure of the faithfulness with which the records of the ministry and teaching of Jesus have been presented.'

[16] About this Dr. E. Schweizer, in TWNT 6, 400, says something very similar to what Mr Flemington, cited in note 15, says about baptism; and see now a short communication on even Luke's restraint regarding 'universalism', read by N. Q. King at 'The Four Gospels' Congress (as in note 1 above). There are also other differences between the Gospel and the Acts which are relevant to our enquiry.

[17] *Das paulinische Evangelion* (1934), 78.

[18] *Christ the Conqueror* (1954), 65. I have omitted the following words, as slightly confusing the issue for my present purposes: 'No doubt Mark has written his gospel with the same intention as John, "that you may believe that Jesus is the Christ, the Son of God," but the account of the last hours of Jesus has a strangely sombre and tragic colour. No beams of light from Easter day penetrate the gloom of Good Friday. There is no halo around the cross, no grandeur in the sad countenance of the crucified, and there are no groaning demons.'

[19] Dr. Vincent Taylor writes in his commentary: 'Mark's christology is a high christology, as high as any in the New Testament, not excluding that of John' (121); '. . . the ἐκθαμβεῖσθαι καὶ ἀδημονεῖν of 14:33, and the death cry of 15:34, reveal that experience of sinbearing which inalienably belongs to the destiny of the Suffering Son of Man. Ultimately, the Markan representation belongs to the cycle of ideas which is worked out in the Epistle to the Hebrews, but it has closer affinities with the Pauline doctrine of *In Christo*' (125).

[20] In Davies and Daube (as in note 4 above), 214 f.

[21] C. C. McCown, in *The Search for the Real Jesus* (1940), 305 f., after allow-ing (what, on my showing, would need to be considerably modified) that the Gospels contain the apostolic faith in an already idealized mystical Christ, goes on to say that they contain 'also a record, meager, but vivid and vital, based upon authentic and largely trustworthy tradition, about a Jesus who actually lived in Palestine nineteen hundred years ago. The Gospels are not merely cult ritual, catechism, and *Kerygma*. They contain all three, but also unimpeachable reminiscence.' I would only question how much 'cult ritual' there is, and whether 'unimpeachable reminiscence' is not itself part of the *Kerygma*.

[22] Cf. Neh. 9, where it is actually woven into a prayer. But see n. 6 above.

[23] See O. Cullmann, *Die Christologie des Neuen Testaments* (1957), 60 f., and the literature there cited.

[24] *The Teaching of Jesus* (1935), 177 ff.

[25] See C. E. B. Cranfield in SJT 4 (1951), 398 ff., 5 (1952), 49 ff. Incidentally, the confusion between seed and recipients is, if anything, a primitive trait, which I should be prepared to believe is *reproduced* rather than *introduced* in Col. 1:6, 10. It may be added that the acceptance of the section Mark 4:10–20 as it stands is made simpler if it is recognized that vv. 10–12 may be treated as a *generalization*. When Jesus was alone those who took the trouble used to ask for explanation of the parables. To them he used to say that the mystery was theirs, while for those who stayed outside everything remained only on the parabolic level (Jeremias' suggestion that this originally meant simply enigmatic is not cogent). Then, in vv. 13 ff., follows a *specific* instance of explanation. This accounts for the sudden change from τὰς παραβολάς (v. 10) to τὴν παραβολὴν ταύτην (v. 13).

[26] Cf. 1 John 2:24 ff. ὑμεῖς ὃ ἠκούσατε ἀπ᾽ ἀρχῆς, ἐν ὑμῖν μενέτω, etc.

[27] The Gospels were (in the words of H. E. W. Turner, *Jesus, Master and Lord* (1953), 31 f.) 'both books for believers by believers and records of a factual nature about a historical figure. Here is a tension between the subjective and objective side.'

[28] To allow this is not necessarily to deny that its thought and words them-selves spring from worship—even (as has been suggested by some) from the eucharistic prayer and meditation of the celebrant.

[29] JTS n.s. 3 (1952).

[30] Even after this point, it is incidentally remarkable (as C. H. Dodd has observed in *Studies in the Gospels* (ed. D. E. Nineham (1955), 25)) that the post-resurrection narratives in Matthew, Luke and John do not borrow the 'brilliant light' which might so easily have been imported from the traditions of St. Paul's Damascus road vision. In the Gospels this is confined to the transfiguration and (in Matthew) the angel of the resurrection.

PAULUS TANQUAM ABORTIVUS
(1 Cor. 15:8)

by

J. MUNCK

<hr />

THE term ἔκτρωμα in 1 Cor. 15:8 is difficult to interpret. This is its sole appearance in the NT, and the context gives no clear indication of its significance. In 1 Cor. 15:1 ff. Paul discusses the resurrection—that of Christ, which has already taken place, and that of the Corinthians, which is still in the future. After having reminded his readers in vv. 3–4 of the tradition of Christ's death and resurrection which he passed on to them during his mission in Corinth, Paul goes on to enumerate witnesses to the resurrection, beginning with Peter and the Twelve. As the last of these witnesses he mentions himself: ἔσχατον δὲ πάντων ὡσπερεὶ τῷ ἐκτρώματι ὤφθη κἀμοί.

While the earlier interpretation of ἔ. stressed the suddenness and violence of Paul's call, which placed him apart from the other apostles, two admirable papers have recently appeared, by Anton Fridrichsen and Gudmund Björck, both until lately eminent members of the University of Uppsala. The word ἔ. is interpreted by both as a term of abuse applied to Paul by his opponents. Thus Fridrichsen, in 'Paulus abortivus. Zu 1 Kor 15,8' (*Symbolae philol. O. A. Danielsson* (1932), 78–85), holds that the idea to be conveyed is that of the demoniac and non-human qualities of an untimely birth, a 'monster'. In quoting the term used by his opponents Paul indicates that it is used metaphorically by adding ὡσπερεί.

Fridrichsen stresses that the image ἔ. contains a denunciation of the apostle in his pre-Christian days as a persecutor, but is not descriptive of him as a Christian or an apostle (p. 79). In addition, he maintains that Paul's opponents have described him as an ἔ. τῆς ἀναγεννήσεως. In his case, the power of baptism has not been able to form him in Christ's image; instead, a diabolical shape came into being. This more problematical part of Fridrichsen's article may possibly be one of the reasons why Schneider (TWNT ii, 463–65) reverts to the earlier interpretation, so rightly opposed by Fridrichsen: 'Paul describes himself as one who "spiritually speaking" was born out of due time because he was not already a disciple while Jesus was alive.' 'His vision of Christ and his call come out of due time and are extraordinary, being moreover characterized by violence' (p. 464, 5–7, 10–11). Schneider has thus overlooked the point in which Fridrichsen is conclusively right, 'that ἔ. describes the result, not the action' (p. 82).

In 'Nochmals Paulus abortivus' (*Coniect. neotest.* 3 (1938), 3–8) Björck begins by saying that in modern Greek the word also signifies 'monster', and traces the semantic history of the word back to older Greek; his contribution marks a real advance, in that he also takes into consideration the synonym ἄμβλωμα, which is accounted correct Attic. ἔ. signifies something abnormal, whose unnatural deformity is congenital, and the word is therefore an excellent epithet for Saul, the persecutor of the Christians. After examining the other uses of the word Björck concludes (p. 7):

It is my opinion that not only is the significance 'freak', 'monster' that which fits the Pauline text best, but that it is also the only one that would occur to a Greek of his period when ἔ. was used to describe a living person, and without any metaphysical significance. There is no reason why we should not assume that the significance which we can trace back to the late classical period also prevailed in the time of Paul, more especially since it must have been far more frequent in daily speech than in what has survived.

Björck's article also marks an advance in that he rejects the usual interpretation of the article with ἔ. (e.g. Bengel: 'Articulus vim habet, etc.'). The article is essential for the significance.

ὡσπερεὶ ἐκτρώματι ὤφθη κἀμοί must mean '. . . he revealed himself to me also as (he would have revealed himself) to a ἔ.' In τῷ ἔ. we have the well-known figure ἡμεῖς οἱ "Ελληνες (Kühner-Gerth i, 602; Gildersleeve § 606) (p. 8).

The two articles by Fridrichsen and Björck have advanced research on this subject, but it can in my opinion be carried still further. Fridrichsen has shown us that ἔ. describes the result and not the action, and Björck that ἄμβλωμα should be included in ἔ.'s semantic history, and that the article with ἔ. has no demonstrative force. It is also important, as assumed by Fridrichsen, that it is

Paul who is speaking, and who uses ἔ. with a significance chosen
by him. But it is questionable whether any opponents ever used
the word ἔ. of Paul. Apart from the hitherto general interpretation of the article with ἔ., there is no reasonable basis for assuming
that Paul's remark indicates the polemical use of a terrible term of
abuse against the apostle.

I

ἔ. and ἄμβλωμα (with the basic verbs and their derivatives) before
the period of the NT generally signified a premature (that is, prematurely born) and stillborn child. It has been maintained that ἔ.
did not mean a prematurely born child, but a stillborn child, but
this distinction is incorrect. The word signifies a child that is born
prematurely, and is therefore normally not alive, but, as will
appear, ἔ. can also signify a premature, living child (see p. 185 f.).
    Björck rightly points out that ἔ. occupies no definite place in
medical terminology, and issues a warning against the precon-
ceived opinion that in the general linguistic instinct ἔ. was always
closely connected with the use of ἐκτιτρώσκειν, 'miscarry', and
ἔκτρωσις, 'miscarriage'. According to Littré's index to Hippo-
crates, Kühn's to Galen, and Hude's to Aretaeus ἔ. (like ἄμβλωμα)
is not used by these medical writers. ἐκτιτρώσκειν on the other
hand is frequently used, and other words of the same stem occasionally.[1] One of the reasons for this is however that these doctors
see the matter from the mother's point of view, and not from the
child's, still less from that of the unborn child.
    Björck here makes a wrong deduction from his correct observa-
tions. It is clear from those ancient dictionaries that discuss non-
Attic words that ἔ. means a stillborn child.[2] This evidence is confirmed by the texts treated below, LXX, Philo and the heretical
sects, whose doctrines are recorded by the Fathers. These texts are
of great importance because taken as a whole they broadly cover
Paul's environment. Lastly, it will be shown that to the exegesis
of the ancient church ἔ. signified a premature, stillborn child (see
pp. 189–190).
    Now, as stated by Björck, ἔ. = 'monster' may have been used
more frequently in ordinary speech than in what has survived. But
the curious thing is that the evidence from a later period which
forms the basis for the theory of the existence of this significance

does not derive from popular circles but from the learned, and those trained in rhetoric. It is only in the more recent periods that 'monster' occurs as a common significance of ἔ., corresponding to a similar usage in several other European languages. If these learned texts can be taken to indicate that ἔ. signified 'monster' at that time, then our earlier and not always literary sources can with equal justice be used to demonstrate that this significance did not yet exist in Paul's days.

II

The basic significance of ἔ., a prematurely born dead foetus, is used in LXX and the later Greek translations of the OT as an image of the deepest human wretchedness. In LXX it is used in Num. 12:12, Job 3:16, and Eccles. 6:3. In addition it occurs in Ps. 57(58):9 in Aquila (A), Theodotion (T) and Symmachus (S), and the last-mentioned also uses the word in his translation of Isa. 14:19.[3] In Num. 12:12 Aaron prays that Miriam may be cured of her leprosy, μὴ γένηται ὡσεὶ ἴσον θανάτῳ, ὡσεὶ ἔκτρωμα (a double translation of *kamēth*) ἐκπορευόμενον ἐκ μήτρας μητρὸς καὶ κατεσθίει τὸ ἥμισυ τῶν σαρκῶν αὐτῆς. According to MT Miriam is here compared to a stillborn child whose flesh at birth is half consumed. In Job 3:16 ἔ. occurs in the passage where Job curses the day he was born (3:1–10) and laments that he was not born dead, or died at birth (3:11–19). Here he expresses the wish that he now rested in peace in his grave, thus in v. 16: ἢ ὥσπερ ἔκτρωμα ἐκπορευόμενον ἐκ μήτρας μητρὸς ἢ ὥσπερ νήπιοι οἳ οὐκ εἶδον φῶς. In accordance with *parallelismus membrorum* the two members of the verse can mean the same, or there can be the same difference as in v. 11 between the stillborn child, who was already dead before birth, and the child that dies at birth. MT reads *kᵉnēphel ṭāmûn*, 'like a hidden (or buried) untimely birth'. In Eccles. 6:3–5 the man whose soul is not filled with good is compared to an untimely birth. The latter is better than he. It is *hanāphel* that in v. 3 is translated as τὸ ἔ.

It is not in LXX but in A, T and S that ἔ. is used in Ps. 57(58):9.[4] In vv. 7–10 the psalmist prays that God will destroy the wicked. V. 9 runs: 'Let them become as the snail, dissolved in slime, as an untimely birth (*nēphel* '*ēšeth*) that never saw the sun.' In LXX the second hemistich runs: ἐπέπεσε πῦρ, the plural form *ḥāzû*, which has given great difficulty to modern interpreters, being understood as applying to the godless and violent men, whose destruction is related in the aorist. Here A reads: ἔκτρωμα γυναικός, S: ἢ ἔ. γ., T: ὡς ἔ. γ. Lastly, S makes use of ἔ. in translating Isa. 14:19. In the song of mockery on the fall of the king of Babylon (14:4–23) it is stated in v. 19: 'but thou art flung aside without a grave, like a miserable foetus'. Here S translates kᵉnēṣer in MT as ὡς ἔ. (Field II, 457), presumably because it has been read as kᵉnēphel. In the Targum of Isaiah (ed. Stenning, 1949, 49–51) the same text or textual interpretation as in S must have formed the basis, since the translation is keyaḥaṭ. The Isaiah text here has the following interesting rendering (Stenning's translation): 'But thou art cast forth out of thy grave like the untimely birth of a woman that is hidden away.' The last part is reminiscent of MT's version of Job 3:16, and may be connected with this.[5]

It is worth noticing that of the OT passages cited Num. 12:12, Job 3:16, Ps. 57(58):9 A, T, S, and Isa. 14:19 S have respectively an introductory ὡσεί, ὥσπερ, ὡς or ὡς before ἔ. In all these passages the OT conception of life is revealed in the fact that a man in the depths of misery is compared to a stillborn child, indeed, in Eccles. 6:3–5 he is less than this. 'Like a stillborn child' is thus the strongest expression for human wretchedness.

III

In Plato's *Theaetetus* Socrates reveals to the young Theaetetus that he, like his mother, acts as midwife. He can therefore immediately establish that Theaetetus is with child, and is suffering from birth-pangs (148E, 151B). Socrates' midwifery differs from his mother's in that he delivers men and not women; he deals with souls in labour, not bodies (150B). If the child should prove to be a phantasm and not a reality it is necessary to expel it (151C). On the other hand, many young people have left Socrates and have then miscarried (ἐξήμβλωτο) of that with which they were pregnant because of bad company (150E). There is reason to believe that in essentials this passage derives from Socrates, since the imagery is parodied by Aristophanes (*Nubes* 137, 139); it may also have been created by him, and need not imply an already existing metaphorical usage of the themes of birth and abortion.[6]

After Plato there is scattered evidence of the metaphorical use of the verb ἀμβλίσκειν, etc., which is reminiscent of the extended use of the English word 'miscarry': (*a*) In Theophrastus, *Hist. plant.* iv, 14, 6 'the eyes (buds) of the vine' fail because of frost.[7] (*b*) In *De lib. educ.* iv (p. 2E) Plutarch writes that bodily strength is enfeebled by neglect (ἐξαμβλοῦται, cf. τελεσφόρα in the text). (*c*) Of thought—as early as Aristophanes, *Nubes* 137, 139; Longinus, Περὶ ὕψους, 14, 3, and of the intellect Philo, *De somniis* i, § 107 (iii, 228, 1) (ἀμβλόω = make barren). In Aelian three times of hope, e.g. αὕτη ἡ ἐλπὶς ἐξήμβλωτο αὐτῇ, fr. 211, 12; and fr. 209, 11, in intrans. active with ἡ σπονδή as subject (W. Schmid, *D. Atticismus*, iii, 1893, 39); Themistius, *Or.* II, 33B (ed. Dindorf, 1830, 39, 27) of words (and thought).

All these examples are concerned with verbs, and it is questionable whether the corresponding substantive ἄμβλωμα (and ἔ.) can be similarly used of something that is a failure. The earliest evidence—not of the term, but of the subject-matter—is a rabbinical statement, *b. Soṭah* 22a Bar (SB i, 496 f.; Epstein, 1936, 111 f.): 'A maiden who gives herself up to prayer, a gadabout widow, and a minor whose months are not completed—behold these bring destruction upon the world', an assertion that is rejected. The last example is further explained as 'a disciple who rebels against the authority of his teachers' or 'who has not attained the qualification to decide questions of law and yet decides them', etc. This imagery may have originated independently of the Greek development already discussed, but it may also be dependent on this. In Palladius' biography of Chrysostom (ed. Coleman-Norton, 1928, 91, 19) certain bishops are described as τὰ τῶν ἀνθρώπων ἐκτρώματα, ἃ μήτε χοίρων ἀλόγων ἢ κυνῶν ἄξια. The text is not clear, but the translation 'failures as human beings, who cannot compare with either foolish swine or dogs' seems to cover the sense.[8] The use of birth as an image has thus many possibilities, and it is not as in Björck simply a question of choosing between the senses 'stillborn child' and 'monster'.

IV

Towards the time of Jesus another birth image becomes very important. Man is to all appearances alive, but is in reality dead. If he is to attain life he must be born anew, perhaps first die in order to live.[9] This religious imagery, which is still in use, also included at that time the idea that this second birth is not one process, but consists of several stages, perhaps several births (thus Philo, *De conf. ling.* § 145 ff (ii, 256 f.)). This imagery is put to a singular use in the so-called 'gnostic' systems in the description of the æons which together form the Pleroma. The last of these, Sophia, has without its σύζυγος[10] produced an οὐσίαν ἄμορφον καὶ ἀκατασκεύαστον.[11] This event threatens the heavens with chaos, and the powers above intervene to restore order. What is formless is given form.[12] It is not possible to discuss here the variations assumed by this doctrine in the different heretical systems, and the difficulties of interpreting the texts of the Fathers of the Church. The common feature of the imagery seems to be that ἔ. does not signify a stillborn child, but a premature child, whose life can still be saved, but which only outside intervention can make fully developed and capable of surviving. Since the events in the Pleroma reflect the salvation of mankind this informs us of the possibilities offered to the adherents of these syncretistic sects. There is here a decisive difference between the Platonic realization of the possibilities latent in man, and the expectation in these sects of help from above. Thus ἔ. here is not something that is for ever a failure, but something which for the time being is not fully developed or perfect. What is inferior or incapable can be stressed because it is certain that the powers above are in the course of fulfilling the possibilities of salvation.

Somewhat later than the NT we find in Eus. HE V, 1, 11 ἐκτιτρώσκειν used of the weak Christians who were not steadfast under persecution, ἐξέτρωσαν ὡς δέκα τὸν ἀριθμόν. Later, however, these apostates confess (V, 1, 45–6): καὶ ἐνεγίνετο πολλὴ χαρὰ τῇ παρθένῳ μητρί, οὓς ὡς νεκροὺς ἐξέτρωσε, τούτους ζῶντας ἀπολαμβανούσῃ. δι᾽ ἐκείνων γὰρ οἱ πλείους τῶν ἠρνημένων ἀνεμετροῦντο καὶ ἀνεκυΐσκοντο καὶ ἀνεζωπυροῦντο καὶ ἐμάνθανον ὁμολογεῖν καὶ ζῶντες ἤδη καὶ τετονωμένοι προσῄεσαν τῷ βήματι κτλ. Here it may also be mentioned that according to V, 1, 49 Alexander stood by the judge's seat and urged those who were being examined to confess, φανερὸς ἦν τοῖς περιεστηκόσιν τὸ βῆμα ὥσπερ ὠδίνων. Martyrdom is here visualized as a birth, and those whose steadfastness fails are stillborn (V, 1, 11 and 45–6 (the opposite ζῶντας, ζῶντες)), but it appears that they can be revived and experience the true birth. The image, like the other metaphorical usages of ἔ., is not executed consistently, but it is important that after the time of Paul ἔ. was used of something as yet embryonic, which by God's help could be transformed into life and perfection.

V

In the scientific view of today there is no connection between a stillborn child and a monster. The former is a child born dead, before its time, or born at the normal time but stillborn owing to special circumstances, while the deformed or at least defective, living child may very well be born at the normal time and at a normal birth. Nevertheless, these two are coupled together, and 'abortion' is applied to a deformed person or in a wider sense to a person of somewhat singular appearance, sometimes simply to a small person. We are familiar with this phenomenon from European culture as a whole; thus Shakespeare, in *Richard III*, Act I, Scene II:

> If ever he have child, abortive be it,
> Prodigious, and untimely brought to light,
> Whose ugly and unnatural aspect
> May fright the hopeful mother at the view.

In his investigation Björck (p. 3 f.) goes back from modern Greek to the period after Paul. It is more natural to attempt to go the opposite way and begin with Aristotle, who in *De gen. anim.* pp. 769b–773a discusses the causes of congenital defects and monsters, and of the birth of several children or young ones, and lays down that the cause is the same as that of abortion (769b; 770b; 771a; 772b–773a). The stillborn child and the monster are thus coupled together as early as the time of Aristotle. That there is a more popular and less logical tendency to confuse the two has already been shown. In the material we possess it is however seldom that ἔ. is used of a monster. But it must be admitted that ἔ. may have been used with this significance. The further sense of a failure, something that has come to nothing, which was discussed above, makes such a change of meaning possible and natural.

But it is this last, vaguer sense which in itself must make us sceptical of Fridrichsen's and Björck's assumption that ἔ. should without further explanation signify 'monster'. Björck's material, in addition to Palladius, whom we interpret otherwise (see p. 185), consists of Tzetzes, a Proclus scholium and *Corpus Hippiatr. Graec.*

(ed. Oder-Hoppe, 1924, p. 374, 8). In the last-mentioned passage Björck prefers the reading: ἀμβλώματα τῆς φύσεως καὶ τέρατα to the παραχαράγματα κτλ. of the text, and points out that Tzetzes has the same expression. Tzetzes (*Histor. var. Chiliades* ed. Kiessling, 1826, VII, 505 f.) turns on his opponents in anger and calls them ἔ-τα, because they are incompetent in their work. In a last burst of anger he calls them both ἀμβλώματα φύσεως and νόθον τέρας. In V, 515 ἔ. occurs again according to Liddell-Scott 'as a term of contempt', but here Björck's interpretation, which assumes it to refer to court jesters, etc.,[13] is probably better. Finally Björck cites a Proclus scholium to Hesiod, *Erga* v. 235, which I have recovered from *Poetæ minores græci*, ed. Gaisford, iii, 1820, 143, 12: τὰ πολλὰ τῶν ἀμβλωθριδίων καὶ τῶν τεράτων ἐξ ἀκρασίας γίνονται καὶ πλησμονῆς.[14]

It seems to me that this material cannot form a proof that ἔ. has the same significance as τέρας. But it confirms what was *a priori* assumed above, that ἔ. can occasionally, as in Tzetzes V, 515, signify a person not normally developed. I attach no great importance to *Corp. Hipp.* and the Proclus scholium. It can thus be assumed that to Paul's contemporaries the word ἔ. might as a faint possibility bring to mind a deformed person, but not something demoniac. Another explanation must be sought for the fact that a persecutor of the Christians is described as an ἔ.

VI

After this investigation of the significance of the term ἔ., we may turn to 1 Cor. 15:8. What makes this verse so difficult to understand is the abrupt introduction of this word, which, as we have seen, is used in several senses. In the list of witnesses to the resurrection Paul mentions himself as the last of all, which may mean of all the witnesses to the resurrection, or of all the apostles (who for Paul are not identical with the Twelve[15]). The next question is whether the next verse, with its 'I am the least of the apostles, that am not meet to be called an apostle, because I persecuted the church of God,' is an explanation of the significance of ἔ., or of the significance of ἔσχατον δὲ πάντων, which could be simply an indication of time, but could also imply an order of precedence.

The difficulty of choosing between these possibilities is not removed by reference to the earliest exegetes. As early as the NT the unknown authors of Eph. and 1 Tim. have used 1 Cor. 15:8, and thus given the first interpretation. But both Eph. 3:8: ἐμοὶ τῷ ἐλαχιστοτέρῳ πάντων ἁγίων ἐδόθη ἡ χάρις αὕτη, τοῖς ἔθνεσιν εὐαγγελίσασθαι, κτλ., and 1 Tim. 1:15: . . . ἁμαρτωλοὺς . . . ὧν πρῶτός εἰμι ἐγώ · ἀλλὰ διὰ τοῦτο ἠλεήθην, ἵνα ἐν ἐμοὶ πρώτῳ ἐνδείξηται Ἰησοῦς Χριστὸς τὴν ἅπασαν μακροθυμίαν, κτλ., show that ἔ. is not considered, but only the contrast between imperfection and mercy.

Ignatius also uses 1 Cor. 15:8, and implies his understanding of Paul's words. In *Rom.* 9:2 he says: οὐδὲ γὰρ ἄξιός εἰμι, ὢν ἔσχατος αὐτῶν (of the Christians of the church in Syria) καὶ ἔκτρωμα, ἀλλὰ ἠλέημαί τις εἶναι, ἐὰν θεοῦ ἐπιτύχω. It is important that Ignatius' condition as ἔ. need not be final. He expresses what must happen to him if he is to find grace in the words: ὁ δὲ τοκετός μοι ἐπίκειται (*Rom.* 6:1). Death for Christ's sake can make him a 'disciple', let him ἐπιτύγχανειν θεοῦ or something similar.[16]

In the patristic commentaries ἔ. receives no comment by J. Damascenus (PG 95, 689D). He merely writes a sentence which is characteristic of several of the Fathers: τοῦτο ταπεινοφροσύνης τὸ ῥῆμά ἐστιν (cf. Chrysostom, PG 61, 327–9; Oecumenius, PG 118, 864–5; Theophylactus, PG 124, 756 f.; Ambrosiaster on v. 9 only: PL 17, 276). Chrysostom tends to the significance 'failure' when he writes τοῦ μὲν ἔκτρωμα εἶναι τὸ ὕστερον αὐτὸν ἰδεῖν τὸν Ἰησοῦν. Cyril of Alexandria (PG 74, 896) renders v. 8: ὤφθη δὲ κἀμοὶ, ὡσπερεὶ τῷ ἐκτρώματι τῶν ἀποστόλων. Theodoret (PG 82, 352) says that Paul wishes to describe himself as the lowest of all men, and therefore passes over all those born in the normal way and compares himself to a stillborn child, which cannot be accounted a human being. Oecumenius (864 f.) repudiates the idea that Paul should have been less than the others because his revelation was later. In that case James would also be less than the 500 brethren (thus already Chrysostom). It is merely excessive humility that makes Paul call himself an ἔ.: ἔκτρωμα, ἤγουν ἐξάμβλωμα καὶ ἀμβλωθρίδιον, ἤγουν τὸ ἀτελὲς ἔμβρυον, τὸ ἄμορφον. Theophylactus defines: Ἔκτρωμα δὲ λέγεται κυρίως, τὸ ἀτελεσφόρητον ἔμβρυον, ὃ ἀποβάλλεται ἡ γυνή. Since Paul considered himself unworthy to be an apostle he used this expression ὡς ἀτελεσφόρητον κατά γε τὸ τοῦ ἀποστόλου ἀξίωμα. Others have interpreted ἔ. as τὸ ὕστερον γέννημα, because he was the last of the apostles.[17]

Among the Latin annotators Ambrosiaster maintains (PL 17,

276): Abortivum se dicit, quia extra tempus natus in Christo, apostolatum accepit jam Christo in coelos recepto cum carne. Pelagius (ed. Souter ii, 214) interprets Tanquam abortiuo: De cuius uita desperatum est. Primasius (PL 68, 543-4) holds: Abortivus dicitur, qui extra tempus nascitur, seu qui mortua matre vivus educitur.[18] Abortivum se nominat, qui extra tempus dominicæ prædicationis credidit.

The general interpretation in the patristic exegesis is that Paul is speaking of himself with humility. No importance is attached to the use of the article, and if *ἔ.* is considered at all it is generally in order to point out that Paul became an apostle at a different time from the other apostles (in the Fathers used of the Twelve), when Christ was no longer among men.

VII

Of the significances of *ἔ.* discussed above, only two need be seriously considered. They are the second and the fourth. If we assume *ἔ.* to refer to the statement in v. 9, that Paul has persecuted the church of God, ὡσπερεὶ τῷ ἐκτρώματι must be taken as expressing that Paul is the most wretched of men, only to be compared to a stillborn child. If so, we have here an OT reminiscence, or rather a 'miniature quotation', comprising in two words an OT passage which in LXX appears in its clearest form in Job 3:16 and Eccles. 6:3. The idea is not alien to the NT. We have in Matt. 26:24[19] and in Mark 14:21 a saying of Jesus, pronouncing woe unto that man by whom the Son of man is betrayed. It were better (for him) if that man had not been born. In using the word *ἔ.* Paul ranks himself with Judas Iscariot.[20]

The other possible interpretation is to be found in the fourth significance of *ἔ.*, as something embryonic, that needs to be formed. This interpretation assumes that ἔσχατον δὲ πάντων anticipates ὁ ἐλάχιστος τῶν ἀποστόλων, while *ἔ.* describes something else in Paul, as he was when Christ met him at Damascus. This interpretation was first put forward by Severian of Gabala (Cramer, *Catenae* V, 286 f.; in Staab, *Pauluskommentare*, 1933, 272 in two versions, of which the shorter version is quoted here): Τὰ ἐκβαλλόμενα βρέφη πρὶν ἢ διαμορφωθῆναι ἐν τῇ γαστρὶ ἐκτρώματα καλεῖται. ἐπεὶ οὖν ἐν μὲν τῷ νόμῳ προεμορφοῦντο αἱ ψυχαὶ πρὸς εὐσέβειαν, ἀναγεννῶντο δὲ ἐξ ὕδατος καὶ πνεύματος, ὁ δὲ Παῦλος ὡς οὐ μορφωθείς[21] ἐν τῷ

νόμῳ ἐδίωκε τὴν ἐκκλησιαν, διὰ τοῦτο εἰκότως ἔκτρωμα ὀνομάζει.
There is however a difference, in that Severian takes Paul to be
one not formed under the Law, and therefore an ἔ.; but it is more
plausible from Paul's view of his relationship to Judaism to regard
him as formed under the Law, but nevertheless an ἔ. because he
had not yet been formed by Christ.

The conception of rebirth is to be found in John 3:4–5 in the
words of Nicodemus, who rejects it crudely: How can a man be
born when he is old? can he enter the second time into his mother's
womb, and be born? Jesus answers that except a man be born of
water and of the Spirit he cannot enter into the kingdom of God.
Paul has a saying that assumes not only a new birth, but a continued process until the desired result is obtained. It occurs in
Gal. 4:19: 'My little children, of whom I travail in birth again
until Christ be formed in you.'

Since ἔ. in 1 Cor. 15:8 describes Paul before Damascus, it must,
as Severian holds, refer to his Jewish past. In the account of his
call in Gal. 1:13 ff. two features of his Jewish past are mentioned:
his persecution of the church of God, and his progress in Judaism,
and we know from the Acts that these two features are characteristic of the tradition of Paul's call.[22] His Jewish past is commonly
conceived as a time of suffering under the yoke of the Law, until
the meeting with Christ. But Phil. 3:7 shows that it was on the
contrary Christ who led him to regard the Law and all other
Jewish advantages as losses. Gal. 1:15 shows that God has separated
Paul from his mother's womb, and called him by his grace. Although the latter expression is used of the Christians in v. 6 (χάρις
Χριστοῦ however) it is most natural, in spite of the commentaries'
differing interpretations (see however G. S. Duncan in *The
Moffatt NT Comm.*), to assume that the call in v. 15 took place
before the call at Damascus, and did not anticipate the latter. At
all events, Paul's Jewish past was also under God's election and
vocation, and it is from the standpoint of the later grace that this
first stage can be described as an ἔκτρωμα.

VIII

This article is only an outline. Much further material could be
cited, and everything said be stated in greater detail. Nevertheless,
I hope some light has been cast on a single word in a single verse

of the NT. Material has been collected from scattered sources, both from Israel and from Greece. The words investigated have been used both as terms of abuse and to express the fundamental nature of life in the terms of the mystery of birth. The scantiness of the material has made it necessary not to confine investigation to the use of the word itself, but to try to discover the ideas connected with birth and miscarriage.

To conclude with two solutions may seem to be a weakness, but it agrees with the vagueness of the word and the text, and yet has the advantage of excluding other interpretations as useless. It is often our task to make it clear how little we know, and merely to indicate the field within which the correct solution must be sought.

NOTES

[1] On ἔ. Galen 17, 1, p. 324, 10 Kühn, see Björck, p. 6, note 1. Altogether, neither Aristotle nor the medical writers have any fixed usage. In addition to ἐκτιτρώσκειν and ἀμβλίσκειν and their derivatives, φθείρω and its derivatives are for instance also used.

[2] Phrynichus, ed. Rutherford, 1881, p. 288 f., warns against using ἐκτρῶσαι and ἔ.; ἐξαμβλῶσαι, ἄμβλωμα and ἀμβλίσκει are to be used instead. ἐξάμβλωμα and ἀμβλωθρίδιον are to be preferred to ἔ. We meet the same warning in Thomas Magister, *Eclog. Voc. Attic.*, ed. Ritschl, 1832, p. 110, 6–7. Hesychius explains ἄμβλωμα by ἔ. (ed. Latte, i, 1953), and ἔ. by παιδίον νεκρὸν ἄωρον [ἐκβολὴ γυναικός] (ed. M. Schmidt, 1858–60). In Suidas (ed. Adler, i, 1928, p. 136, 22) ἀμβλωθρίδια is explained by ἐκτρώματα, τὰ ἐξημβλωμένα ἔμβρυα (thus also Photius, ed. Reitzenstein, 1907, p. 89, 11). Lastly, Zonar (ed. Tittmann, 1808) explains ἔ. on p. 660 by ἀποβολὴ γυναικός, and on p. 661 he annotates ἔ.: ἢ ὡς ἐξάμβλωμα. καὶ ἀμβλωθρίδιον. He points out that Paul describes himself as an ἔ. ὡς ἀτελῆ ἐν ἀποστόλοις καὶ μὴ μορφούμενον τῇ κατὰ Χριστὸν πίστει ἀπ' ἀρχῆς.

[3] S uses ἐξέτρωσε (Job 21:10).

[4] Field, *Origenis Hexaplorum*, etc., ii, 185.

[5] For the rabbis' interpretation of these passages see: for Num. 12:12 SB i, 818, cf. 524, and iv, 751 (note n); for Job 3:16 SB i, 854–5; ii, 80; cf. iii, 71; for Eccles. 6:3–5 I have found nothing; for Isa. 14:19 SB ii, 417–18; cf. i, 95. In ii, 148 Billerbeck sees Paul in Jesus' disciple Neçer, on a basis of 1 Cor. 15:8.

[6] The metaphor in *Theaetetus* is used by Maximus Tyrius X, 4 (Hobein 115–117), and by Philo, *Leg. alleg.* I, § 76 (Cohn-Wendland, i, 81, 7–8), who compare the foolish man to a woman who is always in labour, but never gives birth to a child. As he cannot bring forth a child, the result is merely ἀμβλωθρίδια and ἐκτρώματα, and Philo refers to Num. 12:12, and thus connects a Platonic idea with an OT passage with a different content. Cf. *De congressu* § 127–30 (iii, 98, 6 f.) and § 138 (iii, 100, 21 f.).

[7] Zonar i, 158 writes ἀμβλυώττειν, similarly *Etymol. genuin.* (Reitzenstein, *Gesch. d. griech. Etymologika*, 1897, 20). Cf. Passow-Crönert, sub ἀμβλώσσειν.

[8] Cf. p. 188 on Tzetzes vii, 507.

[9] For this the NT uses e.g. νεϰρός, γεννάω, ἀναγεννάω.

[10] This conception is illustrated by another text, Philo, *Quod det.*, § 147 (i, 291, 22 f.), where it is stressed that God, as the Father (cf. *De conf. ling.*, § 145 ff. (ii, 256 f.)) of all, makes every birth possible, while διανοία is like a χήρα θεοῦ, which either did not receive the divine seed into itself, or else, if it did so, deliberately miscarried (ἐξήμβλωσε). Cf. *De migr. Abr.*, § 33 (ii, 274, 31 f.).

[11] Irenaeus (ed. Stieren) I, 2, 3–4 (p. 22, 1–26, 7); I, 4, 1 (44, 7–48, 5); I, 4, 5 (52, 11–56, 9); cf. II, 20, 3 (351, 6–29); Hippolytus, *Elenchos* VI, 30, 8–31, 8 (C Ber p. 158, 9–159, 25); 36, 5 (166, 7–8); cf. VII, 26, 7 (205, 8).

[12] For the last see Iren. I, 2, 3–4 (20, 15–26, 7); I, 4, 1 (44, 12–46, 3; 46, 10–14); 4, 5 (54, 6–8); 5, 1 (56, 12–58, 9); 7, 2 (82, 4–8); 8, 2 (90, 16–92, 2); 8, 4 (96, 17–20); 14, 1 (164, 1–2); II, 19, 4 (345, 25–6); cf. I, 8, 5)100, 12–14; 102, 10–11); Hippolytus VI, 31, 2 (158, 24–6); 31, 7–8 (159, 16–25); 32, 2–3 (160, 9–15); 36, 3 (166, 7–8); 42, 8 (175, 7–10); 48, 1 (180, 1–5); VII, 9, 4 (228, 12–14); cf. VI, 46, 2 (178, 7–10).

[13] From the Latin Horace, *Sermones* i, iii, 46–7, may be mentioned. Here a father describes his son as 'pullus' when he is as ludicrously small as was abortiuus Sisyphus, who was presumably Marcus Antonius' dwarf. Fridrichsen (80, note 2) quotes Sueton. *Claud.* 3, 2: Mater Antonia portentum eum hominis dictitabat, nec absolutum a natura (= ἀτελής or ἀτελεσφόρητος), sed tantum incohatum. One might also quote Seneca, *Apocolocyntosis*, also on Claudius, 'monstrum' (V, 3) and 'nemo enim unquam illum natum putavit' (III, 2).

[14] In the 'gnostic' texts one could point out, as Fridrichsen does (80, note 1), that the ἄμορφον is described as an imperfect development. On the other hand it can hardly be deformity, as Fridrichsen maintains, since the process that begins does in fact complete the imperfect process of formation, so that there is no permanent defect.

[15] See 'Paul, the Apostles, and the Twelve', *Studia Theol.* 3 (1950), 96–110.

[16] Cf. Philad. 5, 1: ὡς ἔτι ὢν ἀναπάρτιστς · ἀλλ' ἡ προσευχὴ ὑμῶν εἰς θεόν με ἀπαρτίσει ϰτλ.

[17] See in addition Zonar, note 2, and Severian, p. 190 f.

[18] The last explanation is to be found only here.

[19] Cf. Matt. 18:6–7, and cf. SB i, 989–990; 775; 38, 11 f.; 779–80.

[20] In Num. 12:12 it is the enemy of Moses, the servant of God, who is described as ἔ., in Isa. 14:19 the enemy of God's people, and in Ps. 57 (58):9 the godless and violent men. These words are easily transferred to a persecutor of God's church.—Iren. II, 20, 1–5 (350, 4–353, 4), cf. I, 3, 3 (36, 5 f.), shows that in the second century heretics identified Judas with Enthymesis (ἔ.).

[21] Cf. Zonar, p. 661: μὴ μορφούμενον.

[22] See *Paulus und die Heilsgeschichte*, ch. I.

Appendix.—In BGDW, 5th ed., 1958, col. 489, Walter Bauer gives a new example of ἔϰτρωμα, viz.: 'P. Tebt. 800, 30 [142 v], here in the sense of abortion.' This papyrus (The Tebtunis Papyri, Vol. III, Part I, 1933, p. 253–4) is a complaint of assault, by a Jew whose wife in consequence of the blows is suffering severely and her unborn child in danger of dying and being miscarried. Cf. 'the Complaint of Aurelia', Edgar J. Goodspeed, *Greek Papyri from the Cairo Museum*, etc., Chicago, 1902, p. 21, ll. 15–16 (ἐξέτρωσεν τὸ βρέφος).

o

SOME REFLECTIONS ON WORSHIP IN THE NEW TESTAMENT

by

B. REICKE

SEVERAL valuable studies on 'worship' in the New Testament and in the Church have appeared in recent years.[1] In the following discussion, we should like to recapitulate some of the results which have been achieved by these studies, and to emphasize certain points of view which have not always been observed.

I

The most important New Testament *terms* for the idea of 'worship' taken in its general meaning of regular acts performed in honour of God, are λατρεία, λειτουργία, and προσκυνέω.[2] There are also words like δουλεύω, εὐλάβεια, θρησκεία, σέβεσθαι, εὐσέβεια, τιμάω and others, which do not mean exactly 'worship', but have the more general meaning of 'service', 'religion', 'piety', or 'veneration'.[3] Still others like the verbs αἰνέω and δοξάζω, 'to praise, honour', have a more limited meaning than 'worship'. Consequently, to illustrate New Testament terminology for the idea of 'worship' it is important primarily to study the occurrence of the terms λατρεία, λειτουργία, and προσκυνέω.

Turning first to λατρεία and λειτουργία, one is struck by the fact that these terms, frequent in the LXX, occur rather seldom in the New Testament, a fact which is also true of the corresponding verbs, λατρεύω and λειτουργέω. In the cases where these words are found they often have nothing to do with any worship practised within the New Covenant, but refer to the Jewish temple service.[4] There are also cases where Jewish or Christian devotion in general is called a λατρεία or a λειτουργία, but here the words have received a broader and more figurative meaning which is not equivalent to worship in the technical sense of the word.[5] Furthermore, λειτουργία appears sometimes without special reference to worship or temple service, and keeps instead its original meaning of social ministration,[6] as is the case when it signifies a financial subvention.[7] So, curiously enough, there remain only a few places where λατρεία, λειτουργία and their corresponding verbs have the technical meaning of 'worship', as practised by those belonging to the New Covenant.

Even more surprising is the fact that there is but a single passage in the New Testament where any of the terms in question is used for worship practised by the Christian community, and this is Acts 13:2. Here, the prophets and teachers of Antioch are said to have worshipped (λειτουργέω) the Lord and fasted, before they sent out Barnabas and Saul on their first mission. The context makes it probable that this worship was mainly prayer. In the other New Testament examples of worship practised within the New Covenant or the New Aeon, the worshippers are not members of the Church on this earth. Instead, the reference is either to Christ in his function as a new, heavenly High Priest (Heb. 8:2, 6), or to the martyrs standing before the throne of God in heaven (Rev. 7:15, 22:3).

As for the verb προσκυνέω, which occurs much more frequently in the New Testament than the terms treated above, it is necessary first to eliminate many passages where this word refers to a single act of prostration, a 'salaam'. Even if religious veneration is always involved, it is obvious that an isolated act of this kind cannot be termed worship.[8] On the other hand it is very important to observe that the idea of bodily prostration is always more or less attached to προσκυνέω, so that the instances where this verb really means worship also involve doing reverence to the Deity.[9] First among these instances are those where προσκυνέω means the initial act of submission, as in 1 Cor. 14:25 (where a heathen is converted, does reverence to and adores God), or in Rev. 3:9. When this initial act of submission is prolonged into permanent subordination to the Deity, προσκυνέω comes to mean adoration or devotion, as for example in Matt. 4:9 f. and Luke 4:7 f. (where Jesus refuses to adore the Devil, saying that only God is to be adored and worshipped). This meaning of προσκυνέω is rather common in the New Testament; in Revelation such instances are especially frequent, although there the object of adoration in most cases is not God or Christ, but the Beast and similar figures. However, these cases do not illustrate the idea of worship in a technical, cultic sense, because they involve only a certain attitude, and not acts regularly performed. Only in connection with the adoration of Jews or proselytes in Jerusalem, or of Samaritans on Mount Gerizim, does προσκυνέω have a somewhat cultic meaning (John 4:20, 12:20; Acts 8:27). In the continuation of the first of these passages (John 4:21–4), the verb occurs again, but here true worship is said to be something referring not to Jerusalem, Gerizim or any other holy place, but to Spirit and Truth. However, this does not mean that all external forms of worship are rejected within the New Covenant. Rather, the emphasis here is on the presence of God's Spirit in opposition to any geographical limitation of the service of God; and God's Spirit and Truth may be believed to be present in different forms of worship, in elaborate liturgical service as well as in simple prayer. Therefore this saying of Jesus in conversation with the Samaritan woman should not be given that anti-liturgical meaning which 'purists' commonly have found in it.[10] At the same time it must be recognized that nothing is said in this context about worship in a more technical sense of the word. In fact, nowhere in the New Testament does προσκυνέω mean technical worship performed by Christians on this earth. The only passages which allude to a technical worship performed in the sphere of the New Aeon are found in Revelation, where heavenly elders or angels are said to do reverence to God in His celestial temple (Rev. 4:10, 5:14, 7:12, 19:4). But even here προσκυνέω does not in itself signify a permanent worship of God, but only instantaneous reaction to His great eschatological deeds; for the elders and angels in question are only said to do reverence to God and the Throne on the occasions when the signs of the last days are revealed. Hence it may be concluded that προσκυνέω has certain relations to cultic ideas, but is never used for technical worship performed by members of the Christian Church on this earth.

Thus the New Testament does not use any specific term for Christian worship in the technical sense of the word, the only relevant passage being Acts 13:2, where λειτουργέω seems to refer to prayer. Nor is there any elaborate doctrine of worship in the New Testament.

Considering this, one is tempted to ask: Does not 'worship' have any importance for the New Testament authors?

2

Terminological circumstances, however, are not decisive, even if they illustrate several interesting points. The *idea of 'worship'* may well be found in the New Testament, even in the absence of any technical expression for it.

The New Testament authors evidently avoided λατρεία and the other terms in question mainly because these expressions were connected with the Jewish temple, as is proved by the vocabulary of the Septuagint, and partly also by that of the New Testament itself. In view of the necessity of preventing believers from confusing the Gospel with Jewish temple worship, it was hardly advisable to use terms like λατρεία, which inevitably suggested Judaism. Furthermore, in attempting to prevent any confusion with Jewish forms of worship, the New Testament authors in reality also rejected general heathen ideas of worship. To the Jews, technical worship had the meaning of man's bringing sacrifices to God: this was also the view of ancient man in general regarding worship. Accordingly, the Jewish as well as the general human idea of worship is not applicable to the New Testament.[11] In the Areopagus speech, the Apostle emphasized this with the declaration (Acts 17:25): 'God is not worshipped with men's hands, as though he needed any thing.'

But this state of things does not mean that the idea of worship had no importance in the sphere of the New Testament. Rather, the question is one of determining in which sense 'worship' is represented there.[12]

In the New Testament, all emphasis is on *what God does* for man. That excludes any interest in what man, through sacrifices and similar acts, is supposed to do for God (cf. Acts 17:25, quoted above).

Only one kind of sacrifice is required from man in the New Testament, and that is man's offering of his whole person to the service of God, as described in Rom. 12:1: 'Offer your bodies as a living sacrifice, which is holy and agreeable to God.' Here the apostle calls it a logical, that is, a spiritual, worship (λατρεία). This is the sort of worship or sacrifice that may be said to be characteristic of the New Testament as a whole. And in this context liturgical terms are frequently used.[13] But here there is no question of sacrifice in the technical sense of the word. The only sacrifice in the New Testament which may be compared with the Old Testament sacrifices, and which may be regarded as a continuation or rather a fulfilment of them, is the sacrifice of Christ (Rom. 4:25; Eph. 5:2, etc.).[14] Yet the One who performs this sacrifice is God Himself, and the sacrifice of Christ on Golgotha is in no sense a form of worship.

These circumstances show forcefully that in the New Testament all stress is placed on what God does for man in Christ. It is impossible to find here any general instruction as to what man is to do for God in worship.

Nevertheless, according to the New Testament, worship was practised by Jesus, by his Apostles and by the Primitive Church in general. Jesus is said not only to have taken part in the temple and synagogue services (Matt. 26:18 parr.; John 2:13, etc., Matt. 4:23, etc.), but also to have instituted specific forms of worship like Baptism and the Eucharist. Similarly his disciples are reported not only to have taken part in the temple and synagogue services (Acts 3:1, 21:26; 9:20, etc.),[15] but also to have celebrated these Sacraments and other holy ceremonies (Acts 2:38, 42, etc.).

How is this to be defended, seeing that the only important thing is not what man does for God, but what God does for man?

In answering this question, it is valuable to regard the matter of worship in the New Testament from two points of view: (*a*) what God gives to man, and (*b*) how man is to receive the gifts of God.

(*a*) The New Testament describes what God has done for the world in Christ, the central point being Christ's death and resurrection. This not only belongs to the past, but is also of decisive importance for the present and for the future. According to sayings of Jesus quoted in the New Testament, and according to the unanimous conviction of the Apostles and the Church, the justification and salvation offered to the world in Christ is communicated to believers by the preaching of the Word and the administration of the Sacraments. This is so because the New Testament regards the Word that is preached as the kerygma of the One who died and was raised again for the sins of the world (Acts 2:22 ff., etc.), and the Sacraments as means of communion with Him (Rom. 6:5; 1 Cor. 10:16).[16] So the Word and the Sacraments are indeed considered as holy gifts of God: a prolongation of what He has given in Christ on Golgotha, a manifestation of what He gives in the Lord who is always present in his community, and an anticipation of what He will give in the world to come.[17]

(*b*) Now these holy gifts of God cannot be received by man without special arrangements. There must be a human mediator who preaches the Word and administers the Sacraments. And there must be a congregation of people who receive what is offered to them. Such external arrangements are also essential for the worship of the Church.

However, in practice a Christian congregation gathered for worship does not merely receive passively what is conferred on them as believers. There are also *elements of worship* that have a more *active* character, like hymns of praise, confessions, and thanksgivings. In opposition to the principle of 'sacrament', as a symbol of what God is understood to give, theology here often speaks of 'sacrifice'.[18] Can such elements when considered as 'sacrifice' be justified by the New Testament, in view of its quite specific idea of worship as involving only activities of God?

The answer to this question, from the New Testament point of view,[19] is that if in worship the initiative is on God's side, this does not exclude the fact that He expects to be worshipped by angels and men as a *response* to what He does for the world. Certainly this is also characteristic of New Testament ideas of worship. The New Testament often indicates how angels and men show reverence to God and His Son, when they see His wonders. One illustration of this fact is the hymn of the angels in Luke 2:14, which is sung because of the birth of Christ. The same fact may be exemplified further by certain passages in which the verb προσκυνέω is the key word. When the disciples saw Jesus entering the boat after having walked on the sea, they showed reverence to him and called him the Son of God (Matt. 14:33). The women who met the Risen Lord fell at his feet and showed reverence to him (Matt. 28:9). In a similar way the twenty-four elders and other beings in the heavenly Temple prostrate themselves before God every time an eschatological sign is revealed to them (Rev. 4:10, etc.). These and similar cases represent a sort of instantaneous veneration and worship of God, involving a pious response to the great wonders that God does for the world in Christ. As we have seen, the worship of the Church is a prolongation of what God has done for the world long ago through Jesus Christ. In addition, however, there must also be a prolongation of the reaction of those who were

happy to see with their own eyes what God did for the world
through the appearance of the Son of Man and the Risen Lord.
Just as angels and men once were struck with awe when they saw
Christ's miracles and experienced the great mercy of God, so all
later generations must show that they fear and love God, when
they see what He has done for them in Christ, what He still does
and will do. There must also be a prolongation of the veneration
and worship that Christ received from angels and men when he
appeared on this earth, both as Jesus of Nazareth and as the Risen
One. And this prolongation is the worship of God practised by
the Church, in so far as it consists of such things as hymns, doxo-
logies, confessions and thanksgivings. In the New Testament there
is an illustration of this in Eph. 5:15–21.[20]

The fact that Our Lord and his Apostles took part in Jewish
worship before any specific worship of the Church had come into
existence indicates their anticipation of it. For in doing this, they
did not simply adapt themselves to Judaism, but obviously considered Jewish worship to have gained a new import since the
coming of the Messiah (Luke 4:21; Acts 13:38–41). Accordingly,
even this provisional participation in Jewish worship is actually to be
regarded as a response of man to the great deeds of God in Christ.[21]

These, it seems to me, are the principal New Testament reasons
why there must be worship in the Church, regarded as the work
of God and partly also as a response of man.

3

On the other hand it is apparent that within the New Testament
period a certain *evolution of conceptions of worship* took place. The
teaching of Jesus and Paul is not so advanced in this respect, as is
that of the authors of later writings like Hebrews and Revelation,
whose conceptions are explicitly 'liturgical'.

However, the question is whether such differences are great
enough to justify rejecting the liturgical interests of Hebrews and
Revelation, and so to conclude that the development of worship
in the Church was not a legitimate one, as many anti-liturgists are
inclined to say. In view of this problem it is important to ascertain
whether or not certain essential conceptions found in Hebrews
and Revelation were represented earlier by Jesus and Paul.

As to Jesus himself and his views on worship, one has first of all
to consider the following evidence. The belief so characteristic of

Hebrews and Revelation, that the real temple of God is in heaven and that the earthly temple was a copy of the celestial, was represented already in the Old Testament and in Judaism, e.g. Exod. 26:30; Isa. 6:1–13; Ezek. 40–44; Ecclus. 24:1–12; Wisd. of Sol. 9:8; 1 En. 14:10–25; 2 En. 55:2.[22] Our Lord shared this conviction when He called heaven the throne of God (Matt. 5:34, 23:22), when he spoke of angels serving before God in heaven (Matt. 18:10), when he related the meals he celebrated with his disciples to heavenly meals with the patriarchs (Matt. 8:11 parr.), and when he spoke of rebuilding the Temple (Matt. 26:61 parr).[23] Thus the inherited Jewish ideas of a divine liturgy did not disappear from the teaching of Jesus, although he was highly critical of the actual state of things in the Temple of Jerusalem. He also used the symbol of a building, representing the Temple of God erected on this earth, e.g. Matt. 21:42 parr.[24] Even the cleansing of the Temple (Matt. 21:12–19 parr.) proves that he appreciated this holy place and its liturgy, although it had been made a den of thieves.[25] Also important is the fact that when instituting the Holy Eucharist the Lord treated it as a prefiguration of a meal that he expected to celebrate in the Kingdom of God (Luke 22:16, 18). There is no sufficient ground to deny the authenticity of all these details, even if scholars may reject some of the passages quoted as not being 'genuine'. Accordingly, the liturgical ideas of Our Lord were not so different from those of such later New Testament writings as Hebrews and Revelation.

It is further to be observed that all the four Gospels represent traditions according to which Christ directly authorized worship practised by his disciples. This is obvious from the story of Mary and Martha (Luke 10:38–42), and from that of the woman anointing Jesus, told in different forms in Luke 7:36–50 and in Matt. 26:6–13; Mark 14:3–9; John 12:1–8. Both traditions have the same purpose: to show that Jesus stressed the importance of worship as well as social work. Formally these traditions are not identical, but appear to be historically related to each other. In the Synoptic Gospels, the woman anointing Jesus is anonymous. According to John, she was none other than Mary, the sister of Martha. The latter fact was not known to Luke, who reproduced both stories without referring them to each other. This complicated state of things proves that old traditions are involved here which were taken over by the evangelists without being coordinated.

Probably the stories in question were included in the Gospel traditions in a situation where the Church discussed the value of liturgy in relation to that of *diakonia*, which is the very point in these stories. Allusions to such an ecclesiastical situation are found in the remarks that Martha was occupied with much *diakonia* (Luke 10:40), and that the good work of the woman who anointed Jesus would be remembered in every place where the Gospel should be preached (Matt. 26:13). This is nothing extraordinary. It certainly often happened during the collection and the formation of the gospel traditions that problems of the Early Church directed attention to what Jesus had said or done in a corresponding situation. Thus, in order to elucidate the problem regarding the value of worship in relation to that of social work, it was helpful to recollect situations in the life of Our Lord where he had given instructive answers to this problem.

In what situation of the Church did this problem become acute? Particularly suggestive is the discussion referred to in Acts 6:1-6. Because of the growth of the community, a certain tension between the ideals of worship or liturgy and social work or *diakonia* became unavoidable. As a result, the functions of the apostolic ministry were divided so that the Twelve kept to liturgy, whereas *diakonia* was handed over to a new *collegium*, that of the Seven. In this, or in a similar situation, the value of liturgy, which the Twelve had chosen, was easily called in question. In such circumstances it was valuable for the Apostles to cite one or two situations in the life of Jesus in which he had given directions with regard to the problem under discussion. Thus the Twelve were able to convince themselves and others that they had chosen the good part, as Mary is said to have done in Luke 10:42.

This does not exclude the possibility that something of the kind recorded in the story of Mary and Martha really took place in the life of Our Lord. It is only the form of the stories that has been influenced by an ecclesiastical situation. As to the possibility of their essential authenticity, considered from a purely historical and not dogmatic point of view, there is no reason to be sceptical. Especially it must be recognized that presumably from the very beginning the stories were told by the Twelve who, without sufficient reason, should not be stamped as falsifiers of traditions developed only a few years after the death of Jesus.

In any case it should be clear that according to traditions which probably go back to the Apostles, and were taken up at a very early date, Jesus defended the practice of worship alongside the social work that was otherwise so important a part of his teaching.

This, it seems to me, may confirm the testimony of the New Testament that Our Lord himself instituted Baptism and the Eucharist, the principal sacraments of the Church. Even if these liturgical forms were perhaps not instituted exactly in the way described in Matt. 28:16-20 and 26:26-29 parr., there is no sufficient historical reason to justify the anti-liturgical scholars' inclination to disregard these descriptions as cult legends. It is evident from the circumstances referred to above that Jesus was not so unfamiliar with the idea of worship that he could not have instituted sacraments like Baptism and the Eucharist.

Turning now to St. Paul, we must consider the fact that he assigns cosmic importance to the worship of a Christian congregation. Thus in 1 Cor. 11:3-10 he exhorts men and women, gathered to pray and to preach, to behave in accordance with their different positions in creation. A man taking part in worship must show that he is the glory of God, a woman that she is the glory of man, v. 7, the order being supervised by angels, v. 10. Furthermore it is not to be denied that St. Paul had a profound veneration for the sacraments. He goes as far as to explain the destruction of the children of Israel in the wilderness as the result of their having shown contempt for the sacraments (1 Cor. 10:1-11). According to him they had actually participated in Baptism and the Eucharist, though in prefigurative forms. This is evidence for St. Paul's great appreciation of these sacraments. And when he says he had baptized only a few members of the Corinthian congregation (1 Cor. 1:14-17), this is not because he had Baptism in contempt, but, quite the opposite, because he did not wish to handle this sacrament in a careless way. St. Paul's high estimation of Baptism is also evident from Rom. 6:3-10, where Christian ethics are directly related to Baptism as the means of connection with the death of Christ. In a similar way the moral life of Christians is related in 1 Cor. 11:20-34 to the Lord's Supper. No doubt St. Paul found the sacraments so essential that one must call his theology 'liturgical', in a broad sense of the word.

Accordingly, there is every reason to see a continuity between the Jesus of the Gospels and St. Paul on the one hand and writings like Hebrews and Revelation on the other. For the heavenly worship of God which is described in these later writings is already presupposed by Our Lord and His greatest Apostle, and their comments on worship and the sacraments prove that in this respect they represented a way of thinking which must be called 'liturgical'. So it should be acknowledged that the development of liturgical worship in the Church is, historically, a quite legitimate one, which cannot be dismissed as the result of later Jewish or Hellenistic influences, as has often been attempted by anti-liturgical scholars and laymen.

4

Certainly the *forms of worship* cannot possibly have been so rich at the beginning as they were later. In fact, the descriptions in Acts give the impression that these forms of Christian worship were originally *quite simple*. Furthermore it took a long time for them to become more or less fixed. As is proved by St. Paul's Epistles to the Corinthians, a rather free order of service still prevailed in a diaspora community like Corinth, 1 Cor. 14:23-40.

But a *sort of liturgy* was certainly present from the very beginning. This is shown by Acts 2:42, where the believers in Jerusalem are said to have taken part in the instruction of the Apostles, the communion, the breaking of bread and the prayers, the context indicating that provisionally this took place in the Temple. Even if St. Luke had no personal experience of the primitive Jerusalem congregation, it is not probable that this liturgical scenery was his personal invention, for then he should rather have attributed to the primitive community even such details as were characteristic of his environment and of his theology—which he does not do. As long as there are no other documents available referring to the subject, there is nothing to prove that the worship of the primitive Church was essentially other than St. Luke has described it. All *a priori* arguments against the description of Acts, such as the *konsequent* eschatology many think was characteristic of the first community, are indeed quite arbitrary. It is also arbitrary to deny the sacramental character of the breaking of bread alluded to in Acts, even if this activity was not identical with the Holy Eucharist as it appears in later contexts. The members of the Jerusalem congregation broke the bread in communion with the Apostles and in the shadow of the Temple, receiving instruction from the

Apostles and taking part in their prayers which, in Acts 6:2, 4, are described as belonging to a continuous service of the Word of God.[26] It is quite evident that St. Luke represents a tradition according to which the Apostles and the first Christians in Jerusalem from the very beginning took up a liturgical service of God in the Temple. And there is no reason why this should not be true. On the contrary it is very probable that a liturgical service was their way of keeping contact with the Lord and preparing for the salvation of the new Israel that had been created through the resurrection of Christ. Thus it may be concluded that the worship of the first community, though simple, had a liturgical character.

Furthermore, certain *main forms* of service which existed *already* in the church of the *New Testament* may be discerned.[27] These probably were developed in accordance with older Jewish types of worship so that they may have existed even in the environment of Our Lord. (1) Baptism was such a specific form. It may have developed by analogy with lustrations of Jewish priests, Jewish proselyte baptism and purification rites of such revival movements as the community of Qumran and that of John the Baptist.[28] Of course the intimate relation of Christian Baptism to Christ and to the Holy Ghost is something quite new. And in Matt. 28:19 the institution of Christian Baptism doubtless has been described by one who was already acquainted with this fundamental sacrament of the Church. Nevertheless it is evident that from the very beginning, Christian Baptism was practised because Our Lord himself was baptized by John in the river Jordan, a fact which there is no reason to doubt. Thus the Christian sacrament of Baptism has a historical background in Judaism. (2) Another specific form of liturgical service practised by the Early Church was the common meal, to which were attached prayers, lessons and sermons, as indicated for instance by Acts 2:42, 20:7. It cannot be denied that this holy meal was partly a continuation of Our Lord's regular meals with his disciples.[29] These meals, in turn, may be thought to depend on Jewish religious meals, celebrated weekly or daily, such as are known from the Qumran community[30] and from the Pharisaic groups called ḥaburoth.[31] At the same time the Christian holy meal was understood as a continuation of Our Lord's last supper to which he had given a new and higher significance by relating it to Passover and sacrifice motifs.[32] In its later development the ceremony was concentrated on this 'eucharistic' motif, so that it lost its character of a common meal where real food was eaten. St. Paul contributed to the development of such a purely eucharistic ceremony in Corinth (1 Cor. 11:20).[33] There are, accordingly, several forms and factors to be considered in the development of the Eucharist. But the whole process may be regarded as an evolution of items which go back to Judaism, to Jesus himself and his apostles. It is not a question of anything quite new, or anything imported from outside. (3) Probably there were also in the Early Church sermon and prayer meetings without any relation to a common meal.[34] This seems to be probable with regard to Acts 1:14, 2:1–41, 3:11–26, 4:23–31, 5:18–25, 42, 13:2 f., 14:23–40. Here the Christians are described as gathered to pray and to listen to the word, without any meal being mentioned. Further, in Acts 6:4 appears an allusion to the fact that the Twelve chose to occupy themselves only with prayer and the 'service of the word', whereas the Seven took over the organization of the common meals. In the Jerusalem community, this 'service of the word' was obviously developed as a counterpart to the Jewish temple horæ and the synagogue worship, although formal differences existed between them; in a place like Corinth, Hellenistic piety may also have exerted its influence.[35] But the most characteristic thing was that this 'service of the word' had a special importance in missionary endeavours,[36] when outsiders were often present, and might sometimes be converted (Acts 2:5–13, 37–41, 3:11, 4:4, 5:25, 1 Cor. 14:23). The missionary purpose of such prayer meetings did not prevent them from being services of worship,[37] for the community of believers was understood to be present here just as at the common meals. The difference lay in the fact that here outsiders were allowed to participate who probably were not admitted to the holy meals of the elect. On the other hand the service of the word may be seen as intimately related to the common meal, for it may be regarded as a preparation for Baptism and the Eucharist, which were reserved for the believers. In the later main service of the Church, the mass, this preliminary service of the word was actually combined with the eucharistic meal, serving as an introduction to the latter.[38] Thus the mass of the ancient Church consisted of the 'missa catechumenorum', which included a sermon, and at which unbaptized persons could also be present, and the 'missa fidelium', which included the eucharistic meal and was reserved for the baptized. This combination is only a logical consequence of the fact that in practice the service of the word was really a sort of preparation for the Eucharist, its purpose being the conversion of all people, whereas the Eucharist itself served for the edification of fully fledged believers.

All this shows that the development of the liturgical forms of the Church was on the whole quite natural and legitimate, and that its main factors were already present in the environment of Jesus and his Apostles. Judaism also offers clear analogies to them.[39]

However, although these forms of worship may be called liturgical, and may even be traced partially to Jewish ceremonies, they are not at all 'worship' in the traditional sense of the word. They do not mean that man does anything for God in bringing Him sacrifices or in other service. Rather, the believers only *receive* the gifts of God when they take part in Christian worship. In connection with the service of the word they hear the Word of God preached to them by one who speaks in the name of God. Even in the case of prayer it is not the believers who pray, but the Holy Ghost who prays for them (Rom. 8:15 f.). In connection with the Sacraments which are a continuation of the work of God in Jesus Christ, the believers receive the gifts conferred on them by Christ and his Spirit. Man is passive, God is the only one who acts. A Christian does not baptize himself, but is baptized when he is embodied in the communion of saints which is the Church, the Body of Christ. He is presented with the flesh and blood of the Crucified when he takes part in the Lord's Supper. It is not a question of sacrifice performed by individuals, but of one performed by Christ for his congregation. This fact should always be observed when we speak of worship in the New Testament.

Worship is certainly to be found throughout the New Testament, even in the technical sense of liturgical action. But here it presents that peculiar characteristic: God Himself is the agent behind all worship. Man only receives these gifts of God that so abundantly stream upon him from the Cross and through the Holy Ghost. Here is the great mystery, that even when man thinks he is active in worship, it is God and His Holy Ghost that are working in him (Rom. 8:15 f.; cf. Phil. 2:12b–13a).[40] This is the reason why the Church regards its liturgical traditions as venerable and holy.

NOTES

[1] E.g. O. Cullmann, *Urchristentum und Gottesdienst* (1944; 2nd edn., 1950); G. Dix, *The Shape of the Liturgy* (1945); E. Sjöberg, 'Kirche und Kultus im Neuen Testament', *Ein Buch von der Kirche von schwedischen Theologen*, hrsg. von G. Aulén e.a. (1950), 85–109; W. Hahn *Gottesdienst und Opfer Christi* (1951); G. Delling, *Der Gottesdienst im Neuen Testament* (1952); H. Schlier, *Die Verkündigung im Gottesdienst der Kirche* (1953); also in: *Die Zeit der Kirche. Exegetische Aufsätze und Vorträge* (1956), 244–64; P. Brunner, 'Zur Lehre vom Gottesdienst der im Namen Jesu versammelten Gemeinde', *Leiturgia*, i (1954), 83–364; E. Lerle, *Die Predigt im Neuen Testament* (1956); C. E. B. Cranfield, 'Divine and Human Action. The Biblical Concept of Worship', *Interpretation*, xii (1958), 387–98.

[2] H. Strathmann, 'λατρεύω', TWNT iv (1942), 58–66; id. and R. Meyer, 'λειτουργέω', ibid., 221–38; J. Horst, *Proskynein. Zur Anbetung im Urchristentum nach ihrer religionsgeschichtlichen Eigenart* (1932), 172–307.

[3] K. H. Rengstorf, 'δοῦλος', TWNT ii (1935), 268–83; R. Bultmann, 'εὐλαβής', ibid., 749–51; K. L. Schmidt, 'θρησκεία', ibid., iii (1938), 155–9; cf. Horst (n. 2), 179 ff.

[4] Luke 1:23, 74, 2:37; Acts 7:7; Rom. 9:4; Heb. 8:5, 9:1, 6, 9, 21, 10:2, 11, 13:10.

[5] Matt. 4:10; Luke 4:8; John 16:2; Acts 7:42, 24:14, 26:7, 27:23; Rom. 1:9, 25, 12:1; Phil. 3:3; 2 Tim. 1:3; Heb. 9:14, 12:28.

[6] O. Casel, 'Λειτουργία—munus', *Oriens Christ.* iii, 7 (1932), 289–302.

[7] Rom. 15:27; 2 Cor. 9:12; Phil. 2:17, 30. In one of these passages, Phil. 2:17, λειτουργία is coupled with θυσία, but only in a metaphorical sense, for Paul does not regard the subvention he has received from the Philippians as involving worship of his person.

[8] Matt. 8:2, 9:18, etc.

[9] Horst (n. 2), 311.

[10] Horst (n. 2), 293–307 (306: the ἐν πνεύματι of John corresponds to the ἐν Χριστῷ of Paul); R. Bultmann, *Das Evangelium des Johannes* (1941), 140; Cullmann (n. 1), 82; S. Petri, 'Tillbedjan i ande och sanning. En exegeshistorisk skiss till Joh. 4:19–24', *Svensk exeg. årsb.* 11 (1946), 47–76.

[11] Hahn (n. 1), 27 f.

[12] Cullmann (n. 1), 11, 36, 114; Brunner (n. 1), 104 f.

[13] Hahn (n. 1), 24–9.

[14] Hahn (n. 1), 28.

[15] Hahn (n. 1), 34 f., rightly observes that Jesus and the first Christians did not separate Jewish and 'Christian' worship. But he does not explain how this is to be defended from the general New Testament point of view. An attempt to do this is made here below, p. 200.

[16] Sjöberg (n. 1), 88 f.

[17] The relation of Christian worship to Christ's activity in the past and in the future is emphasized by Cullmann (n. 1), 114 f.; Ph. Menoud, 'La définition du sacrement selon le Nouveau Testament', *Rev. de théol et de philos.*, N.S. 38 (1950), 138–47; 'Wunder und Sakrament im Neuen Testament', TZ 8 (1952), 171–8; its relation to the Lord who is always present in his Church by H.

Riesenfeld, 'Kristen gudstjänst i ljuset av Nya Testamentet', *Svensk exeg. årsb.* 16 (1951), 59 f.

[18] This terminology may be traced back to M. Luther, *De capt. bab.* (1520), W.A. vi, 526, 13-17: 'Non ergo sunt confundenda illa duo, missa et oratio, *sacramentum* et opus, testamentum et *sacrificium*. Quia alterum venit a Deo ad nos per ministerium sacerdotis et exigit fidem, alterum procedit a fide nostra ad Deum per sacerdotem et exigit exauditionem. Illud descendit; hoc ascendit.' Cf. id., *Ein Sermon von dem neuen Testament, das ist von der heiligen Messe* (1520), 24-26, W.A. vi, 367-9; Ph. Melanchhon, *Apologia confessionis augustanae* (1531), xxiv, 17-26; and modern theologians mentioned by Brunner (n. 1), 192. Y. Brilioth, *Eucharistic Faith and Practice, Evangelical and Catholic* (1930), has a similar division on p. 17, but criticizes the individualistic consequences of this theory in Protestant theology on p. 131 f.

[19] Valuable systematic theological observations on the 'sacrifice' or 'responsory' elements of worship in Brunner (n. 1), 191-4, 253-67. Cf. Lerle (n. 1), 39 f.; Cranfield (n. 1), 388 f., 391 f.

[20] Schlier (n. 1, 1956), 252-8.

[21] Cf. above, n. 15.

[22] G. Schrenk, 'τὸ ἱερόν', TWNT iii (1938), 239 f.

[23] Sjöberg (n. 1), 87 f.; Schrenk (n. 22), 243 f.

[24] Delling (n. 1), 25-9.

[25] E. Lohmeyer, *Kultus und Evangelium* (1942), 44-52; T. W. Manson, *The Servant-Messiah. A Study of the Public Ministry of Jesus* (1953), 81-3.

[26] B. Reicke, *Diakonie, Festfreude und Zelos in Verbindung mit der altchristlichen Agapenfeier* (1951), 25-31.

[27] T. W. Manson, *The Church's Ministry* (1948), 56-60.

[28] N. A. Dahl, 'The Origin of Baptism', *Norsk teol. tidsskr.* 56 (1955), 36-52 (with bibliography).

[29] N. Johansson, *Det urkristna nattvardsfirandet* (1944), 104 ff.

[30] K. G. Kuhn, Über den ursprünglichen Sinn des Abendmahles und sein Verhältnis zu den Gemeinschaftsmahlen der Sektenschrift', *Ev. Theol.* 10 (1950-51), 508-27 (translated in a revised and enlarged form under the title 'The Lord's Supper and the Communal Meal at Qumran' in *The Scrolls and the New Testament*, ed. K. Stendahl (1958), 65-93 [Ed.]).

[31] Dix (n. 1), 50 ff.; other references in Reicke (n. 26), 70.

[32] A. J. B. Higgins, *The Lord's Supper in the New Testament* (1952), 20 f.

[33] Reicke (n. 26), 255.

[34] W. Bauer, *Der Wortgottesdienst der ältesten Christen* (1930), 6-11; 15-64; R. Bultmann, *Theologie des Neuen Testaments* (1948-53), 121.

[35] Bauer (n. 34), 11-15; 19 ff.

[36] Cullmann (n. 1), 31.

[37] Hahn (n. 1), 33, 35 f.

[38] Just., *Apol.* I, 67, etc.

[39] Manson (n. 27), 65 f. ('. . . some fundamental certainties which are the basis of all future developments of doctrine; some central acts of worship out of which will come the immense treasury of the liturgies').

[40] Brunner (n. 1), 188 f.; Cranfield (n. 1), 389.

P

SABBAT ET JOUR DU SEIGNEUR

par

H. RIESENFELD

D ANS un article sur Mc. 2:27 s., T. W. Manson a élucidé, à l'aide d'exemples tirés de la littérature juive, le sens symbolique attribué au sabbat en tant qu'il est, outre la circoncision et le temple de Jérusalem, un signe distinctif du peuple juif.[1] On trouve, dans les écrits apocryphes et pseudépigraphiques ainsi que dans la littérature rabbinique, l'idée que le sabbat a été créé par Dieu précisément pour Israel, le peuple élu. C'est une satisfaction de pouvoir prendre, comme point de départ de quelques observations dédiées à la mémoire du regretté professeur Manson, ces textes pour aborder en suite la question de la relation entre le sabbat juif et le jour du Seigneur caractéristique de l'église primitive.

Depuis les temps où la législation de l'Ancien Testament s'est formée, le sabbat évoque l'alliance de Dieu avec son peuple. Dans le cadre des idées qui s'y trouvent liées il y a surtout deux motifs: d'une part la création divine, aboutissant dans l'alliance, et de l'autre son achèvement dans le repos promis à Israël. Ceci s'exprime aussi dans l'observance même de ce jour sacré: « Ce jour-ci ils peuvent manger et boire et bénir celui qui a créé toutes les choses » (Jub. 2:17 ss.). Mais comme c'était l'aspect eschatologique qui, dans l'époque qui suit l'exil, prenait de plus en plus d'importance dans l'ensemble des idées religieuses du peuple juif, le sabbat évoquait par l'observance même qui le caractérisait, l'espoir du salut à venir. Le septième jour de la semaine a été conçu comme une figure du monde futur (GenR. XVII), et on parlait du « siècle à venir qui n'est que sabbat et repos » (MTam. VII, 4). De cette façon le sabbat est devenu, au surplus de ses autres fonctions, un *typos*, c'est-à-dire un signe du salut promis à Israël.

Dans le judaïsme du temps de Notre-Seigneur on a continué d'accentuer la sainteté du septième jour par des règles de plus en plus élaborées et restrictives, mais en même temps la notion de repos fut approfondie dans un sens plus humanitaire et philanthropique.[2] On admettait le besoin de reconfort qu'avaient les ouvriers, les esclaves et même les animaux domestiques.

Le fait que le sabbat a été considéré, dans la pensée juive, comme une figure de l'ère messianique, donne la clé de l'enseignement et des œuvres de Jésus dans la mesure où ils concernent le jour sacré de la semaine. Il y a, en ce point, une conformité évidente avec toute la manière dont Jésus réagit contre la législation religieuse de son peuple en la transformant dans une réalité nouvelle. Les guérisons de malades et l'arrachement des épis de blé le jour du sabbat[3] considérés, par ses adversaires, comme des transgressions de la loi, ont pour but de faire ressortir ce qui est le vrai sens du sabbat dans la perspective eschatologique: pas de défenses, pas de restrictions de la vie, mais la plénitude de l'existence, les bénéfices de Dieu caractérisant le salut promis. La signification typologique du sabbat qui fut ainsi élaborée clairement par Jésus même, doit être conçue dans le cadre des idées bibliques de la nouvelle création.[4]

Or on pourrait supposer que le septième jour de la semaine, rempli d'un sens symbolique qui a été souligné expressément par le Christ, serait resté — en admettant que les formes d'observance en fussent changées — le jour sacré de l'église chrétienne. Cela ne fut cependant pas le cas. Dès les premiers temps de l'église le sabbat perdait sa signification religieuse et son caractère distinctif. Les chrétiens se réunirent le premier jour de la semaine ou plutôt dans la nuit qui suit le sabbat, et c'est alors que l'on éprouvait, au sein de la communauté nouvelle, la présence du Seigneur resuscité. Ce fait ressortit des indications qui se trouvent déjà dans les écrits du Nouveau Testament, et il est confirmé par le témoignage des textes appartenant aux époques ultérieures. Dans cette perspective il devient évident que les chrétiens de Troas se réunirent précisément dans cette nuit lors du séjour de saint Paul dans la ville: « Le premier jour de la semaine, nous étions réunis pour rompre le pain. Paul, qui devait partir le lendemain, s'entretenait avec eux. Il prolongea son discours jusqu'au milieu de la nuit » (Act. 20:7). Et quand Paul, dans la première épître aux Corinthiens, trace des règles concernant la collecte en faveur de l'église de Jérusalem, écrit: « Que chaque premier jour de la semaine, chacun de vous mette de côté chez lui ce qu'il aura pu épargner », il pense sans doute au jour de la réunion hebdomadaire.

Cet usage des chrétiens comment s'est-il formé? L'interprétation courante qu'on en donne prétend que les chrétiens, dès la
première génération, ont abandonné le sabbat juif pour des raisons
d'ordre théologique et qu'ils ont choisi un jour sacré qui leur était
propre, celui de la Résurrection. Une preuve en seraient les
apparitions du Christ ressuscité qui sont relatées dans le quatrième
évangile et où il est dit que les disciples s'étaient réunis précisément
le premier jour de la semaine (Jo. 20:19, 26).[5] Cette interprétation
n'est cependant pas satisfaisante. D'une part le premier jour de la
semaine n'est jamais, dans les écrits du Nouveau Testament,
appelé « jour de la Resurrection » — c'est un terme qui n'apparaît
que plus tard. En revanche le jour des réunions chrétiennes continue
à être fixé, par son nom, au sabbat juif, car on l'appele μία σαβ-
βάτον, le premier jour après le sabbat (Act. 20:7; 1 Cor. 16:2).
D'autre part on ne trouve, dans les textes néo-testamentaires trai-
tant de la Résurrection et de son importance, aucun indice du fait
qu'il fallait instituer un nouveau jour sacré en sa mémoire. Tout
au contraire on peut citer, pour caractériser l'attitude du christianisme primitif, les paroles d'Origène: « Pour le chrétien parfait
chaque jour est un jour du Seigneur » (*Contra Cels.* VIII, 22).

On comprend d'après les textes que le premier jour de la
semaine n'était pas, à l'origine, un jour sacré choisi précisément
pour les réunions des chrétiens. Il semble plutôt avoir été adapté
à son but pour des raisins d'ordre rationnel. Pourquoi donc était-il
adapté?

La solution de cette question est probablement donnée par quelques indications du livre des Actes, caractérisant la vie de l'église de
Jérusalem. Là nous lisons que les chrétiens « jour après jour, d'un
seul cœur, fréquentaient assidûment le Temple et rompaient le
pain dans leurs maisons » (Act. 2:46, cf. 3:1). Quoique cela ne soit
pas dit expressément, il va de soi que les chrétiens assistaient au
culte du Temple, et probablement aussi au culte des synagogues de
la capitale juive, à cause des leçons de l'Ecriture et à cause des
prières, car, pour ce qui est des sacrifices, on comprenait de mieux
en mieux qu'ils avaient été remplacés par la mort du Christ.
Après avoir assisté au culte du Temple on allait chez soi, κατ' οἶκον
(Act. 2:46; 5:42), c'est-à-dire dans une maison privée, entre
autres dans la chambre haute (Act. 1:13), et là les chrétiens se
montraient assidus à l'enseignement des apôtres, fidèles à la communion fraternelle, à la fraction du pain et aux prières (Act. 2:42,

cf. 6:1–2). Il y a évidemment un rapport entre l'assistance au culte juif et les réunions chrétiennes proprement dites. On n'abandonna pas, dès le commencement, le Temple et son culte pour y substituer un culte chrétien plus ou moins évolué, mais on continuait à fréquenter le culte juif dans la conviction qu'il était pour ainsi dire accompli au sein même du nouveau peuple de Dieu, qui se constituait autour de données nouvelles: la récitation des paroles de Jésus, la fraction du pain en sa mémoire, les prières, adressées au Christ ressuscité, et l'enseignement de ses apôtres. L'idée que le Christ est l'accomplissement de la Loi et de toute l'Ecriture, idée qui ressort de tous les écrits du Nouveau Testament, a pour complément concret le fait même que les chrétiens des premiers temps, venant du Temple ou des synagogues, dans lesquelles on faisait lecture de l'Ancien Testament, se rendaient à leurs propres réunions, où ils éprouvaient la réalité d'une vie nouvelle.

L'hypothèse d'une évolution de ce genre permet d'expliquer le fait que les réunions des chrétiens avaient lieu surtout dans la soirée et la nuit qui suivent le jour du sabbat. Car le sabbat était, à cause du repos obligatoire qui lui était propre, le jour de culte principal de la semaine pour les gens ordinaires dans le milieu palestinien. Alors on était libre de participer aux trois offices du jour ou au moins à l'office du matin et à celui de l'après-midi.[6] S'il est dit, dans le livre des Actes, que les chrétiens se réunissaient « jour après jour » (Act. 2:46), cela doit être, pour tous ceux qui n'étaient pas les apôtres, une hyperbole. En revanche il est évident que les réunions hebdomadaires de la communauté chrétienne impliquaient, au sens propre du mot, un prolongement du sabbat —prolongement qui a dû être conçu comme l'accomplissement de ce jour, étant donné que l'espoir qui en constituait la signification essentielle s'était réalisé dans la personne du Christ et dans son église. Ainsi il y avait une relation frappante entre les idées eschatologiques et leur réalisation dans le culte chrétien.

Puisqu'il ressort des textes appartenant à une époque ultérieure que les réunions des communautés chrétiennes avaient lieu dans la dernière moitié de la nuit, avant l'aube, on doit conclure que des associations d'idées provenant d'un autre cadre de réflexions christologiques ont fait valoir leur influence. Alors il est évident que l'on s'est aperçu de la coïncidence du jour du culte et du jour de la Résurrection—ou plutôt des deux nuits en question—et qu'on l'a soulignée par l'heure matinale où les chrétiens s'assemblaient. Il est vraisemblable que cette nouvelle symbolique apparaît dans la phrase du rapport officiel que Pline le Jeune a envoyé à l'empereur Trajan vers l'an 112 et où il s'agit sans doute de la célébration du dimanche: « *Quod essent soliti stato die ante lucem convenire carmenque Christo quasi deo dicere.*»[7] L'association du jour du culte et de celui de la Résurrection est cependant manifeste déjà dans Jo. 20: 19.26, passages auxquels nous avons renvoyé plus haut. Le même thème se trouve chez saint Ignace d'Antioche: « Si donc ceux qui vivaient dans l'ancien ordre de choses sont venus à la nouvelle espérance, n'observant plus le sabbat mais le jour du Seigneur (κυριακή), jour où notre vie s'est levée par lui et par sa mort... » Le mot κυριακή désignant le dimanche, qui figure en outre dans Apoc. 1:10 et Did. 14:1, c'est-à-dire à une époque assez tardive, prouve le fait que les chrétiens considéraient, au moins vers la fin du premier siècle, le premier jour de la semaine comme le jour sacré qui leur était propre. Désormais le dimanche était couramment qualifié de jour de la Resurrection.[8] Il faut cependant se rappeler que tous les textes cités jusqu'à maintenant se réfèrent à la nuit précédant le dimanche ou plutôt succédant au sabbat.[9] La journée du dimanche ne se distinguait certainement pas, pour la plupart des chrétiens pendant les deux premiers siècles, des autres jours ordinaires de la semaine, ni dans le milieu juif, où le sabbat continuait d'être le jour de repos, ni dans le monde hellénistique ou romain, où les fêtes officielles donnaient le réconfort nécessaire aux classes de la population, où se recrutait la majeure partie des chrétiens. L'institution du dimanche comme jour sacré officiel fait partie d'une évolution qui appartient à une époque ultérieure. La condition indispensable en était le fait que le christianisme devenait, sous Constantin, la religion officielle de l'empire romain. Alors l'empereur pouvait promulguer son édit, dans lequel il rapprochait la notion de jour du Seigneur et les idées du dieu soleil dans les cultes païens.[10] Ce ne fut qu'en ce temps-là que l'observance du dimanche a affecté l'aspect extérieur du premier jour de la semaine.

Bien que les chrétiens de l'ère apostolique continuassent de fréquenter le Temple ou les synagogues pour y assister au culte sabbatique, il va de soi que l'on s'emancipa très tôt des lois juives qui donnaient au sabbat sa marque caractéristique. En tant que signe de l'ancienne alliance le sabbat fut considéré, par ceux qui croyaient au Christ, comme abandonné, opinion qui doit avoir été préparé par l'enseignement de Jésus. Dans les épîtres du Nouveau Testament et dans leurs parénèses on ne trouve aucune mention explicite de l'observance du sabbat ou du commandement du décalogue qui s'y réfère. Tout au contraire les apôtres et les chefs de l'église étaient jaloux d'extirper les tendances judaïsantes qui se manifestaient çà et là par le souci d'observer le sabbat avec toute l'ancienne rigeur. Cela vaut pour Paul ainsi que pour Ignace.[11] Mais en même temps qu'on s'opposait à une interprétation et à une observance judaïsantes du sabbat, on continuait à se servir de ce jour comme jour de culte au sein même de l'église, abstraction faite des problèmes spéciaux des judéo-chrétiens.[12] On n'a souvent pas tenu compte suffisamment du fait que le septième jour, toujours appelé sabbat, jouait son propre rôle — qui était étroitement lié à celui du jour du Seigneur — dans l'ensemble de la semaine chrétienne.[13] Cela ressort plus clairement à une époque ultérieure où le samedi est célébré, dans l'église orientale, d'une manière qui correspond à l'observance du dimanche.[14]

Il va de soi que le jour du Seigneur, étant le premier jour de la semaine, n'entrait pas dans la typologie élaborée autour du septième jour comme accomplissement de l'œuvre de Dieu. Cela a causé certaines difficultés à la pensée chrétienne du premier siècle. Car le symbolisme du sabbat, signe du salut à venir, qui est à la base de plusieurs d'entre les gestes accomplies par Jésus, figurait comme thème dans l'enseignement de l'église primitive. Qu'on se réfère surtout au chap. 4 de l'épître aux Hébreux, dont le thème est le repos du sabbat réservé au peuple de Dieu (4:9). Un passage tel que Jo. 5:17 doit probablement aussi être examiné dans ce cadre d'idées: « Mon Père travaille toujours, et moi aussi je travaille »,[15] ce qui veut dire que l'œuvre salvatrice du Messie appartient au sixième jour ou plutôt millénaire de l'histoire universelle et qu'elle est la condition du salut futur équivalent au septième jour ou millénaire.

La difficulté causée par le dimanche comme jour du Seigneur apparaît cependant dans l'épître du Pseudo-Barnabée. Dans un passage bien connu mais qui n'a pas encore trouvé une interprétation satisfaisante, l'auteur inconnu traite d'abord de la typologie millénariste de la semaine:[16] chaque jour correspond à mille années; ayant mis une fin au règne du diable, le Fils se reposera le septième jour. Dans ce monde-ci personne ne peut sanctifier

— selon le commandement de Dieu — le sabbat; ayant été sancti-
fiés par le Christ, les chrétiens pourront sanctifier le vrai sabbat, le
millénaire à venir conçu comme le septième jour (Barn. 15:4-7).
Dans la suite une toute autre symbolique entre en vue:[17] Dieu a
dit: « Je ne supporte pas vos nouvelles lunes et vos sabbats »
(Is. 1:13); alors il ne veut pas les sabbats juifs mais celui dans lequel,
ayant accompli tout, il a inaugré un huitième jour, le commencement d'un autre monde. « C'est pourquoi nous observons le
huitième jour en joie, jour où Jésus est ressuscité des morts... »
(15:8 s.). Il est évident que l'auteur s'apercevait qu'il ne pouvait
faire entrer le dimanche chrétien dans la typologie de la semaine
culminant dans le septième jour. C'est pourquoi il se trouvait
obligé de se référer à un tout autre cadre d'idées eschatologiques,
celui de l'*ogdoas* qui, venant de l'Orient, apparait dans l'apocalyp-
tique juive à une époque relativement tardive.[18] Une source juive
de ces idées se trouve dans le Second Hénoch: « J'ai béni le septième jour, qui est le sabbat, et je lui ai ajouté le huitième qui est
celui de la première création. Quand les sept premiers jours
auront été résolus sous la forme de millénaires, commencera le
huitième millénaire... » (33:1).[19] Un trait caractéristique de ce
symbolisme est sa perspective transcendentale. Mais c'est par un
tour de force que l'auteur de l'épître de Barnabée est parvenu à
combiner la typologie traditionelle de la semaine, le dimanche
comme jour du culte chrétien et la mémoire de la Resurrection
du Christ. Désormais le huitième jour était un thème légitime de
l'exégèse faite par les pères de l'église.[20]

NOTES

[1] T. W. Manson, « Mark ii. 27 f. », *Coniect. Neotest.* 11 (1947), 138-46. Cf. en
outre P. Cotton, *From Sabbath to Sunday* (1933); A. A. McArthur, *The Evolution
of the Christian Year* (1953), 13-29.

[2] SB, Index, s.v.; W. O. E. Oesterley, *Le Sabbat* (1935).

[3] Surtout Mc. 2:23-8 parr., 3:1-6 parr.; Jo. 5:1-18.

[4] Cf. Mt. 11:28-30 sur l'arrière-plan de Gen. 3:17 ss.

[5] Pour le premier jour de la semaine comme jour de la Résurrection voir
Mc. 16:2 parr.; Jo. 20:1.

[6] C. W. Dugmore, *The Influence of the Synagogue upon the Divine Office* (1944),
11 ss.

[7] Plin., Ep. XCVI, 7.

[8] Barn. 15:9; Just. Mart., *Apol.* I, LXVII; *Dial.* XXIII, 3, XLI; Clem. Alex.,
Strom. VII, 12. Cf. *Peregr. Aeth.* XXIV, 9 s. Voir en outre Cotton, 81 s.

[9] Beaucoup plus tard on avait toujours connaissance, dans l'église, du fait que

le dimanche chrétien commence en réalité dans la veille qui le précède, voir Cotton, 83 s., McArthur, 15 s.

[10] Cod. Just., III, 12, 2; Eus., *Vit. Const.* IV, 18–21. Voir W. W. Hyde, *Paganism to Christianity in the Roman Empire* (1946), 257–64.

[11] Col. 2:16; Ign., *Magn.* IX, 1. Cf. en outre Just. Mart., *Dial.* XXIII, 3; Diogn. 4:1; Act. Petr. c. Sim. I; Iren., *Adv. haer.*, IV, XVI, 2–3.

[12] Cf. Mt. 24:20; Eus. HE III, XXVII, 5. Voir Cotton, 54 ss.

[13] Dugmore, 28 ss.

[14] Dugmore, 33 ss.; McArthur, 24 ss.; M. Simon, *Verus Israel* (1948), 374 s.

[15] O. Cullmann, « Sabbat und Sonntag nach dem Johannes-Evangelium », *In memoriam Ernst Lohmeyer* (1951), 127–31.

[16] J. Daniélou, « La typologie millénariste de la semaine dans le christianisme primitif », VC 2 (1948), 1–16.

[17] L'inadvertance en a été remarqué par H. Windisch, *Der Barnabasbrief* (*Handb. zum Neuen Testament*, Erg.-Bd., 1920), 384 s.

[18] Voir par ex. B. Reicke, *The Disobedient Spirits and Christian Baptism* (1946), 140 s.; *Reallex. für Ant. und Christent.*, i, s.v. « Achtzahl ».

[19] Daniélou, 3.

[20] Voir surtout Just. Mart., *Apol.* I, LXVII; *Dial.* XLI, 4. Cf. en outre J. Daniélou, « La Fête des Tabernacles dans l'exégèse patristique », *Studia Patristica* (TU 1957), i, 262–79, voir 270 s.

THE BAPTISM OF JOHN AND THE QUMRAN SECT

by

H. H. ROWLEY

SO many writers have voiced the suggestion that it was from the Qumran sect that John the Baptist derived the rite of baptism that some examination of the question seems to be called for.[1] Few writers define what they mean by baptism, and many are content with the merest shadow of evidence, with the result that much confusion has been allowed to surround the question. The argument appears to run somewhat as follows:

(1) There are cisterns for the storage of water at Qumran, with steps running down into them; therefore these were used for baptism. (2) There are references in the Scrolls to ablutions with water; therefore the previous inference is confirmed. (3) The sect of the Scrolls came into existence in the second or first century B.C.; therefore its practice antedated the baptism of John. (4) John lived in the desert in the neighbourhood of Qumran; therefore he could have derived his practice from the sect, and therefore he did. (5) Josephus tells us that some of the Essenes adopted children;[2] therefore John could have been adopted, and therefore he was.

So far as the first of these arguments is concerned, it is as fatuous as it would be to argue that in every modern house which has a bathroom 'baptism' is practised. So far as the second is concerned, it rests on a similar equation of 'ablutions' with 'baptism', which requires to be established. So far as the third is concerned, it is not universally agreed, but the present writer does agree, though this does not mean that the one is the source of the other. So far as the fourth is concerned, it is wholly without cogency, since it tacitly equates the baptism of John with the ablutions of Qumran, when such evidence as we have suggests that they were totally different in subjects and significance. So far as the fifth is concerned, it is entirely without cogency. If conjecture were evidence, any theory could claim to be established.

As for the cisterns of Qumran, it has to be remembered that the large community which had its centre there must have required a good deal of water, and may be presumed to have stored water for various purposes. The steps down into the cisterns do not necessarily prove that they were used for the immersion of the person, though they would be quite consistent with this. Neither the cisterns nor the steps can give us any evidence as to the occasion or occasions when such immersions may have taken place, or who the persons were who were so immersed, or what significance was attached to the immersion. These are the vital questions when we are discussing baptism.

When we turn to the texts of the Qumran community, we find no clear reference to anything comparable with what the word 'baptism' signifies to us. In the *Manual of Discipline*, in the rules for the admission of new members, it is laid down that a candidate is to be examined first by the Inspector, or Superintendent, and, if he is satisfied, is to be instructed as to the rules of the community. Then, after an unspecified period, his case is considered by the members of the sect in a general meeting. If they vote his admission he enters on a further probationary period of two years. Not until the first of those two years has passed is he allowed to share the 'purity' of the community.[3] This is the only possible reference to 'baptism' as an initiatory rite in the *Manual of Discipline*, and it is not agreed as to what it means. Lieberman maintains that the reference is to the solid foodstuffs of the community.[4] This is because we are told below that after a further year's probation, the candidate is admitted to the 'drink' of the community. But the word rendered 'drink' is commonly used for a 'feast', and hence others think the meaning is that at the end of the second stage of his probation the candidate enters the waters of purification, and at the end of the third stage he is admitted to the meals of the sect.[5] This latter view seems to the present writer more probable.

This, however, brings us at once to the vexed question of the relation of the sect of the Scrolls to the Essenes, as described by Philo, Josephus, and Pliny, all writers of the first Christian century. That question cannot be examined here, but to the present writer it seems likely that the sect of the Scrolls is to be identified with the sect of the Essenes, but with the recognition that in the Scrolls we see them at an earlier stage of their history than in the first century writers, and that therefore their practice was not in all points the same in the two periods. So far as the admission of new members is concerned, there is a large measure of agreement between the *Manual of Discipline* and the account of Josephus. For Josephus tells us that after a first year of probation a candidate was allowed to share 'the purer kind of holy water', but that he could not touch 'the common food' for a further period.[6] This would clearly suggest that the 'purity' of the *Manual of Discipline* is the purifying water, while the 'drink' is the communal meal of the sect.

Before we leap to equate this with an initiatory rite of baptism, however, we have to observe that Josephus tells us that the Essenes daily bathed their bodies in cold water before their midday meal, and even implies that they did the same again in the evening before their evening meal.[7] Here we are reminded of the various ritual ablutions laid down in the Pentateuch for states of ceremonial uncleanness, arising from a whole series of voluntary or involuntary experiences. The Essenes appear to have gone far beyond the requirements of the Pentateuch in their determination to maintain complete ritual purity. Indeed, Josephus says that if a senior in the sect were so much as touched by a junior he had to take a bath, as though he had been in contact with an alien.[8] But this cannot be thought of as 'baptism', and it is a confusing of the whole issue to use this word in this connection. What Josephus tells us of the Essenes is more naturally understood to mean that a candidate for membership was not allowed to share in the daily ritual bath in the water used by the members of the sect until after he had passed through a year of probation. Since he was given a loincloth at the beginning of this year,[9] and since we are told by Josephus elsewhere that the loincloth was used in the bath,[10] it would seem that the probationer was expected to bathe—probably daily—but he was not allowed to do this in 'the purer kind of water', which was the water reserved for the members of the sect.

In the *Zadokite Work*, which comes, by almost universal agreement, from the same sect as the Dead Sea Scrolls, there is a reference to ritual ablutions. Here it is said that the members of the sect are not to bathe in dirty water, or in a vessel or shallow pool, and that if an unclean person touches the water it thereby becomes unclean.[11] It is to be noted that bathing in a vessel is here forbidden. This does not rule out the possibility that the cisterns of Qumran were used for ablutions, however. For it is likely that the *Zadokite Work* reflects a stage in the history of the sect before the Qumran centre was used.[12] Once they lived together in communal settlements, where the water in such cisterns as those of Qumran could be preserved from all contact with unclean persons, the reason for objection to ablution in a vessel would vanish. More germane to our immediate purpose is it to suggest that the 'unclean person' of the *Zadokite Work* in the passage mentioned is probably anyone who was not a full member of the sect. There is nothing, however, to suggest that an initiatory rite was intended, and the passage is more naturally read in association with the provision for daily ablutions discussed above.

There are certain other passages in the *Manual of Discipline* that need to be considered. There is provision for an annual review of all the members, when some may be advanced to a higher position in the order of seniority of the sect, and others relegated to a lower position.[13] Here it is laid down that those who have failed to accept the discipline of the community and to conform their conduct to the high standard set before them may be excluded from the sect.[14] For them no atoning offerings or cleansing waters can have any validity. Only they of humble and upright spirit, who submit their life to the statutes of God can be cleansed by being sprinkled with the purifying water.[15] It is hard to suppose that here there can be any reference to an initiatory rite of baptism, since the passage is dealing with those who have already passed into full membership of the sect, whose life and conduct are under review. The reference to sprinkling makes it doubtful whether this passage has any relevance to the question of ritual immersion at all. What does emerge here is the recognition that the ritual act is meaningless without the spirit to validate it.

Elsewhere in the *Manual* it is said that if a member of the sect should waver in his loyalty and then repent, he is to be punished for two years, during the first of which he is to be excluded from the 'purity' of the sect, and during the second from the 'drink'.[16] Here, as in the passage already examined, it is likely that the meaning is that for two years he shall be excluded from the common meals of the members, and for the first of these years he shall be forbidden to share in the daily lustrations. The reference could not

possibly be to an initiatory rite here, since the passage deals with
one who has attained full membership of the sect and is subject to
discipline.

In the Scrolls, therefore, there is no certain reference to an
initiatory rite corresponding to what we mean by baptism. There
is the passage just mentioned, where 'purity' *cannot* have this
meaning, and this would seem to strengthen the likelihood that
in the other passage, dealing with the admission of new members,
it does not have this meaning, and that what is stated is simply
that during the first stage of probation a candidate does not share
the regular ritual ablutions of the members. There is nothing in-
consistent with this in the passage in the *Zadokite Work*, and this
is the most natural interpretation of the account given by Josephus.

Yet, having said this, the present writer is willing to concede the
likelihood that for the new member his first admission to the ablutions of the sect in the water reserved for the members would have
a special character. It would still not be comparable with what we
mean by baptism, which is an unrepeatable rite of admission, but
it would have a special character as the first of a series of ablutions,
to which he was admitted only after solemn inquiry and examination. Moreover, there is not the slightest evidence that it differed
in form from the ablutions that would follow. It was not, therefore, an administered rite, but a bath.

It is clear already that the link with the baptism of John is tenuous in the extreme. For the baptism of John was a rite of initiation
and only a rite of initiation. In the case of the sect of the Scrolls or
the Essenes an initiatory rite is not recorded, and can at best be an
assumption. In the case of John an initiatory rite rests on evidence,
and subsequent ritual ablutions are not recorded, and if they were
would be entirely different in character. For the baptism of John
was not the first of a series, but an unrepeatable rite of commitment. Moreover, it was an administered rite. Whether John
plunged the person beneath the water, or whether he plunged
himself is of no moment. It was clearly more than a private act,
since the New Testament tells us so clearly that John baptized,[17]
or that Jesus was 'baptized by John'.[18]

Moreover, the baptism of John was administered to persons
under completely different conditions from any possible 'baptism'
of the sect of the Scrolls. Even if we could rightly speak of 'baptism' in that sect, it could only be the baptism of those who had

been probationers for a year, and who had been voted on by the members of the sect after a careful discussion in a meeting of the members. There is not the slightest evidence that the people John baptized had passed through a long period of probation, or that John had submitted to anyone the question whether they should be baptized or not, or that their baptism signified admission to a monastic community.

If it is proper to speak of 'baptism' amongst the sect of the Scrolls at all, it was a private rite. There is no reason to suppose that the daily ablutions were performed in public, and certainly if they were performed in the cisterns at Qumran they were not performed in public. Since at the most the 'baptism' of the members was the first of their regular ablutions, there is no reason to suppose that this was performed in public. For there is no reason whatever to suppose that on the occasion when a new member was joining them in their ablutions for the first time they all repaired to a public place. The care that had to be taken to ensure that the water was not touched by one who was 'unclean'—i.e. by a non-member of the sect, most probably—confirms the likelihood that for the sect nothing but a private rite was in mind. But in the case of John, baptism was a public rite. Crowds came out to see him baptize, and judging by the stinging things he is said to have addressed to these crowds,[19] they did not all come to be baptized. Nothing could stand in sharper contrast to any water rite of the sect of the Scrolls or the Essenes of which we have any evidence, or which we can legitimately infer, than the accounts of John's baptism which we read in the New Testament. The only feature it has in common with any ablutions of the sect is that it involved total immersion in water. But this feature is in no way peculiar to John's baptism and the ablutions of the sect. The ritual ablutions of the Jews on occasions of ceremonial uncleanness were also by total immersion. In short, there is not a single feature of John's baptism for which there is the slightest reason to go to Qumran to look for the source, and for every feature but one Qumran could not possibly provide the source, while for that one the common practice of the Jews could provide the more natural source.

It has to be remembered that about the beginning of the Christian era there were various groups of people who practised lustrations far beyond those required by the Law. About the middle of the first century A.D. Josephus was for a time the disciple of one Banus,[20] who lived an ascetic life and who bathed in cold water several times a day. Josephus makes it clear that Banus was not an Essene, and it is also clear that he had disciples. Whether Banus himself had predecessors in this practice, or whether he was the originator of a movement which died with him, cannot be known.

Epiphanius[21] and the author of the *Apostolic Constitutions*[22] tell us of a sect of Hemerobaptists, who practised daily lustrations, and in the Pseudo-Clementines John is said to have been a Hemerobaptist.[23] These Hemerobaptists would appear to be more akin to the Essenes than to John the Baptist, for they are said to have bathed daily before food, and to have purified with water their table utensils and even their seats.[24] Their baptism would not appear to have been the symbol of death to the age that was passing and rebirth to the new age, as John's baptism was, and this alone renders it improbable that he was a Hemerobaptist. In their case we have no record of baptism as a rite of initiation, but only of ablutions of those who belonged to the sect; in his we have no record of ablutions after the rite of initiation, but only of this. Neither in subjects nor in significance, therefore, is there anything in common between the two.

Other groups who practised water lustrations have left some trace, and it would appear that it was a common idea about the beginning of the Christian era that frequent washing was of the essence of godliness.[25] It may well be that it was from the Essenes that this idea spread, since they seem to be the earliest of the groups that practised lustrations far beyond the requirements of the Law. Josephus tells us that the Essenes attached a value to their lustrations above that of animal sacrifices.[26] This distinguishes them at once from the Pharisees, who with all their insistence on ritual cleanliness were far from going to such a point.

Granting, then, that the Essenes or the sect of the Scrolls, assuming that a historical line of development links these two, were the first to extend the lustrations so largely, and that it was probably from them that the other groups derived the idea, though they may each have given some special turn to their practice, we must allow for the possibility that the idea spread from one group to another and not that all derived it directly and immediately from the Essenes. Hence, even if the baptism of John had more of a common character with that of the sect of the Scrolls we should not be justified in concluding that it must have been derived directly from them. But when his baptism is so different in its subjects and in its significance, different too in being a publicly administered rite as against a private practice, there can be no case for the assumption that he must have derived it from them, or even that he *could* have derived it from them. The sect of the Scrolls cannot be supposed to have supplied John with a rite which they did not practise themselves. For it must be repeated that from no source whatever have we any evidence, or even suggestion, that the sect of the Scrolls or the Essenes had any special rite of initiation by immersion in water.

Some elements of the rite of John seem to be closer to Jewish proselyte baptism than to anything which is recorded of the sect of the Scrolls or the Essenes. For Jewish proselyte baptism was a lustration like the ordinary ritual lustrations of the Jews in form, save that it was an administered rite, but unlike the other lustrations in that it was a rite of initiation and therefore not a rite to be repeated. Our information about the character of the rite of proselyte baptism is all post-Christian, and it was formerly believed that the rite itself was of post-Christian origin.[27] It is now widely agreed that it was probably of pre-Christian origin,[28] though the evidence for this is not strong enough to amount to a demonstration.[29] There is evidence which establishes with reasonable assurance that it antedated the destruction of the Temple,[30] and it is unlikely that Judaism first established this rite during the early days of the Church, and borrowed it from a body to which it was so strongly opposed.[31] It is plain from the New Testament that there were large numbers of proselytes to Judaism wherever Jews were to be found, and it is much more likely that proselyte baptism came into being to meet the situation created by these proselytes, than that it was hastily borrowed by the Jews, either from John or from the Church.

Proselyte baptism was in its essence a rite of initiation. It symbolized a man's death to his old life and faith, and rebirth into the faith of Judaism. From now on he would be expected to practice all the lustrations of the Law when he incurred ceremonial uncleanness for any cause. But he would not be expected to undergo proselyte baptism again.[32] It was certainly not something he would have to repeat daily. It was therefore unlike the lustrations of the sect of the Scrolls or of the Essenes, but like the baptism of John

Q

in this respect. For proselyte baptism was more than a lustration.

Our later sources tell us that proselyte baptism was an administered rite. This does not mean that the candidate was plunged beneath the water by another. It is probable that the actual immersion was his own act. But it was an administered rite in the sense that it was witnessed, and in that an essential part of it was the assurance that the candidate understood the significance of what he was doing. The witnesses warned him of the meaning of his act, and made sure that his motives were pure, and while he was in the act of immersion they repeated to him passages from the law of his new faith.[33] While all this is found only in post-Christian sources, there is no reason to doubt that in essence they go back to an earlier time. For from the time that Judaism made baptism one of the requirements of the candidate for admission to its faith, it must have asked for some evidence that the requirement had been met. And this could only be ensured by a witnessed rite. It is antecedently likely, therefore, that the witnesses would be given some responsibility in the matter, and that this could best be met by requiring them to satisfy themselves in some way that the candidate understood the significance of what he was doing. For Judaism was not interested in empty rites alone, and it is unlikely that at any time it was content with evidence that a man had immersed himself, without asking for assurances that with this immersion there went a complete renunciation of his old life and a commitment of himself to the way of the Law. In the ordinary lustrations, which dealt with ceremonial uncleanness, often involuntarily and necessarily incurred, no moral issues were involved. But proselyte baptism had a moral and spiritual significance, and was concerned with more than technical uncleanness. In such cases Judaism always demanded that the spirit should match the act.

Here is something far closer to the baptism of John than anything we can find in any of the sects that practised frequent ablutions in the first century of our era. At the same time it is something quite different from John's baptism. Proselyte baptism was something required of a non-Jew when he was converted to Judaism, but not of one who was born into a Jewish home. John's baptism was demanded of Jew and non-Jew who accepted his message. His baptism was not coupled with the demand for circumcision and a sacrifice in the Temple, as proselyte baptism was, but appears to have been the sole rite in which he was interested. It symbolized not so much death to the old life and rebirth to a new, as death to the age that was passing, and birth into the new age that was on the point of dawning. It was not so much the rite of admission to an organization as a preparation for a kingdom which was soon to be established by divine initiative in the world. Unlike proselyte baptism it was administered in public, and it was the response to a vigorous summons to men to forsake the world that was passing. There was a prophetic quality about John that is not associated with proselyte baptism, and that was certainly not characteristic of the sect of Qumran or the Essenes. Hence, if the baptism of John had features in common with proselyte baptism, it cannot for a moment be equated with it. The form of the rite John may have taken over, but he transformed its administration and still more its significance, as he also transformed its subjects. The fundamental originality of his baptism is not affected by the recognition that its background was probably proselyte baptism.

Still less can the originality of John's baptism be affected by anything that has come to light in the Dead Sea Scrolls or by anything we learn about the Essenes from the first century writers. The sole feature it had in common with their 'baptism' was that it involved the immersion of the body, but this feature it had in common also with the ordinary Jewish lustrations, with Jewish proselyte baptism, and with the lustrations of the other Jewish groups of which we have knowledge. In being solely a rite of initiation, publicly administered on the responsibility of John alone, and apparently without any long period of probation, it differed *toto coelo* from any rite that can reasonably be presumed to have been practised by the Essenes and certainly from any of which we have the slightest evidence. There is no evidence that the baptism of John entailed the entry into a monastic sect, as the assumed 'baptism' of the sect of the Scrolls did. When John called on soldiers to be baptized, he could scarcely have meant that they should spend one night in three studying the Scriptures, or that they should enter into a communal organization and take their meals daily with a religious brotherhood, as the members of the sect of the Scrolls or the Essenes did. There is, indeed, no shadow of evidence that the sect had any rite even remotely comparable with John's baptism, and the whole structure is built on an assumed, but nowhere recorded, initiatory rite that must have been entirely

different in character from the recorded rites if it had provided John
with any relevant precedent. Such an assumption is not evidence
in favour of what is assumed, and until the discussion of the Scrolls
is more rigidly controlled by evidence we are not likely to reach
secure conclusions. All that we can justifiably say is that the sect
of the Scrolls almost certainly existed in pre-Christian days, and
that like other Jews they practised ablutions, but more frequently
than the Law demanded. These ablutions may have taken place in
the cisterns of Khirbet Qumran. John the Baptist may well have
known something about the sect, but there is no evidence that he
ever belonged to them. If he did, he must have left them and
would have been repudiated by them, since his baptism was utterly
unlike their lustrations in publicity, in subjects, and in significance.
His baptism had far more in common with Jewish proselyte baptism. Yet in all that is most characteristic of John's baptism complete independence of both proselyte baptism and Essene baptism
is to be recognized.

NOTES

[1] Cf. e.g., W. H. Brownlee, *Interpretation*, 9 (1955), 71 ff., reprinted in revised
form in *The Scrolls and the New Testament* (ed. by K. Stendahl), 1957, 33 ff.
(p. 52: 'It was John the Essene who proclaimed the coming Messianic Age in
the wilderness'); J. M. Allegro, *The Dead Sea Scrolls* (1956), 163 ff. (p. 164: 'It
does appear, however, that John belonged to the Essene movement'); C. T.
Fritsch, *The Qumrān Community* (1956), 112 ff. (p. 112: 'There is little doubt
that John the Baptist was a key figure through whom many of the practices
and teachings of the Qumrān sect found their way into early Christianity');
A. Powell Davies, *The Meaning of the Dead Sea Scrolls* (1957), 142 f. (p. 142:
'That John was, in the broader sense of the term, an Essene can scarcely be
doubted').

[2] BJ II, viii, 2 (ii, 120).

[3] *Manual* vi, 13 ff.

[4] Cf. JBL 71 (1952), 203.

[5] So, e.g., T. H. Gaster, *The Scriptures of the Dead Sea Sect* (1957), 60 f. and
107 notes 58, 60.

[6] BJ II, viii, 7 (ii, 137 ff.).

[7] BJ II, viii, 5 (ii, 129 ff.).

[8] BJ II, viii, 10 (ii, 150).

[9] BJ II, viii, 7 (ii, 137).

[10] BJ II, viii, 13 (ii, 161).

[11] *Zadokite Work*, x, 10 ff.

[12] Cf. the present writer's essay 'Some Traces of the History of the Qumran
Sect', in TZ, 13 (1957), 530–40.

[13] *Manual*, ii, 19 ff.

[14] *Manual*, ii, 25 ff.
[15] *Manual*, iii, 4 ff.
[16] *Manual*, vii, 18 ff.
[17] John 1:25 f.
[18] Mark 1:9, Matt. 3:13.
[19] Luke 3:7 ff.
[20] *Vita*, 2 (11).
[21] *Panarion*, xvii (ed. Holl, i (C Ber xxv), 1915, 214).
[22] *Const. Apost.* vi, 6 (Migne, PG i, 1857, 917 ff.).
[23] *Hom.* ii, 23 (Migne, PG ii, 1886, 92).
[24] *Const. Apost., loc. cit.*
[25] For an account of these various sects cf. J. Thomas, *Le Mouvement Baptiste en Palestine et Syrie* (150 av. J.-C.–300 ap. J.-C.), 1935.
[26] *Ant.* XVIII, i, 5 (xviii, 18 ff.).
[27] Cf. M. Schneckenburger, *Über das Alter der Jüdischen Proselyten-Taufe und deren Zusammenhang mit dem Johanneischen und christlichen Ritus*, 1828.
[28] Cf. M. Dods, in DCG (ed. by J. Hastings), i (1906), 169a; W. Brandt, *Die jüdischen Baptismen* (1910), 58 f.; W. Heitmüller, in RGG¹, v (1913), 1088; E. Stauffer, RGG² v (1931), 1003; J. Coppens, in *Supplément au Dictionnaire de la Bible* (ed. by L. Pirot), i (1928), 893.
[29] The present writer discusses this question in *Hebrew Union College Annual*, 15 (1940), 313 ff.
[30] Cf. *ibid.*, 316 ff.
[31] Cf. A. Calmet, *Commentaire littéral sur tous les livres de l'Ancien et du Nouveau Testament*, vii (1726), 288: 'Quelques-uns ont crû que les Juifs avoient imité cette cérémonie des Païens ... ou des Chrétiens ... Mais et les Païens et les Chrétiens étaient trop odieux aux Juifs, pour croire que ceux-ci ayent voulu les imiter en cela.'
[32] Marcel Simon would equate proselyte baptism with the ordinary ablutions of the Jew more closely than does the present writer. He says: 'Il est identique aux ablutions lévitiques dans sa forme, rite d'immersion, et aussi dans ses effets; il élimine cette impureté rituelle qui, accidentelle chez un Juif, est chez un *goy* congénitale. La pureté qu' il confère aux prosélytes ne leur est pas acquise une fois pour toutes. Il ne les dispense pas de recourir par la suite aux ablutions usuelles' (*Verus Israel* (1948), 333). It is, however, to be noted that witnesses were essential to proselyte baptism, but not to ordinary lustrations. The special character of the former did not lie merely in the fact that it was the first lustration, and it had a specifically initiatory character which belonged to no other.
[33] BT, Yebamoth, 47 ab.

THE CONCEPT OF THE CHURCH IN THE GOSPEL AND EPISTLES OF ST. JOHN*

by

E. SCHWEIZER

FOR a long time now the difference between the concept of the Church in Jerusalem, and that of Paul, has been realized.[1] But the fact that John had still another view of the Church is usually overlooked.[2] This essay is therefore an attempt to say something about the special nature of John's view of the Church.

I. THE EARLY CHURCH[3]

It is no longer possible to reconstruct the history of the Early Church with certainty, because we have no really reliable sources.

Opinions differ concerning the extent to which preoccupation with the future really formed the heart of the Christology of the Early Church.[4] But even if the Early Church emphasized the importance of past events more than our sources lead us to believe, it is quite clear that the main emphasis was not on the incarnation of the pre-existent Son, nor on the Cross (which rather represented a perplexity which had to be explained); no, the main emphasis was on the exaltation of Christ, which was interpreted as the establishment of his lordship over the Israel of the Last Days. Jesus is understood as the Messiah through whose words and acts God's grace is offered to man and the way is opened for him to become a member of God's New Israel of the Last Days. Throughout, the Early Church is thinking in the temporal scheme of the *Heilsgeschichte*. This is especially the case where the actual event of salvation is seen in the Parousia, without reflection on the short interim period before it comes. This also applies to the later stage when Jesus' life on earth is regarded as the centre of time, against

* Paper read at the Congress 'The Four Gospels in 1957' in Oxford, 19th September, 1957.

which the whole period of Christian missions up to the Parousia stands out in bold relief. But even where the whole stress lies on what has already happened, it is nevertheless understood as the fulfilment of the promise, the end and goal of the *Heilsgeschichte*.

Thus all the time the Church is understood as Israel; it is only the emphasis which varies, whereby the stress is laid on the contrast between this New Israel and the pre-Christian Israel.[5] This emphasis was expressed in the question of church order. Our texts do not invite us to separate in a simple way a hierarchical Church in Jerusalem from a Hellenistic Church under the direct guidance of the Holy Spirit, like the churches founded by Paul. The early history of the Church in Jerusalem was probably strongly marked by an 'ecstatic' spirit-life and by prophetic utterances. But the old order of Israel was taken over more or less unchanged, even when it was re-interpreted. However, the first disciples already knew that there were to be no more titles of honour or differences of rank among them. Thus from the very beginning the Church was free from officialdom and priesthood.[6] But that did not prevent it from continuing at first to live within the framework of Israel and its orders; it was only very gradually that it separated itself, probably under the pressure of persecution; nor did it prevent it from taking over arrangements like the appointment of elders.[7] The action of the Spirit was not regarded as creating tensions with the legal order and tradition, but rather as the new basis for that order.[8]

II. PAUL

Paul also understood the Church as the New Israel.[9] The idea of *Heilsgeschichte* is clearly expressed in his writings, e.g. in Rom. 9–11. Here the time between the crucifixion and the Parousia (which Paul thinks will be very short) is interpreted as a time for missionary enterprise. But in addition there is a new idea.[10] Paul gives a new dimension to Christology—although he only takes up old elements in a new way. Before he became a Christian the Cross had been 'a scandal' to him; he now gave it the central position. Already before Paul's time it had been recognized that Christ died for our sins (1 Cor. 15:3); but it was Paul who really interpreted this fact systematically. In the Hellenistic church there was already probably a tendency to regard salvation as directly connected with the heavenly Redeemer. This tendency regarded the

spirit which had been bestowed upon the church very much as a
'substance'—as a mysterious force which guaranteed this connection with the heavenly world. Paul could accept this view, but at
the same time he corrected it, to correspond with his view of the
Cross. Incorporation in the Body of Christ, effected through baptism, meant entering the 'place' in which the blessing and the lordship of the Crucified and Risen Lord extended their validity
farther and farther. That is why one became a member of the
Church, by dying with Christ. This conception is clearly in terms
of space rather than in terms of time. As the Body of Christ the
Church already to a certain extent stands apart from time and
history. The fact that on the cross Jesus died for believers is here
taken so seriously that the Church is understood as the congregation of those who—because they live by what happened at the
cross—are already removed from the world, are already living in
the sphere of salvation. The Church is no longer so much the
pilgrim-people which has heard God's call, is fulfilling His commission to the world, and is marching towards His Kingdom. The
Church is no longer thought of as a people which is determined
by a call from outside, or by a historical event in the past. It is
only a Church at all by force of its present link with the Risen
Redeemer and its indwelling in him. Christ is therefore a sort of
corporate personality[11] who embodies all his 'members' (in the
spatial sense).

Thus here the Spirit receives an entirely new role. It is no longer
merely an additional gift of God which enables the Church to
fulfil its missionary task (as in Luke).[12] It is what effects the link
between the Church and the Risen Christ. Only Paul no longer
thinks of that substantially; rather he sees it fulfilled in the fact
that the Spirit enables us to perceive the events of salvation. Thus
he is able to retain the statement that the life of the Church is
determined by the historical event of the Cross. But it is typical
that from this angle the gifts of the Spirit are primarily those which
constantly reveal afresh the 'Body of Christ' in worship, and
which thus 'build' the Church. Of course, Paul also knows that
building the Church is ultimately inseparable from missions. And
of course from the very beginning the Early Church realized that
it was the 'favoured flock' which was set apart from the world and
from history. But the emphases are different. Where the Church
is seen to be the 'Body of Christ', the believer does not exactly

enter a Chosen People which God is leading through the ages; he rather enters a 'place' in which he participates in the blessing and the lordship of his heavenly Redeemer.[13] This means that the Spirit and the gifts which it imparts become very essential for church order. There are no longer any official positions based simply on tradition. But the living Spirit requires a clear order. There is no distinction, it is true, between priests and laity. The Spirit is bestowed on every member of the Church. But it is bestowed in very different ways on every individual. An order which is only arranged 'afterwards', in accordance with the gifts of the Spirit, must therefore ensure that every member of the Church fulfils his service as well as he possibly can, and for the good of all the members.[14]

III. JOHN: CHRIST, THE TRUE VINE

The Christology of the fourth Gospel is characterized by the fact that its author stresses much more strongly than Paul that everything decisive has already happened. It is true that John recognizes a consummation which lies in the future,[15] but it is only the confirmation of what has already happened. The Last Judgment has already taken place, and the Parousia is effected through the Christian message. John agrees with Paul that the Christ-event represents God's victory in the great cosmic struggle between God and the world, because it is a proof of the righteousness of God and the unrighteousness of the world.[16] But John does not give the central position to the cross as an atonement or substitution; his main emphasis is on the incarnation and obedience of Jesus, even to the Cross.[17] In his Gospel the concept of time is even more relative.[18] For it is precisely in the Son's absolute obedience, consummated in the complete humiliation of the Cross, that his oneness with the Father is revealed. This is God's message to the world, the revelation of His glory, the pledge of His love to the world.[19] Anyone who comes to the faith here perceives God Himself—in the incarnate Christ.

This leads us to expect a reappearance of the idea found in Paul —the 'Body of Christ'. T. W. Manson maintains the theory that the concept of 'the Son of Man' in the New Testament tradition is to be understood primarily corporatively, in the light of the seventh chapter of Daniel.[20] Even those who (like myself) cannot share his view are grateful to him for showing that the idea of the body of elect can easily be linked up with the figure of the Son of Man. This lends considerable justification to C. H. Dodd's comparison between John 15:1 ff. and Psalm 80:16 (where owing to a mistake in the text the Son of Man is connected and identified with Israel, the vine planted by God).[21] Israel is replaced by Christ, the true vine, who bears the branches with their fruit. Expressed in an entirely different terminology independent of Paul, the same view appears here; Christ is a 'corporate personality' in whom all believers are incorporated. The 'true vine' of God is not Israel, nor a loyal remnant within Israel, but Jesus himself. It is only in him, as branches on the vine which can do nothing without him (John 15:5), that believers can be the Church. The thought here is no longer in terms of *Heilsgeschichte*. It is true, the relation of Jesus to the Israel of the Old Testament is dealt with throughout the Gospel. But there is no analogy to Rom. 9–11. And the unbelieving Jews are only representatives of the world as a whole. On the other hand the believer of 4:46 ff. is no more a pagan contrasted with the unfaithful Jews. Belief or unbelief are possibilities for every man. The election of Israel, which is not denied, is really only perceptible in the fact that its unbelief is the typical unbelief—the rejection *kat' exochēn*. The antithesis is always between faith (which responds to God's call) and unfaith (which closes its ears to Him). In this sense Nicodemus is addressed as 'the master of Israel' (John 3:10), Jesus is greeted as 'the King of Israel' (John 1:49; cf. 19:19–22), and salvation is said to be 'of the Jews' (John 4:22). That is why John, contrary to Paul, never gives a central place either to the antithesis between faith and works, mercy and justice, as was typical in Israel. It is true, Paul also regards the sins of the gentiles as ultimately the same as the sins of Israel. But only at the end. He has to show that the idolatry of the Gentiles contains the same attitude of *kauchēma* as the arrogance of those who obey the letter of the law, and that the pagan's frantic search for earthly security (such as wealth) is due to rejection of God in the same way as the Pharisee's accumulation of good works.[22] But that means that the 'true vine' is not simply a comparison between the New Israel and the old Israel, as two periods of *Heilsgeschichte* on the way of God; the 'true vine' symbolizes the antithesis between the Church and the world, the sphere of God and the sphere of Satan, the sphere of light and the sphere of darkness. Anyone who is cut off from the vine is bound to perish.

IV. The Role of the Individual in the Church, as conceived by John

From what has been said it is understandable that for John the perception of God's revelation in Jesus means everything. Anyone who perceives God in Jesus is already surrounded by God's love, he is already saved, he has already passed from death to life, he lives in God and God lives in him. Such perception is a personal matter. In the Synoptic Gospels we read that whole towns accepted or rejected Jesus. Even when individuals are called to follow him, their personality remains completely obscure. It is truer to say that interest is expressed in the individual and his decision rather when someone turns away from Jesus (Matt. 18:12 ff., 15 ff.; Luke 15; Mark 10:17 ff.). In the Gospel of John, on the other hand, the call is always addressed to the individual, and the question how his resistance is overcome and how he comes to a perception of the revelation is of the greatest importance (John 1:35 ff., 3:1 ff., 4:7 ff., 46 ff., etc.). It is only in the fourth Gospel that some of the disciples are described psychologically.

This is also expressed in the fact that the symbols applied to the Church are taken from the world of nature. John does not compare the Church to a 'Body' which incorporates all the members from the beginning and grows as a whole. In John's Gospel the Church is compared to the vine which keeps sending out fresh branches (15:1 ff.). This is even more distinctly expressed in John 12:24, where the saving significance of Jesus' death is seen in the fact that the corn of wheat does not remain alone, but falls into the ground and produces a whole sheaf of corn. The same applies in the parable of the shepherd; some of the sheep hear his voice and follow him, while others do not know him. Some sheep will even come to him from other folds (John 10:4, 14 ff., 27; cf. 11:52).

John's emphasis on the individual does not apply only when the initial decision of faith has to be made. In the Synoptic Gospels a whole town may decide to listen to Jesus, and it is only later that it becomes clear who will really stay with him. But in the Gospel of John anyone who has perceived God in Jesus has already received everything. This thought is so radical that faith and perception are regarded as ultimates, which only need to be confirmed in the consummation of heavenly glory. Even if many misunderstandings have to be overcome, so that there is something resembling a divine education,[23] nevertheless from the very outset the disciple possesses full perception (John 1:41, 45). In John's view, therefore, there are not different spiritual gifts. There is only one spiritual gift: the revelation of the Father in the Son. Thus Pentecost does not bring any miraculous tongues (20:22 f.). Nor is there any church order like that in Matt. 18, or in 1 Cor. 12 and 14. He who has seen the Father possesses everything. He does not need anything else. They are all equal, perfect units living side by side. One seed grows beside another, one branch beside another, one sheep feeds beside the other. They are held together because they all spring from the same root, the same vine, and are led by the same Shepherd. But they do not serve one another in the same way as the arm serves the fingers, or the mouth serves the stomach. John does not describe the Church as the New Israel or as God's People or God's 'Saints'; he never mentions the word 'Church' at all.[24]

In the New Testament there is hardly a single book which stresses the unity of the Church as strongly as the fourth Gospel (John 10:17, 17:20 ff.). But it is just this which shows that unity has become a problem; the congregation are urged to pray for unity. In the Synoptic Gospels unity is taken much more as a matter of course. That may be due to the later date of John's Gospel. But that alone does not adequately explain it. For at a much earlier date Paul already realized the problems involved in this unity. We must therefore observe the theological approach from which an attempt is made to avoid the threatened breach. In Paul's view, one Church must help the other with the special gifts which it has received. The church in Jerusalem has given the Gentiles a share in spiritual things (πνευματικά); now the Gentiles must help the church in Jerusalem in a material way, through the 'fleshly things' (σαρκικά), through collections (Rom. 15:27). On the other hand the faith of the Gentiles must stimulate Israel to follow the way of faith (Rom. 11:11). Peter has received the gift of the mission to the Jews; Paul that of the mission to the Gentiles (Gal. 2:7 ff.). In the Gospel of John the position is seen quite differently. It cannot be said that one Church needs the services of the others. He regards unity and fraternal love as so important only because they reveal God's will to the world. Jesus himself is the revelation of God's glory to the world; and his church must be so also. Its unity is the unity of the vine itself. It can only bear witness of the Son of God to the world if its members live in brotherly love with one another (17:21, 13:35).

V. THE CHURCH ALREADY CONSUMMATED, ACCORDING TO JOHN

John therefore understands the newness of the Church down to the last detail. It has no priests or officials. There is no longer even any diversity of spiritual gifts, so that one member can learn from another. There is no church order at all—not even a free, mobile order open to the workings of the Spirit, as in the churches founded by Paul. There are no 'offices' except among Jesus' enemies—the Jews, Judas (John 12:6), Diotrephes (3 John 9). The twelve disciples have not disappeared (how could they?), but they are of much less importance than the disciple whom Jesus loved.[25] And he is a living example of the deep spiritual link between the believer and the Lord: he 'leaned on Jesus' bosom' (John 13:23).

This Church has really no further to go, no battle to win, no goal to reach. It has only to 'abide' in Jesus; any tendency to move forward is regarded with suspicion (2 John 9). The Church has already reached its goal. Unlike Paul (e.g. 1 Cor. 9:19 ff.) John does not describe the church as being faced by a missionary struggle for the world. He does not mention either the election (Mark 3:13 ff.) or the sending forth of the disciples (Mark 6:7 ff.). The church has indeed the task of bearing witness.[26] But this means a testifying to the glory of God which includes condemning the world as well as calling the predestined children of God.[27] And even this is really done by the Spirit or by the Son himself (cf. John 16:26 f., 3:11) and is only the initial step which leads immediately to an independent perception of God's glory, whereby the new Christian no longer needs the evidence of a witness (John 4:42).[28] Pentecost, as described by John (20:22 f.) is not a commission to evangelize the world. It is the bestowal of the Spirit, which has power to forgive sins or retain them.[29] This means: just as Jesus himself is the *crisis* simply by his existence, because in him light is separated from darkness, and faith from disbelief, the same is true of Christ in the preaching of the disciples.

Membership of the Church is here understood as an absolute gift of grace. It can be described only as being 'born of God' (1:13). The Father draws to Himself whom He will (6:44) and gives him to Jesus (6:37, 17:2). The Son, when he is lifted up, draws his own to him (12:32; cf. 14:3). On the other hand Jesus himself hands his betrayer a sort of 'satanic sacrament' [30] which impels him to his foul deed (13:26 f.; cf. 6:64, 17:12, 18:9). Those who come to Jesus have always belonged to him; and those who reject him have always been 'of this world'. The world *cannot* recognize him, just because it is the world. It is bound to hate him and his Church (8:23, 14:17, 15:18 ff., 16:3).

The call to love one another is stronger in the Gospel of John than almost anywhere else. But he admonishes us always to love our *brethren* (John 15:17-19). He does not mention loving our enemies (Matt. 5:44 ff.; Rom. 12:14 ff.). 'Greater love hath no man than this, that a man lay down his life for his *friends*' (John 15:13). Towards the world our attitude can only be one of rejection; 'love not the world' (1 John 2:15). The trials of the Church are occasioned only because the world hates it and persecutes it; they are not due to its own 'flesh'. John does not speak of the struggle between the spirit and the flesh (as Paul does), nor does he relate the stories included in the Synoptic Gospels about Peter's sinking (Matt. 14:30), about Jesus addressing Peter as 'Satan' (Mark 8:33; cf. John 6:68 f.) and about the eleven disciples forsaking Jesus (Mark 14:50; cf. John 18:8).

VI. THE EPISTLES OF JOHN

Without going into the question whether they were written by the same person,[31] these Epistles reveal a good deal of the same peculiarities in the conception of the Church as the Gospel of John. In fact even more clearly. Here again the idea is expressed that anyone who has perceived Jesus to be the true God therewith has everything (1 John 5:20), and that he then no longer needs any brother to teach him (2:20, 27). In the Epistles too the sending of the Son is the revelation of God's love (4:9 ff.). Eye-witnesses and witnesses of later generations stand on the same level and perceive the same Son sent by the Father (4:14 and 1:1 ff.). Here again, Christians are urged only to love one another and to keep themselves from the world (2:9 ff.).[32]

It is clear that a more advanced stage of thinking has been reached. This may be shown by certain concessions made to the church doctrine of the Parousia (2:28 ff.). It is also shown by the fact that Christians are urged to love one another by means of practical examples (3:17 f.). Most important of all, the unity of the Church has become much more of a problem. The Church of John is confronted by the problem of false teachers and 'anti-Christs'. Is there not a falling off of perception and a hesitation in the way of faith? Does not this prove that the Church was conceived of on a false basis? But the concept of the Church is strictly retained; these false teachers only stand out because they never were part of the Church; they masked their worldliness, but they never perceived Christ (2:19). Their teaching (probably docetically) draws a distinction between the earthly Jesus and the heavenly Christ, and thus confronts Christology (and therefore ecclesiology) with a question: is not John's conception bound to lead to a heavenly Christ isolated from history, who stands in exactly the same relationship to contemporary Christians as to the disciples of the earthly Jesus, who is seen today just as he was then, and with whom Christians are linked today just as they were then? Does not this destroy the significance of his time on earth? 1 John 4:2 sharply corrects this misconception. But both points reveal a weak spot in John's conception of the Church. Does not the solution in 2:19 simply mean capitulation in face of the task of winning those who have strayed back to membership of the Church (Matt. 18:12 ff.; 2 Cor. 2:6 f.; 2 Tim. 2:25 f.)? And is not 1 John 4:2 a much-emphasized but unbased dogmatic statement rather than convincing mistaken teachers? Perhaps the change in the situation becomes clearest in the problem of church tradition.[33] John's view is that the Spirit cannot teach anything but what has existed 'from the beginning'. A particularly strong appeal must therefore be made to 'abide', and warnings must be made against 'going forward'. But this very 'abiding' has become a problem. It is no longer merely a question of faith and disbelief; there are also false faiths. Some criterion must be set up to distinguish between true and false faith; and that criterion is precisely 'abiding' in what has been since the beginning. But this is no longer abiding 'in him', which can still be interpreted as something living and dynamic; it has become an 'abiding' in the old teaching. In this case the Church tends more and more to become a group of orthodox people, of correct Christians, of conservatives. No wonder that it was necessary to make such strong appeals to show brotherly love.

Lastly, the development is shown by another point. The problem arises of sin after baptism. The author of the Johannine conception of the Church is in some way helpless when confronted by this problem. This is shown in 2:1 where the sins of a Christian look like an exception which should never have happened. I cannot feel convinced that this problem would be solved on the lines of Luther's *simul peccator, simul iustus.*[34] I rather incline to think that the contradictory statements in 1:8 and 3:9 may be explained by pointing to the false teachers against whom the author has to contend. These false teachers declare (again as a wrong and dangerous consequence of Johannine statements) that those who have received the Spirit have a divine character which they cannot lose; it is no longer possible for them to sin. They can therefore be as immoral as they like, in order to demonstrate their complete freedom from the law.[35] In face of such assertions, the Epistle is bound to deny that man is divine and without sin; but it also opposes any frivolous immorality by stressing that sin is lawlessness and nothing else. Both points show wrong and dangerous consequences resulting from John's approach.

VII. Comments

We have seen the strength and the weakness of John's concept of the Church. With impressive, systematic power he solves the difficult question as to how the Church here and now can live by what happened in Jesus of Nazareth at another time and place. There is no longer any problem about bridging over the distance in time and space between the events of salvation and the contemporary Church. For the Church is not a people based on an act of God in history—like the act of rescuing Israel by bringing them safely across the Red Sea. Nor is it a people whose wanderings are determined exclusively by its ultimate goal, namely entrance into the promised land, or the Kingdom of God which dawns with the Parousia. It is not even understood as a people guided by God's rule from day to day, under the protection and the commandment of the Risen Lord. It is the Church only in so far as it lives 'in' the Son and he in it. The Son is present in the Church today just as he was then, through the message—in fact it is only now that his presence is perfect (John 16:7, 13). This avoids the misunderstanding that faith might be merely a matter of approving some doctrine or some ethical pattern or agreement with the historical origin of the Church. It also makes it impossible to escape into a better 'Beyond' which is yet to come. Here the Church is placed in the present time and is proof against all forms of historicism and of millenarianism. But one danger is clear: that the Church may become detached from history. Unless the Church bears strictly in mind that the Christ whom it preaches is none other than Jesus of Nazareth, and that there can be no heavenly 'Son' except the one who became man, it will develop into a group of Gnostics. John wrote a Gospel, not a dogmatic treatise. If this were to be forgotten, if the incarnation were no longer regarded as an act of obedience but merely as an (ultimately non-essential) *epiphania* of a divine nature which is eternally the same,[36] then the Church would be in danger of docetic disintegration.

Equally important is the firm way in which faith is understood by John as a gift, as the 'pull' of God Himself. John firmly rejects any misconception that faith consists in achieving correct ideas which bring *sacrificium intellectus*. He also rejects all pietistic ideas of justification through works. This situation is realized so intensively that the author states that the Church has always been 'born of God', and that the world has always been 'of the devil'. It is this which urges him to abandon the world and to apply love solely to the brethren. The 1st Epistle of John already shows how, from these premises, the author nevertheless has to insist on dogmatic orthodoxy and practical charity. This clearly involves the danger that the pious group will retire into itself and become completely rigid, making no real attempt to care for the spiritual needs of those who think differently from itself, and undertaking no real missionary work because God's children cannot change, neither can the world change. Here the important point in connection with the statements that the Father draws to Him whom He will, that the Son gathers in his own, and that the Spirit leads to all truth, is not to interpret them as automatic, mechanical processes but as living events. Just because faith is a gift, it must never be regarded as a possession which makes further effort unnecessary. Faith must always be expressed afresh—not intellectually but in such a way that the believer realizes that he must constantly be 'drawn' to God afresh and constantly led back to the truth. In this way the brother who thinks differently becomes a help and a task presented by God. The same applies to love. Love must be constantly carried out afresh, but not in the sense of 'good works' based on a law of the old kind; love must be carried out in such

R

a way that the one who loves realizes that he must *let* himself be
constantly loved afresh, so that he can radiate the love which he
has received (1 John 4:9 ff.). In this way the love of him who loved
the world (as John states more clearly than anyone else) will
radiate through the brotherhood and beyond them and touch
the world.

Finally, with a clarity which is found hardly anywhere else,
John insists that anyone who has perceived the glory of the Father
in the Son has *everything*, and needs nothing else. Hence there is no
real development of faith, and no falling from faith.[37] This avoids
the danger of thinking that the message is to be progressively developed and re-adapted to the spirit of every age. It also avoids
over-estimating any curious phenomena which might be regarded
as proofs of the Spirit. Sensational modern formulations have no
place in the Church, nor have sensational psychic phenomena. But
again, everything depends on this: that perception of the Father in
the Son must be understood as something which must constantly
occur afresh. It must be emphasized that, although this perception
contains the whole of salvation, it is nevertheless something which
must grow, as it grew in Jesus' teaching of the disciples (also described by John). Otherwise it is impossible to avoid seeing that
the Church is in danger of developing into a group of complete
Gnostics,[38] of which each individual member has reached the goal
independently. How could a Church *live* if each of its members
already possessed *everything* in the Spirit and no longer needed his
brethren and their encouragement? How could services of worship be held if the assembled congregation expected nothing new,
and merely came to receive confirmation that they were children
of God?

The fascination of the fourth Gospel lies in the fact that it insists
that salvation has been fully accomplished in Jesus Christ, and that
the Church is therefore the absolutely new flock in which God's
Kingdom has already been achieved. This was shown in all three
of the points dealt with. But (as seems strange at first sight) it was
precisely here that the problems arose which later on broke out in
Gnosticism. It is precisely because the unity of the Church follows
so logically from this theological conception, that that unity becomes a problem. For the perfect man needs no other perfection.
Thus unity becomes something which is only asserted in theory,
but not visibly realized. Just here, where the importance of the

Church seems to be greatest (its unity with the Father being a present reality), that importance becomes problematical. For it cannot ultimately bring anything new either in its worship or in its missionary work. Thus its importance becomes merely theoretical; it is not expressed in practice. The Church of the second century gratefully accepted the Gospel and the Epistles of John, and it was certainly right in doing so. Perhaps there are no other writings in the New Testament which can be as stimulating and fruitful as these. But the Early Church placed them beside other writings—the Synoptic gospels and the epistles of Paul. It is only in connection with them, and modified and interpreted in the light of them, that we can understand the message of John.

NOTES

[1] K. Holl, 'Der Kirchenbegriff des Paulus in seinem Verhältnis zur Urgemeinde', Sitzungsberichte der Akademie der Wissenschaften zu Berlin, 1921, 920–7 = *Gesammelte Aufsätze*, II, 1928, 44–67; H. v. Campenhausen, *Kirchliches Amt und geistliche Vollmacht in den ersten drei Jahrhunderten* (1953), 32–134.

[2] B. H. Streeter, *The Primitive Church* (1930), 83 ff., deals with the Epistles of John separately, but regards the Johannine Church as completely incorporated into the Church in Asia Minor. Some information may be found in A. Oepke, *Das neue Gottesvolk* (1950), 231 ff.

[3] The Early Church and Paul can only be dealt with very summarily here. Further details may be found in E. Schweizer: 'Geist und Gemeinde im Neuen Testament und heute', *Theologische Existenz heute*, new series, 32, 1952.

[4] Examples of the most extreme points are A. Schweitzer's book, *The Quest of the Historical Jesus* (1952), 328 ff. and C. H. Dodd, *The Parables of the Kingdom* (1936), 41 ff.

[5] Cf. T. W. Manson, 'The New Testament Basis of the Doctrine of the Church', JEH 1 (1950), 1 f.

[6] In this the Church was completely different from the Qumran sect. This is shown most clearly in the language: the word for 'office', λειτουργία, taken from Greek usage and from the Old Testament, is often found in the New Testament, but is not used to describe the special service of an individual, which is what we call 'office'. For that a word-root occurs which is not found in the Old Testament except in two passages, where it is used purely secularly: διακονία (cf. E. Schweizer, *Das Leben des Herrn in der Gemeinde und ihren Diensten* (1946), 19 ff. On DIAKONIA, iQS 3, 26; Zad. Fragm. 20, 21; Jos. *Ant.* 18, 1, 5; E. Stauffer, TLZ 1952, 201 ff.; W. D. Davies, *Religion in Life*, 21, 265); E. Schweizer, Gemeinde und Gemeindeordnung im NT (in print), II, 2.

[7] Cf. W. Michaelis, *Das Ältestenant*, 1953; G. Bornkamm, TWNT 6, 651 ff.

[8] E. Käsemann, 'Sätze heiligen Rechtes im Neuen Testament', NTS 1 (1954/55), 248 ff.

[9] Gal. 6:16 (with N. A. Dahl in *Judaica* 6 (1950), 161 ff., contrary to G. Schrenk, *ibid.*, 5 (1949), 81 ff. and 6 (1950), 170 ff.); 1 Cor. 10:18; Rom. 9:6 ff.,

11:16 ff.; also 1 Cor. 10:1 ff., etc. On the 'heilsgeschichtlich' view see T. W. Manson, *op. cit.* (note 5), 2 f.

[10] For the juxtaposition of the two lines see E. Dinkler, 'Earliest Christianity', *The Idea of History in the Ancient Near East* (1955), 181 ff.; also T. W. Manson, *The Church's Ministry* (1948), 22 ff.

[11] Of course, some explanation should be given as to the real meaning of this very vague idea. See E. Schweizer, *Erniedrigung und Erhöhung bei Jesus und seinen Nachfolgern* (1955), 75 ff., *Lordship and Discipleship* (in print), ch. 4.

[12] E. Schweizer, πνεῦμα, TWNT 6 (1956), 405 ff.

[13] T. W. Manson points out the danger of stressing the concept of the Body of Christ exclusively (T. W. Manson, *op. cit.* (note 10), 20 ff.).

[14] T. W. Manson, *op. cit.* (note 10), 56 ff., 78 ff. E. Schweizer, *op. cit.* (note 6), 95 ff.; *op. cit.* (note 3), 25 ff.

[15] John 6:27, 12:25, 14:2 f., 17:24; also 11:24. Still clearer are the passages 5:28 f., 6:39 ff. (the genuineness of which is, indeed, disputed).

[16] Th. Preiss, 'Die Rechtfertigung im johanneischen Denken', *Evangelische Theologie*, 16 (1956), 289 ff. = 'Hommage et Reconnaissance', *Cahiers théologiques de l'actualité protestante*, hors-série 2 (1946), 100 ff. English translation in 'Life in Christ' (S.C.M. *Studies in Biblical Theology*, No. 13, 1954), 9 ff.

[17] As is the case in the hymn quoted by Paul in Phil. 2:6–11.

[18] Although perhaps one should not insist on the present tense ὤν in John 1:18 (cf. 2 Cor. 8:9; Luke 24:6, 44; 2 Clem 9, 5; F. Blass-A. Debrunner, *Grammatik des neutest. Griechisch*, § 231), one must take due account of 3:13 and 8:58. As a man on this earth Jesus 'has ascended' to the Father, and before Abraham was, he *is* (not 'was'!). John 3:11 (cf. 9:4) also makes it clear that Jesus goes on living in the 'we' of all his witnesses. Cf. R. H. Lightfoot, *St. John's Gospel* (1956), to 3:13.

[19] Thus the last evening is described as the revelation of the love of the Son and of the Father: 13:1 ff., also 14:21 f., 15:9.

[20] T. W. Manson, *The Teaching of Jesus* (1931), 227 ff.; *Coniectanea Neotestamentica* 11 (1947), 138 ff.; *The Church's Ministry* (1948), 18 ff.; BJRL 32 (1950), 171 ff.; *The Servant-Messiah* (1953), 72 ff.

[21] With regard to my view in EGO EIMI (1939), 37 ff., Dodd's argument (in *The Interpretation of the Fourth Gospel* (1953), 411 f.) has convinced me that the use of the word in the Old Testament is to be considered, especially as in 10:1 ff. the Jewish 'shepherds' seem to serve as a contrast with the true shepherd (*op. cit.*, 358 ff.). This is confirmed by J. A. T. Robinson's analysis (ZNTW 46 (1955), 233 ff.).

[22] In Matthew the sins of the Gentiles are hardly mentioned. In Acts the difference between the Jewish and Gentile audience determines the form of what is said far more than the change in the person of the speaker (E. Schweizer, 'Zu den Reden der Apostelgeschichte', TZ 13 (1957), 10 f.).

[23] Jesus Christ is for John a living person. Therefore being in Christ, although it *is* already the final salvation, always means life. The disciple who *has* believed has to believe time and again (1:51, 2:11, 11:15, 13:19, 14:29, 16:31; cf. 15:2, 8). In 8:12 the future tense is connected with the ἀκολουθεῖν of the believer. Cf. also Lightfoot, *loc. cit.* (note 18) to 14:2. Bernard, ICC to 1:38.

[24] It does not occur again until 3 John 6, 9 f. Particularly striking is the for-

mulation ἐκλεκτὴ κυρία in 2 John 1. Nor does the fact that false prophets are mentioned in 1 John 4:1 in any way prove that there were charismatic prophets in the Church (R. Schnackenburg, *Die Johannesbriefe* (1953), 190 (cf. 216). The tension between the individual and the social view in John is carefully described in D. Faulhaber, *Das Johannes-Evangelium und die Kirche* (1938), 51–6, 60, 65 f.

[25] Only in the postscript (21:15 ff.) is a special commission mentioned. And even this is connected with the special position of the eye-witness. John 20:22 ff. does not belong here; it is not even clear in that passage whether the ten (!) disciples or a larger group are referred to. At any rate the μαθηταί here as everywhere are representative of the church as a whole (C. K. Barrett, *The Gospel according to St. John* (1955), 472 f.). If one wished to regard them merely as office-bearers one would also have to restrict the commandment to love, in Christ's farewell words, only to office-bearers.

[26] M. Barth, The Reformed Review 10 (1957), 5 f.

[27] Like Jesus himself (3:11, 7:7, 14:31, etc.) or the Spirit (16:8–10) the church also is witness for God against the world. It is true, there are men coming out of the world into the church (17:20, 20:29), but the world as a whole remains immersed in evil (17:15). Although the world is loved by God (3:16) and should believe (17:21) it is overcome by Christ (16:33). The disciples are chosen out of the world (17:6). Cf. Barrett, *loc. cit.* (note 25) to 16:33, 17:2; Lightfoot, *loc. cit.* (note 18) to 17:21.

[28] John 1:46 shows the dilemma of the witness who can only point to the disciple's direct encounter with Jesus.

[29] Note the formulation. The judgment does not imply 'binding' as in Matt. 16:19, 18:18. It implies leaving the world in the condition in which it already is. The same formulation occurs in John 3:36: 'the wrath of God *abideth* on him who believeth not.'

[30] W. Wrede, *Vorträge und Studien* (1907), 136 (quoted according to R. Bultmann, *ad loc.*).

[31] The difference in authorship is supported particularly by C. H. Dodd in *The Johannine Epistles*, 1946; also by H. Conzelmann, 'Was von Anfang war', *Neutestamentliche Studien für R. Bultmann* (1954), 194 ff., who regards John as a 'Johannine Pastoral Letter'.

[32] John 16:33 says that Christ has overcome the world. In 1 John 5:4 f. (cf. 2:13 f.) this is applied to the Church.

[33] Cf. Conzelmann, *op. cit.* (note 31).

[34] Cf. R. Bultmann, *Theologie des Neuen Testaments* (1953), 426 (paragraph 50, 3).

[35] Like the Gnostic opponents mentioned by Irenaeus, *Adv. Haer.*, I, 6, 2.

[36] Cf. note 18. For the interpretation of 1:14 see E. Käsemann, 'Aufbau und Anliegen des johanneischen Prologs', *Libertas Christiana* (Festschrift F. Delekat, 1957), 88 ff.; R. Schnackenburg, 'Logos-Hymnus und johanneischer Prolog', *Biblische Zeitschrift*, neue Folge 1 (1957), 79 f.; E. Schweizer, σάρξ, TWNT.

[37] The danger is removed by the word of Christ: 16:1, 4.

[38] According to 3:8, not only the Spirit but also the man born of the Spirit is like the wind, and cannot be judged by his fellow-men. Cf. Barrett, *loc. cit.* (note 25) to 16:23. T. W. Manson warns against this danger, *loc. cit.* (note 5), 8 ff.

THE ORIGINAL ORDER OF Q

by

V. TAYLOR

IN view of the great contribution which Professor T. W. Manson has made to the study of Q, a contribution for which all
students of Gospel Origins are deeply grateful, it seems not inappropriate to offer in this essay a few comments on the Order of
this source. There are several reasons why such an investigation
is desirable. First, it will be agreed that, while many important
contributions have been made to this question, the results cannot
be regarded as completely satisfactory. Again, and not uncon-
nected with this situation, there has been a shift of interest which
has caused a temporary halt to these discussions. For something
like a generation the earlier interest in literary criticism, so virile
during the latter part of the nineteenth century and the opening
decades of the twentieth, has abated owing to the competing
claims of Form Criticism, New Testament Theology, Typology,
and existentialist assessments of the Gospel tradition. These newer
and fruitful interests are not to be regretted and it was perhaps
necessary that the well tilled fields of literary criticism should lie
fallow for a time. Nevertheless, it seems necessary, without
neglecting the later disciplines, to return to the study of the older
problems and to consider how far they are capable of a solution.
Further, in the interval the existence of Q has been vigorously
assailed, notably by such scholars as E. Lummis,[1] H. G. Jameson,[2]
B. C. Butler,[3] and A. Farrer.[4] These scholars have revived the
hypothesis that Luke used the Gospel of Matthew as a source, and
Abbot Butler has gone so far as to describe Q as 'an unnecessary
and vicious hypothesis'.[5] The Two Document Hypothesis has
been strongly attacked. These attacks have not changed the views
of its advocates, but in some quarters a certain uneasiness is manifest. There is a tendency to speak of Q as 'a hypothetical document' and its alleged unity has been questioned.[6] On the other

hand, there has been what must be described as a closer approach to the Q Hypothesis on the part of some Roman Catholic scholars. In the new *Catholic Commentary on Holy Scripture* (1953) Père Benoit has maintained that an original Aramaic Gospel of Matthew was used as a source by the three Synoptists. Similarly Dr. Alfred Wikenhauser,[7] who maintains that the Greek Matthew and Luke are both dependent on Mark, suggests that Matthew composed the *logia* in Aramaic, the Greek translation being the common source used in the Greek Matthew and Luke.

In these circumstances it may be timely to re-examine the order of Q in its bearings on the Q Hypothesis. At any rate this is the theme of the present essay.

I

In this inquiry I shall use the symbol Q to represent those sayings and parables in Matt. and Luke which are commonly assigned to this source, accepting the view that Q was a document as 'a working hypothesis'. I shall leave aside the possibility that Q was preceded by earlier groups of sayings and examine the common source which, by hypothesis, lay before them as a unity. Several arguments have been held to support this hypothesis— the linguistic agreements between Matt. and Luke, the order reflected by the sayings, and the presence of doublets in the two Gospels which point to the use of Mark and at least one other source. I do not propose to discuss all these arguments, but only the question of order, which in many respects is the most objective and decisive argument of all. I shall use the sign M as a convenient symbol for the sayings and parables which are found only in Matt. With Streeter and Bussmann I believe that M was also a document, but it will not be possible within the limits of this essay to discuss this hypothesis, although the investigation will have something to contribute to it. It will not be necessary to examine the L hypothesis, and I must content myself with stating the belief that it was a body of oral tradition which Luke was the first to give a written form. All I wish to attempt is to consider whether the order of the sayings commonly assigned to Q is such as to render probable the view that this source lay before the two Evangelists in the form of a document at the time when they wrote.

In this endeavour I am compelled to refer to an article on 'The Order of Q' which I contributed to the *Journal of Theological Studies*[8] in April, 1953, since the present essay carries further conclusions there suggested. In that article I made a new approach to the question of order by suggesting that we must not be content to study parallel passages in Matt. and Luke in *two* columns, with Luke on the left, as presumably representing better the original order of Q, and Matt. on the right. Such lists point to a common order, as many scholars have argued, but the breaches of order in the lists are so many that the case has been felt to be much less strong and convincing than, in fact, it is. In the article referred to I set down the Lukan passages on the left, but instead of one column for Matt. I used *six*, including the Q sayings in the five great discourses in Matt., in 5–7, 10, 13, 18 and 23–25 and a sixth column containing the Q sayings in the rest of Matt. The result was to show an astonishing range of agreement, not continuous throughout, but visible in groups or series of passages in the same order in both Gospels. In all, only ten sayings stood apart from these series breaking their continuity, and it was suggested that, unless Luke used Matt. as a source, a strong argument existed in favour of the hypothesis that both Evangelists drew upon the document Q as one of their principal sources.

Obviously the tabulated series cannot be the result of happy chance, but, in default of any criticisms of the article known to me, I may perhaps be permitted to say that the table is open to two objections. First, I excluded a group of sayings and parables on the ground that in them by wide consent Matthew's preference, while possibly using Q, is dependent upon another source, with the result that the order of Q, as reflected in Matt. and Luke, may be obscured.[9] Secondly, I did not discuss in detail the ten short sayings which stand in a different order in the two Gospels. The table was left to speak for itself.

In the present essay I shall include all the passages mentioned, with the exception of Matt. 16:2 which is textually suspect. The effect is to break to some extent the regularity of the agreements, although not in one or two cases, but in any case it makes the investigation more complete. I now propose to discuss the order of the Q sayings in Luke as compared with that present in the five great discourses in Matt. and in the rest of this Gospel outside these discourses.

II

THE SERMON ON THE MOUNT

Luke	Matt. 5-7
6:20-3	5:3-6, 11 f.
6:27-30	5:39b-42
6:31	(7:12)
6:32-6	5:44-8
6:37 f.	7:1 f.
6:41 f.	7:3-5
6:43-5	7:16-20
6:46	7:21
6:47-9	7:24-7
11:2-4	6:9-13
11:9-13	(7:7-11)
11:33	(5:15)
11:34 f.	6:22 f.
12:22-31	6:25-33
12:33b, 34	(6:20 f.)
12:57-9	(5:25 f.)
13:23 f.	7:13 f.
13:25-7	7:22 f., [25:10-12]
14:34 f.	(5:13)
16:13	(6:24)
16:17	5:18
16:18	5:32

Notes

1. The greater part of Matthew's Version consists of sayings from M. In particular, 5:21-48 includes six 'Antitheses', together with an introduction in 5:17-20. Into these sections Q sayings have been inserted. It is not surprising, therefore, that in these cases Matthew and Luke do not agree in order.

2. Further, there is an original group of M sayings in 6:1-8, 16-18 (and perhaps also in 19-21). This also affects the order in which Q is used.

3. In these circumstances the agreement in the order of Q in the two Gospels is remarkable. The order is not continuous, but consists of sequences in common, of which the first (broken by 7:12) is considerable, and the second (broken by 7:7-11 and 5:15) is hardly less notable. Two briefer sequences, consisting of two sayings each, follow. The bracketed passages are those which differ in order.

4. It will be seen that Matthew has used practically the whole of

Luke's Sermon on the Plain in Matt. 5 and 7, and in 6 various sayings from Luke 11–14 and 16. This distribution has the appearance of a consciously adopted plan.

5. The passages in brackets obviously call for special discussion, and it will be useful to consider first those in Matt. 5:17–48, and then those in the rest of the Matthaean Sermon.

The Q sayings in Matt. 5:17–48

The six Antitheses are (1) 21 ff. on Murder, (2) 27 ff. on Adultery, (3) 31 f. on Divorce, (4) 33 ff. on Vows and Oaths, (5) 38 ff. on Retribution, and (6) 43 ff. on Love of one's Neighbour. The theme of the Introduction, 5:17–20, is the Attitude to be taken to the Law. Of the Q sayings in 5:17–48 that on reconciliation in 25 f. is loosely appended to 24 in No. 1 and it is not surprising that the Lukan order is broken. What is surprising in that 18 (in the Introduction) and 32 in No. 3 stand in their Lukan order, and that the same is true of 39b–42 and 44–8 in Nos. 5 and 6. Nos. 2 and 4 contain no Q sayings.

These facts are naturally explained if Matthew has edited the Introduction and has himself added Nos. 3, 5, and 6 to an original group of three Antitheses in Nos. 1, 2, and 4. This hypothesis has independently been suggested by M. Albertz[10] and W. L. Knox[11] on literary grounds[12] and receives further support from the order of the Q sayings. With the exception of the editorial use of Matt. 5:25 f., dependence on Q in Matt. 5:17–48 in an order common to Matt. and Luke is a reasonable assumption. Matt. 5:18 and 32 are used earlier than the parallel sayings in Luke because they are inserted by Matthew into this complex.

The Q Sayings in the Rest of the Sermon on the Mount

In their Lukan order these sayings are Matt. 7:12, 7:7–11, 5:15, 6:20 f., 5:13, 6:24; and with these 7:13 f. and 22 f. may with advantage be considered.

1. *Matt. 7:12* (Luke 6:31): 'All things therefore whatsoever ye would that men should do unto you, even so do ye also unto them: for this is the law and the prophets.'

Apart from the Matthaean addition in the final clause, Matt. and Luke agree closely.[13] Dependence on Q is highly probable, and the only question to consider is why Matthew incorporates the saying at a later point. In reply, it is to be noted that both

Evangelists use it as a summary passage. The position in Luke is much to be preferred since it is the conclusion to a group, Luke 6:27–30, arranged in Semitic parallelism and revealing both rhyme and rhythm when translated back into Aramaic.[14] Apparently, Matthew has delayed his use of the saying to sum up the considerable number of Q sayings in 6:22–7:11. In short, he alters Luke's order for editorial reasons.

2. *Matt. 7:7–11* (Luke 11:9–13): *On Answer to Prayer*

The agreement is close, but the clue to the difference of position in the two Gospels is obscure. McNeile says that in Matt. the saying stands in no apparent relation to the context.[15] In Luke it appears in a section on Prayer (11:1–13) following the Lord's Prayer (2–4) and the parable of the Friend at Midnight (5–8). Knox[16] suggests that the section is a (pre-Lukan) tract on Prayer, but, if so, this suggestion does not exclude the probability that in Q Luke 11:9–13 originally followed immediately Luke 11:2–4. Why, then, in Matt. 7:7–11 is it separated from the Prayer (Matt. 6:9–13) by several passages from Q and M, placed immediately after the M saying, 'Give not that which is holy to the dogs', and before the summary saying, 7:12, on doing to others as we wish them to do to us? No completely satisfactory answer has been given to this question, and it may be insoluble. Only a conjecture can be offered. The natural place for the passage in Matt. would be after the Lord's Prayer (Matt. 6:9–13) as in Luke. But at this point Matthew uses a saying from Mark or M on forgiveness (Matt. 6:14 f.). This change of theme leaves the passage on Answer to Prayer on his hands; and he finds no place for it, save, in an unsuitable context, after the extracts from Q and M immediately before 7:12 as indicated above. In any case, and whatever may be the explanation, Matthew's use of 7:7–11 is probably editorial.

3. *Matt. 5:15* (Luke 11:33): 'Neither do men light a lamp, and put it under the bushel, but on the stand; and it shineth unto all that are in the house.'

Matt. 5:15 stands in an M context (Matt. 5:13–16) and may even belong to M. In this case no problem arises: Matthew follows the order of M. More probably, however, the saying has been taken from Q. The parallel passage in Luke 11:33 has a doublet in

Luke 8:16 (= Mark 4:21) and shares with it the words οὐδείς, ἅψας, and εἰσπορευόμενοι and the idea that those who see the light enter from without. This explains the linguistic differences between Luke 11:33 and Matt. 5:15.[17] That a common source is used is suggested by the fact that Matt. 5:15, 6:22 f., and 6:25-33 follow in the same relative order as Luke 11:33, 34 f., and 12:22-31.[18] The earlier position of Matt. 5:15 is caused by its insertion in its present M context (see above).

4. *Matt. 6:20 f.* (Luke 12:33b-34): Treasure on Earth and in Heaven.

Apart from the closing words (Matt. 6:21 and Luke 12:34) the linguistic differences are considerable. These differences and the variation of rhythm[19] in the two forms suggest that Matthew is drawing upon M and Luke on Q. In this case the difference in position is not surprising.

5. *Matt. 5:13* (Luke 14:34 f.): On Salt.

Here again Matthew's source may be M.[20] If he is using Q, the difference of order in Matt. and Luke is due to the M. context in which Matt. 5:13 appears.

6. *Matt. 6:24* (Luke 16:13): On Serving Two Masters.

The two versions are in almost verbatim agreement; the only difference is that Luke has οἰκέτης with οὐδείς. With the last saying this is one of those 'scattered fragments' which Streeter[21] says there is good reason to assign to Q, although they are not found embedded in the mass of other material from that source. Easton[22] soundly observes that its place in Q is quite uncertain.

It is possible to state a case in favour of the order of either of the Evangelists. Luke attaches it to a group of L sayings (Luke 16:10-12) which follow the parable of the Unjust Steward (16:1-9) and the connexion seems determined *ad vocem* by the word 'Mammon'. This arrangement appears to be artificial as compared with that of Matthew who uses the saying to introduce the passage on Anxiety (6:25-34). The two are connected by the phrase διὰ τοῦτο and the idea suggested is that, as we cannot serve two masters, we are not to be anxious for our life. This connexion is good, but somewhat artificial. Luke has the passage on Anxiety earlier (12:22-31) after the parable of the Rich Fool (12:13-21), and in this arrangement διὰ τοῦτο seems to point back to the pre-

ceding Q saying on the guidance of the Holy Spirit in a time of
anxiety (12:11 f.). As in Matt. this connexion is good, but perhaps
superficial. Anxiety about food and clothing and about one's
defence before a legal tribunal are connected by little save the idea
of anxiety itself. No compelling argument enables us to decide
between Matt. and Luke and we must agree with the opinion of
Easton, cited above, that the place of the saying on Serving Two
masters in Q is uncertain. Editorial activity has been at work in
either Matt. and Luke, and perhaps in both.

7. *Matt. 7:13 f.* (Luke 13:23 f.): The Two Ways, and *Matt. 7:22 f.*
   (Luke 13:26 f.): The Shut Door.

Linguistically the two sayings have so little in common that
it is possible that both have been taken from M.[23] Moreover,
Matt. 7:13 f. speaks of the narrow *gate* which leads to the ways of
destruction and life, whereas Luke speaks of the narrow *door* which
many are not able to enter. The sayings on the Shut Door also
agree only in the common use of Ps. 6:9. Phrases in Luke 13:25
recall the parable of the Ten Virgins in M (Matt. 25:1–13).

The two sayings are considered here in order to have as many
facts before us as possible because (*a*) they stand in the same order
in Matt. and Luke, and (*b*) the intervening passages, Matt. 7:16–
20 (Luke 6:43 f.) and Matt. 7:21 (Luke 6:46), *also* stand in the
same order.[24] Moreover, Matt. 7:16–20 and 21 also, like 7:13 f.
and 22 f., may come from M. If the source is Q, Matthew has followed its order; if M he (or the compiler of M) is aware of Q's
order or of a tradition common to Q and M. Probably the editorial work is that of Matthew himself. He connects 7:16–20 and
21 because they stand in that order in the Lukan Sermon on the
Plain (Q) and 7:13 f. and 22 f. because they follow in the same
order in those passages outside of the Lukan Sermon which he
uses in compiling the Sermon on the Mount.

Conclusions regarding the Sermon on the Mount

From the above investigation it would appear that, apart from
cases of conflation with M, and insertions and additions to it,
Matthew has followed the order of Q as it stood in Luke. The
necessity of discussing cases where the order is broken must not
obscure the fact that for the most part the agreement of order is
patent and therefore does not need discussion. In the cases

examined conflation and editorial changes are departures from
the order present in Luke, except on rare occasions when Luke is
responsible for the differences. A point of interest is that M supplies about two-thirds of the whole, which suggests that M itself
contained a version of the Sermon beginning with Beatitudes. If
so, Matthew has followed M in 5:3-11 with additions and modifications suggested by Q.

THE MISSION CHARGE

Luke	Matt. 9:37-10:42
6:40	(10:24 f.)
10:2	9:37 f.
10:3-12	10:9-16
10:16	(10:40)
12:2 f.	10:26 f.
12:4-7	10:28-31
12:8 f.	10:32 f.
12:11 f.	(10:19 f.)
12:51-3	10:34-36
14:26 f.	10:37 f.
17:33	10:39

Notes

1. The Matthaean discourse contains material from M and Mark, but
mainly from Q. (For 10:9-16 see footnote 26.)

2. It will be seen that, apart from 10:24 f., 40, and 19 f., the Q passages
listed (24 verses) agree exactly in order in Matt. and Luke.

3. Obviously the three exceptions (5 verses) call for examination in
order to see why they appear in a different order.

1. *Matt. 10:24 f.* (Luke 6:40): 'A disciple is not above his master, nor a
    servant above his lord. It is enough for the disciple that he be as his
    master, and the servant as his lord' (Matt.); 'The disciple is not above
    his master: but every one when he is perfected shall be as his master'
    (Luke).

It should be noted that Luke 6:39 has a parallel in Matt. 14:14
which is also not in Luke's order. Luke 6:39 f. is a unit, not connected closely with its context in the Lukan Sermon, which Matthew has not included in the Sermon on the Mount. In 15:14 he
applies 39 to the Pharisees[25] and, as we see, sets 40 in the Mission
Charge. Both Matthaean sayings stand in an M context and both
may belong to M;[26] but the artificiality of the construction in

15:12–14 and 10:23–5 raises the question whether after all both have been derived from Q.

A common dependence on Q is suggested by the agreements and by the fact that Matthew's modifications appear to be secondary. Instead of the general application which the sayings have in Luke 6:39 f. he applies 39 to the Pharisees and adapts 40 for use in the Mission Charge in 10:24 f., where the context and the double use of the term 'his lord' suggest that he is thinking of Jesus himself.

All this is true even if Luke 6:39 f. is not in its original order. Creed[27] says that its position is editorial and Easton[28] thinks the connexion is artificial. But there is not a little to be said for the view that Luke retains the order of Q. Luke 6:39 f. follows the saying on Not Judging (6:37 f.) and precedes that on the Mote and the Beam (6:41 f.). The idea appears to be that the man who condemns others is a blind guide who can benefit no one. Teacher and disciple alike will fall into a pit, for the disciple's insight will rise no higher than that of his teacher even if the lesson is learned perfectly. Moreover, the man who judges is blind in another sense. He sees the mote in his brother's eye, but not the beam in his own eye, and thus deceives himself. This connexion of thought seems too subtle to be editorial. It is easier to suppose that Luke is reproducing the order of Q.[29] If so, on his understanding of the sayings, Matthew has regarded them as unsuitable for the Sermon on the Mount and has transferred them to the contexts in which they now stand.

2. *Matt. 10:40* (Luke 10:16): 'He that receiveth you receiveth me, and he that receiveth me receiveth him that sent me' (Matt.); 'He that heareth you heareth me; and he that rejecteth you rejecteth me; and he that rejecteth me rejecteth him that sent me' (Luke). Cf. Mark 9:37, 'Whosoever shall receive one of such little children in my name, receiveth me: and whosoever receiveth me, receiveth not me, but him that sent me.'

It is important to note that, while these versions of the saying are not in the same order in Matt. and Luke, each belongs to the conclusion of the Mission Charge in the two Gospels. Apparently, Matthew has postponed the use of it deliberately until he has used additional sayings from Q, M, and Mark. It is not certain, however, that Q is his source. Matt. 10:40 f. may be from M and

10:42 is probably taken from Mark 9:41. Dr. Manson[30] says that Luke 10:16 is to be assigned to Q, but that one may have doubts whether Matt. 10:40 should be labelled Q or M. He further suggests that Matt. 10:40, Mark 9:37, and Luke 10:16 may go back to a fuller common original. The possibility arises that, if Matt. 10:40 is drawn from M, its position at the close of the Charge is suggested by the place of Luke 10:16. In any case, whether it be from Q or M, its use by Matthew is determined by editorial considerations.

3. *Matt. 10:19 f.* (Luke 12:11 f.): 'But when they deliver you up, be not anxious *how or what* ye shall speak: for it shall be given you in that hour what ye shall speak. For it is not ye that speak, but the Spirit of your Father that speaketh in you' (Matt.); 'And when they bring you before the synagogues, and the rulers, and the authorities, be not anxious *how or what* ye shall answer, or what ye shall say: for the Holy Spirit shall teach you in that very hour what ye ought to say' (Luke). Cf. Mark 13:11 and Luke 21:14 f.

The difference of order in Matt. and Luke is explained by the fact that the closer parallel to Matt. 10:19 f. is Mark 13:11. Matthew's source in 10:17–22 is Mark 13:9–13. It is often maintained that Luke 12:11 f. is from Q because of its small linguistic agreements with Matt. 10:19 f. which are not present in Mark, especially the phrase 'how or what'. This view is weakened if, as Streeter thinks, the phrase is due to textual assimilation,[31] but it is not altogether destroyed. Streeter points out that in both Gospels the saying stands in the same discourse as Luke 12:2 ff. = Matt. 10:26 ff., though separated by a few verses, and argues that the presence of Luke 12:11 f. explains the use of the saying in both Gospels.[32] Q may have suggested to Matthew the use of Mark 13:9–13 in the Mission Charge rather than in the Eschatological discourse in Matt. 24 where it is merely summarized (Matt. 24:9,13).

Conclusions regarding the Mission Charge

In considering the above passages one must not forget that, even more impressively than in the Sermon on the Mount, much the greater number of Q sayings (approximately four-fifths) are in the same order in Matt. and Luke. Where there is a difference of order, the arrangement in Matt. (and possibly occasionally in

Luke) is due to editorial reasons or the use of other sources and that in some cases (10:19 f. and 40) Matthew appears to be aware of the order he deserts. Thus, the differences do not weaken the hypothesis of a common order, but tend to confirm it.

THE DISCOURSE ON TEACHING IN PARABLES

In this, the third of Matthew's five discourses most of the material is taken from the two sources, Mark (4:1-9, 10-12, 13-20, 30-2) and M (Matt. 13:24-30, 36-43, 44, 45 f., 47-50, 51 f.). The Q material is limited to one saying and two parables (The Mustard Seed and the Leaven), of which the Mustard Seed (Matt. 13:31 f.) is a conflation of the Q version with Mark 14:30-2.[33] This material, arranged in the Lukan order, is as follows:

Luke	Matt.	
10:23 f.	13:16 f.	'Blessed are the eyes which see'.
13:18 f.	13:31 f.	The Mustard Seed.
13:20 f.	13:33	The Leaven.

Notes

1. There are no Q passages in an order other than that of Luke.

2. It is reasonable to suppose that in constructing the discourse Matthew takes his point of departure from Mark 4:1, adding a considerable amount of parabolic matter from M, and inserting extracts from Q.

3. He conflates the Q version of the Mustard Seed (Luke 13:18 f.) with Mark 4:30-2, and appends the parable of the Leaven because the two stood together in Q.

4. Already Matthew has on his hands the saying, 'Blessed are your eyes' (Luke 10:23 f. = Matt. 13:16 f.), having replaced this passage by the M saying, 'Come unto me, all ye that labour' (Matt. 11:28-30), after the saying, 'I thank thee, O Father, Lord of heaven and earth' (Luke 10:21 f. = Matt. 11:25-7). He places the saying after the Markan passage on the Purpose of Parables (Mark 4:10-12 = Matt. 13:10-15), adding the phrase 'and your ears, for they hear' and substituting 'righteous men' for 'kings'. As Easton[34] says, the arrangement is obviously artificial. Matthew chooses the best place he can find for the saying previous to the second and third extracts from Q fixed by the use of Mark 4:30-2, the parable of the Mustard Seed.

5. It is to be noted that Matthew had already used all the Q material in Luke which stands before 11:23 f., as well as all the sayings between this passage and the parable of the Mustard Seed (Luke 13:18 f.), with

S

the exception of the saying on the Great Commandment (Luke 10:25–28). Thus, the three extracts from Q stood together ready for use in Matt. 13.

Conclusions on the Discourse on Teaching in Parables

The amount of Q sayings in the discourse is small, but, so far as it goes, it confirms the hypothesis that Matthew follows the order of Q as it is reflected in Luke.

THE DISCOURSE ON DISCIPLESHIP

The fourth Matthaean discourse is constructed like the third. It consists of material taken almost wholly from Mark (9:33–7, 42–8) in 18:1–9 and from M in 18:10–35. A few Q sayings appear to be used in the order in which they are found in Luke.

Luke	Matt.	
14:11	18:4	On humbling oneself.
[15:4–7, 10]	[18:12–14]	The Lost Sheep.
17:1 f.	18:6 f.	On Stumbling-blocks.
17:3 f.	18:15, 21	On Forgiveness.

The extent to which Matthew uses Q in these passages is debatable.

It is open to question if the second belongs to Q. Matt. 18:4 differs considerably from Luke 14:11, and Matt. 18:6 f. and 15, 21 are conflations of material from Q and M.

All the more remarkable is the agreement in order shown above. Moreover, Matthew had not to search for the Q sayings: they probably lay immediately before the eye. He had already drawn upon all the sayings in Q which precede Luke 14:11 and those also which lie between this saying and Luke 17:1 with the exception of the sayings which apparently he intended to use in 23–25. Thus, the three sayings listed above stood in succession ready for use in 18.

In view of the difficult questions which arise in these sayings it is necessary to examine them in detail.

1. *Matt. 18:4* (Luke 14:11): 'Whosoever therefore shall humble himself *as this little child, the same is the greatest in the kingdom of heaven*' (Matt.); 'For every one that exalteth himself shall be humbled; and he that humbleth himself shall be exalted' (Luke). Cf. Luke 18:14b

and Matt. 23:12, which are in almost verbatim agreement with Luke 14:11.

Luke 14:11 is attached loosely to the section on Table Manners (14:7–10) and similarly the doublet in Luke 18:14b is a pendant to the parable of the Pharisee and the Taxgatherer (18:9–14a). Matt. 23:12 stands at the end of an M section which condemns the habit of seeking respect from others, and Matt. 18:4, which is the passage under review, in an insertion in the story derived from Mark 9:33–7 on True Greatness.

Many scholars describe the passage as 'a floating saying'[35] or as 'a short proverbial saying' for which there is no need to postulate a written source at all.[36]

On the whole it seems best to assign Luke 14:11 = Matt. 18:4 to Q and to explain Luke 18:14b and Matt. 23:12 as repetitions of the saying. Hesitation to take this view is natural, for at first sight Mat. 18:4 seems widely different from Luke 14:11. But the differences, underlined above, are modifications due to the Markan context in which it appears (cf. Mark 9:34, 36). Thus, Matt. 18:4 is more than 'a reminiscence of Q';[37] it is a conscious modification of Q for editorial reasons.

2. Matt. 18:12–14 (Luke 15:4–7, 10); The Lost Sheep.

This parable is widely assigned to Q,[38] but the opinion of Streeter,[39] endorsed by T. W. Manson,[40] that Matthew's version belongs to M and Luke's to L, is highly probable. The words common to both are those without which the story could not be told, and where the versions can differ, they do. Some of the differences are apparently translation variants.[41] The setting and the moral of the two versions are also different. In Matt. the parable is set in an M context and is related to the despising of 'little ones'; in Luke it precedes two other similar parables from L (The Lost Coin and the Lost Son) and its theme is the mercy of God in forgiving sinners. An inordinate amount of editorial modification has to be assigned to Luke if both versions are drawn from a common source, whereas the differences are intelligible if they come from different cycles of tradition.

If this view is taken, the variation in order is irrelevant. Just because this fact is consistent with the main contentions of this essay it is necessary to consider what follows if the common source is Q. In this case the different order is the result of editorial adjustments with the other sources mentioned above on the part of one or both of the Evangelists.

3. *Matt. 18:6 f.* (Luke 17:1 f.); On Offences.

Matthew's version is widely held to be a conflation of Mark and Q, a view which accounts for the reverse form in which the saying appears in Matt. and Luke.[42]

4. *Matt. 18:15, 21 f.* (Luke 17:3 f.): On Forgiveness.

The verbal agreements are slight, and from these it is impossible to maintain that the two versions are derived from one common source. Moreover, the number of the acts of forgiveness differs (Matt., seventy times seven, or seventy-seven; Luke, seven times), and 'I repent' is peculiar to Luke. But there is agreement in the succession of themes (Offences and Forgiveness).[43] The presumption is that Matthew is giving the fuller M version in 18:15–22 in preference to that of Q for liturgical reasons.

Conclusions regarding the Discourse on Discipleship

Although the Q sayings used or reflected in the discourse are few, they follow without exception the Lukan order. It is possible that order of thought in Q, humility, offences, and forgiveness, is the clue to Matthew's disposal of Markan and M material in 18:1–9 (Mark) and 10–35 (M).

THE ESCHATOLOGICAL DISCOURSE

Whether Matt. 23 (the Condemnation of the Scribes and Pharisees) should be separated from the Eschatological Discourse proper in Matt. 24–5 is a disputed question. Certainly 23 is self-contained, but it is not concluded by the formula, 'And it came to pass, when Jesus had finished all these words', which appears at the end of the five great discourses (cf. 26:1). It appears to be Matthew's intention to connect 23 with 24–5 (cf. 23:38). Since, however, it forms a whole, it will be useful to examine it separately.

Luke	Matt.
11:39–48	23:4–31
11:49–51	23:34–6
11:52	(23:13)
13:34 f.	23:37–9

Notes

1. It will be seen that there is a relative agreement of order broken, apparently, at Matt. 23:13.

2. The table, however, is delusive unless we consider Matt. 23:4–31 (to which verse 13 belongs) in detail, since M forms the backbone of this section. Mark 12:38b–40 is inserted in 23:6–7a and 13(f) almost verbatim. Several of the parallels in Luke xi, which presumably are from Q, are slight and not in the Lukan order. In these circumstances it will be helpful to set out the whole of Matt. 23 in a table indicating the parallel sayings in Luke and the extent to which they agree linguistically.

In their Matthaean order the parallel sayings are as follows:

Matt. 23

Matt. 23	Luke	Agreement
1		
2 f.		
4	11:46	Small
5		
6–7a	11:43	Small
7b–10		
11		
12	(cf. 14:11)	Almost verbatim
13 (f.)	11:52	Small
15–22		
23	11:42	Considerable
24		
25 f.	11:39–41	Considerable
27 f.	11:44	Negligible
29–31	11:47 f.	Small
32 f.		
34–6	11:49–51	Considerable
37–9	13:34 f.	Almost verbatim

Note. The horizontal lines separate the seven 'Woes' in Matt. from the rest of the chapter.

From this table it can be seen that the first five parallels stand in a different order in Matt. and Luke. They appear to be cases in which a definite preference has been given to the order and text of M. Only Matt. 23:12 is a probable insertion from Q and 23:23 may be a conflation of Q and M. In these circumstances the difference or order in the five parallels is not in the least surprising.

All the more remarkable is the complete agreement of order in the last five parallels. Moreover, apart from Matt. 23:27 f. and 29–31 the linguistic agreement is much greater. Apparently in these two sayings Matthew is still dependent on M. The agreement in order might be accidental or due to the original tradition lying behind M and Q, but the considerable degree of linguistic agreement of 23:25 f., 34–6, and 37–9[44] with their Lukan counterparts suggests rather a knowledge of the order of the five sayings in Q, and 23:23 may well have drawn Matthew's attention to this series.

We must conclude that, although Matthew follows M in the main in 23, he is well aware of the order of Q and observes it in the latter part of the discourse.

Matt. 24–25

In the Eschatological Discourse proper the parallel passages in their Lukan order are:

Luke	Matt.
12:39 f.	24:43 f.
12:42–6	24:45–51
17:23 f.	24:26 f.
17:26 f.	24:37–9
17:34 f.	24:40 f.
17:37	(24:28)
19:12–27	25:14–30

Notes

1. There are two parallel series, the second of which is broken by Matt. 24:28 (The Gathering Vultures).

2. The questions to be discussed are why 24:43–51 (The Parables of the Thief and the Faithful and Unfaithful Servants) appears later in Matt., and why 24:28 is used earlier than in Luke.

1. *Matt. 24:43-51*

The first question is easily answered. The two parables are attached to the Markan saying (13:35) in Matt. 24:42 to form the first and second of a group of five parables (the last three of which, the Ten Virgins, the Talents.[45] and the Sheep and the Goats, are from M) in Matt. 24:43-25:46 (i.e. at the end of the Discourse).

2. *Matt. 24:28:* 'Wheresoever the carcase is, there will be the vultures gathered together' (Matt.); 'And they answering say unto him, Where, Lord? And he said unto them, Where the body is, thither will the vultures also be gathered together' (Luke).

In Matt., without an opening question, it stands in a good connexion after the saying on the suddenness of the Coming of the Son of Man; in Luke it closes the Eschatological Discourse. In Matt. it affirms the inevitability of the Parousia; in Luke it amounts to a refusal to answer the question, 'Where, Lord?' Commentators are very divided on the question of its original position, and this is not strange since the saying is a proverbial utterance. The roughness of Luke's enigmatic form may be more original than Matthew's smoother version, but a certain decision is perhaps not possible. In any case the editorial activity of one or other of the Evangelists is responsible for the difference of position.

Conclusions regarding the Eschatological Discourse

As in 23 Matthew has used material from M and Mark with which he has connected extracts from Q. In the latter Matthew and Luke agree in order apart from editorial rearrangements in Matt. 24:43-51 due to use of M, and perhaps also in 24:28 where Q alone is in question.

In all the five discourses we meet with the same features— —respect in the main for the order of Q as it appears in Luke and editorial activity usually on the part of Matthew where the order is different. It remains now to ask if the same is true of the use of Q in the rest of Matt. outside the five great discourses.

THE REST OF MATTHEW

The Q passages in the Lukan order are as follows:

Luke	Matt.
3:7–9, 12, 16f.	3:7–12
3:21 f.	3:16 f.
4:1–13	4:1–11
6:39	(15:14)
6:43–5	(12:33–5)
7:1–10	8:5–10, 13
7:18–23	11:2–6
7:24–8	11:7–11
7:31–5	11:16–19
9:57–60	(8:19–22)
10:13–15	11:21–3
10:21 f.	11:25–7
10:25–7	(22:34–9)
11:14–23	12:22–30
11:24–6	12:43–5
11:29–32	12:38–42
12:10	(12:32)
13:28 f.	(8:11 f.)
13:30	(20:16)
14:15–24	[22:1–10]
16:16	(11:12 f.)
17:5 f.	17:20
22:28, 30b	19:28

Notes

1. It is a remarkable fact that, with the exception of the passages in brackets and the inversion of Matt. 12:43–5 and 38–42, all the sayings stand in the same order in Matt. and Luke.

2. The passage in square brackets is the parable of the Marriage Feast (Matt. 22:1–10, Luke 14:15–24, the Great Supper). It is included for the sake of completeness. Linguistically Matt. and Luke have very little in common and conflation in Matt. of Q with another parable is a probable explanation.[46]

3. Of the remaining passages in brackets Matt. 12:32 (cf. Mark 3:28 f.) and 22:34–9 (cf. Mark 12:28–34) are conflations of Q and Mark which, as many examples have shown, result in a difference of order.

4. The passages left for discussion are Matt. 15:14, 12:33–5, 8:19–22, 8:11 f., 20:16, and 11:12 f.

The inversion of Matt. 12:43-7, 38-42 and Luke 11:24-6, 29-32

Editorial rearrangement is the cause of the inversion. In Matt. the sections on the Sign of Jonah and the Ninevites are brought together because they relate to Jonah and the addition, 'Even so shall it be also unto this generation', brings the saying on Demon Possession (12:43-5) into harmony with the whole. In Luke the saying on Demon Possession stands first after the section on Collusion with Beelzebul, presumably because both deal with exorcism. Opinions will differ regarding the original order of Q. Matthew, I think, is responsible for the inversion, but in either case a common order is presupposed.

1. *Matt. 15:14* (Luke 6:39): 'Let them alone: they are blind guides. And if the blind guide the blind, both shall fall into a pit' (Matt.); 'And he spoke also a parable unto them, Can the blind guide the blind? shall they not both fall into a pit?' (Luke).

It will be recalled that the saying which follows (Luke 6:40 = Matt. 10:24 f.) was discussed earlier, and that the view taken was that Luke 6:39 f. preserves the order of Q, Matt. 10:24 f. owing its position to the M context in which it stands. A similar explanation accounts for the position of Matt. 15:14 which reflects editorial rearrangement.[47]

2. *Matt. 12:33-5* (Good and Corrupt Trees). Cf. Matt. 7:16-20 and Luke 6:43-5 discussed earlier.

The relationships between Matt. 7:16-20 and 12:33-5 are difficult to determine. Easton[48] suggests different forms in which the saying was spoken. With greater probability Hawkins[49] suggests that Matthew uses the saying twice, adapting it to the context in which he places it, in 7:16-18 to bring out the criterion of true and false teachers, in 12:33-5 to bring out the importance of words as proofs of the state of men's hearts.[50] If this is so, editorial activity accounts for the fact that 12:33-5 is not in the Lukan order.

3. *Matt. 8:19-22* (Candidates for Discipleship). Cf. Luke 9:57-60.

Why does Matthew place these sayings at an earlier point than that of Luke? Easton[51] gives the answer when he says that in both Matt. and Luke this is the last discourse section before the Mission Charge. *After* the Charge Matthew places those relating to the Baptist (11:2-6, 7-11, 16-19), while Luke has the parallel sayings *before* it (7:18–23, 24–8, 31–5). Further, Matthew has used 8:19–22 as a preface to a considerable group from Mark and M containing many miracle-stories. The purpose of this arrangement is to prepare the way for 11:5 f. (Luke 7:22 f.), which is the message to John about the mighty works being wrought by Jesus. Luke meets the same need by the editorial passage, 7:21, 'In that hour he cured many of diseases and plagues and evil spirits; and on many that were blind he bestowed sight.' Both Evangelists exercise editorial freedom, but in Matt. the order of Q is affected.

4. *Matt. 8:11 f.* (Luke 13:28 f.): 'Many shall come from the east and the west. . . .'

Matthew has used the saying earlier by inserting it into the story of the Centurion's Servant (8:5–10, 13) and has inverted the sentences in order to get a better connexion.

5. *Matt. 20:16* (Luke 13:30) (The Last First and the First Last).

The transposition of No. 4 (above) left the saying[52] isolated and Matthew has attached it to the parable of the Labourers in the Vineyard (20:1–15).

6. *Matt. 11:12 f.* (Luke 16:16): 'From the days of John the Baptist.'

In the interests of a better order Matthew has transferred the saying to an earlier point after the testimony of Jesus to John (11:7–11). Luke would hardly have moved it from this position if Q had so placed it.[53]

Conclusions regarding the Rest of Matthew

The use of Q in its Lukan order is as pronounced as in any of the five great discourses. It may be conjectured that, if the discourses were constructed first, the Q sayings were left standing as they appear in Luke. The changes of order are editorial or due to conflation with Mark. They arise from the necessity of inserting the sayings in the Markan framework and the desire to bring together and to adjust those relating to the Baptist.

III

CONCLUSIONS REGARDING Q AS A WHOLE

The investigation has confirmed the view that Luke has preserved the order of Q and has followed it with great fidelity. It has shown further that Matthew knew the same order and was aware of it when he made editorial adjustments and conflated Q with Mark and M. If we reject, as we must, the hypothesis of Luke's dependence on Matt., the result of a comparison of the order of the sayings in Matt. and Luke is to demonstrate the existence of Q, so far as this is possible in the case of a source known to us only from its use in the two Gospels. Q is not 'an unnecessary and vicious hypothesis', but a collection of sayings and parables which actually existed when Matthew and Luke wrote. Its earlier history is a matter for conjecture; it is not excluded that earlier groups of sayings and parables have been combined in it. But this stage was past when the Gospels were compiled, and what we are able to recover is the form in which Q was current at least as early as the decade A.D. 50–60 and perhaps even earlier. It is probable that some of the sayings peculiar to Luke belong to it, including 6:24–6, 9:61 f., 12:35–8, 47 f., and 54–6, but not sayings found only in Matt.

It is desirable that M should be investigated more closely. This task has been waiting for a generation,[54] and it will always prove difficult, since the M sayings are found in Matt. only.

NOTES

[1] *How Luke was Written* (1915).

[2] *The Origin of the Synoptic Gospels* (1922).

[3] *The Originality of St. Matthew* (1951).

[4] *A Study in St. Mark* (1951).

[5] *Op. cit.,* 170.

[6] See the important essay of C. K. Barrett, 'Q: A Re-examination', ET vol. liv, 320–3.

[7] *Einleitung in das Neue Testament* (1953), 162–82.

[8] Vol. IV, N.S., 27–31.

[9] The passages omitted were the Great Commandment (Luke 10:25–8, Matt. 22:34–9), the Signs of the Times (Luke 12:54–6, Matt. 16:2 f.), the Narrow Gate (Luke 13:23 f., Matt. 7:13 f.), the Shut Door (Luke 13:25–7, Matt. 25:10–12), the Great Supper (Luke 14:15–24, Matt. 22:1–10), the Lost Sheep (Luke 15:4–7, 10, Matt. 18:12–14), and the Pounds (Luke 19:12–27, Matt. 25:14–30).

[10] *Die synoptischen Streitgespräche* (1921), 146–9. The hypothesis is discussed in my *Formation of the Gospel Tradition* (1933), 97–9.

[11] *The Sources of the Synoptic Gospels,* II (1957), 19–25.

[12] T. W. Manson, *The Sayings of Jesus* (1949) [first published as Part II of *The Mission and Message of Jesus,* 1937], 162, suggests that the original arrangement was: introduction, 17 and 20, No. 1, 21 f., No. 2, 27 f., No. 3, 31 f., No. 4, 33 f., No. 5, 38 f., No. 6, 43 f., Conclusion, 48.

[13] Dr. Manson, *op. cit.*, 18 f., suggests that 'whatsoever' (Matt.) and 'as' (Luke) may be alternative renderings of an Aramaic original, and that 'all things' and 'therefore' are probably editorial.

[14] Cf. Manson, *op. cit.*, 50; C. F. Burney, *The Poetry of our Lord*, 113, 169; M. Black, *An Aramaic Approach to the Gospels and Acts*, 137 f.

[15] *The Gospel according to St. Matthew*, 91.

[16] *Op. cit.*, 60 f.

[17] Matthew is probably nearer to the original in his use of the impersonal plural καίουσιν.

[18] It is noteworthy that if the differences of position of 7:7–11, 5:15, 6:20 f., 5:25 f. are editorial, the agreement in order extends from 6:9–13 to 7:22 f.

[19] Cf. Burney, *op. cit.*, 115.

[20] Cf. Manson, *op. cit.*, 132.

[21] *The Four Gospels*, 285–9.

[22] *The Gospel according to St. Luke*, 246.

[23] For this reason they were omitted with five other sayings in the JTS article mentioned at the outset (Group A).

[24] See the table on p. 249. The correspondences (with the Matthaean passages on the left) may be represented as follows:

Matt.	Luke		Luke
7:13 f.			13:23 f.
7:16–20	6:43 f.		
7:21	6:46		
7:22 f.			13:26 f.

[25] This passage is considered later in the section headed 'The Rest of Matthew', p. 264 f.

[26] Cf. Manson, *op. cit.*, 57. Manson also suggests that Matt. 10:9–16 is a conflation of material from Mk, Q, and M, *op. cit.*, 180.

[27] *The Gospel according to St. Luke*, 97.

[28] *Op. cit.*, 92.

[29] The opinion that 'He spake also a parable to them' (Luke 6:39) is editorial is supported by Luke 5:36, 8:4, 12:16, 13:6, 14:7, 15:3, and 18:1; but Bussmann, *Synoptische Studien*, ii, 48, n. 1, suggests that perhaps it is original and lost through Matthew's change of position. It may be a necessary connecting link in the sense of 'Take an illustration'.

[30] *Op. cit.*, 78, 183.

[31] *Op. cit.*, 280.

[32] *Ibid.*

[33] Cf. Streeter, *op. cit.*, 246–8.

[34] *Op. cit.*, 168.

[35] Cf. Manson, *op. cit.*, 312.

[36] Cf. Streeter, *op. cit.*, 285.

[37] Easton, *op. cit.*, 227.

[38] Cf. Bussmann, *op. cit.*, II, 86 f.; Easton, *op. cit.*, xix, 235 f.; Creed, *op. cit.*, lxv; G. D. Kilpatrick, *The Origins of the Gospel according to St. Matthew*, 28 f.; S. E. Johnson, *The Interpreter's Bible*, vii, 471.

[39] *Op. cit.*, 244 f.

[40] *Op. cit.*, 283.

[41] Cf. Manson, *op. cit.*, 208; J. Jeremias, *The Parables of Jesus*, 29, 106.

[42] Cf. Streeter, *op. cit.*, 265, 281 n.; Easton, *op. cit.*, 256; Creed, *op. cit.*, 214; Klostermann, *Das Lukasevangelium*, 170.

[43] Cf. Streeter, *op. cit.*, 281, 'Seeing there is no very obvious connection of thought between the two topics, the connection (Offences-Forgiveness) must have been made in the common source Q'.

[44] Dr. Manson, *op. cit.*, 102, points out that, taking Luke's shorter version as the standard, the amount of agreement in Matt. 23:34–6 = Luke 11:49–51 is under 50 per cent and in Matt. 23:37–9 = Luke 23:34 f. it is near 90 per cent.

[45] The parable of the Talents (in Luke the Pounds) appears to be a conflation of M and Q (cf. Matt. 25:24–9 and Luke 19:20–6).

[46] Cf. Manson, *op. cit.*, 129, 225.

[47] Cf. Manson, *op. cit.*, 57

[48] *Op. cit.*, 92.

[49] *Horae Synopticae*, 85.

[50] Cf. Manson, *op. cit.*, 59, 'It is difficult to resist the conclusion that the Q material given here (Luke 6:43–5) in Luke has been freely adapted in Matt. to other purposes'.

[51] *Op. cit.*, 155.

[52] The source of the doublet in Matt. 19:30 is Mark 10:31 where, as in Matt., the clauses are inverted (the First Last and the Last First).

[53] Cf. Streeter, *Oxford Studies in the Synoptic Problem* (ed. W. Sanday), 156 f.

[54] An important contribution has been made by Professor Pierson Parker in *The Gospel before Mark* (1953), who has shown that 'since Q has not been assimilated to Matthaean types of expression', and 'the style of Q does not pervade M, therefore Q and M have different origins' and that 'Q is really from an autonomous source' (p. 30 f.).

DOMINUS VOBISCUM: THE BACKGROUND OF A LITURGICAL FORMULA

by

W. C. VAN UNNIK

THE new service-book of the Dutch Reformed Church[1] gives in several of its formularies as an optional introduction to prayer the dialogue between minister and congregation:

'The Lord be with you.'
R. 'And with thy spirit.'
'Let us pray.'

To Roman Catholic, Anglican and Lutheran Christians it is a familiar part of the liturgy, because it belongs to the age-old heritage of Latin Christianity. As such it was taken over by the committee which prepared the revision of the Dutch Reformed Liturgy. But *what is the meaning of this dialogue both in its constituent elements and in its sequence?* It is not out of place to raise this question, because the church of our days is not helped by ancient formularies as such, but only by a living expression of its faith.[2] It is somewhat startling to read in this connection the following statement by a Jesuit who is one of the leading authorities in the liturgical field:

> In einem aus heutigem Empfinden geschaffenen Gottesdienst würden wir kaum auf den Gedanken kommen, dass der Vorbeter zuerst die Gemeinde begrüssen soll, noch weniger würden wir daran denken, ihn diesen Gruss im Verlauf der Gebetsstunde öfters wiederholen zu lassen.[3]

I have consulted many books and various experts, but did not receive a satisfactory answer; it seemed as though this formula is so customary and revered that nobody asks for its proper meaning.

The first occurrence of the dialogue is—according to the present knowledge of sources—found in the Church Order of Hippolytus (*c.* 200): it goes before and is connected with the preface to the great eucharistic prayer.[4] In later stages of liturgical development it is used on several other occasions as an introduction to prayer and to the reading of the Gospel. It is remarkable that this particular form is restricted to the Western and Egyptian traditions; in the other Eastern liturgies the salutation has a different wording, viz.: *'Peace be with you'* or the formula of 2 Cor. 13:13.[5] Which is the older form, or are they rival developments? These and other interesting questions about the spread and use of this introductory greeting in the course of history cannot be investigated here, though much is still obscure.[6] For the present paper it is sufficient to establish the existence of the formula at about 200 A.D.;[7] here attention will be focused on the origin and meaning of these short sentences.

The interpretation of the dialogue does not appear so simple as its wording. It is usual to refer to the Old Testament, generally to Judges 6:12 and Ruth 2:4.[8] To be sure there the greeting 'the Lord with you'[9] occurs, but it should be observed that in the former it is not followed by an answer resembling that of the liturgy and in the latter the response of Boaz' reapers is: 'The Lord bless you.' What is the origin of 'and with thy spirit'? Here one is suddenly sent to the New Testament, 2 Tim. 4:22: 'the Lord with thy spirit', but this text is not a response; it is a special form of greeting. Nowhere is it explained how these texts, derived from such different surroundings, or others which are sometimes mentioned like Luke 1:28, Gal. 6:18, 2 Thess. 3:16 have become fused into this one dialogue. Influence of an unimportant book like Ruth is quite incredible. Frör finds the background of the priestly salutation in the liturgical practice of the apostolic church as mirrored in the pauline letters, and says that the response of the people probably goes back to 'die älteste urchristliche Zeit'.[10] This last statement is a mere guess apart from its vagueness, because the texts adduced (Gal. 6:18, Philem. 25, 2 Tim. 4:22) do mention the Spirit, but are not answers of the people; they stand, as seen from the formal side, on the same level as the texts he quotes for the greeting of the priest. Jungmann cites these texts as evidence for greetings in ordinary daily life. According to this author the priest calls for attention in prayer and listening to the Gospel; the form of a greeting is very appropriate, he says, because it calls for an echo and these two elements create an atmosphere 'heiliger Gottesnähe, in der sich die Liturgie vollziehen soll'.[11] The

answer is a semitic expression for: 'and also with you'. Frör finds
this too flat. The salutation is an acclamation, of the same force as
'Maranatha': 'Die Gabe dieses jetzt unter uns gegenwärtigen
Herrn, seine eschatologische Heilsgabe soll unter euch sein'; in
combination with the response it means that in the presence of the
risen Lord 'sich jedesmal der Knoten der Liebe und Eintracht
zwischen Pfarrer und Gemeinde aufs Neue schürzt'.[12]

There is every reason to take up this question again, since these
explanations do not appear to be satisfactory. Frör's interpretation
suffers from a certain 'pan-liturgism' which sees everywhere in the
pauline epistles the background of the liturgy whenever a simple
parallel in wording between them and the *much later* liturgies is
found.[13] But even if one takes the wider view about the 'Sitz im
Leben', viz the ordinary daily salutation, one touches upon the
difficulty—often met in form-criticism—that the form as such
prevails over the contents. It seems to me far more important to
ask what was expressed in this greeting than to state that it is a
greeting. Besides that it may be necessary to distinguish between
a greeting at entering and at departing, since the two have not the
same force.[14] The pauline salutations stand at the end of his letters
and the supposed connection with a (reconstructed) liturgy is
without foundation in the texts.

It would be obvious to look for a solution to the Jewish liturgy
which in so many ways offered the pattern for Christian worship.
But search in that direction is in vain. Neither in the liturgy of the
Temple nor in that of the synagogue is the slightest trace of such
a dialogue to be found.[15] In daily life the greetings are always
answered,[16] but they were not given in the form 'the Lord with
you'; it is always: 'Peace on you'.[17] This was also the manner of
Jesus' greeting according to John 20:19, 26 (Luke 24:36 varies in
many manuscripts), cf. John 14:27 which is a possible reference
to the practice of greeting. In Luke 10:5 He commands His
apostles to use that form. It would be somewhat puzzling that the
early Christian communities should have invented and had a form
so different from that of the (risen) Lord.[18] There is no point of
contact here.

The phrasing of the salutation raises a number of questions:
(A) Who is 'the Lord': God the Father or Jesus Christ?[19]
(B) What mood of the verb 'to be' should be supplied: 'is' or
'be'?

(C) What is contained in this 'to be with somebody', when said of the Lord?

(D) Why is this former part followed by '*and* with thy spirit', this second part of response being coupled to the former by καί and this continuation suggesting that there is a certain parallelism.[20] But how and why? Is this spirit the special grace of the priest given at his ordination?[21]

Let me first give some brief comments upon these questions. The first two are familiar in this connection. As to (A), it may be remarked that it is often difficult in Paul's letters to decide who is the κύριος.[22] Question (B), fact or wish, has often been discussed in connection with the final blessing of the congregation.

With regard to (D) it is called a semitism,[23] practically amounting to 'with yourself'. This is stated without further notice, but in view of the linguistic evidence this interpretation is highly improbable, not to say impossible. If *psyche* (*nēpheš*) had been used, it would have been correct, since this often expresses 'self' or 'person' in semitic texts, but I do not know a single unambiguous text where *pneuma* (*rûaḥ*) has this meaning.[24] So we must look for another explanation.

The crucial question is (C). It is somewhat surprising that always the same small group of texts is quoted, but the full evidence is not surveyed. The expression is found in numerous places of the OT and NT. What is even more surprising, the commentators on the Bible are so sure that every reader knows exactly what is meant that they have practically no comments to make.[25] But is it really so crystal-clear? Let us specify this question somewhat more precisely.

(*a*) It goes without saying that the Bible and the Christian Church firmly believed in God's transcendence. God is in heaven and Jesus who was once on earth is now at the right hand of the Father in heaven (Eph. 1:20). But what did Jesus promise to His disciples when he said: 'And lo, *I am with you* alway, even unto the end of the world' (Matt. 28:20)? This *concluding* verse comes after the declaration that Jesus has received all power (v. 18) and commissioned His disciples (v. 19). It is introduced with that 'and lo' which is always in the Bible the indication of something extraordinary and unexpected. It must be something far more than Christ's 'perpetual presence'[26] which makes the mission possible. Nor can we agree with Dodd who says: 'The church is clearly

T

conceived as the *locus* of the presence of Christ during the interval between His resurrection and παρουσία'.[27] It is fairly common, I know, to speak in this way about the church and Christ's presence. But is it not, I dare to ask, *loose* thinking? Are we to credit the early Christians who so clearly knew about Jesus' separation from the *earth* and His glorification in *heaven*, with such a conflicting view? On the other hand, Jesus does not speak to the church (a word Matthew knows), but to the apostles as missionaries. The use of the word 'locus' suggests a static presence while, as will appear from the following pages, Jesus' 'being with them' has quite different associations. This was seen by O. Michel who based himself on some OT texts and explained the expression as 'protection'.[28] Since he, however, did not cover all the evidence, this explanation is insufficient.

(*b*) The Lord's 'being with a person' cannot be interpreted from the point of view that the liturgy is 'heaven on earth', a favourite idea in Orthodox theology. Such an interpretation conflicts with the sequence in Hippolytus: 'sursum corda', etc., and cannot explain its introduction before prayer and Gospel-reading.

(*c*) In some places the salutation reads as follows: 'the peace' or 'the grace of the Lord with you' (or something similar). That is perfectly clear: a *gift* of the glorified Lord which can be received on earth. But it is not the same as 'the Lord (Himself) with you', because there the Lord is thought to 'be with somebody' on earth and at the same time in heaven. It is well-known that later Jewish thought introduced all sorts of intermediaries, such as the Name, the *Shekhina*, etc., to safeguard His transcendence and His nearness.[29] God's power is expressed by 'the hand of the Lord was with . . .'.[30] Elsewhere the 'angel of the Lord' is a substitute for God Himself, a tendency already to be detected in the OT;[31] if it is said that he is with somebody,[32] there is no difficulty at all. But in the 'Dominus vobiscum' we do not find such a substitute. Does this 'to be with . . .' express the same ontological presence as in the expression: 'the angel is with . . .' or 'the peace is with . . .', and how can it be reconciled with God's transcendence or Christ's ascension? It will be clear that this difficulty cannot be overcome by philosophical categories or scholastic reasonings, since this kind of thinking stands far apart from the biblical way of thought.

(*d*) There are some texts in the NT which call for special attention, because there God's 'being with a person' is employed in a rather curious way and resists any interpretation we have met so far:

(1) In Acts 10:38, the speech of Peter in the house of Cornelius—perhaps a reflection of the ancient *kerygma*[33]—describes Jesus' appearance in these words: 'How that God anointed him with the Holy Ghost and with power: who went about doing good and healing all that were oppressed of the devil, for *God was with him*'. Here it is meant to explain why Jesus could develop this extraordinary activity. It does not say that God was *in* Him, but *with* Him; it is also more positive than 'protection'. The man Jesus of Nazareth is enabled to do these mighty works because of God's assistance. The second interesting feature is the reference to Jesus' being anointed with the Spirit. This suggests a connection between the Holy Ghost and the 'God with him'. Is this accidental? Or is there a close relation between the Holy Spirit and this 'God was with Him'?

(2) In the brief summary of Joseph's life given by Stephen the phrase recurs as a quotation from the OT. Therefore we shall return to it later (p. 285), but at the present moment it is well worth noticing that in the NT story this expression is far more prominent than in the OT. There it is found four times in connection with the unhappy fortunes of his life, but in the NT it is, one may say, the leading motive of his whole life which is described here in one sentence while in the OT it fills several chapters: 'and the patriarchs, moved with jealousy against Joseph, sold him into Egypt: and *God was with him* and delivered him out of all his afflictions and gave him wisdom and favour before Pharaoh, king of Egypt: and he made him governor over Egypt and all his house' (Acts 7:9 f.). Joseph is treated most inhumanly by his brethren, but not forsaken by God. The term does not describe only God's presence or protection, but the divine assistance which delivers him from evil (negative aspect) and makes him successful (positive aspect).[34]

(3) When Nicodemus comes to Jesus, he says according to John 3:2: 'Rabbi, we know that thou art a teacher come from God (ἀπὸ θεοῦ ἐλήλυθας) for no man can do these signs that thou doest except *God be* (= ᾖ, subj. depending on ἐὰν μή) *with him*.' Here the paradoxical situation which the term provokes at first sight (cf. p. 273) is clearly formulated: 'come from God' (ἀπό = away!), and at the same time: 'God with him.' These signs (wonders) make manifest the unique character of Jesus' ministry. The moving

power behind it which makes these deeds of Jesus such conspicuous signs, different from the miracles of others, is this: 'God with
him.' This has been discovered by Nicodemus in that teacher
Jesus of Nazareth, the son of Joseph (1:45). Again it puts into
words a positive force and not God's omnipresence. In this category the Jewish rabbi could conceive and explain the remarkable
deeds of Jesus. This verse presupposes acquaintance with more
'signs' than have been told in John so far. It also shows the existence of a general rule that could be applied to the special case of
Jesus. Billerbeck does not offer any parallel. In the OT there is,
however, a text connecting both elements, *viz.* 1 Sam. 10:7: 'and
let it be, when these *signs* are come unto thee that thou do as occasion serve thee: for *God is with thee*', the sign being Saul's prophetic enthusiasm,[35] which came so unexpectedly (v. 11). Here it
is related with the Spirit of God (v. 6). Is this also the case in John
3:2 as in Acts 10:38? I think it is, because in John Jesus is the bearer
of the Spirit in a very special sense, cf. 1:32: 'John bare witness,
saying, I have beheld the Spirit descending as a dove out of heaven;
and it abode upon him'; and the Spirit is typically bound to Jesus
during His lifetime on earth (7:39, 16:7).

On closer inspection it can be seen that these applications of the
phrase are not so peculiar, but are in full agreement with the usage
in the OT. Let us see what light is shed by the OT on our questions.

Very frequently it is said in the OT that God (or the Lord) 'is
with a person'.[36] From this abundant material[37] it becomes perfectly clear that this expression *does not define a static presence, but
a dynamic power*, as is in harmony with the active character of OT
revelation.[38] As a short-hand note it indicates *one reality*, but on
analysing this unit one discovers *various aspects* in this expression
of God's dealing with man. They can be distinguished in the
following manner:

(*a*) protection, help, deliverance;
(*b*) taking sides with;
(*c*) blessing and success, generally very concrete in worldly
affairs;
(*d*) assurance that there is no reason to fear;
(*e*) exhortation to valour;
(*f*) sometimes conditioned by man's obedience.

It is double-sided in two respects: (1) it is positive and negative;

(2) it has an effect upon the person's *psyche* and on his outward circumstances.

It would take too much space to discuss all the O.T. texts. Some characteristic illustrations for every aspect will suffice. This analytical distribution should not be taken too rigorously, since the phrase is a unit, several aspects may be found together in the same text.

(*a*) Gen. 28:15: 'And behold, *I am with thee* and will keep thee whithersoever thou goest' (to Jacob at Bethel).

Exod. 3:11 f., the call of Moses: 'And Moses said unto God, Who am I, that I should go unto Pharaoh and that I should bring forth the children of Israel out of Egypt? And he said: Certainly *I will be with thee.*'

Deut. 2:7: 'For the Lord thy God has blessed thee in all the work of thy hand: he has known thy walking through this great wilderness: these forty years *the Lord thy God has been with thee:* thou hast lacked nothing.'

Judges 2:18: 'And when the Lord raised them up judges, then *the Lord was with the judge,* and saved them out of the hands of their enemies.'

1 Sam. 17:37: 'And David said: the Lord that delivered me out of the paw of the lion . . . he will deliver me out of the hand of this Philistine. And Saul said unto David, Go and *the Lord shall be with thee.*'

1 Chron. 22:18: '*Is not the Lord our God with you* and has he not given you rest on every side? for he has delivered the inhabitants of the land into mine hands.'

Judith 13:11 (when Judith returns to the city after the slaying of Holophernes): 'Open, open now the gate: *God is with us,* even our God, to show his power yet in Israel, and his might against the enemy.'

3 Macc. 6:13, 15: 'Let the heathen to-day fear thy invincible might, thou glorious one who hast mighty works for the salvation of the race of Israel. . . . Let it be shown to all heathen that *thou art with us,* O Lord, and hast not turned thy face away from us; but as thou hast said, Not even when they were in the land of their enemies have I forgotten them (Lev. 26:44), even so bring it to pass.'

Ps. 90(91):15: '*I will be with him* in trouble; I will deliver him, and honour him.'

Isa. 43:1–2: 'Fear not, for I have redeemed thee. . . . When thou passest through the waters, *I will be with thee.*'

Jer. 15:20: 'I will make thee unto this people a fenced brazen wall, and they shall fight against thee: but they shall not prevail against thee: for *I am with thee* to save thee and to deliver thee, saith the Lord.'

See also Gen. 28:20, 35:3 (with addition of LXX 'and he saved me'); Num. 23:21; Deut. 1:42, 32:12; Joshua 1:5; 1 Sam. 3:19; 20:13; 1 Kings

8:57; 2 Chron. 25:7; Esther 6:13; Judith 5:17; Hag. 1:13; Isa. 8:8, 10 (where the name 'Immanuel' has been translated in LXX, while in 7:15 LXX has transliterated it), 43:5; Jer. 1:8, 19, 49:11 (MT 42:11).

(*b*) Num. 14:42: 'Go not up, for *the Lord is not with you*'; 2 Chron. 13:12: 'Behold, *God is with us* at our head'; 2 Chron. 32:8: 'with him (Sennacherib) is an arm of flesh, but *with us is the Lord, our God*, to help us and to fight our battles'; Zech. 10:5: 'they shall be as mighty men, treading down their enemies in the mire of the streets in the battle; and they shall fight, because *the Lord is with them*; and the riders on horses shall be confounded.'

Jer. 20:11: 'But *the Lord is with me* as a mighty man ($\mu\alpha\chi\eta\tau\acute{\eta}\varsigma$) and a terrible; therefore my persecutors shall stumble and they shall not prevail.'

See also Deut. 1:42; Judges 1:19, 6:16; 2 Chron. 36:23; Isa. 43:5.

(*c*) Gen. 21:20: '*God was with the lad* (Ishmael) and he grew.'

Gen. 26:3: 'God said: *I will be with thee*, and will bless thee.'

Gen. 39:23: 'The keeper of the prison looked not to any thing that was under his hand (Joseph), because *the Lord was with him*; and that which he did, the Lord made it prosper.'

Joshua 3:7: 'The Lord said to Joshua, This day will I begin to magnify thee in the sight of all Israel, that they may know that, as *I was with Moses*, so *I will be with thee*.'

Judges 6:12 f.: 'The angel of the Lord appeared unto him (Gideon) and said unto him, *The Lord is with thee*, thou mighty man of valour. And Gideon said unto him, Oh, my Lord, if *the Lord be with us*, why then is all this befallen us? and where be all his wondrous works which our fathers told us of . . .; v. 16: 'Surely, *I will be with thee*, and thou shalt smite the Midianites as one man.'

Ruth 2:4: 'Boaz said unto the reapers, *The Lord be with you*. And they answered him, The Lord bless thee.'

1 Sam. 16:18: 'Behold, I have seen a son of Jesse . . . that is cunning in playing, and a mighty man of valour, and a man of war, and prudent in speech, and a comely person, and *the Lord is with him*.'

2 Kings 18:7: '*The Lord was with him* (Hezekiah): whithersoever he went forth he prospered.'

2 Chron. 1:1: 'And Solomon, the son of David was strengthened in his kingdom, and *the Lord his God was with him* and magnified him exceedingly.'

2 Chron. 20:17: 'Ye shall not need to fight in this battle: set yourselves, stand ye still, and see the salvation of the Lord with you, O Judah and Jerusalem: fear not, nor be dismayed: to-morrow go out against them: for *the Lord is with you*.'

2 Chron. 35:21 = 1 Ezra 1:25 a word of Pharaoh Neco (*sic!*): 'What

have I to do with thee, thou king of Judah? I come not against thee this day, but against the house wherewith I have war; and God has commanded me to make haste: forbear thee from meddling with *God who is with me*, that he destroy thee not.'

See also Gen. 21:22, 26:28, 31:5, 39:2–3; Joshua 1:9, 7:12, 14:12; 1 Sam. 10:7, 18:14, 28; 2 Sam. 5:10, 7:9, 14:17; 1 Kings 1:37 (cf. 3:6), 11:38; 1 Chron. 11:9, 17:2, 8, 22:11, 16; 2 Chron. 13:12; Judith 5:17, 13:11; Isa. 58:11 LXX.

(*d*) Deut. 20:1: 'When thou goest forth to battle against thine enemies, and seest horses and chariots, and a people more than thou, thou shalt not be afraid of them: for *the Lord thy God is with thee*; which brought thee up out of the land of Egypt.'

1 Chron. 28:20: 'David said to Solomon his son, Be strong and of good courage, and do it; fear not, nor be dismayed: for *the Lord is with thee*; he will not fail thee nor forsake thee, until all the work for the service of the house of the Lord be finished.'

Ps. 22(23):4: 'I will fear no evil, for *thou art with me*.'

Jer. 1:8 (calling of Jeremiah): 'Be not afraid because of them, for *I am with thee*.'

See also 2 Chron. 19:11, 20:17; Ps. 45(46): 8, 12; Jer. 1:7 LXX, 26(46):28, 49:11; Isa. 43:1 f.

(*e*) Deut. 31:23: 'He gave Joshua, the son of Nun, a charge, and said, Be strong and of a good courage; for thou shalt bring the children of Israel into the land which I sware unto them: and *I will be with thee*.'

Hag. 2:4 f.: 'Yet now be strong, O Zerubbabel, saith the Lord; and be strong, O Joshua, son of Jehozadak, . . . be strong, all ye people of the land, saith the Lord, and work, for *I am with you*, saith the Lord of hosts; according to the word that I covenanted with you, when ye came out of Egypt, and my spirit abode among you; fear ye not.'

(*f*) 1 Kings 11:38: 'And it shall be, if thou wilt hearken unto all that I command thee, and wilt walk in my ways, and do that which is right in mine eyes, to keep my statutes and my commandments, as David my servant did, that *I will be with thee* and will build thee a sure house, as I built for David.'

2 Chron. 15:2: 'Hear ye me, Asa, and all Judah and Benjamin: *the Lord is with you*, while ye be with him; and if ye seek him he will be found of you; but if ye forsake him, he will forsake you.'

2 Chron. 19:11: Jehoshaphat in appointing judges who must do their work in complete accordance with God's law: 'Deal courageously and *the Lord shall be with the good* (*man*).'

Amos 5:14: 'Seek good, and not evil, that ye may live: and so *the Lord, the God of hosts, shall be with you*, as ye say.'

See also 2 Chron. 17:3, 25:7.

It is interesting to see how this term was interpreted in later times. In the paraphrase of the Targum Onkelos, e.g., the element of 'help' comes to the fore. Instead of 'the Lord is with you' it has: 'the Memra of the Lord is to your help' (bs'dkh[39]). In the Midrash Rabba Gen. 28:15 is explained as a word of assurance and protection[40] and an annotation on Exod. 3:12 says: 'an expression used only to one who is afraid'.[41] Gen. 39:3 is explained in this way: his master suspected Joseph of witchcraft 'until he saw the Shekinah standing on him'.[42]

In Philo and Josephus, representing Hellenistic Judaism, the paraphrases of some relevant texts show that they do not retain the original wording—which was probably unintelligible to their readers—but bring out the element of divine assistance and the happiness it creates.

Philo, *de somniis*, I, 30, § 179, on Gen. 20:15: μεγίστη δέ ἐστιν εὐεργεσία ψυχῇ πονούσῃ καὶ διαθλούσῃ συνοδοιπόρον ἔχειν τὸν ἐφθακότα παντῇ θεόν.

Quod. det. pot. insid. soleat, 2, § 3, on Gen. 31:5: Laban is the world of senses; μετὰ σοῦ ὁ θεός means a soul in which God walks (ἐμπεριπατεῖ).

De post. Caini, 23, § 80, on Gen. 39:2: αὐτὸς ἄνδρα ἐπιτυγχάνοντα εἶπε τὸν Ἰωσὴφ οὐκ ἐν ἅπασιν, ἀλλ᾽ ἐν οἷς ὁ θεὸς τὸ εὐοδεῖν ἐχαρίζετο.

De fuga et inv., 25, § 140, on Exod. 3:12: ἡ θεοῦ μόνου σύνοδος.

De agricultura, 17, § 78, on Deut. 20:1: τοὺς ἔχοντας τὴν τοῦ μεγάλου βασιλέως θεοῦ δύναμιν ὑπερασπίζουσαν καὶ προαγωνιζομένην ἀεὶ καὶ πανταχοῦ · στρατὸς δὲ θεῖος αἱ ἀρεταὶ φιλοθέων ὑπέρμαχοι ψυχῶν.

De migrat. Abrah., 11, § 62-63, on Deut. 20:1, speaks of God as σύμμαχος ... τούτου γὰρ ἡ σύνοδος καθαιρεῖ πολέμους, εἰρήνην ἀνοικοδομεῖ, τὰ πολλὰ καὶ συνήθη κακὰ ἀνατρέπει, τὸ σπάνιον καὶ θεοφιλὲς γένος ἀνασῴζει.

Josephus, *Ant.*, I, 19, 2, § 283 = Gen. 28:15, προνοία—II, 12, 1, § 268 = Exod. 3:12, τοῦ θεοῦ συμπαρόντος—V, 6, 2, § 213 = Judges 6:12, εὐδαίμονα καὶ φίλον τῷ θεῷ—VII, 4, 4, § 91 = 2 Sam. 7:3, ὡς τοῦ θεοῦ πρὸς ἅπαντα αὐτῷ συνεργοῦ παρόντος—VII, 14, 5, § 357 = 1 Kings 1:37, τὸν θεὸν Σολομῶνι εὐμενῆ γενέσθαι—IX, 1, 2, § 11 = 2 Chron. 20:17, αὐτοῖς μάχεται τὸ θεῖον. These are not all his paraphrases; we merely choose some examples; the others show the same character. It is interesting to see that Josephus nearly always paraphrases the text of the OT and does not take over the OT phrase itself. This is the more striking, because in another passage of his own invention he uses the term himself. In its context and explanation it is very illuminating:

Ant., XV, 5, 3, § 138, is part of a speech which king Herod delivers to encourage his troops in the warfare against the Arabs.[43] The Arabs have murdered some ambassadors of Herod, but the Jews are afraid to attack them. Then Herod is reported to have said: 'Now perhaps somebody will say: "What is right in the eyes of God and men is on our side, but they happen to be braver and more numerous." It is, however, in the first place, unfitting for you to say so, because on the side of those with whom the right is, stands God; and where God is present, there are both numbers and bravery.' (*ἴσως τοίνυν ἐρεῖ τις, τὸ μὲν ὅσιον καὶ δίκαιον*[44] *μεθ' ἡμῶν, ἀνδρειότεροι καὶ πλείονες ἐκεῖνοι τετυχήκασιν. ἀλλὰ πρῶτον μὲν ἀνάξιον ὑμῖν ταῦτα λέγειν · μεθ' ὧν γὰρ τὸ δίκαιόν ἐστι, μετ' ἐκείνων ὁ θεός, θεοῦ δὲ παρόντος καὶ πλῆθος κὶ ἀνδρεία πάρεστιν.*)

The parallel passage in BJ I, 19, 3 ff., has nothing comparable.[45]

This later Jewish exegetical material is important for the conception of the phrase in NT times. It also clearly points to the avoidance of the wording of the OT and gives the expression a more or less 'neutral' turn. Presumably the difficulty formulated on p. 273 was felt already by these ancient authors. There is a marked difference here from the NT where the phrase is so freely used. At the later stage we shall see a wider implication of this difference and explain its great significance (see p. 293).

A survey of the material in the OT leads to some remarkable observations:

(1) The formula uses the words 'God' and 'the Lord' promiscuously and without distinction in meaning; sometimes both words are combined.

(2) The verb 'to be' is sometimes used, sometimes left out (see below, no. 7). It is employed in all three tenses, depending on the situation. The Lord's active help was there in the past, is experienced in the present and will be there in the future. In past and present it can be seen. As to the future it is not always formulated as a wish (see below, no. 6), but mostly as a definite declaration.

(3) Frequent though the expression is, it occurs only twice in greetings, viz. Judges 6:12 and Ruth 2:4, the usual greeting-form being: 'peace'.[46] In the former case it is certainly something exceptional, because Gideon is not simply greeted, but called to be a judge and saviour (cf. p. 278). He cannot accept this (v. 15:

'Behold, my family is the poorest in Manasseh, and I am the least in my father's house'. He understands the full weight of the word of the angel, but he does not discover its truth. For the words 'the Lord is with you' imply blessing in outward things, and the desolate situation of his country and the poor state of his family run counter to this existence of blessedness (cf. v. 13). The whole passage is clear evidence that this form of greeting was unique for a man like him in those circumstances.—As to Ruth 2:4 there is no such indication. It may be that this later book [47] wished to tell this story of the period of the Judges with colours derived from that book. It is also possible to interpret this word as a stimulus to the reapers for their work. Or is there an indication in the name of Boaz? According to a common explanation this name means: 'In him is power.' [48] Can he pronounce that unusual greeting, because he has great power (of Yahweh) in himself?

(4) The Gideon-story is highly significant, because it shows that God's 'being with a person' was not conceived as a permanent fact, but as a dynamic experience that acts in special cases which can be sharply discerned. The declaration of the angel (see below, no. 6) does not appear in his person and situation (v. 13). Then follows in v. 16: 'The Lord said unto him, Surely *I will be with thee*, and thou shalt smite the Midianites.' At that particular time in the future it will become evident ($\check{\varepsilon}\sigma o\mu a\iota$, not $\varepsilon\check{\iota}\mu\iota$). Another patent example can be found in 1 Sam. 10:6 f. (see p. 205) and Judith 13:11. This dynamic conception, this not permanent, but suddenly appearing presence, when once observed, characterizes also the contents of other texts.

(5) The fact that 'the Lord is with a person' can be discovered by others. It manifests itself outwardly, and even unbelievers see it.

Gen. 21:22: 'And it came to pass at that time that Abimelech and Phicol the captain of his host spake unto Abraham, saying, *God is with thee* in all that thou doest', cf. 26:28.

Num. 23:21, words of Balaam: '*The Lord his God is with him* (Israel) and the shout of a king is among them.'

Joshua 22:31: 'This day we know that *the Lord is with us*, because ye have not committed this trespass against the Lord.'

2 Chron. 15:9: 'And he gathered all Judah and Benjamin and them that sojourned with them out of Ephraim and Manasseh, and out of Simeon: for they fell to him out of Israel in abundance, when they saw that *the Lord his God was with him*.'

Zech. 8:23: 'Ten men shall take hold, out of all the languages of the nations, shall even take hold of the skirt of him that is a Jew, saying, We will go with you, for we have heard that *God is with you*' (this is more than a movement among the pagans for monotheism; it is seeking protection and blessing from that God who blesses so manifestly His people).

See also Gen. 39:3; Joshua 3:7; 1 Sam. 3:19 f., 16:18, 18:28; 3 Macc. 6:15.

(6) In some places the term is given in the form of a wish. There it is interesting to look at the interpretative work of the LXX. In Exod. 10:10 and Joshua 1:17 it has ἔστω, in 1 Kings 1:37 εἴη, in 1 Kings 8:57 γένοιτο as an exact translation of the Hebrew, but we observe that in places like 1 Sam. 20:13; 1 Chron. 22:11, 16; 2 Chron. 19:11 the Hebrew iussive *yᵉhî* ('be') is rendered by the positive ἔσται. An odd example of this difference in translation may be seen in a text which is found three times in LXX: 2 Chron. 36:23 = 2 Ezra 1:3 = 1 Ezra 2:3; in the first two cases ἔσται, in the last ἔστω. It is important to see that this note of certainty about future help and blessing is far stronger than the subjective forms of wish and possibility. The expression is used with the future tense in Gen. 26:3, 31:13, 48:21; Exod. 3:12, 18:19; Deut. 31:23; Joshua 1:5, 3:7; Judges 6:16; 1 Sam. 17:37, 20:13; 2 Sam. 14:17; 1 Kings 11:38; Amos 5:14; Isa. 58:11. It is not only declared by God Himself, but also by men. The certainty existing already in the Hebrew text is underlined and strengthened in LXX. This is important for the rest of our discussion (this is a tendency opposite to that which can be observed with 'āmēn—γένοιτο).

(7) It is also important to note the instances where the copula is missing in the Greek text (in literal translation of the Hebrew). That feature is not uncommon. In all these cases it is practically always a declaration, as appears from the context and therefore the later translators rightly add 'was' or 'is'.[49]

In 1 Chron. 22:16 the end of the exhortation of David to Solomon is usually translated in an optative form: 'arise and be doing, and *the Lord be with you*', but in view of v. 12 f. ('fear not, etc.', cf. p. 279) and v. 18 which is certainly declarative, it seems better to translate: 'the Lord will be with you' (if Solomon follows the commandments of Moses; this 'conditional' form is very marked in Chron., see p. 279). In Judges 6:12 the greeting is not a wish, but a declaration and so it is conceived by Gideon, as follows from his answer ('if the Lord is with us', as you say, why this miserable situation); this was also the understanding of Josephus (p. 280). The salutation in Ruth 2:4 is ambiguous; since the answer of the reapers is optative[50] one is inclined to translate the former part in the same way, but in view of Judges 6:12 it may be a declaration, when Boaz sees the work of the reapers.

(8) As will be seen from p. 300, n. 37, there is a curious distribution throughout the OT. It is fairly seldom found in Psalms and prophets, where one would expect it, and rather frequent in the historical books with a marked preponderance in Gen., Joshua, Sam., and Chron. There is no connection with liturgical contexts. It is striking that this 'being of God with . . .' is not bound up with the Ark[51] or the Temple; in those cases the OT speaks about the 'dwelling' of God and this difference once more brings to light the *active* character of the expression we are investigating, in contrast with the static conception, suggested to us by the verb 'to be'. Everywhere in the OT the phrase expresses the same dynamic reality (apart from one element which will be mentioned below, no. 10).

(9) If one makes a list of those 'with whom God is', it is typical that the number of instances where the people of Israel as a whole, the chosen people of God is intended, forms a minority[52]. In the large majority of texts the term is used of *individuals,* and even where the people is meant it is sometimes individualized as in Deutero-Isa. and Jer. 26:28. The line does not go from the people as a whole to the individual, but rather the other way. It is not applied to every pious man in general, but to very *special persons.* It is a marked feature in the history of Jacob, Joseph (Moses), Joshua, the Judges (2:18 in general), Gideon, Saul and David (in 2 Chron. also of several other kings). Among the prophets it is precisely Jeremiah, the best known personality among the prophets, who yields some texts. It is often mentioned in connection with a special divine task, in which the particular man is assured of God's assistance, see e.g. Gen. 28:15; Exod. 3:12; Joshua 1:5; Judges 6:12 ff.; I Sam. 10:7; Jer. 1:8, 17, 19; the man himself is afraid to accept the task, because he has no strength in himself.

The OT itself shows that there exists some link between these individuals. It says that the Lord was with Joshua as He was with Moses (Deut. 31:23; Joshua 1:17, 3:7); something similar is said about Saul and David (I Sam. 20:13) and David and Solomon

(1 Kings 1:37). Is it possible to detect here a typical common factor?

(10) Here we come to a point that is of vital importance for the exact and full understanding of the expression. *Most of the individuals of whom it is declared that 'God was with them' were specially endowed with the Spirit of God.* It is the Spirit with his manifold manifestations (cf. Isa. 11:2); the Spirit of wisdom and strength; the Spirit which makes men speak the words of God as a prophet and do His deeds.

Joseph: 4 times it is mentioned that 'God was with him' (Gen. 39:2, 3, 21, 23) and in Gen. 41:38 after his interpreting of Pharaoh's dreams he is called 'a man in whom the spirit of God is'. It is interesting to see that these separate elements (the former is exclusively used for the prison-period; the latter for the explanation of the dreams and the reward of authority as governor) are understood by the early Christians as a unity, as appears from Acts 7:9 f. (p. 275). The Spirit is not mentioned by Stephen, in all probability because it was implied in the words 'God was with him'.

Moses: Num. 11:17: 'And I will take of the spirit which is upon thee'; in v. 25 that happens: 'and it came to pass, that, when the spirit rested upon them (the elders), they prophesied'. Cf. Deut. 34:10, Moses was a prophet.

Joshua: Deut. 34:9: 'And Joshua, the son of Nun, was full of the spirit of wisdom; for Moses had laid his hands upon him.'

Judges: cf. Judges 2:18; the Spirit is mentioned in the cases of Othniel (3:10), Jephthah (11:29), Samson (13:25, 14:6, 19, 15:14).

Gideon: Judges 6:34, when he enters upon his task: 'the spirit of the Lord came upon Gideon' (ἐνέδυσεν, cod. B ἐνεδυνάμωσεν).[53]

Samuel: 1 Sam. 3:19 f.: 'And Samuel grew, and the Lord was with him, and did let none of his words fall to the ground. And all Israel ... knew that Samuel was established to be a prophet of the Lord.'

Saul: 1 Sam. 10:6 f.: 'And the spirit of the Lord will come mightily upon thee, and thou shalt prophesy with them, and shalt be turned into another man. And let it be, when these signs are come unto thee, that thou do as occasion serve thee; for the Lord is with thee'; cf. also the story 19:20 ff.

David: 1 Sam. 16:13, after his anointing: 'and the spirit of the Lord came mightily upon David from that day forward'; cf. the description of his person in v. 18, quoted p. 278. Important in this connection is the relation of Saul and David which is characterized by that spirit; 1 Sam. 16:14, after the anointing of David: 'Now the spirit of the Lord had departed from Saul, and an evil spirit from the Lord (note the difference!) troubled him' (cf. vv. 15, 16, 23 and 18:10, 19:9). In 28:16 Samuel says: 'The Lord is departed from thee and is with thy neighbour' (reading of LXX), because Saul had not obeyed God's command (v. 18).

Israel: 2 Ezra 19:20 (= Neh. 9:20): 'Thou gavest also thy good spirit to instruct them and withheldest not thy manna from their mouth' (about the period in the wilderness); cf. also Isa. 63:10 ff.

Isa. 44:3: 'I will pour my spirit upon thy seed and my blessing upon thine offspring', cf. 32:15, 59:21.

In other cases we have to do with the Patriarchs who have a special place in Jewish theology,[54] and Jacob was credited with the spirit in later thought;[55] with anointed kings (if they are obedient) and with Jeremiah who was a prophet (1:5, 7).

Peculiar is the utterance about Pharaoh Neco, 2 Chron. 35:21, but see v. 22: Josiah 'hearkened not unto the words of Neco, *from the mouth of God*', so it is prophetic.

Important also is the connection in Hag. 2:4 f., quoted on p. 279 and the same in 1:13 f. which show that the relation was still felt at that time.

The man to whom this 'the Lord is with you' is said becomes a pneumatic; he is—as in the graphic description of Saul—'turned into another man'. The man who is anxious becomes a hero; receives supernatural insight and is able to speak the word of the Lord. Through that quickening power of the Spirit unexpected results can come about.

This relation between 'God's being with a person' and the Spirit is too frequent in the OT to be incidental or accidental. It may be left to OT scholarship to investigate whether this conception belonged to a certain period of religious development. For the NT scholar it is sufficient to know that this close connection is there, since the early Christians did not read the OT from the historical point of view, but saw it as a unit. In passing, however, it may be remarked that apparently there has been an important change of emphasis. It seems as though this bond between 'God with a person' and the Spirit was loosened after the exile (see Chron.). It is not mentioned by the authors in the NT period (p. 281). If this is correct, it would not be surprising, since it was widely held among the Jews in NT times that there was no revelation of the Spirit in the present time, this being reserved for the eschatological future.[56]

After this detailed discussion of the OT material the NT texts which employ the term need not detain us long. With the OT conception and its associations in mind we discover that in the NT the same reality is met with. Since that has generally been overlooked it will be our task to demonstrate that the term in the NT has still its vital force and that the living understanding of this expression throws into relief its full content.

In the texts quoted before (p. 275 f.) we observed a connection between Jesus' wondrous actions and the Holy Spirit which enabled Him to do them and which was recognized as such. This is not surprising, but in line with the OT conception. The promise to the disciples in Matt. 28:20 gets its full force in this perspective: after having set that enormous task (v. 19), Jesus who has now all authority comforts His weak followers (cf. 26:56) and assures them of His powerful assistance (note: εἰμι, not ἔσομαι) which will make their activity both possible and successful. That is the surprising declaration at the moment of departure. Matthew returns at the end to the beginning: Jesus was (1:23) and is 'Immanuel' (see below), not only as the suffering Servant, but also as the triumphant king.[57]

Here follow the other texts containing the expression in the NT.

(1) Matt. 1:23, a quotation from Isa. 7:14. The insertion of this quotation is an addition of the evangelist, i.e. it expresses his own conception and the message he wished to convey. It is also important to see that *he* offers the translation of the name which was left untranslated in LXX (see p. 278). This proves that he attached great value to the proper understanding of the name. This prooftext serves as the divine confirmation of what happened to Mary; her awkward position from the human point of view was according to the divine plan. Matthew not only quotes from Isaiah the first part about the virginity,[58] but also the second part with the name (which was not the usual name for Jesus![59]), and wants his readers to understand it: 'God with us'. Both parts of the citation run parallel with the preceding story: v. 18, 'when his mother Mary had been betrothed to Joseph, *before they came together* she was found with child *of the Holy Ghost*' . . . v. 20 (message of the angel to Joseph), '*fear not* to take unto thee Mary thy wife: for that which is conceived in her is *of the Holy Ghost*'. Because the unusual conception is the work of the Holy Spirit (mentioned twice), Jesus was 'God with us'. Against the OT background we

discover what this means: it is the power of God who comes into action to deliver, to grant His blessing, to call for a new obedience to His will. The fact that Matthew could use this expression and brought it to the fore, without elucidation, shows that the ideas associated with the term were living conceptions for the Christians of the apostolic age.

Jesus' healing work in silence, described in Matt. 12, is seen as a fulfilment of Isa. 42:1 ff.: 'Behold, my Servant whom I have chosen, My beloved in whom my soul is well pleased, *I will put my Spirit upon Him*', cf. 3:16 f., Jesus' baptism with the Spirit.—In 12:28 Jesus asks: 'But if I by the Spirit of God cast out devils, then is the kingdom of God come upon you', pointing at the Agent who works through Him.—This conception is closely akin to that of Acts 10:38.

Matt. 18:20 may also be quoted in this connection: 'For where two or three are gathered together in my name, there am I in the midst of them'. This ἐν μέσῳ stands parallel to μετά which is sometimes in LXX a translation of 'in the midst', p. 300, n. 36. In Matt. this verse is the motivation ('for') of the preceding one; it explains why that prayer will be answered. In itself v. 19 is not self-evident. Where the smallest number of Christians are gathered in Jesus' name, they may be sure of *His* active assistance which is a spiritual power, bringing unity of spirit ('agree', v. 19) and contact with the Father.—The rabbinic parallel Aboth III, 2, which is often quoted, shows as much difference of content as similarity!

(2) Luke 1:28, the angel saluting Mary: χαῖρε, κεχαριτωμένη, ὁ κύριος μετὰ σοῦ. The sequence of this saying is very illuminating. Mary is troubled by that 'manner (!) of salutation', in all likelihood because it was unusual.[60] Then the angel gives an explanation: '*Fear not*, Mary: for thou hast found favour with God' (this χάρις explains the κεχαριτωμένη); her child will be the wonderful fulfilment of the promises given to David. When Mary asks how that will come to pass to her, the virgin, the angel continues: 'The *Holy Ghost* shall come upon thee and the power of the Most High shall overshadow thee; wherefore also that which is to be born shall be called holy, the Son of God' (v. 35). The fact that her kinswoman Elisabeth, the barren, is pregnant, is a sign[61] that 'no word from God shall be void of power' (v. 37). Typical in this passage is that 'fear not' which is often connected with 'the Lord with thee' (p. 279). The 'word from God' which is not void, is here the greeting and assurance 'the Lord with thee', and its con-

tent is defined by the great blessings (v. 32 f.), wrought by the Holy Ghost. This extensive passage again shows the heavy dynamic weight attached to these words and the sympathetic understanding of the NT writers. This simple maiden of Nazareth could not rank with the great men of Sacred History 'with whom the Lord was', but God's election brings her there. This is the story of Mary's calling (cf. p. 284; that of Gideon especially may be compared, cf. v. 48). She is afraid and does not know how it shall be, just like men in the OT, but she accepts the task: 'be it unto me according to thy word' (v. 38). The saying 'The Lord with thee' takes away fear and gives strength; its effect is blessing for Mary, the people, the world.

For the special relation between Jesus and the Spirit, see His baptism, Luke 3:22, and His first public appearance, 4:1 (twice), 14 and particularly v. 18, a quotation of Isa. 61:1: 'The Spirit of the Lord is upon me, because He anointed me', etc., with the declaration in v. 21: 'To-day hath this Scripture been fulfilled in your ears.' This is fundamental for the whole of Jesus' activity in Luke.

(3) John 8:29: 'He that sent me *is with me*; he has not left me alone, for I do always the things that are pleasing to him.' Jesus speaks what the Father has taught him (v. 28; he is the Prophet, cf., e.g., 4:44, 7:40, 52). The association of ideas is familiar from the OT. He is not forsaken by the Father, as was Saul (1 Sam. 18:28; cf. 1 Chron. 28:20 (p. 279)). For ἀρεστά, a well-known word in LXX for obedience to God's will,[62] see texts on p. 279, under *f*.

(4) John 14:16 contains the phrase, but the whole context is relevant: v. 12, 'Verily, verily, I say unto you, he that believeth on me, the *works* that I do shall he do also; and greater works than these shall he do, because I go unto the Father. . . . (v. 15). If ye love me, ye will *keep my commandments* (v. 16). And I will pray the Father, and he shall give you another Comforter,[63] that he may *be with you for ever* (v. 17), even *the Spirit* of truth . . . ye know him, for he abideth with you and shall be in you (v. 18). I *will not leave you desolate*' (cf. also 16:13 f.). The Holy Spirit takes Jesus' place, but is there for ever, not on certain occasions (p. 282). It is the prophetic Spirit, as is seen from the teaching in these chapters 14–16. The conditions for and the effect of that abiding of the Spirit are the same as those connected with 'The Lord with you' in the OT.

(5) John 16:32: 'Behold, the hour cometh, yea, is come that ye
U

shall be scattered . . . and shall leave me alone; and *I am not alone,
because the Father is with me.*' See above on 8:29. Jesus, left by His
followers, is sure of God's protection (cf. the remarkable transposition of the word about the cup in 18:11 as compared with that
of the Synoptics, Mark 14:35 ff., and its parallels).

(6) Acts 18:9 f., in a critical situation of Paul's life at Corinth:
'And the Lord said unto Paul in the night by a vision: *Be not afraid,
but speak* and hold not thy peace: for *I am with you,* and no man
shall set on thee to harm thee: for I have much people in this city.'
Paul must continue his divine, prophetic mission. The expression
implies both protection, comfort and success; mark the combination with 'fear not' (p. 279). Is this modelled after the experience
of Jeremiah (cf. Acts 26:17; Gal. 1:15)? It is superfluous to give
many texts for Paul's activity as a pneumatic, see, e.g., Acts 9:17,
16:6 f.[64]

(7) Four Pauline texts may be taken together:

Rom. 15:33: '*The God of peace with you all.*'

2 Cor. 13:11: 'Finally, brethren, rejoice,[65] be perfected, be com-
forted, be of the same mind, live in peace; and *the God of love and
peace shall be* (ἔσται) *with you.*'

Phil. 4:9: 'The things which ye both learned and received and
heard and saw in me, these things do; and *the God of peace shall be*
(ἔσται) *with you.*'

2 Thess. 3:16: 'Now the Lord of peace himself give you peace
at all times in all ways. *The Lord with you all.*'

These four texts are all at the end of the respective epistles but
they do not give the final greeting,[66] as is most clearly seen from
Phil. 4:9. Besides the phrase 'the Lord with you' they have also in
common the combination with 'the God of peace'. This is a
favourite expression of Paul: the God he preaches is 'the God of
peace'. This does not envisage an inward peace of mind,[67] as
appears from 1 Cor. 14:33: 'God is not a God of disorder, but of
peace.' In Rom. 16:20 and 1 Thess. 5:23 Paul describes what the
'God of peace' accomplishes: the future subjection of Satan and
the complete preservation of the Christian.[68] These last verses
illustrate the texts we are studying. The peace is connected with
the very concrete situation of the people addressed. Through
strife and disunity the 'peace' of the church is broken, as is patent
from the epistles to the Corinthians, Philippians (strong appeal for
unity!) and Thessalonians. If the readers fulfil the commandments

of the apostle, he assures them of God's assistance and protection (2 Cor. 13:11; Phil. 4:9); this is in agreement with the OT conception (p. 277 f.). It is not purely eschatological (Phil. 4:9), but this 'welfare' can be realized among them now, 'the unity of the Spirit in the bond of peace' (Eph. 4:3). It has a declarative force. That he could use it in Rom. 15:33 and 2 Thess. 3:16 without further explanation shows that this phrase was understood by his readers; that there is no copula there is not surprising, see p. 283, and does not diminish its character of declaration. The Spirit has been given to the Christian community (Rom. 8:14 ff.; 1 Cor. 2:12 ff., 12:13).

Later rabbis saw in the phrase a word of assurance (p. 280) which would have been impossible if it were just a wish. The proper understanding of Matt. 1:23 and Luke 1:28 also brings to light the existing and active assistance of God's Spirit which is not wished or hoped for, but is present.[69] The Pauline texts have the same value: they are a firm declaration of God's saving power. That is in line with the whole biblical conception of the term, with the two texts where ἔσται is used and with Paul's unwavering conviction about the reality of Christ's redeeming work which is on its way to final victory.

The optative δῴη in 2 Thess. 3:16, cf. Num. 6:26, does not militate against this interpretation. Paul hopes that the Lord of peace will give peace in every manner (that is the important point!) and he can express this wish just because he is sure that this Lord *is* 'with them'.

It is usual in this and other cases to add in translating the subjunctive 'be', but that can only be done because the phrase 'the Lord with you' is considered just a pious exclamation (just as in Dutch the saying 'Adieu' in bidding farewell has lost its value) and is completely under-estimated.

In passing I may say that the final greetings have the same force: 'the grace of the Lord is with you all'. The subjective interpretation falls short of the certitude of Paul's faith. As a last farewell he assures the readers again of the sole, but firm ground of their Christian existence, cf. Acts 20:32. In all probability stress must be laid on the word 'all'.

A parallel may be drawn from the use of 'peace' in greetings. This word has a strong dynamic force, as was clearly pointed out by W. S. van Leeuwen (p. 303, note 67). The peace given in greeting is not a desired thing, but an existing reality: it is sent out and may come back to the giver, Luke 10:5; its working depends on the receiver, but there is no doubt about the reality of the gift.

This 'being of God with the Christians' is the present reality of the Holy Spirit in the church. The proof is found in 1 Cor. 14:25.

In a church-gathering the Spirit gives prophetic power to the believers by which they reveal the secrets of the unbeliever's heart. This is so surprising and shocking to him that thereby he is moved to adoration, 'declaring that *God is among you* indeed' (ὄντως = in reality and not only professed). This recognition of the divine presence is well known from the OT (p. 282 f.).[70] Here the presence of the Lord is bound up with the prophetic experience (p. 284 ff.) and manifests itself to the outsider. This picture of a service in the apostolic age shows that these Christians came together in a pneumatic atmosphere, filled by the Pneuma of God (cf. also 2 Cor. 1:21 f.: 'He that stablisheth us with you in Christ, and *anointed* us, is God who also sealed us and gave us the earnest of the *Spirit* in our hearts').

(8) 2 Tim. 4:22: '*The Lord with thy spirit*. The grace with you all.' This combination of singular and plural form is somewhat surprising, especially after this personal letter. It is found in all three Pastoral Epistles, highly interesting being Tit. 3:15. It is an indication that these personal letters were also meant to be read in the community. Is 'with thy spirit' here the same as 'with you'? One is led to think so, because in some greetings Paul writes: 'the grace with you all', but in Gal. 6:28; Phil. 4:23; Philem. 25 'the grace with your spirit'.[71] One may say that there is identity, but not in the sense that 'thy spirit' = 'thyself' (see p. 273), but that 'you' are the Christians, i.e. men and women endowed with the Spirit (see above and 1 Cor. 5:5; 1 Thess. 5:23). Now, there is a diversity of gifts of the Spirit (1 Cor. 12:4 ff.) and therefore it is possible that Paul is thinking here of the divine assistance to Timothy's special charisma, cf. 1 Tim. 4:14; 2 Tim. 1:6 f. For the discharge of his task Timothy will need fortitude, wisdom, longsuffering, etc. It is an assurance that there is no reason to fear; an assurance also of God's protection and blessing for his work (cf. 2:22 ff.).

In the so-called 'Apostolic Fathers' there is only one text with the expression which may be mentioned here: Barnabas 21:9: 'the Lord of glory and all grace with your (plur.) spirit.' This final greeting is not copied from one of the NT texts. 'Spirit' must be here the spirit living in the church as a whole to which this letter is addressed. The words following the admonition: σώζεσθε, 'children of love and peace', are an assurance, that He Who has given love and peace can preserve them, safe and well, for the coming Age.

In reviewing these texts from the NT[72] we discover that in the light of OT usage they receive their full force. The phrase is like a short-hand note. At face-value it does not seem of great importance and is therefore passed over in the commentaries. On closer inspection, however, it turns out that the NT authors themselves understood its full meaning perfectly well and were sure that their readers would understand it as well. They did not use an out-worn phrase, but wrote it down as expressing a self-evident truth. There is a marked difference here from later Judaism (p. 286). In its humble wording it contains the fulness and certitude of the Christian faith.

Jesus, the Messiah = Christ = Anointed One with the Spirit, the mediator of the new Covenant, is the IMMANUEL and does His work of salvation; His followers, anointed with the Spirit, form the new Israel and stand in the line of the prophets, heroes and kings of the old Israel, obedient to God's will and assured by His blessing.

Let us now turn back to our starting-point: the dialogue between minister and congregation.

In the course of our argument many passages with the phrase: 'the Lord with somebody' were passed in review. They revealed a number of different applications of the same weighty conception. It will be impossible to use it inadvertently. It is impermissible to confine the interpretation of the dialogue to the use of the phrase in greetings. As a matter of fact it only occurs in greetings in very few instances and there the contexts show the exceptional character of this salutation. The term defines *the dynamic activity of God's Spirit given to particular chosen individuals or the people of God, enabling them to do a work of God in word or deed by protecting, assisting and blessing them; this presence of the Spirit manifests itself in the individual and to the outside world.*

This is the answer to the third question, formulated on p. 273. These texts also solve the other riddles. The 'Lord' is here not so much the Father or the Son; it is the manifestation of the Lord in the Spirit (cf. 2 Cor. 3:17, an interpretation of an OT text!). The greeting is a declaration (p. 283 f.) that the Spirit of God is really present. The response of the congregation is very much to the point: when the minister assures them of the presence of the Spirit who 'is with them', i.e. with their spirit as Christian folk, they in their turn assure him of the same divine assistance with his spirit, he having a special charisma[73] and standing in need of that assistance because of his prophetic work.

This dialogue has not been made after a biblical model, since that is not found anywhere. But it is deeply rooted in the biblical revelation. It has been formulated by the early Christians led by a deep experience of the Spirit. In the present state of the available material it is impossible to say when or where it first took shape. It has no parallels in the world of Greek or Jewish religion. It is a spontaneous creation of the Christian Church.

These short sentences which for the first time are met as an introduction to the Prayer of Thanksgiving (εὐχαριστία) are, if properly understood, highly significant for the ancient church service. There we find its *Sitz im Leben*. Other texts from the first and second centuries will help us to understand more fully in what surroundings it originated.

On the early Christians the new era had dawned. For them the New Covenant had come, 'not of the letter, but of the Spirit' (2 Cor. 3:6). This explains why in the NT the phrase has again its full weight and connection with the Spirit, while in later Judaism it had lost this relation (p. 280 f). The early Christians lived under the guiding inspiration of the Holy Spirit. That was not only so in the apostolic age, but also in later generations. It is often said that after the time of the apostles there is a decline of charismatic force; that Christian life becomes more institutionalized. To a certain extent that may be true, but on the other hand it must be said that we often get a false picture through the fragmentary state of the surviving source-material. Yet even so there are sufficient statements about the living experience of the Spirit in the church. I Clement 2:2 shows this, when he speaks about a 'full effusion of the Holy Spirit on all' (cf. also 46:6). Much illustrative and relevant material has been collected long ago by Weinel in an excellent book that is unduly neglected at present.[74]

Christian worship, too, stood in this magnetic field of the Holy Spirit, and was its centre. This determining factor of the early liturgy is often overlooked in recent discussion of this subject. Prayer especially is a work of the Spirit. This is conspicuous in Paul. Two passages in Rom. 8 help us to see the background of the dialogue: vv. 15 f.: 'Ye received the *spirit of adoption, whereby we cry*, Abba, Father. *The Spirit himself beareth witness with our spirit*, that we are children of God', and v. 26 f.: 'In like manner the Spirit also helpeth our infirmity; for we know not how to pray as we ought: but *the Spirit himself maketh intercession for us* with groanings which cannot be uttered; and he who searcheth the hearts knoweth what is the mind of the Spirit, because he maketh intercession for the saints according to the will of God.' To offer a right prayer, acceptable to God, the assistance of the Holy Spirit is necessary; it must be a combined action of Divine and human spirit. This 'spiritual' character of prayer comes to light also in 1 Cor. 14:14 f. It is typical of Christian prayer, as Harder in his important monograph has rightly observed,[75] and must be explained not from hellenistic presuppositions about 'spiritualization', but from the basic idea of the New Covenant. Very relevant also is Eph. 5:18: 'Be filled with the *Spirit*, speaking one to another in psalms and hymns and *spiritual* songs (i.e. inspired by the Spirit) . . . *giving thanks* always for all things in the name of our Lord Jesus Christ to God the Father'; 2:18: 'for through Him (Jesus, our peace) we both (Christians from Jewish and pagan stock) have *in one Spirit* our access unto the Father', and 6:18: 'With all prayer and supplications praying at all seasons *in the Spirit*.' This effectual presence of the Spirit in a church service is brought out by 1 Cor. 14:25 (see p. 292).

This feeling of the presence of the Spirit during divine worship continued in later times. One of the rules in Hippolytus' Church-Order says: 'They shall be zealous to go to the assembly (ἐκκλησία) where the Spirit abounds' (Lat. tr., *floret*).[76] A text from the prophet Hermas (middle second century) is very enlightening.[77] In picturing the difference between the true and the false prophet he lets the former 'having the Divine Spirit' enter 'into an assembly of righteous men who have faith in the Divine Spirit'; when 'this assembly offers up prayer to God, then the angel of the prophetic Spirit who is destined for him, fills the man: and the man being filled with the Holy Spirit speaks to the multitude as the Lord wishes' (Mand, xi, 9).[78] This prophet does not speak on his own authority; what he potentially possesses is suddenly stirred up when the assembly is praying. In the case of the false prophet that does not happen, but then 'the earthly spirit flees from him through fear, and that man is made dumb' (§ 14). The true prophet finds a sympathetic environment in such an assembly, but the spirit of the false prophet cannot stand it: 'the empty prophets, when they come to the spirits of the righteous, are found on leaving to be such as they were when they came' (§ 15); in the Spirit from God there is power, but the earthly spirit is powerless (§ 17). The critical moment for the prophet is that of prayer; then the whole meeting-place is filled with the Spirit and the spirit of the incoming prophet must be in tune with that of the congregation. For effective prayer an interplay between the Holy Spirit and that of man is indispensable. This becomes clear from the previous Mandatum. Here Hermas combats grief, because it crushes out the Holy Ghost 'which was given to man a cheerful spirit' and he continues: 'Grieving the Holy Spirit he works iniquity, neither entreating the Lord nor giving thanks[79] to Him. For the entreaty of the sorrowful man has no power to ascend to the altar of God.' [80] The reason for this is that a mixture of grief with this entreaty makes it impure; grief cannot be mixed with the Holy Spirit any more than vinegar with wine (Mand., x, 3).[81] This grief is a sister of doubt and anger; people like Hermas do not understand, because their minds are occupied with worldly business.[82] 'Those, on the other hand, who have the fear of God, and search after Godhead and truth, and have their hearts turned to the Lord (*καὶ τὴν καρδίαν ἔχοντες πρὸς κύριον*),[83] quickly perceive. . . . For where the Lord dwells, there is much understanding' (Mand., x, 1). The 'Holy Spirit' here is that which dwells in man (Mand., x, 2, 5) and is subject to all sorts of human emotions. This peculiar conception[84] is clearly conceived by Hermas as the characteristic Christian 'spirit' which the newly-baptized has received as that element which stamps him as a Christian (cf. p. 292). The sequence of thought in Hermas often lacks clearness. But in the main his way of looking at things is simple: in the Christian dwells the 'Holy Spirit', given by God to make him pure, obedient to God's will, together with all sorts of other 'spirits', leading forces; for a prayer acceptable to God this 'Holy Spirit' must be free from other influences; when the Christian comes to the church, where other Christians, the people of God, are gathered, and the Holy Spirit in its fulness is present, then it becomes clear whether the individual 'spirit' is in tune with the Holy Spirit.

This conception of prayer and service was not a private idea of Hermas. In Didache, x, 7, it appears that saying the 'eucharist' was not bound to certain formularies, if a prophet was doing it.[85] This presupposes that it was part of the activity of the Spirit. From

Tertullian, *De Oratione*, 16, it follows that Hermas had a very deep influence upon the practice of prayer,[86] and though Tertullian combatted this slavish imitation of the Roman author, he shares with him certain important ideas.[87]

The material available for the reconstruction of the history of the liturgy does not enable us to determine the exact date and place of the origin of the dialogue. It may be anywhere in the first or second century. The connections with ideas in Hermas make a date in the middle of the second century quite probable.

Within the picture presented to us by Hermas, the dialogue finds its natural place and explanation.[88] A real Eucharist (prayer of thanksgiving) can only be offered in the right spiritual atmosphere both in the congregation as a whole and in its individual members. And 'spiritual' means here that the Spirit of God is present; He is the life-blood of the church. That Spirit must flow and not be hampered by emotions and worldly thoughts. That spirit has been given, but must be vivified.

The Lord with you, says the minister with a word of assurance: here where the people of God is gathered in the name of Jesus IMMANUEL the dynamic presence of the Spirit is found which enables them to perform the holy work of the spiritual sacrifices; He assists these weak men and women; He will keep their spirits in the right condition.

And with thy spirit, rings the answer: like them the minister called to that work of the Spirit, to say the prayer, needs to be assured of that assisting power of the Spirit which keeps his spirit from all worldly thoughts, etc.

Lift up your hearts, now calls the minister: when the church again sees what it means to be the church of Christ and stands in the right atmosphere, they are called to direct their hearts[89] to the heavenly altar where the prayers are offered.

We lift them up unto the Lord, is their answer: to Him, Whom they are about to thank for His wonderful work in creation and re-creation. After this preparation the Thanksgiving can be said.

If this spiritual background has been discovered one also understands how this same introduction can be used before the reading of the Gospel. 'The natural man receiveth not the things of the Spirit of God: for they are foolishness unto him; and he cannot know them, because they are spiritually judged' (1 Cor. 2:13).

The history and work of Jesus Who was anointed with the Spirit is pre-eminently spiritual.[90] Is everyone in our churches where these old and revered words are repeated hundreds of times aware of their deep, heart-searching meaning? I wish they were. But if not, let these words not be used in vain, for 'the letter killeth, but the Spirit gives life'. That is a judgment and the hope of the Church!

NOTES

[1] *Dienstboek voor de Nederlandse Hervormde Kerk* (*in ontwerp*, 's Gravenhage 1955), 9, 11, 13, etc. The legend of Dutch silver coins has also 'God met ons' (God with us), and as my colleague Prof. Quispel reminded me, the same version 'Gott mit uns' was on the belts of German soldiers, even during the Nazi period. The origin of these applications cannot be traced here; it is however interesting to see the application of the same formula in widely divergent places.

[2] Tertullian, De virg. vel. 1: 'Sed dominus noster Christus veritatem se, non consuetudinem, cognominavit.' This is still a valuable, all-too-often forgotten rule.

[3] J. A. Jungmann, *Missarum Solemnia*[2] (1949), Bd. i, 447.

[4] Hippolytus, *Apostolic Tradition*, ed. G. Dix (1937), 7, cf. also 39, 50. Because the salutation is always regarded as a special unit, I will do the same. At the end of this paper however it will be seen (p. 297) that the two parts in Hippolytus belong together and cannot be separated.—On various forms of the 'Sursum Corda', see C. A. Bouman, 'Variants in the Introduction to the Eucharistic Prayer', VC 4 (1950), 97 ff.

[5] The material has been collected in a very convenient form by K. Frör, *Salutationen, Benediktionen, Amen*, in K. F. Müller-W. Blankenburg (eds.), *Leiturgia, Handbuch des evangelischen Gottesdienstes* (1955), Bd. ii, 570–81.—In the course of the following discussion I refer to Jungmann and Frör, because they offer the latest and most complete discussion of the subject.—In passing it may be remarked that the short article of H. Leclercq, 'Dominus Vobiscum', in F. Cabrol-H. Leclercq, *Dictionnaire d'Archéologie chrétienne et de Liturgie*, is quite unsatisfactory.

[6] Cf. K. Frör, *op. cit.*, 575, Ak. 33: 'In der Geschichte der Salutationen sind viele und wesentliche Zusammenhänge noch nicht geklärt'.

[7] Though the ascription of this reconstructed work to Hippolytus by Schwarz and Connolly has been challenged, I believe with the majority of scholars at present, that it is correct.

[8] P. Morrishoe, 'Dominus Vobiscum', in *Catholic Encyclopedia*, v, 114 writes: 'Its origin is evidently Scriptural, being clearly borrowed from Ruth ii 4 and 2 Paral. xv 2.'

[9] Biblical texts are quoted from the Revised Version; in some places, however, I have left out the copula in order to bring out the original wording.

[10] K. Frör, *op. cit.*, 575.

[11] J. A. Jungmann, *op. cit.*, 448.—On p. 446 ff. he mentions several other explanations, e.g.: 'dass . . . wenn der Priester das Gebet aller Gott darbringt, der Herr ihnen nahe sein und Gottes Gnade Ihr Beten begleiten möge', but he remarks that this idea does not explain the *greeting*-form.

[12] K. Frör, *op. cit.*, 573; this last interpretation is quoted from the German liturgical reformer Wilhelm Löhe (1853).—Frör's parallel with the *Maranatha* is derived from Wetter; this Swedish scholar (*Altchristliche Liturgien*, I *das christliche Mysterium* (1921)) gave an interpretation of the early Christian liturgy as an ancient mystery-cult; though his book contains several interesting observations, his method was arbitrary and his views have rightly been abandoned.

[13] It is of course certain that Paul wanted his letters to be read to the whole congregation and even to others (Col. 4:16), but is it reasonable to suppose that 1 Cor. was read as an introduction to a communion service? It would take us too far, if we were to discuss this point here; let it only be said that the chronological difference should not be overlooked.

[14] A farewell greeting with religious content, like our Dutch 'Adieu' (= à Dieu) or the old 'God bless you' and 'God speed' are greetings that can only be used in that situation. The meaning does not depend on the form, but on the situation.

[15] Neither W. O. E. Oesterley, *The Jewish background of the Christian Liturgy* (1925) nor C. W. Dugmore, *The influence of the synagogue upon the divine office* (1944) mentions it.

[16] Cf. W. Ewing, 'Greeting', in J. Hastings, DCG (1906), i, 692 f.

[17] The rabbinic material in SB i, 380 ff., on Matt. 5:47 and ii, 584 f., on John 20:19.—Billerbeck mentions one text, Mishna Berakoth, ix, 5, where influence of Ruth 2:4 is found, but he adds: it 'ist so unbestimmt gehalten, dass sie ziemlich wertlos erscheint. In der rabbin. Literatur haben wir kein Beispiel gefunden, dass man sich beim Gruss irgendwie nach jener Verordnung gerichtet hätte.'— In the OT the formula 'Peace on you' is the usual form of greeting, Gen. 43:23; Judges 19:20; 1 Sam. 25:6, etc.; see the important pages on greeting written by J. Pedersen, *Israel, its life and culture* (1926), i–ii, 202 f., 303 f., 524 f.—In the other semitic languages the same form is found.

[18] See also Acta Thomae 27: 'And the Lord was revealed to them by a voice, saying: Peace be unto you, brethren' (tr. M. R. James, p. 376) after the sealing of Gundaphorus and Gad. Later on they see the appearance of a youth who is Jesus. Cf. with this the use of the Dialogue in Hippolytus, ed. Dix, 39.

[19] Cf. Jungmann, *op. cit.*, 449.

[20] F. Blass and A. Debrunner, *Neutestamentliche Grammatik*[7] (1943), § 442, 10: 'und ebenso'.

[21] So Chrysostomus, In 2 Tim. hom. 10, 3 (PG, 62, 659), as cited by Jungmann, *op. cit.*, 449, n. 16, and Theodorus Mops., *Commentary on the Lord's Prayer and on the Sacraments*, ed. A. Mingana (1933), vol. vi of *Woodbrooke Studies*, 90 ff.: he speaks of 'an ordinance found in the church from the beginning'.

[22] Especially in the citing of OT texts, see W. Foerster in TWNT iii, 1085 ff.

[23] So by Jungmann, *op. cit.*, 449 and F. L. Cross (ed.), *The Oxford Dictionary of the Christian Church* (1957), 414, s.v. *Dominus Vobiscum*.

[24] Cf. the Hebrew Lexicon of L. Köhler, that on the NT by Walter Bauer and on the Syriac of J. Payne Smith, s.vv.

[25] It is significant that the voluminous TWNT does not contain the word μετά and has nothing relevant under εἰμι in Bd. ii, 396 ff.

[26] A. H. McNeile, *The Gospel according to St. Matthew* (1915), 437.—Cf. the interesting remark of the Syriac Didascalia 21, ed. R. H. Connolly (1929), 180. 'But now *by His working is He with us, but visibly He is absent*, because He has ascended to the heights of heaven and sat at the right hand of His Father.'

[27] C. H. Dodd, 'Matthew and Paul', in *New Testament Studies* (1953), 61.

[28] O. Michel, 'Der Abschluss des Matthäusevangeliums', in *Evangelische Theologie* 10 (1950–51), 16–26, n. 86.—BGDW (1957), col. 1006, gives the translation 'Beistand'; that is right so far as it goes, but not sufficient, as the rest of this paper will prove.

[29] Cf. G. F. Moore, *Judaism* (1932), i, 434 ff. and index, ii, 446, s.v., 'Name', i, 429 f.

[30] E.g. 1 Chron. 4:10; Luke 1:66; Acts 11:21, and the note of A. Plummer, *The Gospel according to St. Luke* (1922), 38.

[31] Cf. Moore, *op. cit.*, i, 401 ff.; Th. C. Vriezen, *Hoofdlÿnen der Theologie van het Oude Testament*,[2] (1954), 259.

[32] See Epist. Jer. 6 to the exiles in Babylon: 'For my angel is with you'.— Apoc. Abrah. X, transl. G. H. Box (London 1919), p. 79: 'Stand up, Abraham! Go without fear; be right glad and rejoice; and *I am with thee*', says the angel Jaoel, bearer of the ineffable Name (p. 46) who has 'been sent to thee to strengthen thee and bless thee in the name of God.'—In Hermas, Mand. v, 1, 7, vi, 2, 3, xii, 3, 3; Sim. v, 3, 4, v, 7, 6 speak of the guiding angel of Hermas.

[33] C. H. Dodd, *The Apostolic Preaching and its Developments* (new edn. 1944), 27 f.

[34] The great attention given here to Joseph makes him a type of Christ, who also suffered from the zeal of his brethren (Matt. 27:18), Whose way went through ignominy to glory (Luke 24:26); cf. also Acts 7:9 f., 10:38; Luke 2:52.

[35] 1 Sam. 10:6 f. LXX: καὶ ἐφαλεῖται ἐπὶ σὲ πνεῦμα κυρίου καὶ προφητεύσεις μετ' αὐτῶν καὶ στραφήσῃ εἰς ἄνδρα ἄλλον. καὶ ἔσται ὅταν ἥξει τὰ σημεῖα ταῦτα ἐπὶ σέ, ποίει πάντα, ὅσα ἐὰν εὕρῃ ἡ χείρ σου, ὅτι θεὸς μετὰ σοῦ = Josephus, Ant. VI, 7, 2, § 56–57, καὶ γενόμενος ἔνθους προφητεύσεις σὺν αὐτοῖς, ὡς πάνθ' ὀντιοῦν ὁρῶντα ἐκπλήττεσθαί τε καὶ θαυμάζειν, λέγοντα πόθεν εἰς τοῦτ' εὐδαιμονίας ὁ Κείσου παῖς παρῆλθεν · ὅταν δέ σοι ταῦτα γένηται τὰ σημεῖα, τὸν θεὸν ἴσθι μετὰ σοῦ τυγχάνοντα.

[36] Because the early Christians read the Bible in its Greek form, we take the LXX as a basis. In most cases the expression renders *hāyāh 'im*; sometimes like Gen. 21:20, 39:2–3; Judges 1:19; Hag. 1:13, 2:4 it stands for the preposition *'eth*, without change of meaning. In Joshua 22:31 it is a translation of *bᵉthûkh*; in Num. 14:42; Deut. 1:42 of *bᵉkirbᵉkhem*. In Gen. 35:3 LXX has an interesting explanatory gloss: MT God 'was with me in the way which I went' = LXX ἦν μετ' ἐμοῦ καὶ διέσωσέν με ἐν τῇ ὁδῷ. It is added by the LXX in Esther 6:13; Isa. 58:11 and Jer. 1:17; the texts in Judith and 3 Macc. are of course additional material of LXX.

[37] For the sake of completeness, since not all texts can be mentioned in the text, I give here the full list of texts where the expression is found in the OT. The distribution is interesting (see p. 284): Gen. 21:20, 22, 26:3, 24, 28,

28:15, 20, 31:3, 5, 13, 35:3, 39:2, 3, 21, 23, 48:21; Exod. 3:12, 10:10, 18:19; Num. 14:42, 23:21; Deut. 1:42, 2:7, 20:1, 31:23 32:12; Joshua 1:5, 9, 17, 3:7, 6:27, 7:12, 14:12, 22:31; Judges 1:19, 2:10, 6:12, 13, 16; Ruth 2:4; 1 Sam. 3:19, 10:7, 16:18, 17:37, 18:14, 28, 20:13 (28:16); 2 Sam. 5:10, 7:3, 9, 14:17; 1 Kings 1:37, 8:57, 11:38; 2 Kings 18:7; 1 Chron. 11:9, 17:2, 8, 22:11, 16, 18, 28:20; 2 Chron. 1:1, 13:12, 15:2, 9, 17:3, 19:11, 20:17, 25:7, 32:8, 35:21, 36:23; 1 Ezra 1:25, 2:3; 2 Ezra 1:3; Esther 6:13; Judith 5:17, 13:11; 3 Macc. 6:15; Ps. 22 (23):4, 45(46):8, 12, 90(91):15; Amos 5:14; Hag. 1:13, 2:4; Zech. 8:23, 10:5; Isa. 8:8, 10, 43:2, 5, 58:11; Jer. 1:8, 17, 19, 15:20, 20:11, 26:28, 49:11.

[38] Cf., e.g., G. E. Wright, *God who acts* (1952); J. de Groot-A. R. Hulst, *Macht en wil, de verkondiging van het O.T. aangaande God*, (n.y.).

[39] G. H. Dalman, *Aramäisch-neuhebräisches Handwörterbuch*[2] (1922), 296 b.

[40] Midrash Rabbah, Genesis, tr. H. Freedman (1939), ii, 633, 637 f., 701 f.— In Gen. 31:5 '*immādhî* was read as '*immūdhî* my pillar, support, *l.c.*, 677.

[41] Midrash Rabbah, Exodus, tr. S. M. Lehrman (1939), 63.

[42] Midrash Rabbah, Genesis, p. 807.

[43] See E. Schürer, *Geschichte des jüdischen Volkes im Zeitalter Jesu Christi*[3-4] (1901), 303.

[44] A well-known Greek combination, see: H. G. Liddell-R. Scott, *A Greek-English Lexicon* (1940), ii, 1260, and frequent in Josephus, cf. A. Schlatter, *Die Theologie des Judentums nach dem Bericht des Josephus* (1932), 37, 96 ff.

[45] In Ant. XIII, 10, 7 § 300 speaking about the three offices God had given to John Hyrcanus (high-priest, king and prophet), he says: συνῆν γὰρ αὐτῷ τὸ θεῖον, καὶ τὴν τῶν μελλόντων πρόγνωσιν παρεῖχεν αὐτῷ τ᾽ εἰδέναι καὶ προλέγειν, = B.J. I, 2, 8, § 69, ὁμίλει γὰρ αὐτῷ τὸ δαιμόνιον ὡς μηδὲν τῶν μελλόντων ἀγνοεῖν. It is remarkable that it is not the phrase εἶναι μετά which is used, but συνεῖναι. Was the latter expression more appropriate according to Josephus, more intimate? If this inference is correct it sheds some light upon our investigation.

[46] See above, p. 272.

[47] Th. C. Vriezen, *Oud-Israelietische Geschriften* (1948), 220; H. H. Rowley, *The Growth of the Old Testament* (1950), 150; O. Eissfeld, *Einleitung in das Alte Testament* (1956), 595: all post-exilic date with perhaps older material in it.

[48] The etymology of Boaz as 'in him is power' is rejected as old-fashioned by H. A. Redpath, 'Boaz', in HDB i, 308, but in the newest dictionary known to me: *Bijbels Woordenboek* (1954–1957), kol. 198 it is still maintained.

[49] See: Gen. 21:22, 39:2 (cf. v. 3); Num. 23:21; Deut. 2:7, 20:1; Joshua 22:31; 1 Sam. 10:7, 16:18, 18:28; 2 Sam. 5:10, 7:3; 1 Chron. 11:9, 17:2; 2 Chron. 1:1, 13:12, 15:9, 20:17, 35:21; Esther 6:13; Judith 13:11; Ps. 45(46)8, 12; Zech. 8:23; Isa. 8:8, 10; Jer. 20:11.

[50] εὐλογήσαι; for the ending see: Blass-Debrunner, *op. cit.*, § 85.

[51] In view of Num. 10:35 f. (cf. A. H. Edelkoort, *Numeri* (1930), 118 f.) and 1 Sam. 4:6 as compared with vs. 3 one would have expected such a connection. But Num. 14:42; Deut. 1:42 show that there is no such direct relation. There is here also a distance between popular belief and God's revelation, as is clearly witnessed by Amos 5:14, cf. also Jer. 7. Obedience is essential (1 Sam. 15:22 f.,

important because the 'being of God with him' plays such a large part in the story of Saul, p. 285 f.), cf. p. 279.

[52] Num. 14:42, 23:21; Deut. 1:42, 2:7, 20:1, 32:12; Joshua 7:12, 22:31; 1 Kings 8:57; 2 Chron. 25:7, 32:8; Judith 5:17, 13:11; 3 Macc. 6:15; Amos 5:14; Zech. 8:23, 10:5; Isa. 8:8, 10, 43:2, 5, 58:11; Jer. 49:11. Compare p. 300, n. 37.

[53] Cf. Pedersen, *op. cit.*, iii–iv, 35: 'Yahweh's promise to be with Gideon means: that he needs the blessing for his deed, but it is further added that he is to act with a special force. . . . It was Yahweh's soul which filled him and was active in him.'

[54] Moore, *op. cit.*, i, 536 ff.

[55] F. Büchsel, *Der Geist Gottes im Neuen Testament* (1926), 122.

[56] For late Jewish material see the references in SB iv, 2, 1229 f., Register s.v. Geist, heiliger; also H. Gunkel, *Die Wirkungen des heiligen Geistes nach der populären Anschauung der apostolischen Zeit und der Lehre des Apostels Paulus*[3] (1909), 50 f.; Büchsel, *op. cit.*, 123 ff.

[57] See the article of O. Michel, quoted above p. 300, n. 28, adopted by J. Jeremias, *Jesu Verheissung für die Völker* (1956), 33.

[58] It is interesting to see that Justin Martyr who quoted Isa. 7:14 on several occasions (Dial. 43:8, 67:1, 71:3, 84) always cites the first half about the virgin birth only. In Apol. 33 the full text is quoted, though not with the name IMMANUEL (p. 278) but with the Greek translation; in the course of his explanation he speaks about the 'power' of God by which it happened and cites Luke 1:31 f.; then he explains the name 'Jesus' but does not speak about 'God with us'.

[59] The name 'Jesus' is explained in Matt. 1:21; Matthew is the only one among the Evangelists who does so and this is the more striking since the idea of 'saving' is not prominent in his gospel, see my paper: *L'usage de σώζειν 'sauver' et ses dérivés dans les évangiles synoptiques*, in *La Formation des Evangiles* (1957), 178 ff. These names had a meaning which is of the utmost importance for the understanding of the gospel.

[60] Vs. 29 διελογίζετο ποταπὸς εἴη ὁ ἀσπασμὸς οὗτος, cf. p. 272 and 281 f.

[61] J. M. Creed, *The Gospel according to St. Luke* (1930), 20: 'The angel authenticates his message.' Note the introduction with 'behold'. In the stories of Moses, Gideon, Saul and Jeremiah too one finds this authentication by a sign when they do not dare to believe the message.

[62] See HRCS, s.v.

[63] J. Behm in TWNT v, 812, and W. Bauer, *op. cit.*, col. 1227, s.v. παράκλητος translate it by 'Helfer'; He is called to the aid of the disciples.

[64] Cf. E. Benz, 'Paulus als Visionär', in *Abhandlungen der Akademie der Wissenschaften und der Literatur in Mainz*, Geisteswissenschaftliche Klasse 1952, No. 2, 81–121.

[65] RV translates 'farewell', taking it in the ordinary Greek sense at the end of letters. In view of the following imperatives and Phil. 4:4 'rejoice' seems preferable; the greeting comes in vs. 13. This interpretation is given by H. Windisch, *Der zweite Korintherbrief* (1924), 426 and E. B. Allo, *Second Epître aux Corinthiens* (1956), 343.

[66] As far as Rom. 15:33 is concerned this depends of course on the decision whether Rom. 16 is taken as a separate epistle or as an original part of Romans. I do not accept the hypothesis that ch. 16 was an epistle to Ephesus, but cannot argue the question here, see: H. Lietzmann, *An die Römer*[3] (1928), 128 ff.

[67] See on the expression 'God of peace', O. Michel, *Der Brief an die Römer* (1955), 337, n. 3; on 'peace' the fine monograph of W. S. van Leeuwen, *Eirene in het Nieuwe Testament* (1940 (Leyden thesis)).

[68] See my remarks on 1 Thess. 5:23 in 'Aramaeismen bij Paulus', in *Vox Theologica* 14 (1943), 122 f.

[69] Blass-Debrunner, *op. cit.*, § 128, 5 suggests that in Luke 1:28 we should add εἴη, as is usually done, but see above p. 283.

[70] Cf. Isa. 45:14; Zech. 8:23 and the commentary of J. Moffat, *The First Epistle of Paul to the Corinthians* (1938), 224 f.; F. W. Grosheide, *De Eerste Brief aan de Kerk van Korinthe* (1957), 371.

[71] See N. A. Waaning, *Onderzoek naar het gebruik van ΠΝΕΥΜΑ bij Paulus* (1939 (thesis: Amsterdam Free University)), 132 f.—In this text 'your' is plural.

[72] We left one text undiscussed, Rev. 21:3, because it is purely eschatological and therefore on a different level from those we are discussing.

[73] Cf. the consecration prayers in the Church Order of Hippolytus. This is the origin of the patristic interpretation, p. 299, n. 21. The variety of the gifts of the one Holy Spirit is given by Paul, 1 Cor. 12:8 ff. and parallel texts.

[74] H. Weinel, *Die Wirkungen des Geistes und der Geister im nachapostolischen Zeitlater bis auf Irenäus* (1899).

[75] G. Harder, *Paulus und das Gebet* (1936), 163 ff.

[76] Cf. also the Syriac Didascalia ch. 1, ed. R. H. Connolly (1929), p. 2: 'God's planting and the holy vineyard of His Catholic Church, the elect who rely on the simplicity of the fear of the Lord, who by their faith inherit His everlasting kingdom, who *have received the power and fellowship of His holy Spirit*, and by Him are armed and made firm in the fear of Him', etc., and ch. 26, p. 246: '*A believer is filled with the Holy Spirit* and an unbeliever with an unclean spirit', etc.; the whole following paragraph is relevant, because it shows that this teaching was not a pious theory, but reality, for on that basis he combats the view of over-anxious people who want to re-introduce all sorts of baptismal rites in the Christian church, a Jewish practice which brings them again under the slavery of the 'Second Legislation'.

[77] I cannot remember having come across this text in recent discussions on the liturgy of early Christianity. This side of the picture is not found in Justin Martyr's famous account in his Apology, but it should not be forgotten that these contemporaries wrote for different readers, Justin's information being destined for outsiders, Hermas addressing his fellow-Christians. It may be, however, that Justin's phrase about the 'president' who prays ὅση δύναμις αὐτῷ has a double meaning: not only according to his personal ability (cf. Apol. 13:1, 55:8, Dial. 80:3), but also according to the power of the Spirit granted to him (67:5).

[78] The English quotations are taken from the *Ante-Nicene Christian Library*, vol. i.—Extremely helpful is the commentary of M. Dibelius, *Der Hirt des Hermas* (1923) who pointed out the special character of this conception.

304   *W. C. van Unnik*

[79] For this translation see Dibelius, *op. cit.*, 535.

[80] Prayers are conceived here as 'spiritual sacrifices', see the note of E. G. Selwyn, *The First Epistle of St. Peter* (1946), 160 ff. on 1 Pet. 2:5 and Tertullian, De Oratione, 28.

[81] Tertullian, De Oratione, 12.

[82] Cf. also Hermas, Sim. ii, 5 ff. about the prayer of the poor and the rich: 'the poor man is rich in intercession and thanksgiving, and his intercession has great power with God . . . the intercession of the poor man is acceptable and influential with God'; that of the rich man misses this power, because he is distracted by his riches and worldly cares, but he can be helped by giving alms to the poor man: 'and the poor man, being helped by the rich, intercedes for him, giving thanks to God for him who bestows gifts upon him'.

[83] Cf. the same expression in Hermas, Vis. iii, 10, 9: 'Your doubts make you senseless and the fact that you have not your hearts turned towards the Lord': Dibelius, following Funk here, refers to the 'Sursum Corda'. They are 'senseless' as regards heavenly revelations: they are not understood, because there is doubt (the spirit is not in the right state) and their heart (see below, n. 89) is not directed towards the Lord. In the note of Dibelius the connection with the Preface is not clarified; there is no direct dependence on either side, but both spring from the same 'spiritual' source.

[84] Cf. the interesting 'Exkurs' of Dibelius on the Pneumatology of Hermas, *p. cit.*, 517 ff.

[85] In Did. ix–x some formularies for the thanksgiving are given, but at the end it is said: 'but permit the prophets to thank as much as they wish'; this is of course not the prophet's private wish; he speaks 'in the Spirit'. This rule resembles Justin's 'according to his own ability' (Apol. 67:5) and that in Hippolytus' Church Order, ed. Dix, 19. These testimonies show that there was not yet any fixed formulary absolutely prescribed. Hippolytus has to shield bishops who use formularies against criticism, which shows that the general feeling was against these set forms. The fact that in Rome in the second century the bishops formulated the eucharistic prayer 'according to their ability' puts them on a line with the prophets of the Didache; it shows again that this prayer was seen as an action inspired by the Holy Spirit.

[86] For the 'mos quibusdam' to sit down on a couch after prayer they appealed to Hermas, Sim., v, 1; his book was considered part of Scripture, see the commentary of G. F. Diercks, *Tertullianus De Oratione* (1947), 159 ff. (thesis: Amsterdam). The canonical authority of Hermas in many circles of the early church is well-known, see A. Harnack, *Geschichte der altchristlichen Literatur*, Bd. I *Ueberlieferung und Bestand* (1893), 51 ff. If, *teste* Tertullian, Hermas was followed in such a minor point, his ideas must have been very influential.

[87] See above, n. 81, cf. also ch. 1 and 28 f. for the primary importance of the Spirit in prayer.—In the writings of Tertullian there is no trace of the dialogue; see E. Dekkers, *Tertullianus en de geschiedenis der Liturgie* (1947). This may be purely accidental in view of his works as a liturgical source. At any rate I do not venture to draw any inference from his silence.

[88] The 'salutation' and the 'sursum corda' are taken together, as they stand in Hippolytus, cf. p. 298, n. 4.

[89] W. Bauer, *op. cit.*, col. 797: 'Mittelpunkt u. Quelle des geistigen Lebens

mit seinem Denken, Wollen, Fühlen . . . beim natürl. wie beim erlösten Menschen.'

[90] When we have so explained the meaning of the 'Dominus vobiscum' and its legitimate place in the worship of the second-century church, it seems permissible to infer that the formulae of the Eastern Liturgies using the form with 'Peace' or 'the grace of the Lord with you' are later developments, adopting either the ordinary salutation or a more 'rational' text (cf. p. 274) in the dialogue. If this inference is sound, it witnesses to a change in the conception of the Liturgy. The decision on this point must be left to further research.

DIDACHE, KERYGMA AND EVANGELION

by

H. G. WOOD

I DO not propose to re-examine the use in early Christian litera-ture of the three terms which provide a title for this paper. I am starting from the now generally accepted theory that the Kerygma and the Didache, denoting the Apostolic Preaching and the Apos-tolic Teaching, are to be distinguished and that the traditions in which the one and the other were embodied, whether in oral or literary form, were, so to speak, separate entities, serving distinct purposes—traditions which were eventually associated in the gospel, when Matthew and Luke re-edited and enlarged Mark's gospel. This view of the relation of Didache and Kerygma to Evangelion is summarized conveniently in this passage from Bultmann, *Theology of the New Testament*, i, 86:

> The reason that the sayings of the Lord, which at first were handed down separately from the Christological Kerugma, came more and more to be taken up into 'the gospel' (in Mark, still sparingly, whereas Matthew and Luke combine the Kerugma and the tradition of Jesus' sayings into a unity) is that, while missionary preaching continued, preaching to Christian congregations took on ever-increasing impor-tance, and for these already believing congregations, Jesus in the role of 'Teacher' had become important again.

While I am not inclined to follow Dom. Butler and Dr. Austin Farrer in their attempts to persuade us to dispense with Q, I am disposed to think that the Didache and the Kerygma have been too rigidly separated, that some elements of the teaching of Jesus may have been incorporated in the Christological Kerygma from the first, and that the taking up of the sayings of the Lord into the gospel, while it may well have been desirable in preaching to Christian congregations, was discovered to be an element of in-creasing importance in missionary preaching. It was precisely because missionary preaching continued, that the gospel needed to be presented in the forms given to it by Matthew and Luke.

In C. H. Dodd's masterly and still indispensable study of the Apostolic Preaching and its developments, the Kerygma as analysed in the table at the end of the book, contains no direct reference to the sayings of Jesus. In Acts, there is in the Kerygma an appeal to the mighty works which God did through Jesus, and this is evidence of the Divine approval of Jesus and of the presence of God with him. For the rest, the main themes are the Crucifixion and the Resurrection: the offer of the remission of sins in the name of Jesus: the assertions that Jesus is to be our judge, and that all that has happened, has happened according to the Scriptures. The Kerygma according to Paul concentrates on these main themes, and omits the mighty works as well as the words of the Lord. It is, however, unwise to assume that the primitive Christological Kerygma was at any time confined within such limits. Recent studies of what may be called the Apostolic Paradosis suggest that Kerygma and Didache were distilled out of a tradition that included both. Such is the contention of Harald Riesenfeld in his paper, *The Gospel Tradition and its Beginnings*. He suggests that many of the logia of Jesus, particularly passages which manifest poetic form, were not only memorable but actually designed to be memorized. Jesus, like a Rabbi, entrusted his word to chosen disciples. An interesting argument leads him to the following conclusion: 'It was owing to the tradition of the words and deeds of Jesus which began from Jesus himself that the primitive Church had the basis for its faith'.[1] In an important article '*Paradosis et Kyrios*', Oscar Cullmann argued that when Paul 1 Cor. 11:23 says, 'I received from the Lord' he is identifying Kyrios and Paradosis. The account of the Last Supper which Paul received from the Lord, came to him not by special revelation or vision, but from the Apostolic Tradition, and the Apostolic Tradition is regarded as the word of the Lord. However, Cullmann thinks that the designation *Kyrios* does not point to the historic Jesus, as the chronological starting-point and first link in the chain of transmission. It refers rather to the Lord raised to the right hand of God, who would be for Paul the true author of the whole tradition as it develops in the bosom of the Apostolic Church. In Cullmann's view this hypothesis gives the best explanation of the fact that the Apostolic Paradosis could be identified by Paul

purely and simply with the Kyrios. The Lord is to be found behind and active in the transmission of the tradition, and not only
at its commencement. The risen Christ is himself the author of
the Gospel, of which he is at the same time the theme.[2] This interpretation of Paul's view of the relation of Paradosis to Kyrios may
be accepted without thereby excluding Riesenfeld's suggestion
that the Apostolic Tradition was initiated by Jesus himself during
his ministry. For Paul the tradition is Apostolic because it is based
on the recollections of those who knew the Lord in the days of
his flesh and who were qualified to be witnesses of his resurrection. It is as a witness to the resurrection that Paul claims his place
among the Apostles, and there can be no successors to the
Apostles so far as their original calling and function are concerned.

What, then, did the Paradosis, the Apostolic Tradition, contain? It is natural to conceive it as parallel to Rabbinic tradition
with the two strands, the Halacha and the Haggada, the first concerned with ethical teaching, and the second with stories and doctrine. So of the Christian Paradosis in the time of Paul, Cullmann
says:

On the one hand, it is concerned with moral rules, which like the
Halacha, bear on the life of the faithful (see 1 Cor. 11:2; 2 Thess. 3:6;
Rom. 6:17; Phil. 4:9; Col. 2:6). On the other, we have a summary of
the Christian message, conceived in the fashion of a credal formula and
bringing together the facts of the life of Jesus and their theological
interpretation (1 Cor. 15:3 f.). Finally, we have isolated stories of the
life of Jesus: (1 Cor. 11:23 f.).

Cullmann adds:

The primitive Paradosis probably consisted of the summary of the
Kerygma. But by the time of the Apostle Paul, the tradition has already
advanced a step: from now on it is concerned equally with the logia of
Jesus and stories of his life.[3]

Here Cullmann seems to be identifying the primitive Paradosis
with the Kerygma, the Apostolic Preaching as Dodd summarized
it in the table at the end of his book, with what Bultmann calls
the Christological Kerygma. But this Christological Kerygma is
in the first instance, the presentation of the Gospel to Jewish
hearers. It emphasizes certain elements in the Apostolic Paradosis,
the mighty works, the crucifixion and resurrection of Jesus, and
the evidence from prophecy that in these events God's purpose

may be discerned, which formed the kernel of the Kerygma, but this Kerygma need never have constituted the whole of the primitive Paradosis. As Bultmann and Dodd both hold, the Didache which corresponds to the Halacha belonged to the primitive Paradosis from the beginning, though it figures little in the Christological Kerygma. It should be noted, however, that a Kerygma which concentrated on the story of the Passion, on the events which led up to it, and on stories of healing, cannot have been silent with regard to sayings of Jesus. Too many logia are too closely associated with the deeds of Jesus and the events of his life, to be ignored in the Christological Kerygma. So I doubt whether concern with the logia of Jesus and with stories of his life represents a development of the primitive Paradosis. It contained both Didache and Kerygma from the start.

Perhaps we have paid too little attention to Luke's sentences introductory to his gospel and to Acts. He claims to be basing his narrative on the Apostolic Paradosis, on tradition handed on by those who from the beginning were eye-witnesses and ministers of the word, but he implies that those traditions were not in order. Incidentally, if only Luke had said that the eye-witnesses and ministers of the word were among the many who had undertaken to compile a narrative of the things which have been accomplished among us, it would have strengthened Dr. Austin Farrer's case enormously. For having claimed that Luke, when he said 'many' must have meant two—like those hosts and hostesses who say 'Take as many as you like, take two'—Dr. Farrer might then have added that one of the two was by an eye-witness, namely Matthew, and the other by a minister of the word, namely Mark, who went with Paul and Barnabas to Cyprus as minister.[4] But unfortunately, it is the traditions, not the narratives, that Luke attributes to eye-witnesses and ministers, and on these traditions some sort of order has to be imposed. Luke implies that the Paradosis included many elements and that the traditions regarding the words and works of Jesus were not an ordered whole, but consisted of detached groups of sayings or incidents and often of isolated sayings or incidents. When Luke says he has tried to write things in order, he may not be contrasting his narrative with earlier narratives, but simply claiming to put together the disorderly fragments of the Paradosis in an orderly manner. When he describes his gospel in the opening of Acts, he says it was a record of all that Jesus began to do and to teach. It is tempting, though probably mistaken, to see in this phrase a reference to his two main sources, Mark and Q! Manifestly, when Luke wrote of the things accomplished in the Christian dispensation, he was not thinking only of the death and resurrection of Jesus. He had in mind both the mighty works and the teachings of Jesus. For Luke these are an essential part of the Kerygma, and so of the Evangelion.

It is of course not surprising that by the time the gospel of Luke is written, the teaching of Jesus is associated with the record of all that Jesus began to do. But this is not the intrusion of an alien element into the primitive Christological Kerygma, nor is it without its place in the presentation of the gospel to the Gentiles. In the *Demonstration of the Apostolic Preaching*, Irenæus describes the Apostles as witnesses in the following terms:

His disciples, the witnesses of all His good deeds and of His teachings and His sufferings and death and resurrection, and of his ascension into heaven after His bodily resurrection—these were the apostles, who after (receiving) the power of the Holy Spirit were sent forth by Him into all the world, and wrought the calling of the Gentiles, showing to mankind the way of life, to turn them from idols and fornication and covetousness, cleansing their souls and bodies by the baptism of water and of the Holy Spirit: which Holy Spirit they had received of the Lord, and they distributed and imparted It to them that believed: and thus they ordered and established the Churches.[5]

Here, Irenæus takes it for granted that the teachings are included in the Apostolic witness and are indeed a vital element in the Kerygma for the Gentiles. It should be noted that the Kerygma for the Gentiles differed from the Kerygma for Jewish hearers in two particulars. First, the faith in God the Creator which was implied in the Kerygma as represented in the speeches in Acts had to be made explicit when the preachers turned to the Gentiles. Acts 14:15–7 is also an early proclamation of the gospel, and it claims to convert Gentiles from the worship of idols to faith in the living God. Paul mentions this point when describing the conversion of the Thessalonians,[6] and Irenaeus regards this as the normal foundation of the effective calling of all Gentiles. But whereas Paul puts second the Christian hope—the Thessalonians have turned from idols to the living and true God and *await His Son from Heaven*—Irenaeus puts second the moral change, the turning from fornication and covetousness through the way of life for mankind revealed in the teachings of Jesus. Clearly the tradition of the teaching of Jesus belongs now to the Kerygma. It has its place in missionary preaching and makes an effective appeal to Gentile hearers.

That the sayings of Jesus had an arresting and converting power is manifest, and Gentiles responded more readily than Jews. Trypho the Jew admits that the precepts contained in what Christians call the gospel are wonderful and great, but so great and wonderful that it is doubtful whether any one can keep them.[7] Irenaeus, on the other hand, speaks for Gentiles when he contrasts the simplicity and directness of the teaching of Jesus with the complexities of the Jewish Law.

That not by the much-speaking of the law, but by the brevity of faith and love, men were to be saved, Isaiah says thus: 'A word brief and short in righteousness: for a short word will God make in the whole world.' And therefore the apostle Paul says: 'Love is the fulfilling of the law': for he who loves God has fulfilled the law. Moreover the Lord when he was asked which is the first commandment, said: 'Thou shalt love the Lord thy God with all thy heart and with all thy strength. And the second is like unto it: Thou shalt love thy neighbour as thyself. On these two commandments, He says, all the law hangeth and the prophets.' So then by our faith in Him, He has made our love to God and our neighbour to grow, making us godly and righteous and good. And therefore a *short word* has God made on the earth in the world.[8]

Justin Martyr bears witness to the same characteristic of the sayings of Jesus, when he says in his first *Apology*: 'Short and concise are the words that have come from Him: for he was no Sophist, but His speech was God's power.'[9] The sayings have converting power. In the three chapters that follow Justin cites many of the teachings of Jesus. No doubt he selects such teachings as may convince the Emperor of the innocent life and character of Christians. Naturally he included 'Render unto Caesar' as proof of the loyalty of Christians. The Emperor has nothing to fear from such citizens. But when Justin starts from the Lord's demand for chastity and purity, and continues with teachings about universal love, nonresistance, generous charity and freedom from care for riches, he is thinking of the same deliverance from fornication and covetousness which Irenaeus singled out as essential features of conversion among Gentiles. Incidentally, Justin also emphasizes faith in God as creator. This is clear from the form in which he cites the first great commandment. 'Thou shalt worship the Lord God and Him only should thou serve with thy whole heart and with all thy strength,—*the Lord God who made thee.*' In the same context he makes a similar addition to the saying, There is none good save only *God who made all things.*[10] The gospel, the Christological Kerygma itself made ethical monotheism an effective reality for men who were living in what Klausner rightly called 'a world decaying for lack of God and social morality.' If in ethical monotheism we find the treasures of Israel, then it is true that Jesus took the treasures of Israel and made them available for mankind.

There is a story told of Olive Schreiner as a young girl, reading the Sermon on the Mount and rushing into her mother's drawing-room and saying, 'Look, Mother! Now we can live like this!' It seems to me that it is in some such spirit that Justin cites the brief concise words of Jesus and that Irenaeus writes of the short word of God, which through faith in Christ and the fellowship of the Holy Spirit in the Church, makes our love to God and our neighbour grow, making us godly and righteous and good. Didache and Kerygma together make up Evangelion.

NOTES

[1] Professor Harald Riesenfeld's address delivered at the Opening Session of the Congress on 'The Four Gospels in 1957' in Oxford on September 6 has been published by A. R. Mowbray Co., Ltd. under the title, *The Gospel Tradition and its Beginnings: a study in the Limits of 'Form-geschichte.'* In it he argues the case for recognizing that the primitive Gospel-tradition, the original Apostolic Paradosis, must have been a kind of Holy Word, recording both the words and deeds of Jesus. As a negative result of his investigations he claimed that 'The Sitz-im-Leben' and the original source of the Gospel tradition was neither mission preaching nor the communal instruction of the primitive Church' (p. 16). In other words, Kerygma and Didache derive from the Gospel tradition, and did not produce the Gospel tradition by their coalescence.

There is much to be said for the view that the primitive Church had as the basis of its faith a tradition of the words and deeds of Jesus which began from Jesus himself (p. 29). But if we accept this in principle, the limits and the form of the Gospel tradition have still to be determined.

[2] Professor Oscar Cullmann's article, 'Paradosis et Kyrios: le problème de la Tradition dans le Paulinisme', was published in RHPR 1950, No. 1. I have summarized in the text the following passage from p. 15 of the article. '[Le désignation Kyrios] ne viserait pas le Jésus historique, commencement chronologique et premier chaînon de la chaîne de transmission, mais le Seigneur élevé

à la droite de Dieu; ce serait lui le véritable agent de toute la tradion qui se développe au sein de l'Église apostolique. Nous pensons que cette hypothèse explique de la meilleure façon le fait que le paradosis apostolique ait pu être identifiée par Saint Paul purement et simplement avec le Kyrios... Selon l'apôtre, le 'Seigneur' est lui-même à l'oeuvre dans le transmission de ses paroles et de ses oeuvres par la communauté primitive, qu'il agit à travers elle.'

[3] *Op. cit.*, p. 18. 'Quel est, d'apris Saint Paul, le *contenu* de la Paradosis? D'une part, il s'agit de règles morales, qui, à la façon de la 'halacha' se rapporte à la vie des fidèles.... D'autre part, nous avons un résumé du message chrétien conçu à la manière d'une formule de confession et réunissant des faits de la vie de Jésus et leur interprétation theologique... Enfin, des récits isolés de la vie de Jésus.

La paradosis primitive était problement constituée par le résumé du Kerygma. Mais, à l'époque de l'apôtre Paul, la tradition a déjà fait un pas en avant; elle a désormais pour objet également des logia de Jésus et des récits touchant sa vie.'

The material of this article, which also appeared in SJT 1950, 180–97, was incorporated by Dr. Cullmann in his essay 'The Tradition' in *The Early Church*, ed. A. J. B. Higgins (1956), 55–99 [Ed.].

[4] Dr. Austin Farrer's paper, 'On Dispensing with Q' is included in *Studies in the Gospels*: Essays in Memory of R. H. Lightfoot, ed. D. E. Nineham.

Dr. Farrer believes that 'the literary history of the Gospels will turn out to be a simpler matter than we had supposed. St. Matthew will be seen to be an amplified version of St. Mark, based on a decade of habitual preaching, and incorporating oral material, but presupposing no other literary source beside St. Mark himself. St. Luke, in turn, will be found to presuppose St. Matthew and St. Mark, and St. John to presuppose the three others. The whole literary history of the canonical Gospel tradition will be found to be contained in the fourfold canon itself, except in so far as it lies in the Old Testament, the Pseudepigrapha, and the other New Testament writings' (p. 85). But the natural interpretation of Luke's preface to his gospel is that he knew of more than two literary sources. He certainly claims to draw on the original apostolic tradition and there is no reason to suppose that he knew this tradition only in oral form. When Dr. Farrer asks, 'What did the primitive Christians write, beside letters and homilies and gospels?' (p. 61), the answer is, in all probability they had in writing, collections of the logia of Jesus, such as are found in the first four chapters of the Teaching of the Twelve Apostles; collections of Testimonia, or proof-texts from the Old Testament to show that the events of the life of Jesus happened according to the Scriptures: isolated stories like the Pericope Adulterae: and quite possibly documents of a liturgical character or concerned with Church-government.

[5] Irenaeus, *The Apostolic Preaching*, translated by J. Armitage Robinson, 41, p. 106.

[6] 1 Thess. 1:9, 10.

[7] Justin Martyr, *Dialogue with Trypho*, c. 10: Ὑμῶν δὲ καὶ τὰ ἐν τῷ λεγομένῳ εὐαγγελίῳ παραγγέλματα θαυμαστὰ οὕτως καὶ μεγάλα ἐπίσταμαι εἶναι, ὡς ὑπολαμβάνειν μηδένα δύνασθαι φυλάξαι αὐτά.

[8] Irenaeus, *The Apostolic Preaching*, c. 87, p. 141.

[9] Justin Martyr, *Apology* I, c. 14, *ad fin.*: Βραχεῖς δὲ καὶ σύντομοι παρ'

x*

αὐτοῦ λόγοι γεγόνασιν   οὐ γὰρ σοφιστὴς ὑπῆρχεν, ἀλλὰ δύναμις θεοῦ ὁ λόγος αὐτοῦ ἦν.

[10] Justin Martyr, *Apology* I, c. 16: Κύριον τὸν θεόν σόν προσκυνήσεις . . . κύριον τὸν θεὸν τὸν ποιήσαντά σε. Οὐδεὶς ἀγαθὸς εἰ μὴ μόνος ὁ θεὸς ὁ ποιήσας τὰ πάντα. It is not too much to say that in the preaching of the gospel to the Hellenistic world, the thought of God as Creator and Preserver became of primary importance; cf. Bultmann, *Theology of the New Testament*, i, 66–72. In this, the Christian evangelists were continuing the propaganda of Hellenistic Judaism. What Jewish Christian and Hellenistic Jew had in common, faith in the living and true God, stood in the forefront of the gospel for the Gentiles. See further, *The Mind of the Early Converts* by Campbell N. Moody, an original and penetrating study of the Apostolic Fathers and the Apologists, illuminated by the writer's experience as a missionary in Formosa.

LIST OF SUBSCRIBERS

Dr. Sverre Aalan, Vollsveien 79, Jar, Oslo, Norway.
The Rev. D. W. Allen, St. Stephen's House, Oxford.
Rabbi Dr. A. Altmann, 38 Waterpark Road, Salford, 7.
The Rev. J. Amstutz, St. Benet's Hall, Oxford.
D. R. Ap-Thomas, Llansadwrn, Menai Bridge, Anglesey.
L. J. Austin, Department of French Studies, The University, Manchester.

R. S. Barbour, 56 Blacket Place, Edinburgh, 9.
The Rev. J. M. Barkley, Assembly's College, Botanic Avenue, Belfast.
The Rev. Allan Barr, 4 Templeland Road, Edinburgh, 12.
The Rev. Markus Barth, 4846 S. Kimbark Avenue, Chicago, 15. Illinois, U.S.A.
The Rev. G. R. Beasley-Murray, Spurgeon's College, South Norwood Hill, London, S.E.25.
The Rev. Ernest Best, Minterburn Manse, Caledon, N. Ireland.
The Rev. Canon J. S. Bezzant, St. John's College, Cambridge.
Mrs. R. Bilton, 2 Broadway, Tynemouth—*and the following, all sisters of Professor Manson:*
    Mrs. J. Glover, 6 Jackson Street West, North Shields.
    Mrs. S. A. Pullen, The Manse, St. Michael's Road, Aldershot.
    Mrs. J. F. Jackson, Moore House, Whalton, Northumberland.
    Mrs. J. Crosby, 48 Ramsdale Crescent, Sherwood, Nottingham.
    Mrs. J. Spark, 12 Kennersdene, Tynemouth.
    Mrs. G. Sutton, 48 Briarfield Road, Gosforth, Newcastle-upon-Tyne.
The Rev. J. N. Birdsall, Department of Theology, The University, Leeds.
The Rev. E. C. Blackman, 50 Millway, Mill Hill, London, N.W.7.
D. J. Bowden, 118 Highfield Road, Farnworth, Lancs.
John Wick Bowman, 10 Kensington Court, San Anselmo, California, U.S.A.
S. G. F. Brandon, Department of Comparative Religion, The University, Manchester.
Robert G. Bratcher, 317 Zorn Avenue, Louisville, 6, Kentucky, U.S.A.
The Rev. Canon G. E. Brigstocke, Bede College, Durham City.
G. L. Brook, Department of English, The University, Manchester.

The Rev. L. E. Browne, Lucaslands, Highbrook, Ardingly, Sussex.
The Rev. W. R. F. Browning, Great Haseley Rectory, Oxford.
F. F. Bruce, Department of Biblical History and Literature, The University, Sheffield.
R. P. Adrien-M. Brunet, O.P. (University of Montreal), 5375 Notre-Dame-de-Grâce Avenue, Montreal, Canada.
Mrs. Burdess, St. Mary's College, Bangor, N. Wales.
G. Norman Burkhardt, 28 Manor Drive, Manchester, 21.
The Rev. T. A. Burkhill, Ray Lodge, Woodford Green, Essex.
Mrs. Butt, 11 Pitt Street, Gloucester.
The Rev. F. C. Buxton, The Manse, 39 Oakfields Avenue, Knebworth, Herts.

Henry J. Cadbury, 774 Millbrook Lane, Haverford, Pa., U.S.A.
The Rev. Dr. W. H. Cadman, 197 Woodstock Road, Oxford.
Colin P. Campbell, Department of Pathology, The University, Manchester.
H. Chadwick, Christ Church, Oxford.
John V. Chamberlain, Goucher College, Towson, 4, Maryland, U.S.A.
Dr. Henri Clavier, Faculté de Théologie Protestante, Université de Strasbourg.
The Rev. R. E. Clements, 5 Buchanan Road, Sheffield, 5.
The Venerable J. O. Cobham, The College, Durham.
The Rev. R. J. Coggins, St. Stephen's House, Oxford.
The Rev. Richard J. Connell, Meadow, Upper Drive, Angmering-on-Sea, Sussex.
Hans Conzelmann, The University, Zurich.
W. Mansfield Cooper, The Vice-Chancellor, The University, Manchester.
R. A. Cordingley, Department of Architecture, The University, Manchester.
The Rev. R. Corke, 10 Kirkmoor Road, Clitheroe, Lancs.
The Rev. John B. Corston, Pine Hill Divinity Hall, Halifax, Canada.
The Rev. John Coutts, Holybourne Vicarage Alton, Hants.
The Rev. C. E. B. Cranfield, 1 Pelaw Terrace, Durham City.
The Rev. K. R. J. Cripps, The Rectory, 27 Ladybarn Road, Manchester, 14.
C. J. T. Cronshaw, Alnwick, Prestwich Park, Prestwich, Lancs.
The Rev. F. L. Cross, Christ Church, Oxford.
Mr. and Mrs. S. Currington, Mead Croft, West Clandon, Nr. Guildford, Surrey.

N. A. Dahl, Rektorhaugen 17, Oslo.

Edward R. Dalglish, Eastern Baptist Theological Seminary, Lancaster Avenue, Philadelphia, 21, Pa., U.S.A.

I. M. Davies, 11 Collier Road, Cambridge.

W. D. Davies, 54 College Road, Princeton, New Jersey, U.S.A.

Dr. Erich Dinkler, Ahornweg 33, Bonn-Venusberg.

J. D. Douglas, Tyndale Library, 16 Selwyn Gardens, Cambridge.

The Rev. A. B. Downing, 16 Styal Road, Wilmslow, Cheshire.

Downside Abbey, Bath.

C. Driver, Didsbury Training College, Manchester, 20.

The Rev. G. Duckworth, The Manse, Kings Road, Chandler's Ford, Hants.

The Rev. C. W. Dugmore, University of London King's College, London, W.C.2.

The Very Rev. G. S. Duncan, Inchdowrie, Fettercairn, Scotland.

Dom Jacques Dupont, Abbaye de Saint-André, Bruges, 3, Belgium.

The Rev. K. C. Dykes, Manchester Baptist College, Manchester, 14.

The Rev. J. W. Earp, 2 Willowbrook, Eton College, Windsor, Berks.

The Rev. George Brinkmann Ehlhardt, Theological Seminary of the University of Dubuque, Iowa, U.S.A.

E. Earle Ellis, Southern Baptist Theological Seminary, 2825 Lexington Road, Louisville, 6, Kentucky, U.S.A.

Dorothy M. Emmett, Department of Philosophy, The University, Manchester.

The Rev. T. Noel Evans, Gwylfa, Llangefni, Anglesey.

The Rev. Owen E. Evans, 7 Demesne Road, Manchester, 16.

The Rev. George Farr, 10 Chandos Road, Manchester, 21.

The Rev. J. E. Farrar, 58 Warwick Road, Bishop's Stortford.

The Rev. John Farrimond, 20 Cairngorm Road, Glasgow, S.3.

S. Vernon Fawcett, Union College of British Columbia, Vancouver, 8, B.C., Canada.

The Rev. Charles Feilding, Trinity College, Toronto, 5, Canada.

The Rev. W. F. Flemington, Wesley House, Cambridge.

The Rev. J. Flitcroft, Hulme Hall, Victoria Park, Manchester, 14.

The Rev. R. H. Fuller, Seabury-Western Theological Seminary, 600 Haven Street, Evanston, Illinois.

Wilfrid Gaisford, Department of Child Health, St. Mary's Hospital, Manchester.

The Rev. Bertil Gärtner, Tiundagatan 61, Uppsala, Sweden.

Le Père A. George, La Faculté Catholique de Théologie de Lyon, 74 Ch. du Grand Roule, Sainte-Foy-Les-Lyon (Rhône), France.

The Rev. A. Gilmore, 105 Queens Park Parade, Northampton.

The Rev. M. J. Gilyead, 73 Longsight, Harwood, Bolton, Lancs.

The Rev. Eugene Van Ness Goetchius, The Episcopal Theological School, 3 Mason Street, Cambridge, 38, Massachusetts, U.S.A.

Victor R. Gold, Pacific Lutheran Theological Seminary, 2770 Marin Avenue, Berkeley 8, California, U.S.A.

Kathleen G. Gough, Ashburne Hall, Fallowfield, Manchester.

The Rev. A. A. K. Graham, Worcester College, Oxford.

The Rev. K. Grayston, Didsbury College, Westbury-on-Trym, Bristol.

The Rev. S. L. Greenslade, The Black Hostelry, The College, Ely.

Dr. Heinrich Greeven, Kiel University, Germany.

J. H. Grice, 8 Welholme Road, Grimsby, Lincs.

The Rev. D. R. Griffiths, 71 Redlands Road, Penarth, Nr. Cardiff.

Dr. F. W. Grosheide, 175 Ceintuurbaan, Amsterdam-Z., Holland.

The Rev. W. Guy, St. Anne's Rectory, Newton Heath, Manchester.

Dr. D. Rafael Gyllenberg, Auragatan 22, Abö, Finland.

Canon T. Halliwell, Trinity College, Carmarthen, S. Wales.

The Rev. John P. Hastings, Madhupur E.R., Santal Parganas, Bihar, N. India.

Michael E. Heard, Baptist College, Manchester, 14.

The Rev. A. S. Herbert, Central House, Selly Oak Colleges, Birmingham, 29.

D. J. Hodges, Baptist College, Manchester, 14.

S. H. Hooke, Westbrook Cottage, Buckland, Faringdon, Berks.

J. J. B. Hudson, 121 Moseley Avenue, Coventry.

The Rev. James T. Hudson, 128 Lytham Road, Southport, Lancs.

The Rev. R. H. Hughes, Gogerddan, Menai Bridge, Anglesey.

J. Williams Hughes, Baptist College, Bangor, N. Wales.

E. J. Hugman, 509 St. Helens Road, Bolton.

Edmond Jacob, Faculté des Lettres, L'Université, Strasbourg, France.

Aubrey R. Johnson, 207 Cyncoed Road, Cardiff.

The Rev. Clifford D. Johnson, Warden, Bermondsey Settlement, London, S.E.16.

The Rev. George Johnston, Emmanuel College, Toronto, 5, Ontario.

The Very Rev. H. A. Jones, The Cathedral, Manchester.

R. G. Jones, 166 Southey Hill, Sheffield.
Dr. M. de Jonge, Voorstraat 31, Blija (Fr.), The Netherlands.

The Rev. J. N. D. Kelly, Principal's Lodgings, St. Edmund's Hall, Oxford.
The Rev. F. Kenworthy, Unitarian College, Victoria Park, Manchester.
The Rev. R. E. Ker, Edgehill College, Lennox Vale, Belfast.
Miss Joyce Kewley, Neville's Cross College, Durham.
J. H. Kellgren, 19 Rathen Road, Manchester, 20.
N. Q. King, University College, Achimota, Ghana, West Africa.
The Rev. Harold Kirkman, The Vicarage, Horsedge Street, Oldham, Lancs.
Dr. A. F. J. Klijn, Joh. Wagenaarkade 89, Utrecht, The Netherlands.
The Rev. Sydney H. Knight, Stand Parsonage, Whitefield, Manchester.
The Rev. S. J. Knox, The Manse, Cremore Park, Glasnevin, Dublin

O. Jessie Lace, William Temple College, Rugby.
V. F. Lambert, 334 Upper Brook Street, Manchester, 13.
R. E. Lane, 6 Linden Road, Didsbury, Manchester, 20.
H. W. Lang, McMaster University, Hamilton, Ontario, Canada.
The Rt. Rev. The Bishop of Leicester.
The Rev. M. Pennant Lewis, St. Paul's Manse, Bangor, N. Wales.
The Rev. W. Lillie, Department of Biblical Study, Kings College, Old Aberdeen, Scotland.
A. C. B. Lovell, Jodrell Bank, Cheshire.
The Rev. L. F. Lovell, 280 Liverpool Road South, Burscough, Lancs.
Evald Lövestam, Karl XII Gatan 6, Lund, Sweden.
The Very Rev. John Lowe, Christ Church, Oxford.

The Rev. C. S. Mann, O.S.B., Nashdom Abbey, Burnham, Bucks.
The Rev. J. H. Manson, 11 Donovan Avenue, Muswell Hill, London, N.10.
The Rev. Bernard P. Marks, 192 Thorpe Road, Norwich.
The Rev. John Marsh, The Principal's Lodgings, Mansfield College, Oxford.
The Rev. Roland H. F. Martin, Wesleyville, Orchard Street, Dewsbury, Yorks.
The Rev. S. H. Mayor, 131 Queen's Drive, Walton, Liverpool, 4.

The Rev. George McCabe, 147 Lanehouse Road, Thornaby-on-Tees.
J. D. McCaughey, 1 Ormond College Grounds, Carlton, N.3, Victoria, Australia.
The Rev. R. J. McCoy, The Librarian, Ripon Hall, Boar's Hill, Oxford.
The Rev. John F. McHugh, Ushaw College, Durham.
D. McIlhagga, 41 Claremont Road, Wallasey, Cheshire.
The Rev. James McIntyre, The Cathedral, Gloucester.
The Rev. J. W. Mellowes, Moravian Manse, 12 Parsons Street, Woodford Halse, Rugby.
Philippe H. Menoud, Côte 46b, Neuchâtel, Switzerland.
Bruce M. Metzger, Princeton Theological Seminary, N.J., U.S.A.
Dr. Otto Michel, Haufftneistrasse 12, Tubingen, Germany.
The Rev. E. R. Micklem, The Old Parsonage, Shaftesbury, Dorset.
Adam W. Miller, Anderson College, School of Theology Library, Anderson, Indiana, U.S.A.
The Rev. C. Millington, C.R., The Librarian, House of the Resurrection, Mirfield, Yorks.
The Rev. C. L. Milton, Handsworth College, Birmingham, 20.
The Rev. Hugh Montefiore, Gonville and Caius College, Cambridge.
The Rev. A. C. Moore, The Manse, Tapanui, West Otago, New Zealand.
The Rev. J. L. Moreau, Seabury Western Theological Seminary, 600 Haven Street, Evanston, Illinois, U.S.A.
Dr. R. Morgenthaler, Pfarrer, Hilterfingen, Switzerland.
The Rev. Colin Morris, P.O. Box 326, Chingola, N. Rhodesia.
C. Moss, The Department of Oriental Printed Books and MSS., London, W.C.1.
The Rev. Oswald Mowan, Buckfast Abbey, Buckfastleigh, Devon.
Walter G. Mühlau, Holtenauer Strasse 116, Ecke Beselerallee, Germany.
The Rev. R. T. Murphy, O.P., St. Rose Priory, Dubuque, Iowa, U.S.A.

Hideyasu Nakagawa, W5, N15 Sapporo, Hokkaido, Japan.
The Rev. Arthur Nelson, Tillydrine, Todholes Road, Cleator Moor.
The Rev. Harold G. Newsham, 200 N. Beacon Street, Hartford, Connecticut, U.S.A.
Dr. Bent Noack, Bregnerodvej 23, Birkerod, Denmark.
Arthur D. Nock, K-21 Eliot House, Harvard University, Cambridge, Mass.
Principal Johs. Nørgaard, Baptist Theological Seminary, Tølløse, Denmark.

The Rev. Alan J. Odell, 341 Aylsham Road, Norwich, Norfolk.
The Rev. George Ogg, The Manse, Anstruther Easher, Fife.
H. P. Owen, University College, Bangor, N. Wales.

Maurice P. Pariser, 7 Brazennose Street, Manchester, 2.
Alfred L. Parry, Woodlands, Brislington, Bristol, 4.
The Rev. E. A. Payne, The Baptist Union, 4 Southampton Row, London, W.C.1.
The Rev. A. W. Penn, Kirkdale Vicarage, Nawton, York.
Lektor Ernst Percy, Drottninggatan 33^{II}, Hälsingborg, Sweden.
Mary A. Perkins, 57 Shenley Fields Road, Selly Oak, Birmingham, 29.
The Rev. C. S. Petrie, St. Matthew's Manse, Stawell, Victoria, Australia.
The Rev. Walter Phillips, 11 Derwent Road, Haresfinch, St. Helens, Lancs.
Miss E. I. Pinthus, Ashburne Hall, Manchester.
Otto A. Piper, 58 Mercer Street, Princeton, N.J., U.S.A.
The Rev. Albert E. Potts, 391 Brook Street, Broughty Ferry, Dundee, Angus.
Muriel Poulter, 114 Howard Road, London, E.17.
The Rev. E. J. Powe, 37 Field Engineering Regiment, B.F.P.O. 53.
The Rev. J. W. Povah, 26 Broad Street, Bromyard, Herefordshire.
The Rev. Douglas H. Prescott, Mission Protestante Méthodiste, Dassa Zoumé, Dahomey, W. Africa.
Miss Miriam D. Prescott, The Hollies, Baxworth, Nr. Shropshire.
The Rev. R. H. Preston, St. Anselm Hall, Victoria Park, Manchester, 14.
The Rev. B. F. Price, Theology Department, Serampore College, Serampore, West Bengal.
A. N. Prior, Department of Philosophy, The University, Manchester.

The Rev. Donald J. Rabson, R.A.F., El Adem, B.F.B.O. 56.
I. T. Ramsey, Oriel College, Oxford.
J. W. Rees, The University, Manchester.
The Rev. C. Bernard Reynolds, 3865 West 15th Avenue, Vancouver, 8, Canada.
Dr. Karl Heinrich Rengstorf, Melcherstrasse 23, Munster, Westf., Germany.
The Rev. W. L. Richards, Greete Rectory, Ludlow, Salop.
B. Rigaux, Professeur d'Ecriture Sainte, 2 Avenue Chant-d'Oiseau, Brussels, Belgium.

Bleddyn J. Roberts, Department of Biblical Studies, University College of North Wales, Bangor.

Edward Robertson, The John Rylands Library, Manchester, 3.

The Rev. J. A. T. Robinson, Clare College, Cambridge.

The Rev. W. G. Robinson, The Northern Congregational College, Whalley Range, Manchester, 16.

The Rev. Wilfred H. Robinson, Leysian Mission, 112 City Road, E.C.1.

J. W. Rogerson, St. Anselm Hall, Victoria Park, Manchester, 14.

The Rev. Erik Routley, 17 Norham Road, Oxford.

The Rev. Raymond G. Rowland, 22 Lime Tree Avenue, Peterborough.

The Rev. H. H. Rowley, The University, Manchester.

The Rev. E. T. Ryder, Penlledwen, Peterston-super-Ely, Cardiff.

Samuel Sandmel, Hebrew Union College, 3101 Clifton Avenue, Cincinnati, 20, Ohio.

Wilbur E. Saunders, President, Colgate Rochester Divinity School, Rochester, 20, New York.

The Rev. Canon Eric Saxon, St. Ann's Rectory, Kinnaird Road, Manchester, 20.

Dr. R. Schippers, Albr. Dürerstraat 25, Amsterdam, Holland.

Walter Schlapp, The University, Manchester, 13.

Josef Schmid, 12/i Franz Marcstrasse, Munich 19, Germany.

Dr. R. Schnackenburg, Sonnenstrasse 15, 13a Wurzburg, Germany.

S.C.M. Press, 56–8 Bloomsbury Street, London, W.C.1.

R. B. Y. Scott, 31 McCosh Hall, Princeton University, N.J., U.S.A.

Dr. G. Sevenster, Witte Singel 61, Leiden, Holland.

The Rev. Michael J. Sheen, 21 Garden Road, Sheringham, Norfolk.

Marcel Simon, The University (Faculté des Lettres), Strasbourg.

J. B. Skemp, 9 St. Nicholas Drive, Whitesmocks, Durham.

R. Gregor Smith, 12 The University, Glasgow, W.2.

The Rt. Rev. the Bishop of St. Davids.

The Rev. D. Howard Smith, Department of Comparative Religion, The University, Manchester, 13.

The Rev. Charles W. F. Smith, Episcopal Theological School, Cambridge, 38, Mass., U.S.A.

James S. Stewart, 36 St. Alban's Road, Edinburgh, 9.

Lord Stopford of Fallowfield, Knott Lea, Arnside via Carnforth.

Miss Marjorie H. Sykes, 142 Parkville Road, Withington, Manchester, 20.

The Rev. Charles Taylor, 55 Charlton Road, Keynsham, Bristol.
M. H. Taylor, Baptist College, Manchester, 14.
T. A. Taylor, Baptist College, Manchester, 14.
The Rev. D. Hubert Thomas, 197 Sheen Lane, London, S.W.14.
Walter Till, Department of Coptic Studies, The University, Manchester, 13.
The Rev. B. Timmins, St. Elisabeth's Rectory, Reddish, Stockport.
M. Bernard Thomas, London Mission Post Bag 164, Salem 1, Madras State, India.
The Rev. Philip N. Tindall, 27 Parkfield Road, Liverpool, 17.
R. F. Torrington, Montgomery House, Alexandra Park, Manchester.
The Rev. R. John Tudor, 101 Victoria Road East, Thornton, Nr. Blackpool, Lancs.
The Rev. F. W. Tuswell, Pierrepont House School, Frensham, Farnham, Surrey.
Dr. Moses Tyson, The Librarian, Arts Library, Manchester University.

Eugène Vinaver, The University, Manchester.
The Rev. John J. Vincent, Baguley Hall Methodist Church, Bowland Road, Wythenshawe, Manchester.
The Rev. T. Vine, The Librarian, The Theological College, Ely, Cambs.
The Rev. Ant. Van der Voort, S.C.J., Liesboschlaan 315, Breda, Holland.
The Rev. Edward James Vorba, Union Congregational Church, 2727 Georgia Avenue, West Palm Beach, Florida, U.S.A.

The Rev. N. Walker, 300 Chessington Road, West Ewell, Surrey.
The Rev. D. S. Wallace-Hadrill, Eston Vicarage, Nr. Middlesborough, Yorks.
J. M. Wallace-Hadrill, Department of History, The University, Manchester.
The Rev. A. Marcus Ward, Richmond College, Surrey.
H. D. Westlake, Department of Greek, The University, Manchester.
Mrs. P. M. White, Langdale Hall, Victoria Park, Manchester.
The Rev. D. E. H. Whiteley, Jesus College, Oxford.
Miss Kathleen M. Whiteley, University of London, King's College, Strand, London, W.C.2.
Keith N. Wicks, Baptist College, Manchester, 14.

The Rev. A. G. Widdess, St. Nicholas Vicarage, Leicester.
Amos N. Wilder, Harvard Divinity School, Cambridge, 38, Mass., U.S.A.
The Rev. O. D. Wiles, D.S.O., The Baptist Church House, 4 Southampton Row, London, W.C.1.
The Rev. Principal J. T. Wilkinson, Hartley Victoria College, Manchester, 16.
Miss V. Wilkinson, 3 Garford Road, Oxford.
The Rev. C. Kingsley Williams, 12 Tower Park, Fowey, Cornwall.
F. C. Williams, Department of Electrical Engineering, The University, Manchester.
Miss Wendy I. Williams, 18 Dawson Road, Long Lane, Cheadle, Cheshire.
R. McL. Wilson, St. Mary's College, St. Andrews.
H. G. Wood, 26 Linden Road, Birmingham, 30.
H. P. Wood, Jordanhill Training College, Glasgow, W.3.
James Wood, 3 East Savile Road, Edinburgh, 9.
The Principal, Wycliffe Hall, Oxford.

The Most Rev. The Archbishop of York.
The Rev. Alexander Yule, The Manse, Winchelsea, Victoria, Australia.

LIBRARIES

Abbaye Saint-Pierre, Solesmes, Sarthe, France.

Aberdeen, King's College Library.

Andover-Harvard Library, 45 Francis Avenue, Cambridge, 38, Massachusetts, U.S.A.

Andover-Newton Theological Library, Newton Center, Massachusetts, U.S.A.

Århus, The State and University Library, Denmark.

Ashburne Hall, Manchester.

Baptist Theological Seminary Library, Ruschlikon-Zurich, Switzerland.

Basel University, Oeffentliche Bibliothek, Schohbeinstrasse 20, Switzerland.

Birmingham, City Reference Library.

Birmingham, The University Library.

Bonifacius-Druckerei, Paderborn, Germany.

Bosworth Memorial Library, The College of the Bible, 631 South Limestone Street, Lexington, Kentucky, U.S.A.

Bristol, The University Library.

British and Foreign Bible Society, 146 Queen Victoria Street, London, E.C.4.

California Baptist Theological Seminary Library, Seminary Knolls, Covina, California, U.S.A.

Colgate Rochester Divinity School, Rochester, 20, New York, U.S.A.

The Divinity School (Faculty Board of Divinity), St. John's Street, Cambridge.

Ecole Biblique et Archéologique Française, Jerusalem (zone arabe), P.O. Box 53, Via Amman, Jordan.

Erlangen University Library, Germany.

Erlangen Seminary for New Testament Studies, Germany.

Evangelische Buchhandlung, Sihlstrasse 33, Zurich, Switzerland.
Exeter College Library, Oxford.

The Faculty of Theology, The University, Manchester.

Handsworth College Library, Birmingham.
Hartford Theological Seminary, Hartford, Connecticut, U.S.A.
Hartley Victoria College, Alexandra Road South, Manchester, 16.
Heidelberg University Library, Germany.
Hull, The University Library.

Indiana, West Baden Theologians Library, West Baden Springs, U.S.A.
The Institute of Jewish Studies, Singleton Road, Salford, 7.

Leeds University, The Brotherton Library.
Lincoln, the Theological College.
The London Library, 14 St. James Square, London, S.W.1.
London University, King's College Library.
Louvain, The University Library.
Lucy Stites Barret Memorial Library, 109 East Broadway, Louis-
    ville, 2, Kentucky, U.S.A.

Manchester College, Oxford.
Manchester University, The Arts Library.
Mansfield College, Oxford.
Marburg a. d. Lahn, University Seminary for New Testament Studies,
    Germany.
McCormick Theological Seminary, Virginia Library, 2330 North
    Halsted Street, Chicago, 14, Illinois, U.S.A.
Munster, The University Library, Munster, Westf., Germany.

Newcastle-upon-Tyne, King's College Library.
New College, London, 527 Finchley Road, N.W.3.
North Western Theological Seminary Library, 116 East 22nd Street,
    Minneapolis, Minnesota, U.S.A.

Oriel College Library, Oxford.

Libraries

Paton Congregational College, 487 Derby Road, Lenton, Nottingham.
Philadelphia Divinity School, William Bacon Stevens Library, 4205
    Spruce Street, Philadelphia, 4, U.S.A.
Pittsburgh-Xenia Theological Seminary 616 n. Highland, Pittsburgh
    6, Pa.
Faculté Libre de Theologie Protestante de Paris, 83 Boulevard Arago,
    Paris, 14e, France.
Protestant Theological Faculty, Boulevard de la Cambre 32, Brussels,
    Belgium.

San Francisco Theological Seminary Library, San Anselmo, Cali-
    fornia, U.S.A.
Selly Oak Colleges Library, Birmingham, 29.
Sheffield, The University Library.
The Warden, St. Deiniol's Library, Hawarden, Chester.
The Librarian, St. Edmund Hall, Oxford.
The Librarian, St. John's College, York.
The Librarian, University College of South Wales, Cardiff

The Thorold and Lyttelton Library, 9 The Close, Winchester.
Trinity College, the Librarian, Toronto, 5, Canada.

United Theological Seminary Library, 1810 Harvard Boulevard,
    Dayton, 6, Ohio, U.S.A.

Virginia Theological Seminary Library, Alexandria, Virginia, U.S.A.
Vrije University Library, Keizersgracht 164, Amsterdam, C, Holland.

Wesley College, The Librarian, Headingley, Leeds, 6.
Westminster College, Cambridge.
Weston College Library, Weston 93, Cambridge, Massachusetts,
    U.S.A.
John Gordon Wright Library, Episcopal Theological School, Cam-
    bridge, 38, Massachusetts, U.S.A.